WE
THE
PEOPLE

WE
THE
PEOPLE

The Modern-Day Figures Who Have
Reshaped and Affirmed the
Founding Fathers' Vision of America

JUAN WILLIAMS

CROWN PUBLISHERS
NEW YORK

All rights reserved.
Published in the United States by Crown Publishers,
an imprint of the Crown Publishing Group,
a division of Penguin Random House LLC, New York.
www.crownpublishing.com

CROWN is a registered trademark and the Crown colophon
is a trademark of Penguin Random House LLC.

Library of Congress Cataloging-in-Publication Data
is available upon request.

ISBN 978-0-307-95204-2
eBook ISBN 978-0-307-95206-6

PRINTED IN THE UNITED STATES OF AMERICA

Book design by Anna Thompson
Jacket design by Christopher Brand
Jacket illustration by Vivienne Flesher

10   9   8   7   6   5   4   3   2

First Edition

Roger and Alma Williams—the fighter and the girl he loved—my parents.
You opened the way for generations to come.

CONTENTS

For unto whomever much is given, of him shall be much required.

—LUKE 12:48

Well-done, good and faithful servant . . . Come and share your master's happiness.

—MATTHEW 25:21

CHAPTER 1

THE FOUNDING FATHERS AND MODERN AMERICA

W hat happened to my America?"

"Why don't those people speak English?"

And "Mr. Williams, don't take this the wrong way, but . . . you know, at the donut shop, at the gas station, in the schoolyard—have you ever seen so many immigrants, especially the Latinos everywhere?"

"These kids are so thuggish. . . . Do you see any reason to be confident in this country's future?"

After the 2012 presidential election I heard those kinds of urgent questions from older white conservatives. They seemed disoriented. With obvious anxiety they felt the cycle of history spinning away from them, leaving them dizzy and angry at being pushed away from the center of politics and culture by the emerging "New America."

One poll found 53 percent of white Americans saying the changes in culture, economics, demographics, and politics were coming too quickly and damaging America's "character and values."

This sense of disillusionment is not limited to older white conservatives. In the same 2011 poll, done by Heartland Monitor, the *National Journal,* and Allstate, 51 percent of African Americans said they too felt all the demographic and political churning was too much and the "trends are troubling."

A 2015 poll done by Reuters and Ipsos found that 62 percent of Republicans, 53 percent of Independents, and 37 percent of Democrats "feel like a stranger in [their] own country." Another 72 percent of Republicans, 58 percent of Independents, and 45 percent of Democrats "don't identify with what America has become."

I myself am hardly immune from this national anxiety over change, and it hit me personally eight years before the 2012 election, in 2004. That year I turned fifty and felt the new realities of life pushing against me everywhere.

Just think about how much the world changed during my first fifty years on Earth.

When I was born, in 1954, people who looked like me sat at the back of the bus, drank out of separate water fountains, and went to separate schools. Eighty-nine years after the end of the Civil War, my father, an immigrant black man, could not get anything but a low-end job in most American companies. He could not go to most American schools, could not live in most American neighborhoods, and was not allowed to swim in most pools, golf on most courses, or go to most amusement parks.

My mother, who was born in Panama, did not see Latinos as a major force in American life. The census did not even bother to count the number of Latinos in the United States during the 1950s. In 1970 Latinos in the United States added up to less than 5 percent of the population. Today Latinos make up over 17 percent of the U.S. population, outnumbering blacks as the largest minority group.

In 1954 abortion was not a critical political issue. The idea of women controlling the rights to their own fertility and their bodies was not a "culture war" argument splitting conservatives and liberals. Fifty years ago U.S. government policy, supported by conservatives, promoted family planning. It was seen as a boon to parents, allowing them to better provide for a smaller number of children.

In the 1950s there was no controversy over homosexuality, largely because society was not willing to have the conversation. My mom had a gay male friend who came by the apartment regularly to design and sew dresses. Yet I never heard him or anyone else talk about gay rights. Gays remained in the closet for fear of persecution.

What a different America I saw in 2004. The leaps in the nation's demographics, economy, and culture made it feel to me like *hundreds* of years had passed.

America went from allowing smoking everywhere to banning smoking everywhere. Gambling went from the street corner "numbers man" to government-run lotteries. The rising presence and influence of women in corporate America, the military, and the media shifted the power equation between the sexes, as more women decided they did not need a man to support themselves, to live a full life, or even to have a child. In fact, women began to outnumber men in colleges and graduate schools. They became the majority of the workforce as male-dominated blue-collar jobs went to Asia. Conversations about gay rights morphed into court cases about the right of gays to have legal, state-approved marriages.

Essential fibers of the social fabric—public schools, for example— began to fray, leading to calls for reform (charter schools, magnet schools, and vouchers) that would allow parents and students greater choice to find the best school for their needs. America experienced its first major gun control movement, saw the rise of a national gun lobby, and endured a spike in mass shootings in schools around the country.

And there was wholesale change in the federal government in the decades following World War II. We saw postwar America become the global "arsenal of democracy" that President Franklin D. Roosevelt had promised it would back in 1940, protecting far-flung regions of the world from Soviet communism. We witnessed the South become a Republican stronghold. That led to a conservative political revolution that culminated in the presidency of Ronald Reagan.

New technology emerged, changing the way Americans communicate, process information, and form relationships. It seemed that within just a few years suddenly everyone had a cell phone. New cable television channels, hundreds of them, appeared in everyone's home. Internet and podcast programming moved entertainment to new platforms. And today we can use apps such as OkCupid and Tinder to find people to date in our local area.

The economy got hot in 2004, thanks to revolutions in finance, high-tech companies, hedge fund investments, and ever-higher housing prices. The bubble, of course, would soon burst.

As the economic ways of the past unraveled early in the twenty-first century, the white working class, though buoyed for a while by rising home prices and cheap credit, has faced a rude reality of stagnant wages due to a dim job market, an end to pensions, and the decline of unions. The same has been true for African Americans. Despite the rise of the black middle class in the 1970s, after the 2008 recession the African American unemployment rate soared as high as it had been in the 1960s. In 2005, Hurricane Katrina blew the cover off ingrained black poverty in New Orleans, exposing nationwide roots of black poverty tied to record high rates of unwed mothers and failing schools. The big racial arguments of the latter half of the twentieth century, which had focused on the continuing impact of the history of segregation and the need for affirmative action in college admission and hiring, faded. The focus on black poverty shifted to questions about family structure. And at the same time, ironically, the promise of equality under the law had come ever closer to being fully realized for educated blacks, Latinos, and Asians. That is why immigrants kept coming to America in waves. Change was hitting the country from multiple directions.

During these years I traveled the country as part of a National Public Radio (NPR) series called *The Changing Face of America*. The shows examined issues ranging from the increased use of personal technology on a daily basis to changes in how Americans worshiped to the increased acceptance of legal, state-supported gambling across the country. For the series I met with Mexican immigrants who had been given amnesty under President Reagan's 1986 Immigration Reform and Control Act. I talked with the first generation of Americans who grew up using cell phones and the Internet after the 1996 Telecommunications Act. I reported on poor people, especially young minorities, who lost the right to welfare support because of the welfare-to-work laws crafted by Republican House Speaker Newt Gingrich and President Clinton in the 1990s.

Looking back, it seems that the folks I met through *The Changing Face of America* were living out the theories of Buckminster Fuller and Ray Kurzweil, two futurists who have argued that because of exponential leaps in technology and our understanding of biology, change is coming at a faster rate now than ever before in human history. Kurzweil calls it the "law of accelerating returns." In a 2001 essay he wrote,

"We won't experience 100 years of progress in the 21st century—it will be more like 20,000 years of progress (at today's rate)."

So how long ago and far away is the America of 1776? How distant is the Founding Fathers' America from the reality of twenty-first-century America? I can only imagine how different the people I met while working on that show would be if I reconnected with them today. Imagine the dizziness the Founding Fathers would experience.

The NPR series won critical acclaim. These stories of change in American life from east to west, from urban to rural, and among young and old reminded me that American life was being transformed in exponential leaps. As a journalist, I was particularly alert to the new reality of fragmented politics and niche media. Experiences that at one time served to unify large segments of the population, such as watching one of the three network evening news programs, began to dissolve, with audiences for news programs breaking into politically separate groups, listening to their preferred views on talk radio or watching politically tilted cable news shows.

Even the surge of American nationalism following the 9/11 attacks and the decision to go into two wars faded quickly. At first flags flew everywhere and people stood to applaud the troops at sporting events. But as time passed the wars didn't feel so real anymore. No one was drafted. College campus protests like those that emerged in opposition to the war in Vietnam never took place because the professional force fighting the war and dying generally did not come from elite colleges—or colleges at all, for that matter.

Similarly, the once widespread trust in institutions began to slide. The public schools suffered because of poor performance, the Catholic Church because of pedophile scandals. Baseball stars found themselves before Congress, accused of cheating with performance-enhancing steroids. Our confidence in the goodwill of Wall Street bankers and other financial leaders eroded. Trust in the word of government officials fell when people found out they had been misled about the presence of weapons of mass destruction in Iraq, and later when the government was shown to be have been asleep at the switch when the economic crash came in 2008.

As a black man, I was particularly struck that the once reliable framework of racial identity in America—white majority and black minority dealing with the aftermath of slavery and legal segregation—began to blur as Latinos and Asians began to exercise new cultural and economic influence on the nation.

For the next few years I continued filing away stories that fit the pattern of these foundational shifts in American life. I wanted to weave this collection of colorful threads into a vivid tapestry that revealed the new look of modern American life.

What became clear to me was that America was engaged in a new beginning. This was not the country where I grew up. America has been reborn any number of times over the course of its existence. The westward expansion, the Civil War, the New Deal—all had their turn at reinventing the country. Here, at the beginning of the twenty-first century, I found myself looking at one of those extraordinary moments of national transformation. A new America had emerged, at times painfully bursting from past realities and shedding cultural norms, as it entered stage after stage of uncertain change.

To me, this radical transformation was something to celebrate. Yes, political polarization and fear of rapid change were making people anxious. But overall, middle-class Americans continued to enjoy a high standard of living compared to other people around the globe. Plus the policies that forced people of color and women into subservience have all but vanished. And we Americans have a chance to create, like artists with an untouched canvas, a new, potentially better reality for ourselves.

Then, in 2010, I had an epiphany that forced me to look deeper at the radical changes taking place in the structure of the country. It began with that year's U.S. census report—an unlikely starting point for an epiphany. The census results on the age of the American people jumped out at me. They showed that over a quarter of the American population was younger than the age of eighteen.

At first I didn't believe it. But the census graphs indicated that children, high school age or younger, made up the largest single cohort of any of the demographic categories. I had thought people my age, baby boomers, accounted for the lion's share of the population. I had believed that the declining birth rate among whites should be shrinking the number of young people. But the census told a different story. The influx of immigrants with sky-high birth rates had created an incredibly young nation with a total population of over 300 million American citizens.

I remember expressing my shock at the young age of the population to friends and fellow journalists and having them react with surprise at my surprise. "Have you gone to the movies lately?" one fellow journalist asked. "Every other movie is about vampires or zombie hunters. Whom do you think they're being marketed to? They're not making movies for you and me, buddy. They're made for those young people." My wife asked me if I had gone to the mall lately. The businesses that were bustling, even during the recession, she informed me, sold clothing and accessories to young people—stores like J.Crew, H&M, and Urban Outfitters. To my embarrassment, she told me that I'd have a hard time buying a pair of jeans. The newer denim styles are designed to fit tight young bodies, she said with laughter; older people have to shop for "comfort" jeans. And, she added, it's obvious that merchants understand how family life is changing. Busy moms no longer take charge of buying clothes for their teenage children. Instead, parents give money to their children and let them go to the mall.

It occurred to me that to be a good journalist early in the twenty-first century I needed to better understand young Americans. I wasn't totally in the dark. I did know that younger voters, especially first-time voters, constituted a crucial part of the coalition that elected Barack Obama in 2008. According to exit polls, Obama carried two-thirds of the youth vote against Republican John McCain—about 15 million ballots. Both Obama's supporters and his critics described him as a "rock star" because of his ability to connect with younger votes who had previously been written off by politicians as too lazy and disengaged to show up at the polls on election day. Obama attracted thousands of them at a time to his rallies and enthralled them, surrounding himself with the kind of adoration you'd sooner associate with Taylor Swift. But I also had a hunch that America's youth-heavy population had affected more than Obama's 2008 victory. I needed to meet with these young people and listen to them to hear in their own words how they see their role in this new American story. The rising social and economic power of young people was intersecting with their growing political power.

I decided to visit a high school in the middle of the country, expecting that the big increase in immigrants and racial minorities among young people would be evident there. I visited Washburn High School, a public school for grades 9–12 in Minneapolis, Minnesota. Minneapolis is the largest city in the state and its demographics are roughly at parity with those of the nation as a whole. Politically, it is very much a purple city, having voted for both Democratic and Republican candidates in recent elections for all levels of government. It seemed a good microcosm for the entire nation. I had asked to spend a day there conducting group interviews and listening sessions with student leaders in academics, athletics, student government, and community service. I wanted to get a range of opinions from the whole student body. As an outsider, I found that they seemed similar in mannerisms and dress—texting cavalierly on their smartphones, wearing the same brand names of casual clothing, and drinking the same cans of caffeinated energy drinks. But as I engaged them in conversation, I discovered they saw themselves as unique, and they couldn't understand how I saw similarities in their behavior.

I had a fascinating conversation with a woman who worked as a guidance counselor at the high school. She had been a student at the school in the 1970s, as had her children in the 1980s and '90s. I asked her, "What was the biggest difference between Washburn High then and Washburn High now?" Her first response was, "Mr. Williams, I'm sure it was obvious to you." When I told her it wasn't, she went on, "You asked to meet with student leaders—the students with the highest GPAs and SAT scores, the best student athletes, the ones who were being awarded scholarships and getting internships. Didn't you notice that the majority of all the groups you met with were young women?" One group of ten high achievers had eight girls and two boys; in others, six or seven out of ten were girls. Within those groups, there was a cohort of Hispanic and Asian students, all of whom were the children and grandchildren of immigrants. "That is what is different," the counselor told me. Suddenly the light went on for me, illuminating yet another part of transformation in the nation's structure.

It is not just that young people are the single biggest group of Americans, but that among those young people women clearly outperformed the men. They had better grades and test scores, and they more often demonstrated the maturity to run school groups, get internships, and become leaders. Women are taking the lead in competing for educational and economic opportunities afforded by new technology and a new order of domestic and international politics.

In this transformed, twenty-first-century America, women are now earning the majority of both undergraduate and graduate degrees. One college administrator joked with me that if their admissions panel went strictly on test scores, writing samples, and extracurricular activities, their entire student body would consist of women. He went on to say, only half joking, that they had to have an affirmative action program for young men. When I asked him why that was, he said, "Because girls like boys."

As I drove to the airport to fly back to Washington, D.C., I thought about the world I was returning to inside the Beltway. At the time, the U.S. Congress had over ninety female members—the highest number in American history. One of them, Nancy Pelosi, was the Speaker of the House. The secretary of state, the face of America to the rest of the world, was a woman, Hillary Clinton. Before her, the secretary of state had been a black woman, Condoleezza Rice. Before her, it had been a black man, Colin Powell. And before him, it had been Madeleine Albright, the first woman to hold the post. When he became secretary of state in 2013, John Kerry was the first white man to serve in that role in sixteen years. President Obama had nominated the third female Supreme Court justice in history, Sonia Sotomayor, a Hispanic woman. A year later, Obama would nominate the fourth female justice, Elena Kagan.

Recently enough, two of the three anchors for the network evening news broadcasts were women—Katie Couric at CBS and Diane Sawyer at ABC. Women now make up roughly half of the American workforce. There are a record number of women and minorities serving as CEOs of Fortune 500 companies. Educated young women were the swing vote in the 2008, 2010, and 2012 elections. Those women, along with older women who are widowed, divorced, or never married, have become the deciding vote in every election since the early 1970s. They constitute the fulcrum of modern electoral politics. In fact, millions of dollars are spent each election cycle trying to appeal to women, with a special emphasis on independent-minded, working women—dubbed "soccer moms" during the economic boom of the 1990s, "security moms" after 9/11, or "mortgage moms" after the 2008 financial crisis. They are highly likely to vote, because they care about how government impacts the way their families live.

The changing look of life for American women is but one subplot within the larger demographic shifts in America. Another new plot is the change in white America's centuries-old role as the dominant player in race relations in America.

In 2012 the GOP's presidential candidate, Mitt Romney, won 59 percent of the white vote, the biggest bloc of white voters for a Republican since 1988. And yet it was not enough to win the White House. When President Dwight D. Eisenhower won 57 percent of the white vote in 1952 he took the election in a landslide. Today white voters are a smaller share of the electorate. For example, Romney won among white men by 27 percentage points. He might have won the election if the election had taken place when white men made up nearly half of all voters (46 percent). But that was 1976. In 2012, white men made up only 34 percent of the electorate.

President Obama won his two presidential elections by overcoming middling to poor support from whites. In 2008 he lost the white vote by 12 percentage points, and in 2012 he lost the white vote by over 20 percentage points. He won the election by overwhelmingly claiming votes from a "New America" coalition featuring young people, college-educated white women, and Asian, black, and Latino voters.

The rise of that youthful, multiracial voting coalition in national politics is a reflection of powerful shifts in the demographics of the country. They countered the previous dominance of white America not only at the voting booth but also when it comes to setting the political agenda. The issues important to that "New America" coalition suddenly dominated the national political conversation: universal healthcare, contraception as a mandatory part of employee healthcare insurance packages, immigration reform, school reform, and climate change. The younger American coalition wanted to confront previously taboo social issues such as gay rights, women having the right to serve in combat, and the legalization of marijuana.

This shift in the national conversation left the older, white, and conservative center of political life—with its intense focus on a strong military, low taxes, deregulation, and small government—increasingly out of touch and concerned that this political and demographic change signals the passing of the "true" America. It stirred nostalgia for the past, beginning with the Founding Fathers and the Constitution. It created a yearning for the 1950s—an era before antiwar protests, the civil rights movement, feminism, and new types of immigrants had destroyed the faith in capitalism, democracy, and the traditional family that Americans once held so dear.

For the generation born in the 1950s and 1960s, the start of the twenty-first century means the loss of small towns and Rust Belt factory communities once at the heart of industrial America. Today big cities, fueled by jobs for highly educated young people and the influx of immigrants and racial minorities, are the center of national life. And that has led to anger at immigrants—officially expressed as anger at illegal immigrants—as whites began to witness the declining influence of Western European traditions and a rise in the visibility of music, fashion, and religions from Latin America, Asia, and Africa. Today Latino and Asian faces dominate among the newcomers.

Of course, this lament over the loss of tradition and stability in American life is hardly new to the twenty-first century. It has been a common refrain throughout much of American history. It was evident in the aftermath of the Civil War. It split the nation's politics after the Great Depression with the advent of the New Deal. The "silent generation" of the 1960s and 1970s were discontented with the social turmoil of the civil rights movement, anti–Vietnam War protests, and sexual revolution. Put another way, parents never like their kids' music.

Political coalitions and the clout of demographic groups come and go, shifting traditions and the axis of electoral power. The Federalists, America's first political party, got locked into a small ruling elite of wealthy northeastern power players. As the nation expanded, Democratic-Republicans, a group with a strong populist base in the South, overtook the Federalists. And just before the Civil War the Whigs, a party formed in opposition to Andrew Jackson's Democrats, joined with the new Republican Party in support of abolishing slavery, creating a new power center. This is the way the wheel of history turns in the United States.

What distinguishes this twenty-first-century lament over changing traditions and loss of stability is how ferociously it divides young and old. The generational divide took center stage in 2008 with the election of Barack Obama, whose only true rival in reaching office came from a person who would have been the first female president, Hillary Clinton. The millennial generation of Americans, those born after 1980, is made up of 40 percent people of color. They have little problem with gay marriage and less, if any at all, with interracial dating and marriage. They grew up with women leaders, and they strongly support President Obama.

Their political opposites are the "silent generation" of Americans, who became adults after World War II. They are far more conservative than the millennials. Polls consistently find the silent generation's resistance to the changes in the nation matched by their resistance to President Obama. For many, the first black president, the son of a globe-trotting, well-educated white woman and a black African Harvard doctoral student, personifies a huge divide at the start of the twenty-first century between the nation's past and its future. This silent generation is even more conservative than the generation that came before them, what Tom Brokaw labeled the "Greatest Generation," which fought in World War II and remembered the New Deal as government activism that helped the workingman.

Time magazine ran a cover story a year before the 2012 elections based on a Pew Research Center poll of today's polarized generations. "Silent Generation members are twice as likely as millennials to call themselves 'angry' with the government, and they trust Republicans more than Democrats on nearly every key issue," author Michael Crowley wrote. "Obama appears to be a contributing factor in their discontent." The poll found the strongest disapproval of the president among white voters over the age of sixty-five. The same group overwhelmingly disapproved of the demographic changes to the nation, with only 22 percent approving of the rising immigrant population and only 29 percent comfortable with interracial marriage. "Some combination of the change [President Obama] has championed and the change he actually represents is too much for some of these voters to accept," Crowley explained.

This group of older Americans—largely conservative Republicans, some of them members of the Tea Party—has led the fight against the president's plan for universal healthcare. They have questioned his legitimacy as president (the "birthers" said he was not born in the United States and therefore was not qualified to be president). And they've painted him as a socialist, secretly seeking to undermine capitalism. They believe, in the words of the 2012 Republican presidential nominee Mitt Romney, that President Obama is creating an "entitlement society" to reward the "47 percent," the increasing number of Americans living off of government handouts who are "takers, not makers."

This polarizing political divide was evident as early as the closing days of the Clinton administration, when Congress impeached the president for lying about his sexual behavior. Americans, young and old, separated into camps over the question of whether the impeachment was a waste of time or a real constitutional crisis.

The divide grew during the George W. Bush years. The fracturing of American political life has led to arguments about whether or not the demographic and economic changes in the country are, on balance, making for a better nation. These arguments almost inevitably work themselves back to the question of the fundamental meaning of America, and to the meaning first established by the Founders themselves— the ever-reliable touchstone of Americanness.

Every day, it seems, top American news outlets publish headlines like this one from the *Wall Street Journal*: "What Would the Founding Fathers Think of Election Day 2012?" Or this one from the *Washington Post*: "Who Would the Founding Fathers Deport?" Or this one, published in the *Boston Globe* following the controversial end to John Boehner's tenure as House Speaker: "Speaker's Resignation Is a Testament to Founding Fathers' Wisdom." Journalists aren't the only ones to shower praise on our Founding Fathers. During his first inaugural address, President Obama spoke of the Founding Fathers who "faced with perils that we can scarcely imagine, drafted a charter to assure the rule of law and the rights of man."

And who are these original Founding Fathers? Most historians consider the original Founding Fathers to include the fifty-six men who signed the Declaration of Independence in 1776 and the fifty-five men who attended the Constitutional Convention in 1787. A handful of them participated in both historic events. And many, like George Washington, Thomas Jefferson, John Adams, James Madison, and Alexander Hamilton, earned key spots in the new federal government.

Some historians like to include other figures who neither signed the Declaration nor participated in the Constitutional Convention. Even so, they still played various pivotal roles in the nation's founding: early justices of the Supreme Court like John Marshall; contrarian members of state ratifying conventions like Patrick Henry; and philosophers, like Thomas Paine, who gave the Revolution its intellectual backbone. All in all, there are well over a hundred original Founding Fathers.

The Founding Fathers are with us everywhere we go. If you empty your pockets right now, you'll see portraits of Washington, Hamilton, and Jefferson staring back at you from your nickels, quarters, dollar bills, and ten-dollar bills. Emanuel Gottlieb Leutze's 1851 oil painting of George Washington standing astride a boat to bravely cross the icy Delaware River during the American Revolution is one of the most recognizable images in the American saga. Today, the U.S. Capitol houses an eighteen-by-twenty-six-foot painting by Howard Chandler Christy that depicts the Founding Fathers signing the Constitution back in 1787. Books about the Founding Fathers by prominent authors, including Joseph Ellis's *American Sphinx: The Character of Thomas Jefferson* and David McCullough's *1776* and *John Adams,* are consistent bestsellers. In fact, McCullough's book on Adams was made into a top-rated HBO miniseries.

America's love of its Founding Fathers shapes contemporary politics as well as culture. In her book on the Tea Party Movement, Harvard history professor Jill Lepore describes how the Tea Party, a far-right movement formed in the wake of Obama's 2008 victory, frequently cites the Founding Fathers in order to give their movement authority and recruit new members. "From the start," Lepore writes, "the Tea Party's chief political asset was its name: the echo of the [American] Revolution conferred upon a scattered, diffuse, and confused movement a degree of legitimacy and the appearance . . . of coherence. Aside from the name and the costume, the Tea Party offered an analogy: rejecting the bailout is like dumping the tea; healthcare reform is like the Tea Act; our struggle is like theirs."

Yes, the Founding Fathers have become stone pillars in a world of rapid change and uncertainty. But what would the Founders have thought of the military-industrial complex? What would they have thought of the fights over religious freedom versus secular freedom? Do we uphold the Second Amendment as they intended? How would they have confronted the question of gay marriage? How would they view the use of electronic surveillance to monitor citizens' communications? The Founding Fathers would find modern America a totally strange land.

In 1790, the nation the Founding Fathers led had 3.9 million people, including 694,280 slaves. Most Americans lived on farms or in small towns. They could go for days without seeing neighbors. Less than nine people lived in every square mile of the former colonies. And there was no racial diversity. Sixty percent of the Founding Fathers' fellow Americans were whites from Britain. The second-largest group, another 14 percent, identified as whites of Scottish or Scots-Irish background. The third-largest group, at 9 percent, were people of German ancestry. Another 5.4 percent came from the Netherlands, France, and Sweden. Only the presence of black slaves kept America from being an all-white country of western European origins and culture.

If the Founding Fathers could travel through time to present-day America, they'd land in a country with more than a hundred times the number of people—over 322 million. When they walked around they might feel a little squeezed by the 87.4 people per square mile; today most Americans live in big cities clogged with traffic. And they would be almost certain to bump into a lot of blacks, Hispanics, and Asians, who make up more than a third of the population.

Imagine a Founding Father—say, Ben Franklin—taking a walk in Philadelphia during the Colonial era, when the city was the biggest in the nation. Starting by the river, he had to walk west only half a mile to reach the city limits. If he walked along the river, it was only a mile before he left behind the sailors, traders, and businessmen. That was the whole of the big city. Today skyscrapers are the core of downtown Philadelphia and its 1.5 million people. And California, a state the Founding Fathers never heard of, has the ninth-largest economy in the world.

In the federal government known to the Founding Fathers, the president had an attorney general and a cabinet made up of three departments: State, Treasury, and War. There were no administrative departments in the government. In the 1st Congress, which met in New

York and then Philadelphia rather than Washington, D.C., there were only twenty senators and fifty-nine members of the House of Representatives. The Supreme Court had six justices—including the chief justice—and there were three circuit courts for the entire country. Making their way to modern Washington, the Founding Fathers would find a black president presiding over fifteen departments and several other agencies that have cabinet-level positions, from the chairman of the Council of Economic Advisers to the administrator of the Environmental Protection Agency.

During the 1st Congress, from 1789 to 1791, 144 bills and resolutions were introduced. The 112th Congress saw 10,400 bills and resolutions introduced. The Founding Fathers would likely have a hard time grasping that federal taxes exceeded $3 trillion in 2014. In the days of the Founding Fathers the single biggest source of money for the federal government was customs revenue. There was no income tax, no federal taxes. Today the U.S. military is the biggest in the world; the government spends more on its armed forces than the world's next seven largest combat forces combined.

And when it comes to technology, the Founding Fathers, who thought of pamphlets and newspapers as the cutting-edge media of their time, would not be able to comprehend two recent American inventions, Facebook and Twitter, yet more than a billion people use them worldwide.

As one might surmise, the Founders would have been ill equipped to answer many of the questions I posed above. Harking back to the legacy of the Founders is a source of tremendous inspiration and guidance, and something that I think we should do reverentially and frequently. But it should also be done with a sense of caution. They were great men but hardly infallible in their public and private lives.

Far too often in political debates the Founders are given the veneer of purity and infallibility. And they are assumed to have all been in agreement on the big issues by people who use them as ideological filters to put a sacred light on a favorite position in the latest political argument.

Take, for instance, former Rep. Michele Bachmann (R-Minn.), a potential GOP nominee in 2012. In one speech, Bachmann contrasted President Obama's flawed presidency with the Founding Fathers, who "worked tirelessly until slavery was no more." Though Bachmann was implying that she, like the Founding Fathers, would fight tirelessly for freedom, what Rep. Bachmann didn't seem to realize is that the Founding Fathers did not "work tirelessly" to end slavery. As any diligent reader of history knows, the Founders were often at odds with one another—they differed over how to shape the nation as well as the proper role of the federal government, and especially on the issue of slavery. Faced with a divisive issue, they agreed to a compromise that allowed slavery. Most of them, in fact, owned slaves.

Thurgood Marshall, the first African American to serve on the Supreme Court and a lawyer who spoke lovingly of the ideals of the Constitution, reminded everyone that America's Founding Fathers were, like all other men, imperfect. During the Constitution's bicentennial celebration in 1987, some members of the Court agreed to go to Philadelphia and dress in Colonial-period clothing as part of a reenactment of the Founding Fathers' signing the Constitution. Justice Marshall turned down the invitation, saying, "If you are going to do what you did 200 years ago somebody is going to have to give me short pants and a tray so I can serve coffee." In another speech, Marshall called the Constitution "defective from the start" for its failure to end slavery and grant women the right to vote.

On issues such as slavery, the Founders realized they had no control over the new realities of life in America that would come to pass in the years ahead. They understood the inherent impermanence of their work. They put in our founding documents a brilliant flexibility with which future generations could remain true to principles and yet evolve as the world changed. That is why they opened the door to the idea of constitutional amendments. Real-time revision—the acceptance of the idea of new births of freedom in future generations—is part of the incredible beauty of the American experiment. Thomas Jefferson was vocal on this point: "No society can make a perpetual constitution, or even a perpetual law," he wrote. That fit with his understanding that "the earth belongs . . . to the living." He even put forward that the "dead hand of the past" should not be a weight on future generations.

In 1841, Scottish historian Thomas Carlyle thought the best way to tell the history of his era was to recount the stories of the transformational figures whose words and deeds had come together to form

Western civilization up until that point. His treatise *On Heroes, Hero-Worship and the Heroic in History* was a history of the ages, but it was also commentary on how these men (they were all men) related to their times and how their times related to them. Carlyle's work covered heroes in virtually every field of human endeavor, including Napoleon, Shakespeare, and even the Prophet Muhammad. In writing about these men, Carlyle concluded that great men shaped the course of history.

As I look at the history of the United States after World War II, I see a similar constellation of great men and women who forged the nation we have today in 2016. The more I read, the more I begin to connect dots that previously were separate in my mind. The more lines I draw, the more I become convinced that there is an important story to tell here. In telling that story, I can explore how we got here—to this time of profound change—and forecast where we are heading as a nation.

Behind our high rates of immigration, our global economics, our massive military, and the law enforcement apparatus that has our jails packed, the current state of national affairs is tied to the people who set in motion the changes we are living with every day. Some of those people are famous, while others are not so well known. In some cases their lives are so recent that history has not had time to make the judgments needed to celebrate or curse them. None of them was purely virtuous or purely wicked in either their private or public deeds, though some leaned more heavily in one direction or the other. Their stories cannot be adequately told as either hagiography or pathology. They were reflections of changes building the country in the times in which they lived. What distinguishes each of these founders—both new and old—is that at some point during their lives each of them took action, developed ideas, or organized movements that set the groundwork for the way we Americans live in the twenty-first century.

To my mind, the great men and women of postwar America include Eleanor Roosevelt, Thurgood Marshall, Daniel Patrick Moynihan, Ted Kennedy, Martin Luther King Jr., Ronald Reagan, Richard Nixon, Bill Bratton, Billy Graham, and many others. To understand them is to understand America in the twenty-first century. It is the story of a family—a new founding family for today's America. They have kept faith with the ideals of the Founding Fathers while reshaping the country. They advanced the Founding Fathers' audacious concept of a nation of free people forever able to maintain their own independence and liberty. These recent innovators have met the never-ending challenges, even threats, to the idea of a strong, free, creative people.

By recognizing the story of this new founding family, we do not ignore or diminish the contributions of the great men and women who came before them. For as long as the Republic stands, every American—statesman or layman—will be in the debt of the original Founding Fathers: Washington, Jefferson, Adams, Madison, Hamilton, Franklin, and the rest of them. Through their courage and wisdom and sacrifice, they began what Alexis de Tocqueville called "the great American experiment." The country they founded was built to endure long after they had passed from this world. And so it has. The experiment is still ongoing, and by recognizing its progress, we are paying tribute to their memory. The original Founders bound the pages into a book and penned the all-important first chapters—but they left it to future generations of founders to continue the story.

These towering figures have now passed their mantles fully to us. Future historians will look back at the present day as a coming-of-age story for the new America. During my lifetime, this new America has struggled through all of the changes, conflicts, joys, and pains that attend the passage into adulthood. But now we are beyond simply following instructions left by the Founding Fathers. As their admiring heirs in a changing world, we are keepers and protectors of a sacred trust given to us by them. Upon this rests the revitalization and future of our nation.

So who are the people who led us to America as it is today? Were they misguided or mistaken? Have we taken their visions too far? Not far enough? And, most important, where do we go from here?

In the pages ahead, I explore and chronicle the exploits of what I think of as this new founding family, the people who pushed America to a new crossroads and a new identity. By understanding these new founders, I hope we might better appreciate the big picture of our moment in time and better take stock of our nation. Through this framework, I believe we can have a more relevant, pressing, and fruitful conversation regarding the changes we are living through and which are driving us together as a people.

CHAPTER 2

THE GREAT AMERICAN MELTING POT

JFK, Ted Kennedy, and the Immigration Reform That Changed America

The Founding Fathers would have loved John F. Kennedy and his younger brother, Ted Kennedy. The two ambitious Irish Americans are famous for their political success. John became an iconic president. Ted became a long-serving, very influential U.S. senator.

While there are many innovative senators and presidents in the American saga, I would argue that the Kennedy brothers are unique in the ways they used their political power to bring new blood into the body of American life. The brothers drastically reformed America's immigration policy in the second half of the twentieth century. And while that new policy has sparked decades of political disputes over who deserves a chance to come to America, conservative and liberal politicians agree that the Kennedys' changes in immigration policy have changed the nation. And their redesigned policy fit with the original Founding Fathers' desire to have America remain always open to hardworking people bringing energy, ambition, and ideas to the new land. The men who declared independence from the British king wanted their new nation to never be constrained by what Thomas Jefferson called the "dead hand of the past." For that radical success, the Kennedy brothers deserve spots in America's new founding family.

The Kennedy family arrived in the United States in the 1840s as Irish immigrants fleeing famine. "For all intents and purposes, it [U.S. law allowing Irish immigration to the United States] was wide open when my great-great-grandparents came here in 1848," Ted Kennedy told an interviewer near the end of his life. He still knew the location of the "Golden Stairs," the steps used by his Irish ancestors as they arrived by boat and climbed the piers of East Boston.

For white people, few limits on immigration existed in the United States when the Kennedy family arrived. In the first half of the nineteenth century, there were no quotas on immigrants from Britain, Ireland, and other countries in northern Europe. The Founding Fathers encouraged people from other lands to join the growing American nation. One of the only constraints they put on immigration was to impose a waiting period before granting citizenship, to make sure newcomers shared their views of democratic government before they became naturalized. If you were black or a Native American, however, the rules did not apply. According to the Naturalization Act of 1790, passed by the 1st Congress, only "free white persons of good character" could become citizens.

But even though they were allowed to immigrate to the United States and become naturalized citizens, the Kennedys—because they were Irish—were treated differently than the earlier, mostly British immigrants. When the Kennedy family settled in Massachusetts, nearly a century after the Revolutionary War, their Irish Catholic immigrant experience had nothing to do with rebelling against British Colonial rule. Their fight late in the nineteenth century was with the "Boston Brahmins," the business and political elite in Boston, who came from British ancestors. The city's powerful British families viewed Irish immigrants as lower-class.

"There was an enormous sense of discrimination against . . . the Irish—which I remember hearing about in great detail from my grandfather [John Francis 'Honey Fitz' Fitzgerald]," Ted Kennedy recounted. His grandfather recalled the signs that read "No Irish Need Apply." Irish immigrants were "ostracized and discriminated against [in employment] and every other aspect of social-political and economic life. My grandfather Fitzgerald was the first son of immigrants that was elected to the Congress of the United States, and also [the first elected] mayor of a major city, which was a major breakthrough. But the sting of discrimination they felt was very powerful and stayed with them."

The sting was also felt by Fitzgerald's grandsons. As a senator preparing to run for president in the late 1950s, John F. Kennedy faced prejudice against Catholics in a nation with a Protestant majority. Ever since Catholics from Ireland and southern Europe began arriving in America in the nineteenth century, they were treated worse than the Protestants who had originally populated the British colonies.

By the time JFK was considering the race, just one Catholic, New York governor Alfred E. Smith, had ever seriously run for president. During his 1928 campaign, folks accused Smith of planning to build a tunnel between the White House and the Vatican. These anti-Catholic prejudices, which threatened to undercut Kennedy's political future, motivated the candidate to take a stand against Americans' fear of foreigners.

"The Irish were the first to endure the scorn and discrimination later to be inflicted, to some degree at least, on each successive wave of immigrants by already settled 'Americans,'" wrote Kennedy in a surprisingly angry 1958 essay on immigration that he drafted for the Anti-Defamation League, a Jewish group bent on building allies to fight immigration laws that limited the flow of Jews from eastern Europe—and which, less than two decades earlier, had prevented many Jews from escaping the Holocaust by immigrating to the United States. Kennedy wrote that Irish immigrants were the "only people in our history with the distinction of having a political party, the Know-Nothings, formed against them. Their religion was later also the target of the American Protective Association and, in this century, the Ku Klux Klan." And even in the 1950s U.S. immigration laws amounted to a thinly veiled racist effort to keep America "pure."

The Irish and the Jews found political support for their immigration reform movement from groups of U.S. immigrants from Italy, Greece, Poland, and Portugal. Those groups, too, were fighting immigration quotas, set up at the beginning of the twentieth century, that produced long waiting lines for relatives and friends in their native countries while visas for people from northern Europe remained unused.

Their experience of being discriminated against by government-enforced immigration quotas fit with the rising civil rights movement during the 1950s against government-enforced laws segregating black Americans. Just as Thurgood Marshall, the lead lawyer for the NAACP, claimed headlines with legal cases based on constitutional appeals calling for an end to racial segregation in schools, the immigration rights movement pointed out the same lack of equality in American immigration law. And just as civil rights leaders appealed for equal rights under the law—the first major civil rights legislation since the late 1800s and Reconstruction was passed only in 1957—the immigration reformers cited the current immigration law's lack of fidelity with the notion of equal rights and with the Founding Fathers' distaste for privileged classes. The calls for revising immigration law focused on ending regional and racial quotas limiting who had the right to enter the United States and become an American.

In *A Nation of Immigrants,* published after his death, JFK explicitly made the case that immigration exclusions amounted to an unjustified assault on the human dignity of foreigners who wanted to achieve the American dream. They "violate[d] the spirit expressed in the Declaration of Independence that 'all men are created equal,'" as Kennedy had written in his 1958 essay.

Referring to the words carved into the base of the Statue of Liberty— "Give me your tired, your poor, your huddled masses yearning to breathe free"—Kennedy wrote: "Under present law it would be appropriate to add: 'As long as they come from Northern Europe, are not too tired or too poor or slightly ill, never stole a loaf of bread, never joined any questionable organization' . . . [T]he national origins quota system has strong overtones of an indefensible racial preference."

If the Founding Fathers were able to walk America's streets today, the most obvious change to the human landscape would be the nation's incredible diversity. People are drawn here from around the globe, from a variety of ethnic and religious backgrounds. Every year about one million foreigners gain legal status in America—that's roughly 2,740 people per day. The *New York Times* reports that there may be as many as eight hundred languages spoken in New York City.

The two people most responsible for this wholesale shift in the face of the nation are JFK and Ted Kennedy, followed closely by President Lyndon Baines Johnson. Together they shaped the demographics of the

America we live in today. And the heart of their political transformation is the Immigration and Nationality Act of 1965.

The 1965 immigration law "set America on a very different demographic course than the previous 300 years," Simon Rosenberg, president of the think tank New Democrat Network, told the *Boston Globe*. By opening our doors to Asian, Latino, and African immigrants, Rosenberg argues, the 1965 Immigration Act transformed America from a nation that oppressed anyone other than whites from western and northern Europe to one that not only accepts but celebrates its racial diversity.

Rosenberg said that adding new nationalities and races to the U.S. population "changed the racial narrative in America from one of oppression—the white-black divide dating to slavery—to one of diversity." And he labeled the 1965 Immigration Act as "the most important piece of legislation no one's ever heard of."

Census data support Rosenberg's claim. Until President Johnson signed the bill into law, immigrants to the United States were primarily from Europe, and 70 percent of those immigrants settled in the Northeast and Midwest. Today the nation has shifted its demographic picture with a young, rising population of Latinos and Asians. Sixty-seven percent of all of today's immigrants settle in the West and the South.

In the 1960 census, the nation's total immigrant population—which included a six-year-old me—was close to 10 million, or 5.4 percent of the total population. By 1990, thirty years later, the number of people living in the United States who were born in other countries had grown to 20 million. And by 2010, that number had doubled again, to 40 million. Today, immigrants make up 13.1 percent of the U.S. population. In other words, between 1960—when the last census was taken before the 1965 Immigration Act—and 2010, the makeup of the United States has been dramatically recast.

Today's pursuit of the American dream is being staged by a very different cast of characters. "In 1960 there were fewer than 1 million foreign born from Latin America, but by 2010, there were 21.2 million," the U.S. Census Bureau reported in 2012. "There were fewer than one-half million [foreign born from Asia] in 1960, but by 2010 there were 11.3 million. By comparison, the foreign-born population from Europe declined from 7.3 million in 1960 to . . . between 4 and 5 million from 1990 to 2010."

The changing demographics masterminded by the Kennedys and Johnson is reflected as well by a rise in births of American-born children of immigrants. In 1970, the first census taken after the passage of the 1965 Immigration Act, immigrants and their children made up 16 percent of the population. By 2010 that group had jumped to 24 percent of the population. "In other words, over one-third of the growth in the total population of the United States between 1970 and 2010 was due to the increase in the foreign-born population and their native-born children," according to the U.S. census.

At the time of the Founding Fathers in the 1700s, the American population was almost exclusively made up of British and Scottish immigrants. The only limits in the Naturalization Act of 1790 concerned those who were not "free white persons" of "good moral character." By the middle 1800s a new wave of immigrants had begun to arrive— millions of Germans and Irish who settled in New York, Boston, and other big Eastern seaboard cities. The census reported that at times up to 30 percent of all immigrants between 1870 and 1900 came from Germany; and at times as much as 33 percent came from Ireland.

The U.S. government often took extreme measures against immigrant groups thought to be potentially violent. When groups of Chinese immigrants settled in California during the mid–nineteenth century and started getting into fights with white laborers, Congress responded with the 1882 Chinese Exclusion Act, which banned Chinese laborers from immigrating to the United States. No U.S. politician felt the political pressure to defend the rights of Chinese Americans because, due to the Naturalization Act of 1790, nonwhites—including Chinese immigrants—were barred from obtaining U.S. citizenship. They could not vote. Thus lawmakers didn't need to represent the demands of Chinese Americans. The Chinese Exclusion Act was not lifted until 1943.

As the nineteenth century came to a close, a new stream of immigrants began to arrive from Italy, Poland, Russia, and other Eastern European countries. By 1910 the nation had 13.5 million foreign-born people on its shores, and almost 90 percent of them came from Europe. "Nativist Americans . . . thought many of the Europeans who were being admitted were inferior, and the Immigration Restriction League was formed to argue against the undesirables, most of whom were Southern and Eastern Europeans," *Newsweek* editor Jon Meacham wrote in a 2009 piece on America's history of immigration. "In 1909, Sen. Henry Cabot Lodge proposed a literacy test to restrict the influx of 'Italians, Russians, Poles, Hungarians, Greeks and Asiatics,'" particularly those who did not speak English, while leaving the door open to British, French, German, and Scandinavian people. That test became law in 1917, inspiring Congress to pass more legislative limits on immigration in the 1920s. The result was fewer immigrants making their way across the Atlantic and Pacific Oceans to the United States. The Great Depression and World War II acted to further cut the arrival of immigrants.

When World War II ended and the U.S. economy picked up again, Congress reviewed its hodgepodge of immigration laws aimed at keeping out different nationalities. In 1952 the Senate passed the notorious McCarran-Walter Act, which gave immigration and State Department officials wide latitude to deny visas to potential immigrants who had associated with communists in their native countries, labeling them "immoral." Among the people excluded on the basis of the act were two writers who won the Nobel Prize for Literature, Chile's Pablo Neruda and Gabriel Garcia Marquez of Colombia, and the famed British novelist Graham Greene.

One limited good that came from the McCarran-Walter Act was the end of Asian Exclusion—a policy established by laws in 1917 and 1924 that had expanded the earlier Chinese Exclusion Act by completely barring immigration from China, Japan, the Philippines, Thailand, Vietnam, Laos, Cambodia, Singapore, Korea, Burma, India, and Malaysia. Building on the Fourteenth Amendment, which allowed African Americans born in the United States to become citizens, and the 1943 Magnuson Act, which allowed Chinese Americans to become citizens, the new law nullified the "free white persons" clause of the 1790 Naturalization Act. Nonwhite immigrants could now attain American citizenship. But the law retained racial preferences. Stephen Klineberg, a professor of sociology at Rice University, described U.S. immigration law through the early 1960s as "unbelievable in its clarity of racism." According to Klineberg, these laws defined "Northern Europeans [as] a superior subspecies of the White race. The Nordics were superior to the Alpines, who in turn were superior to the Mediterraneans, and all of them were superior to the Jews and the Asians."

When Congress attempted to pass the McCarran-Walter Act in 1952, President Truman vetoed the bill because of its restrictive quotas on immigrants from outside of northern Europe. "Today, we are 'protecting' ourselves as we were in 1924, against being flooded by immigrants from Eastern Europe," the president said. "We do not need to be protected against immigrants from these countries—on the contrary we want to stretch out a helping hand . . . to succor those who are brave enough to escape from barbarism." Truman added that "in no other realm of our national life are we so hampered and stultified by the dead hand of the past as we are in this field of immigration."

But the Senate, including California senator Richard Nixon, overrode Truman's veto. Reflecting the sentiments expressed in the 1952 law, Sen. Pat McCarran later argued that America—"the last hope of Western civilization"—was at risk of being "overrun, perverted, contaminated or destroyed . . . we have in the United States today hardcore, indigestible blocs which have not become integrated into the American way of life but which . . . are its deadly enemies."

The retention of so many restraints on immigration set the table for new debates on immigration among a new, postwar generation of political voices. Those voices included a young, politically ambitious John F. Kennedy. It was in this climate that Kennedy wrote his 1958 essay for the Anti-Defamation League calling for opening the doors to newcomers on an equal basis. The Massachusetts senator wrote: "Immigration policy should be generous; it should be fair; it should be flexible. . . . Such a policy would be but a reaffirmation of old principles." Drawing from the Founding Fathers, Kennedy cited George Washington to make the case against preferential immigration policies for white Europeans. The nation's focus on the Cold War against the Soviets during the 1950s gave Kennedy an opening to argue for extending the immigration system in the name of liberty for all. A nonracial immigration policy with equal opportunity for people from any country in the world, he argued, offered a favorable view of American democracy to people in Asian and African countries emerging from colonial rule and choosing whether to align their interests with communism or Western democracies.

By 1960 the pressure for changes in immigration law was attracting support across party lines. President Dwight Eisenhower, a Republican, told Congress that the "liberalization of some of our restrictions upon immigration" was in the nation's best traditions, and he asked for legislation to allow more refugees from political oppression to come to America. And in June 1963, JFK, now president, spoke of the "good many brothers and sisters of American citizens who are unable to get here ... [B]ecause of the maldistribution of quotas in the European area we have this situation which has become nearly intolerable."

In July 1963 President Kennedy sent Congress a proposal for immigration reform. The existing immigration system, he told Congress, "is without basis in either logic or reason" and is "an anachronism for it discriminates among applicants for admission into the United States on the basis of the accident of birth." Kennedy's proposed legislation was based on the principle of family reunification, allowing family members of individuals already in the United States to join them. It also gave preference to immigration applications from skilled workers.

"The enactment of this legislation will not resolve all of our important problems in the field of immigration law," the president said. "It will, however, provide a sound basis upon which we can build in developing an immigration law that serves the national interest and reflects in every detail the principles of equality and human dignity to which our nation subscribes."

When JFK was assassinated in November 1963, he was busy revising his 1958 essay on immigration. His goal was to publish it as a book and use the excitement around its release to stir public support for his immigration reform bill and pressure Congress to pass it. The president's assassination gave appeals for passage of this new immigration legislation added emotional power, as it did also for the passage of the historic 1964 Civil Rights Act ending segregation between the races in hotels and other public places.

"In a time when this country is attempting to wipe away ancient wrongs against Negro citizens its conscience will not permit a sign at all ports of entry reading: 'Only whites from Northwestern Europe are welcome,'" the *New York Times* wrote in a June 1965 editorial supporting changes to the immigration law as the Senate debated the bill.

The president's brother Ted Kennedy, who had won the Senate seat from Massachusetts vacated by JFK's ascension to the White House, became floor manager of the bill in the Senate. It was the first time in his career that he had taken the lead on a bill, and he made its passage a personal campaign; a reporter later described it as a "milestone in the remarkable career of the junior Senator from Massachusetts." Ted Kennedy also wrote an introduction for *A Nation of Immigrants* that captured the passion he and his late brother shared to correct old injustices against their immigrant ancestors and others suffering the same discrimination.

"Immigration is in our blood," Ted Kennedy wrote, speaking of both the Kennedy family and the nation. "It's part of our founding story. In the early 1600s, courageous men and women sailed in search of freedom and a better life. Arriving in Jamestown and Plymouth, they founded a great nation. For centuries ever since, countless other brave men and women have made the difficult decision to leave their homes and seek better lives in this Promised Land. . . . From Jamestown to the Pilgrims to the Irish to today's workers, people have come to this country in search of opportunity. They have sought nothing more than the chance to work hard and bring a better life to themselves and their families."

Ted Kennedy's strongest ally in the Senate was Sen. Philip Hart, a Michigan Democrat and grandson of Irish immigrants who was known as the "conscience of the Senate." In the House, Sen. Kennedy's primary ally was New York Democrat Emanuel Celler, a grandson of three German Jewish immigrants, who represented the borough of Brooklyn and its large immigrant population. Senator Kennedy also rallied churches and Italian, Polish, and Greek organizations, particularly those with strong union ties, behind the bill. And the senator found support in the Johnson White House by promoting the immigration bill both as his fallen brother's legacy and as part of LBJ's effort to create a "Great Society."

"This bill goes to the very central ideals of our country," Ted Kennedy pleaded during a Senate floor debate. "Our streets may not be paved with gold, but they are paved with the promise that men and women who live here—even strangers and newcomers—can rise as fast, as far as their skills will allow, no matter what their color is, no matter what the place of their birth."

The 1965 Hart-Celler Act eliminated the discriminatory national quota system then in use. Instead, Congress enacted a policy that privileged immigrants seeking to reunite across borders with their American families. It eased entry for scientists, artists, highly skilled professionals, and even unskilled immigrants with proven experience in jobs where U.S. employers needed workers.

Opposition to the bill came from conservatives concerned with high poverty rates and the cost of welfare for the poor. Presciently, they argued that the bill would produce a dramatic rise in immigration that would change the nation's racial makeup. The critics had public opinion on their side. A May 1965 Harris Poll found 58 percent of Americans opposed to revising limits on immigration from outside northern and western Europe.

At one Senate hearing, Myra Hacker, the vice chair of the New Jersey Coalition of Patriotic Societies, a conservative group, cited "mounting welfare costs" and asked, "Are we prepared to embrace so great a horde of the world's unfortunates?" Her dissent, she said, was not about bias against any group. "Whatever may be our benevolent intent toward many people, [the bill] fails to give due consideration to the economic needs, the cultural traditions, and the public sentiment of the citizens of the United States."

Rep. William Miller, son of a man who swept factory floors for a living, was worried about the impact all the immigrants might have on low-wage workers. Miller, the Republican vice presidential candidate in 1964, told reporters during a debate on the bill: "We estimate that if the President gets his way and the current immigration laws are repealed, the number of immigrants next year will increase threefold and in subsequent years will increase even more. . . . [Don't you think we should] look at this situation realistically and begin solving our own unemployment problems before we start tackling the world's?"

North Carolina Democratic senator Sam Ervin claimed that opening the door to people from all over the world would "discriminate against the [western European] people who had first settled and shaped the country." West Virginia Democratic senator Robert Byrd said it was foolish to forget that western Europeans are "more easily and readily assimilated into the American population."

The opponents predicted a sharp increase in immigration that would threaten to shake the stability of the United States with a first-in-history social experiment in mixing nationalities and races. Ted Kennedy and his supporters dismissed those predictions as scare tactics. They called on the memory of the Founding Fathers to condemn the critics as racists who are "out of line with the obligations of responsible citizenship. They breed hate of our heritage." During a Senate hearing, Ted Kennedy said: "First, our cities will not be flooded with a million immigrants annually. Under the proposed bill, the present level of immigration remains substantially the same. . . . Secondly, the ethnic mix of the country will not be upset . . . [by people coming from] the most populated and economically deprived nations of Africa and Asia."

Having succeeded in the House, the bill passed the Senate by a vote of 76–18. President Johnson signed the bill in October 1965 on Liberty Island in New York Harbor, site of the Statue of Liberty. Ted Kennedy and his brother Robert F. Kennedy, the former attorney general and newly elected junior senator from New York, both attended. Their presence captured media attention, as the bill was seen as a tribute to President Kennedy's memory and to the Kennedy family's immigrant background.

"Our beautiful America was built by a nation of strangers," President Johnson intoned on a glowing fall Sunday afternoon with the statue above him and the brilliant sun reflecting off the horizon of wealth and opportunity represented by the New York City skyline. "From a hundred different places or more they have poured forth into an empty land, joining and blending in one mighty and irresistible tide." The new law's emphasis on bringing families together, the president said, was certain to prevent a rush of people other than the mostly white Europeans whose families were already in the United States. Though Johnson recognized that the new law would put an end to the racism in the American immigration system, it was not going to dramatically change the country. "It will not reshape the structure of our daily lives, or really add importantly to either our wealth or our power."

But in fact the law did change America, ending the long-held preference for white immigrants from northern Europe. Despite assurances that no more than a few thousand Asian immigrants would enter the country under the new law, 2.6 million Asian immigrants came to the United States in the 1980s. In 1960, Asians made up 5 percent of the total number of immigrants coming to the United States; by 2010, the figure was 28.2 percent. In 2013, the Pew Research Center reported, the percentage of Asian immigrants, legal and illegal, coming to the United States had surpassed the percentage of Hispanic immigrants.

Ted Kennedy continued his work on immigration. In 1979 he led the fight in the Senate for changes to the immigration law to allow more political refugees to enter the country. In the same year he was at the center of efforts to increase the number of visas available to people seeking to enter the United States from Mexico and Canada. In 1986 he led negotiations with President Reagan that resulted in a bill allowing more than 2.7 million people then in the United States illegally, without a proper visa, to become legal residents. Critics today call the Kennedy-engineered bill "blanket amnesty" for people who broke America's immigration laws.

Kennedy was so passionate in his defense of immigrants that, once he was certain the 1986 bill had enough votes to pass, he himself voted against it. A provision in the bill provided for sanctions against employers who hired illegal immigrants, and Kennedy worried that this might lead some companies to avoid hiring any Hispanics.

Kennedy was also involved in the immigration reform in 1990 that resulted in an international lottery for fifty thousand "green cards," the documents granting immigrants permanent resident status and the right to work in the United States. Kennedy was again a central figure in President Bush's failed efforts at a 2007 immigration reform bill to give what was then estimated to be twelve million illegal immigrants the chance to become citizens.

Thanks to Ted Kennedy's efforts, the nation's newcomers reinvented American commerce and culture (and cuisine—hot sauce now outsells the once all-American condiment: ketchup). Kennedy's work ended policies that many saw as overtly prejudicial. He succeeded in triggering a pronounced shift in the American identity by changing which regions of the world sent immigrants to America. In 1960 the European share of total U.S. immigration was 74.5 percent. In 2010—forty-five years after passage of the 1965 immigration bill—the European share of total U.S. immigration was down to 12.1 percent.

To be sure, the disruption caused by Kennedy's tireless advocacy of immigration reform has led to a rise in anti-immigrant sentiments and widespread criticism of the constant cultural changes brought on by the presence of all these newcomers. Among leading political conservatives there has emerged nostalgia for the era before the 1965 Immigration Act. During a 2012 Republican primary debate, Representative Michele Bachmann claimed that "immigration law worked beautifully" before the 1965 Act.

The anxiety produced by high rates of immigration, both legal and illegal, goes far beyond Bachmann's conservative political supporters. The Pew Research Center, a nonpartisan think tank, estimates that in 2050, when the U.S. population will likely be well over 400 million people, more than 80 percent of the population growth between 2005 and 2050 will have come from immigrants and their U.S.-born children.

According to critics, the impact of such immigrants has weighed down the nation's social services, overburdened its schools, and increased crime rates. Harvard professor George Borjas, in his book on U.S. immigration policy, *Heaven's Door,* argues that since 1965, immigrants coming to America have depressed wages for unskilled American workers, are more likely to end up on public assistance, are more likely to resist assimilation, and are slower to learn to speak English than immigrants who arrived before 1965.

But the Kennedy legacy on immigration also includes vital contributions to American commerce, intellectual life, and culture from America's dynamic new population. Whole areas of the nation, particularly small towns and the South, have been revived by an infusion of immigrants. In 2012 the *Wall Street Journal* reported: "Since the 1990s Latinos have flocked to places like Dalton, Ga., to work in the carpet mills, and to the Piedmont section of North Carolina to work in furniture manufacturing. . . . Between 2000 and 2010, the Hispanic population in the Midwest swelled 49%, more than 12 times the 4% overall population growth there, according to the census."

President Obama's political victories in 2008 and 2012 are directly tied to the young, heavily immigrant vote he captured in his two campaigns. It is estimated that more than 20 percent of voters age eighteen to twenty-nine, a group President Obama won by overwhelming margins, are children of immigrants.

The original Founding Fathers came from various walks of life. They arrived in the American colonies from different countries (nine of the fifty-five delegates to the constitutional convention were born overseas) and lived in different states as they formed the Union. Today's modern-day founding fathers and mothers similarly bring a variety of backgrounds, strengths, virtues, and flaws to the essential task of extending the American dream.

As the original Founding Fathers began passing from the scene in the early 1800s, Daniel Webster spoke of an American civic duty to preserve and defend their creation. That included preserving the right for ordinary Americans to adjust it, to change it, and to build on their past efforts at good government. What they created grants the power to open our doors to new people, and no one embraced that idea more than Ted Kennedy.

In an interview toward the end of his life, Senator Kennedy was asked if it had been a mistake to open the doors so widely to immigrants of all lands. He conceded that he had not anticipated that a decrease in domestic births and the rise of immigration would lead to such a dramatic shift in the composition of the American population. But he embraced his work as the architect who widened the doors to American life, helping to create the America we live in today. Kennedy said: "To be energized we need new workers, younger workers . . . The fact is, this country, with each new wave of immigrants, has been energized and advanced, quite frankly, in terms of its economic, social, cultural and political life. . . . I don't think we ought to fear it, we ought to welcome it."

CHAPTER 3

THE LIVING
CONSTITUTION

Earl Warren, Thurgood Marshall,
Martin Luther King Jr., Lyndon Johnson,
and the Fight for Civil Rights

Most of the Founding Fathers owned slaves. They could have owned me. Had President Obama been alive at the time of the Founding Fathers, he too might have been a slave.

Thomas Jefferson, author of the Declaration of Independence, wrote these inspiring words: "We hold these truths to be self-evident, that all men are created equal; that they are endowed by their creator with certain unalienable rights; that among these are life, liberty and the pursuit of happiness." But even as he made those lofty promises, Jefferson owned black people. Jefferson denounced slavery as a "hideous blot" on America. At another point he called it a practice of "unremitting despotism on the one part, and degrading submissions on the other." Yet he owned slaves, hundreds of them.

You may be surprised to learn that Ben Franklin owned slaves. So did the father of our nation, George Washington. Some of the Founding Fathers opposed slavery as exploitation and a matter of morality. But the Constitution they wrote allowed it.

If time travel were possible and the Founding Fathers arrived in the United States today, the sight of a dark-skinned president would certainly make no sense to them. For successful, educated white men in eighteenth-century America, the concept of racial and gender equality just did not exist. Their understanding of what was rational, given the social hierarchy of the time that placed white male landowners at the top and black slaves at the bottom, would have ruled out the idea of a black man as the leader of our country and commander in chief of its military force.

Similarly, the thought of a black woman such as Condoleezza Rice or a white woman such as Hillary Clinton as secretary of state might make them laugh. To their thinking, it would have been an absurdity. Nancy Pelosi, political leader of the House Democrats, would also have made no sense to the Founding Fathers. When they signed on to the idea that "all men are created equal," that meant all *men*—it did not include women. No woman stood as an equal among the Founding Fathers, nor in any other group of white men. The Founders did not give women participation in government through the right to vote.

This historical disconnect across the centuries is not a condemnation of the Founding Fathers. By all measures they were the best of their generation. But the concept of racial equality, the idea of women's rights, and more generally the notion that individuals are granted certain rights that government cannot take away are concepts that hadn't yet developed in the Founders' era.

That is why the Founding Fathers did not think it contradictory to write "We hold these truths to be self-evident, that all men are created equal" even though many of them were slaveholders. That passionate declaration, even if it came from the minds of slave-owning men, inspired people around the world. It set a standard for human rights that inspires us—that inspires me—to this day.

Still, not everyone in 1776 was blind to the striking gap between the ideals of personal liberty expressed in the Declaration and the reality of slavery in early America. One of the Founding Fathers' contemporary critics, a British abolitionist named Thomas Day, wrote that "if there be an object truly ridiculous in nature, it is an American patriot, signing resolutions of independency with the one hand, and with the other brandishing a whip over his affrighted slaves." Two hundred years later, Supreme Court Justice Thurgood Marshall, speaking on the bicentennial of the Constitution, in 1987, was equally pointed in his assessment of the difference between the Founding Fathers' words and actions. In Justice Marshall's view, the heroes of 1776 "could not have imagined, nor would they have accepted, that the document they were drafting would one day be construed by a Supreme Court to which had been appointed a woman and the descendent of an African slave."

Speaking to a group of prominent lawyers, the first black Supreme Court justice added: "And so we must be careful, when focusing on the events which took place in Philadelphia two centuries ago, that we not overlook the momentous events which followed . . . [T]he true miracle was not the birth of the Constitution, but its life. . . . I plan to celebrate the bicentennial of the Constitution as a living document, including the Bill of Rights and the other amendments protecting individual freedoms and human rights."

The greatness of the Declaration of Independence, former chief justice Earl Warren said in an interview at the end of his career, is as "an emotional and a spiritual expression of the American people." It is an articulation of a desire for liberty and protected rights. But it lacks specifics about how to achieve equality for all. It does not lay down rules on how to manage differences of opinions among the states. It does not offer a road map for settling disputes between the states and a federal government on how to achieve these idealistic goals.

The Constitution does include the specifics about how to achieve equality among certain types of people, as well as the checks and balances against tyranny by any person or group in control of government power. The Constitution's precepts resulted from a "series of a lot of compromises that are absolutely essential in order to bring about a nation," Chief Justice Warren explained. But it took another eighty years, until the post–Civil War era, for the American people to realize that the rights of men needed to include African American men as well. And it would take yet another hundred years after that for lawmakers to fully protect the rights of African Americans, as well as other oppressed groups.

To be sure, moving the legal mountains of entrenched racial, sex, and ethnic segregation required a huge set of historical actors. And it is difficult if not impossible to single out a handful of people in this movement as somehow more important than the rest. Doing so risks omitting thousands of people who led by example, as well as the countless activists, religious leaders, politicians, financial backers, novelists, celebrities, and newspaper editors who offered visionary concepts of how to shift the nation's laws and culture. But four men stand out, in my opinion, as leaders in the effort to build a new structure of twenty-first-century civil liberties. They took the lead in creating a "new normal" for racial equality in twenty-first-century America. They brought to life the Declaration of Independence's ideal of all men being equal, of having unalienable rights of life, liberty, and the pursuit of happiness. Those four men are Chief Justice Earl Warren, Justice Thurgood Marshall, President Lyndon Johnson, and Dr. Martin Luther King Jr.

Warren, Marshall, Johnson, and King largely focused on the problem of racial equality. But their work has served as a model for other oppressed groups that, like African Americans, have ensured that the government protects their right to live and thrive in contemporary America.

Justice Marshall, Chief Justice Warren, President Johnson, and Dr. King were not the first figures to use Congress and the Court to seriously alter America's conception of civil liberties. In fact, Warren argued that America's legal history is best understood as a series of steps taken by the Supreme Court in different historical eras to elaborate on the original Constitution.

The cases that came before the first Supreme Court and the first chief justice, John Marshall, Warren said in an interview, "were cases that determined actually the viability of the federal government." During the decades surrounding the Civil War, the Supreme Court and Congress looked into the question of slavery, as well as race relations more generally. Things went back and forth for many decades. Though in the 1857 case *Dred Scott v. Sanford* the Court decided that blacks, whether enslaved or free, could never become citizens, the Thirteenth, Fourteenth, and Fifteenth Amendments, which were passed after the war ended, abolished slavery and gave blacks citizenship and the right to vote. Though it seemed like the Civil War had given blacks their rights, these rights were effectively taken away by *Plessy v. Ferguson*, an 1896 Supreme Court ruling that separate institutions for blacks and whites were legal as long as they were equal.

Not every law and Court decision involved race. During the late nineteenth century, in the midst of the industrial revolution, the Court ruled on "the relationship of corporations to the state . . . whether they were persons or not. And most of [the decisions involved] the rights of business and the rights of corporations rather than the rights of individuals. Not because the Court chose it that way . . . but because that's the kind of litigation that came to [the Court] because of the thinking of the times," commented Warren. "And then along came the Roosevelt era. And from that time on you have the rights of individuals, the rights of the poor, the rights of minority groups and all."

In 1920, the long-term effort of famous feminists such as Elizabeth Cady Stanton, Susan B. Anthony, and Carrie Chapman Catt paid off with the passage of the Nineteenth Amendment, which gave women the right to vote.

But after World War II, as the United States emerged victorious from its battle with global oppression and fascism, Warren explained, "people all over the world were thinking in terms of freedom, it took hold of people in our country and they started thinking that if we could make the whole world free we ought to be making our own people free." This postwar desire for freedom set up our new founding fathers—Warren, Marshall, King, and Johnson—to radically transform the concept of civil liberties.

One overriding event pulled these four into a single orbit, where they went to work, spinning the ideas, events, and personal agendas that produced a changed America. That one event is the 1954 *Brown* decision.

The *Brown* decision created heightened expectation for racial equality. It unleashed volcanic pressures in American society for social change. It also generated powerful opposition to changing the traditional divide in race relations.

EARL WARREN CAME into his role as the driver of this historic shift in America's basic beliefs from an unlikely background.

Born in Los Angeles, the future chief justice was the district attorney for Alameda County, California, where the city of Oakland is located, from 1925 to 1939, making a name for himself as a prosecutor known for busting bootleggers. He used wiretaps and allegedly even forced confessions from suspects. In one celebrated case he successfully prosecuted a deputy sheriff for taking bribes. In 1931, a Columbia law professor described Warren as "the most intelligent and politically independent district attorney in the United States."

In 1938 Warren was elected California's attorney general. He riveted the state's attention with sensational cases against illegal gambling operations on boats anchored near Santa Monica, California. He first gained national attention after the 1941 Japanese attack on Pearl Harbor, Hawaii. In Warren's public pronouncements, he expressed his fear about the large number of Japanese Americans living in California, claiming they were a hidden threat to the state. He argued for the arrest and confinement—the "internment"—of all Americans of Japanese ancestry living within 150 miles of the California coast.

Speaking two months after Pearl Harbor at a news conference, Warren conceded there was no evidence of sabotage or subversion by Japanese Americans in California. But calling the presence of a large Japanese American population in the state "the Achilles' heel of the entire civilian defense effort," he concluded the Japanese government was simply waiting to attack. In another speech, Warren observed that "it looks very much to me as though it is a studied effort not to have any [attacks] until the zero hour arrives."

The public alarm Warren sounded as the state's chief criminal watchdog was central to the federal government's decision to send Japanese Americans to internment camps away from the coast, as far as Arkansas, Colorado, and Idaho. The attorney general's justification was simple: in a time of war "every citizen must give up some of his normal rights." It is the only time in American history that the government confined a group of Americans on the basis of that group's ethnic identity.

The interned Japanese Americans lost their land, their homes, and their rights when they were deported to cramped, overcrowded camps. Japanese American children were taken out of schools and sent away from friends. Even when U.S. forces began to push the Japanese out of the Pacific in 1943 and critics called for the release of fellow Americans who posed no threat, Warren, now California's governor, resisted.

"If the Japs are released," Governor Warren said, "no one will be able to tell a saboteur from any other Jap. . . . We don't want to have a second Pearl Harbor in California. We don't propose to have Japs back in California during this war if there is any lawful means of preventing it." In fact, the law supported Warren's position. In 1944 the Supreme Court upheld the constitutionality of the Japanese American internment in *Korematsu v. U.S.*

Warren was reelected governor in 1946, winning an astounding 90 percent of the vote. His popularity led to his selection as Thomas Dewey's vice presidential running mate on the GOP's losing ticket in the 1948 presidential election. In 1951, well after the interned Japanese Americans were released, the governor made a trip to Japan to "demonstrate that California no longer harbored ill feelings for the Japanese people." He also became active in urging companies to hire Japanese Americans returning from the internment camps at the end of World War II. He later acknowledged: "It was wrong to react so impulsively, without positive evidence of disloyalty, even though we felt we had a good motive in the security of our state."

The popular California governor campaigned for the GOP presidential nomination in 1952 but lost to General Eisenhower. When Eisenhower won the White House, he named Governor Warren as his solicitor general. But in September 1953, Supreme Court chief justice Fred Vinson had a heart attack and died. President Eisenhower, looking for a Republican able to win Senate confirmation without a political fight, picked the tall, silver-haired Californian. Warren's background as a prosecutor, coupled with his support for Japanese internment, led conservatives to give him their support. But he had also gained liberal support for his investment in public works projects and the state's higher education system during his time as governor of California. As a result, the Senate unanimously confirmed Warren as the Supreme Court's chief justice.

When Warren arrived at the Supreme Court, the big issue facing the Court was the constitutionality of having state, local, and federal government agencies enforce laws requiring racial segregation. The lead lawyer in cases around that issue was the NAACP's Thurgood Marshall.

In 1944 the Court had ruled that Texas Democrats could not hold a whites-only primary. In 1946 the justices said that it was not constitutional for any state to enforce segregation on buses and trains traveling interstate routes. By 1948 they prohibited any court from enforcing contracts limiting the purchase of homes to whites. And in two 1950 cases the high court ruled in favor of African Americans who had been barred from admission from graduate schools in Oklahoma and Texas because of the color of their skin.

These cases had all been brought to the Court by the NAACP and its top lawyer, Marshall. It was Marshall who set the table for the constitutional challenges on equal rights that Warren faced as he took his seat as chief justice.

Thurgood Marshall's success before the Court put pressure on him to attack one of the main pillars of public segregation: separate public schools for black and white children. Marshall was reluctant to move too quickly, fearing that it could lead to a defeat that might set back progress in asserting equal rights for black Americans. But his fellow civil rights lawyers pushed him, and ultimately he brought cases from four different states and the District of Columbia to the Supreme Court to challenge the constitutionality of public school segregation.

The master strategy for the legal challenge to segregation had been put in place while Marshall was in law school. Things got started when Charles Garland, a white Harvard College student, created a liberal foundation with the fortune he had inherited from his father. One of its first grants, in the amount of $100,000, went to the NAACP in 1929 to fund studies on how to end oppressive codes of racial separation being enforced in the South by state and local law enforcement. The grant's goal was to give a black man in the South "his constitutional rights, his political and civil equality, and therewith a self-consciousness and self-respect which would inevitably tend to effect a revolution in the economic life of the country." Due to the Great Depression, the NAACP only received $27,000 of the $100,000 that the Garland Fund had initially promised. But the initial money was enough to fund work by a white Harvard-educated lawyer, Nathan Ross Margold, who came up with a strategy to defeat *Plessy v. Ferguson*'s "separate but equal" doctrine.

Plessy had involved a man who looked white but had one black great-grandmother. The one-eighth-black man was dragged by police from a whites-only train car in New Orleans and put in jail for violating the laws of racial segregation. The Supreme Court ruled against the plaintiff, Homer Plessy. The majority opinion explained that while the

Constitution and the Fourteenth Amendment provided equal rights for all, they did not outlaw local Jim Crow ordinances in the South that kept black and white people separate in public places ranging from restaurants to bathrooms to trains. "A statute which implies merely a legal distinction between the white and colored races [does not] ... destroy the legal equality of the two races," the opinion held.

Dissenting in the *Plessy* case, Justice John Marshall Harlan wrote that allowing local enforcement of racial segregation also allowed the "seed of race hate to be planted under the sanction of law." He asked, "What can more certainly arouse race hate, what more certainly create and perpetuate a feeling of distrust between these races, than state enactments which, in fact, proceed on the ground that colored citizens are so inferior and degraded that they cannot be allowed to sit in public coaches occupied by white citizens?"

Harlan's dissent was only a legal footnote, as the *Plessy* ruling sanctioned the spread of Jim Crow laws. In the state of Florida separate textbooks were printed for black and white students. In South Carolina black workers at cotton mills could be jailed for looking out the same windows as whites. Opposition to the laws of racial segregation slowly took shape at the start of the twentieth century. Booker T. Washington, a black educator who gained wide fame with his calls for blacks to establish their own schools and businesses, called for a conciliatory (many would say overly conciliatory) approach to civil rights. A countermovement took shape in 1905, when black intellectual and activist W. E. B. Du Bois co-founded the Niagara Movement, an interracial group of men and women seeking full racial equality. In 1909 that group founded the National Association for the Advancement of Colored People in order to "secure for all people the rights guaranteed in the 13th, 14th and 15th Amendments to the United States Constitution, which promised an end to slavery, the equal protection of the law and universal adult male suffrage, respectively."

But the question was how to do it. The group lacked a legal strategy, until Margold decided to ask the courts to force the states to spend money to provide separate facilities that were really equal for both white and black citizens. Margold wrote to the NAACP's leaders that whites always had superior facilities, from better schools to better seats on trains and buses. In his opinion, that amounted to a violation of "separate but equal" and was grounds for legal challenges to the segregation laws.

After the Great Depression began with the stock market crash in late 1929, the NAACP began to act on the Margold strategy. The first step, in 1935, was to recruit the dean of Howard University Law School, a black World War I veteran, Charles Hamilton Houston, to put the plan into action. Houston decided to start with lawsuits against segregation in graduate and professional schools. One of the cases brought Houston's top law student, Thurgood Marshall, to join him as co-counsel in arguing for an end to the ban on blacks attending the University of Maryland's law school, located in Baltimore, Marshall's hometown. They won that case in 1935 in local court. It was followed by a defeat in Missouri courts in a challenge to racial segregation at the all-white University of Missouri law school, in 1938. On appeal, the Missouri case went all the way to the Supreme Court. Marshall and Houston won when the Court ruled that black residents of the state had the right to be educated in their state's law school.

In 1940 Marshall succeeded Houston as the NAACP's lead counsel, continuing the strategy of attacking "separate but equal." The legal argument never shifted. Segregation, Marshall contended, violated the Fourteenth Amendment's requirements for equal rights under the Constitution. By 1950 Marshall had won ten Supreme Court cases in which he argued for the right of black Americans to serve on juries, vote in previously all-white primaries, and sit anywhere they wanted to on interstate buses. In 1951 Marshall told reporters the NAACP had launched a "legal action program calling for an immediate attack on all racial segregation practices at the state and municipal level." In 1951, a *New York Times* story reported on the NAACP's "recently adopted courtroom theme that racial segregation at any level creates 'psychological roadblocks' that prevent Negroes from attaining equal status in society as guaranteed by the Fourteenth Amendment."

The first set of arguments before the Supreme Court on the five cases that collectively made up the *Brown* decision took place in December 1952. The high court, under Chief Justice Fred Vinson, had ruled in favor of integrating graduate schools in Texas and Oklahoma because the states lacked equal schools for blacks. But Vinson's Court never declared the doctrine of "separate but equal" to be illegal and a violation of constitutional protections of individual rights. Marshall argued that the cases went beyond equalizing schools for whites and blacks. He said segregation of black and white children was "actual injury" to a black child's development because it amounted to "humiliation." In June 1953 the Court surprised Marshall and the political world by setting an October date for the case to be reargued. The justices asked the lawyers to answer questions about the history of the Fourteenth Amendment, specifically if Congress had intended to end school segregation. The NAACP hired historians, including John Hope Franklin, an esteemed black academic, who quickly found no evidence that the men who wrote the amendment wanted schools to be racially integrated. And the states that ratified the Fourteenth Amendment had not interpreted it as requiring school integration.

But in September 1953, a month before the second set of arguments, the players in the case dramatically shifted with Chief Justice Vinson's death. "We knew he [Vinson] was against us, but we managed to get it reargued," Marshall later told an interviewer. "And then he died. The Lord was on my side!" That was when President Eisenhower named Earl Warren as chief justice, bringing Marshall and Warren, two titans of twentieth-century law, into the same powerful orbit.

Marshall first had to figure out where the new chief justice stood on "separate but equal." After all, Warren was still the man who had called for the internment of Japanese Americans without evidence that they posed a real threat to American security. In fact, he consistently and loudly justified the action when questioned about it. That made the NAACP lawyers nervous. Their questions about Warren's racial views sent Marshall to California to talk to the state's political and civil rights leaders about how to win over Warren. But Marshall got strong, positive reviews of Warren as a law-and-order, good-government politician with no history of bias against blacks or Latinos. Labor leaders said Warren, the son of a railroad worker and union organizer, had always been fair to them. But when it came to his approach to the law, Warren was a mystery. He had never been a judge. The most that California NAACP leaders and Democrats could tell Marshall about Warren was that as attorney general and governor he had always responded to principled arguments made on the basis of the law. That fit with President

Eisenhower's description of Warren at the announcement of the appointment as a man who "has a national name for integrity, uprightness and courage that, again, I believe we need on the Court."

Warren took his seat October 5, 1953. He was the only former politician among the members of the Court. Two months later, Chief Justice Warren and Marshall came face-to-face at the Court as Marshall argued that the Fourteenth Amendment was intended to protect individual rights in all cases, even if schools had remained segregated after its ratification. The opposing lawyer argued that even after the Fourteenth Amendment became law, the Supreme Court had ruled that segregation was legal. In his rebuttal Marshall said: "Ever since the Emancipation Proclamation, the Negro has been trying to get . . . the same status as anybody else regardless of race." He dismissed school segregation as an attempt to deny equal rights to blacks and keep "the people who were formerly in slavery . . . as near that stage as is possible."

Later accounts by members of the Court indicated that before Warren's arrival—with Chief Justice Vinson in charge and prior to the second set of arguments—the Court was leaning toward upholding school segregation. But after hearing Marshall's arguments Warren began telling the other justices in conference and then in one-on-one meetings that as a matter of legal principle under the Constitution racial segregation made no sense to him.

Chief Justice Warren was critical of past Supreme Court justices who had chosen to "run away from [the high court's] jurisdiction just because it affects a social condition." He felt that if the Supreme Court had decided the first civil rights cases properly in the nineteenth century, "we would have avoided much that we're troubled by at the present time," referring to 1950s and 1960s protests calling for equal rights and the violence of segregationists opposed to equal rights for minorities.

The reason the Supreme Court failed to act in dealing with the rights of black citizens after the Civil War and the passage of the amendments guaranteeing black men equal rights and voting rights, Chief Justice Warren concluded, was that "Negroes were so poor and there were so few Negro lawyers" that legal cases about violations of the minority's rights did not reach the lower courts, much less the Supreme Court. People thought, "What's the use of bringing them," as Warren put it.

The chief justice also had support from an Eisenhower Justice Department friend-of-the-court brief that Warren had requested when he came to the Court. The brief sided with Marshall's argument that "compulsory segregation" of black schoolchildren was illegal under the Fourteenth Amendment because it violated the guarantee of equal rights. The new chief justice, a successful politician with experience in building alliances, spoke to the members of the Court about issues beyond the law. He asked the other justices to think about the morality of racial segregation. It was an amazing transition for the man who, as attorney general, had stripped Japanese Americans of their constitutional rights. In memoirs written years later, Warren's brethren on the high court said he told them any approval of segregation under law had to be based on the assumption that blacks are inferior to whites. One prominent legal scholar, Bernard Schwartz, later described Warren as challenging the other jurists for the first time to think in terms of "fairness" and an evolving set of constitutional principles for a new era of life in America.

Warren's political experience also came into play in the *Brown* case. The former attorney general and governor persuaded his fellow justices that it was in the best political interest of the high court to speak with one clear voice in a unanimous opinion on such a divisive subject. That he said this out of concern for the reputation of the Supreme Court gave him added standing with his new colleagues. The chief justice managed to cajole even Justice Stanley Reed, a Kentucky native who belonged to an all-white golf club and the man Marshall considered most likely to dissent, to join in the unanimous ruling as a sign to the nation that the Court stood on principle, apart from racial traditions and racial politics, to present a strong, unified voice.

On May 17, 1954, Marshall arrived at the Supreme Court to hear the *Brown* ruling. Chief Justice Warren, seated with the associate justices of the Court, personally read the decision out loud. "In approaching this problem we cannot turn the clock back to 1868, when the [Fourteenth] Amendment was adopted, or even to 1896, when *Plessy v. Ferguson* was written. We must consider public education in light of its . . . present place in American life. . . . We conclude that, in the field of public education, the doctrine of 'separate but equal' has no place. Separate educational facilities are inherently unequal."

Brown v. Board of Education constitutes a continental divide in the landscape of American law. First, it began the Court's swing away from a focus on property rights to an era of concern over an individual's civil rights. Second, the *Brown* ruling triggered waves of change, even turmoil, in American politics and American race relations. It started the modern civil rights movement for blacks as well as for other minority groups, the poor, and women.

In his memoir, Warren writes that he "deeply regretted [the internment of Japanese Americans] and my own testimony advocating it, because it was not in keeping with our American concept of freedom and the right of citizens." Yet Warren's remorse for his hard-line support for internment during World War II motivated his defense of individual civil liberties in *Brown* and other Supreme Court decisions. His personal transition on the issue of civil rights helped to transform the Supreme Court. And the Court's new interpretation of racial equality set in motion a tremendous wave of social reform that changed the nation.

In 1955, one year after *Brown,* a minister named Dr. Martin Luther King Jr. joined the fray by leading a yearlong protest against segregated buses in Montgomery, Alabama. Aided by Marshall and the NAACP, in 1956 a district court, citing *Brown,* ruled that segregated buses violated the Fourteenth Amendment. The Warren Court affirmed the lower court's ruling and ordered the integration of Montgomery buses. The Montgomery bus boycott, which made King a celebrity, motivated others to take stands against Jim Crow around the South. In August 1963 this era of lawsuit, protest, and political activism came to a historic moment of national attention when King spoke to the largest demonstration Washington had ever seen: the March on Washington.

President Kennedy, a supporter of Dr. King, had proposed a Civil Rights Act in June 1963. But when he was assassinated in November 1963, President Lyndon Johnson picked up the effort and called on Congress to act as a tribute to the martyred president. "No memorial or eulogy could more eloquently honor President Kennedy's memory than the earliest possible passage of the civil rights bill for which he fought," Johnson told a joint session of Congress five days after the assassination. "We have talked for one hundred years or more. Yes, it is time now to write the next chapter—and to write it in books of law."

PRESIDENT JOHNSON WAS more than a political bystander to the Supreme Court's *Brown* decision, the civil rights movement, and the passage of the Civil Rights Act.

As a political leader in the Senate he had not risked political capital to support racial equality among his fellow southern Democrats, showing only passing interest in a watered-down 1957 civil rights bill. By most accounts Johnson had a hand in weakening the bill before it passed.

But all that changed in 1964. The civil rights bill he proposed was stronger than the bill first proposed by President Kennedy. President Johnson's bill went beyond banning segregation in hotels, restaurants, theaters, and retail stores. It required the government to stop funding for federal programs that allowed racial discrimination. And it gave the attorney general the power to file suits calling for racial integration in local school districts, as required by the Supreme Court's *Brown* decision. The act was passed by Congress in July 1964. The intense opposition from the segregationist South reportedly led Johnson to turn to an aide immediately after the signing of the bill to say, "We have lost the South for a generation."

To this day President Johnson is remembered in Washington for his limitless ambition. As a young politician he allegedly stole a Senate election. As a deal maker in the Senate he was known for playing political hardball. His fierce pursuit of the war in Vietnam despite its high cost in lost lives and minimal results forced him to announce he would not run for a second term as president in 1968. For all his flaws, though, the domineering, outsized Texan took the civil rights movement deeply to heart.

But the movement hardly ended with the passage of the 1964 Civil Rights Act. In March 1965, the nation watched as Sunday night television shows were interrupted by video of state troopers brutally attacking a group of six hundred peaceful protestors in Selma, Alabama, leaving many of them bloody. The marchers were calling for voting rights for African Americans. President Johnson responded to the violence within days with a speech to Congress that was watched by seventy million people. "Their cause," the president said, "must be our cause, too, because it's not just Negroes, but it's really all of us who must overcome the crippling legacy of bigotry and injustice. And we shall overcome."

Martin Luther King Jr., watching the speech on television with a group of black ministers, began to cry when President Johnson used the gospel-inspired words of the movement—"we shall overcome." "A tear ran down his cheek," recalled Rev. C. T. Vivian. "It was a victory like none other. It was an affirmation of the movement."

In August 1965 President Johnson signed the Voting Rights Act, which banned the various methods (literacy tests, for instance) that southern states had used to block African Americans from voting. The president signed the Voting Rights Act in the President's Room off the Capitol Rotunda, the same room where President Lincoln had signed the Emancipation Proclamation 102 years earlier. "The vote is the most powerful instrument ever devised by man for breaking down injustice and destroying the terrible walls which imprison men because they are different from other men." President Johnson said. That makes the Voting Rights Act, he concluded, "one of the most monumental laws in the entire history of American freedom."

President Johnson's strong stand on voting rights for blacks infuriated segregationists, particularly his fellow southern Democrats in Congress. They were already upset with the administration's push for passage of the 1964 Civil Rights Act. The president's political instinct was to delay action on the voting rights bill. He wanted to give the South time to adjust to the 1964 bill and the reality of interracial hotels and restaurants. But Dr. King and other activists insisted on taking advantage of the civil rights movement's momentum and moving immediately to begin work on a voting rights bill. They forced the issue by staging protests in Selma and other towns where local white political leaders kept political power through violent opposition to black voter registration.

After the deaths of several voting rights activists, President Johnson showed surprising compassion. He connected the movement to the Founding Fathers' promise that in America "all men are created equal." In a news conference a week after highly publicized beatings, he described voting rights for all Americans as more than his administration's policy. "It is in the heart and purpose and the meaning of America itself," he said in announcing plans to send the 1965 voting rights bill to the Congress.

President Johnson's knowledge of racial injustice was in part derived from his experience as head of the President's Committee on Equal Employment Opportunity, where Johnson, then vice president, came to know national civil rights leaders, including Dr. King, personally as he began to apply his political skills to their issues. It also awakened a part of his own past. In the 1920s, as a young man, Johnson had taught Latino fifth through seventh graders in south Texas.

When Johnson returned to Welhausen Elementary in Cotulla, Texas, as president, he told those in the audience that his experience there had stayed with him. "Right here I had my first lessons in poverty," he said. "I had my first lessons in the high price we pay for poverty and prejudice right here. Thirty-eight years later our nation is still paying that price . . . over half of all the Mexican-American children have less than 8 years of school. How long can we pay that price? . . . [T]he conscience of America has slept long enough while the children of Mexican-Americans have been taught that the end of life is a beet row, a spinach field, or a cotton patch." As president he made improving the quality of schools for Latino, black, and white children one of the keys to his domestic agenda, which he called "the Great Society."

Johnson's Great Society programs included Head Start, to help poor children prepare for school; food stamps, to make sure the poor had food; Medicare, to help seniors pay their healthcare bills; and Medicaid, to help the poor get medical services. During his presidency the poverty rate was cut in half, dropping from 23 percent to 12 percent. He named the first black cabinet secretary—Robert Weaver, as secretary of housing and urban development—and nominated the first black Supreme Court justice, Thurgood Marshall.

President Johnson's use of his considerable political muscle and the emotional aftermath of President Kennedy's assassination to get passage of the Civil Rights Act and Voting Rights Act transformed the hard-wiring of American law on race. President Johnson's political achievements—combined with the powerful and transformative work being done by Chief Justice Earl Warren, NAACP lawyer Thurgood Marshall, and the public activist Dr. King—succeeded in shifting the nation's understanding of the Constitution from acceptance of legal segregation of the races to the foundation of racial equality under law.

That shift changed America. It reversed a history that started with a Constitution that had deprived black people of full citizenship rights and even denied them full humanity, counting black slaves as three-fifths of a person. The post–Civil War amendments had given freed slaves equal rights under law, but the reality of strict segregation left blacks living as an oppressed racial minority, with the power of the courts and the government aligned against them, forcing their submission.

"What is striking is the role legal principles have played throughout American history in determining the condition of Negroes," Thurgood Marshall, by then a member of the Supreme Court, noted in a 1987 speech celebrating the Constitution's bicentennial. Blacks "were enslaved by law, emancipated by law, disenfranchised and segregated by law; and, finally, they have begun to win equality by law. Along the way, new constitutional principles have emerged to meet the challenges of a changing society. The progress has been dramatic, and it will continue."

The shift led by Warren, Marshall, King, and Johnson in the mid-twentieth century changed that history. It revised the idea of American freedom, for the first time making it the government's role to protect equal rights and equal opportunity for people of different races. It put a new face on civil liberties and legal rights and changed everyday life in the United States for people of all races.

The world of individual and civil rights under law affirmed by the Warren Court is beyond the imagination of America's first-generation Founding Fathers. The Supreme Court under the "Super Chief," as Warren is known, ended laws supporting public school segregation and set the law for reapportionment of congressional districts to equalize political power between urban and rural areas. His Court gave poor people the right to public counsel, agreed to Miranda warnings for criminal suspects as protection against self-incrimination, said no to mandatory school prayer, and created a right of privacy for citizens.

Marshall, who won twenty-nine of the thirty-two cases he argued before the Court as a civil rights lawyer, led the fight while serving on the Supreme Court to expand legal protection for the press, for immigrants, for a woman's right to abortion, for the homeless, and of course for minorities.

Apart from his work on civil rights, President Johnson helped found

Medicare, Medicaid, and Head Start, and pushed for the Education Act of 1965, which helps low-income students attend college.

Dr. King is memorialized in marble on the National Mall in Washington; his birthday is a national holiday in honor of the cultural sea change he helped to bring about in the nation's culture and conscience. The nation's openness to equal protection under the law for women, for gays, and for the disabled is but a part of Dr. King's legacy.

These four men are responsible for foundational shifts in American culture. They changed the face of America and the laws under which we live. They are in the front ranks of the new founders who have reshaped America in the twenty-first century.

CHAPTER 4

BROKEN WINDOWS, URBAN CRIME, AND HARD DATA

Bill Bratton and Modern Policing

Every time I open a door or window in my house a sharp, beeping noise goes off. There is an alarm on my car, too. My cell phone requires a passcode. So does my computer and my employer's website.

That is just the beginning of security in twenty-first-century America.

When I drive to work I make a point of slowing down as I approach several speed cameras. There are red-light cameras, too, ready to snap pictures of my car if I run a stoplight. And there are cameras that read my license tag number and keep it for later review in case a crime is committed. When I drive to work I gain entry to the garage with a pass containing a computer chip. It tracks when I arrive and leave. Another pass gives me access to the elevators inside the office building. And still another pass allows me through the doors to the suite of offices where I work.

The Founding Fathers never experienced being constantly watched. There were no police force and no security guards in their day. In fact, there were no prisons. The first prison did not appear until 1790—the Walnut Street Jail in Philadelphia. And even the idea of crime was different, and punishments varied from colony to colony and case to case. Adultery was a crime. In the late seventeenth century Massachusetts juries ordered the execution of twenty colonists for witchcraft. Thieves were whipped or made to hang in the stocks. And murderers were often executed. But that was it for justice.

Today stopping crime in America is a billion-dollar business. There are even more private guards than police. IBM, Microsoft, and other tech companies make huge profits selling law enforcement agencies gadgets to keep track of people walking city streets, riding public transit, and browsing computer sites. By the Founding Fathers' standards, this is all done with relatively little protest.

Terrorism, specifically 9/11, led Americans to accept high-tech policing techniques that earlier citizens would have rejected for violating the Fourth Amendment's protections against government surveillance. The Uniting and Strengthening America by Providing Appropriate Tools Required to Intercept and Obstruct Terrorism (USA Patriot) Act, signed by President Bush a month and a half after 9/11, allowed the government to legally intercept private conversations and correspondence and even to enter homes and businesses for what was described by the Founding Fathers as unreasonable search and seizure.

While the Founding Fathers focused their concern on the individual rights of citizens facing a powerful government, the current concern over crime and terrorism has produced a radical change in Americans, who are willing to accept more intrusions by government in exchange for the promise of security, both at home and abroad.

Now citizens willingly turn to the government—the police, the military, and secret agencies—for protection against crime directed at them, as well as crime directed at corporations. Americans generally go along with government's self-protective steps. We put up with X-ray searches, metal detectors, and random pat-downs, knowing that these measures are intended to stop terrorism, protect us, and maintain the very idea of the United States as a superpower.

Until recently, these heightened security measures prompted relatively little protest. Americans rarely charge the government with violating their civil liberties; after all, this approach to protecting citizens seems to be working. Though anxiety over crime remains high, crime rates are the lowest they've been in decades.

Due in part to stricter policing techniques, today more than 2.2 million Americans are behind bars. Another 4.7 million Americans, though not technically in prison, are under "community correctional supervision," meaning that, as punishment for a crime they have committed, they cannot vote and are not eligible for public housing or food stamps.

So how did this come to be? What changed in the American mind to upend previous generations' understanding of Fourth Amendment protections of personal privacy?

The individual who more than anyone else demonstrated that the collection and use of increasing amounts of data could yield tangible results in fighting crime and preventing terrorism is Bill Bratton. To me, the current New York City police commissioner and former chief of police in Boston, New York, and Los Angeles belongs to America's new founding family for introducing and spreading the use of data to combat criminal activity. It was also Bratton who put the theory of "broken windows" policing into practice. This policy drove down crime rates by cracking down on small criminal violations, from panhandling to loitering and loud music, in order to discourage criminals from committing larger crimes.

Bratton's success in driving down crime rates in American cities during the 1990s transformed modern policing. His top aides have become police chiefs in cities and towns nationwide. They've spread Bratton's crime-fighting techniques coast to coast. In the process they pushed citizens to trade off constitutional privacy rights in exchange for protection from terrorist attacks and street crime. The new police tactics spoke to a primary concern for this generation of Americans: freedom from fear of becoming the victim of an attack.

Before the rise of Bratton's data-driven approach to policing, several big cities, from New York to Detroit and L.A., were, as the newspapers put it, on the brink of "chaos," experiencing a "breakdown of civility and authority."

Beginning in the 1960s, the crime rate in the United States began to rise, and it continued to rise until the arrival of Bratton's new style of policing in the 1990s. Based on the numbers of aggravated assaults, robberies, and murders, the crime rate especially went up in the nation's biggest city, New York. The federal National Institute of Justice blamed the rise in crime rates on a breakdown of respect for police authority. Wealthy and middle-class taxpayers were leaving for the suburbs, as were major retail stores. New York City lost 10 percent of its population in the 1970s—mostly white middle-class citizens who felt the city was too dangerous and who moved to the outlying suburbs.

"The civil rights and antiwar movements challenged police," the federal agency concluded. "This challenge took several forms. The legitimacy of police was questioned: students resisted police, minorities rioted against them, and the public, observing police via live television for the first time, questioned their tactics."

With the middle class leaving, cities became home to higher percentages of poor people, racial minorities, and recent immigrants. The changing population highlighted the lack of racial diversity in big-city police departments, which were dominated by Irish and Italians. Crime became a big story in these cities during the 1980s. Several notorious murder cases, carjackings, and muggings generated sensationalistic headlines about the dangers of city streets. Racial fears added to the tension. With poor black neighborhoods as the center of the highest rate of street crime and an overwhelmingly white police force, charges of police brutality became a constant refrain. At the same time, some black leaders charged that white police and white politicians did nothing to stop crime in black neighborhoods.

Drugs added to the hellish mix in big cities as crack cocaine emerged as a cheap, addictive high that drove an outbreak of small crime—purse-snatching, stealing car radios, and selling drugs in the open—by people looking to pay for their habit. Fights between rival drug dealers with easy access to guns led to drive-by shootings and fear of random violence. Folks referred to Harlem as a "jungle"—you entered at your own risk.

In turn, black people accused white society of assuming that they were all thugs. Several young black men thought to be criminals were killed by groups of whites in New York during the 1980s. In 1984 Bernhard Goetz, a white man who became known in tabloid newspapers as the "Subway Vigilante," shot and seriously injured four black teenage boys who tried to rob him on the subway. While some were outraged at Goetz's actions, others expressed sympathy at Goetz's efforts to defend himself.

As the percentage of black voters in New York City grew with the departure of white middle-class residents, there was also a political shift. New York, Cleveland, L.A., and several other big cities got their first black mayors and chiefs of police. U.S. courts began to hand out stiff sentences for selling and using drugs, sending more people into jail than any other country in the world. But even that did not halt the increasing crime rate.

In his book *The Prince of the City*, journalist Fred Siegel writes that the New York police "ceased policing all but the most serious crimes in the inner city . . . Early violations of the law were treated with indifference; 'minor crimes' such as stealing car radios and low-level burglaries were effectively decriminalized. The upshot was that violent crime quadrupled between 1966 and 1990, reaching its peak with the crack epidemic. . . .

"In the summer of 1990 'wolf packs' of young teen toughs armed with easily accessible guns roamed the city. . . . [I]n the first six months of 1990 more than forty children were killed by random gunfire," Siegel reports. He believes that New York's lawless attitude, in part, made the city "become filthy . . . streets had become public toilets with the right to urinate in public vigorously defended by the city's army of earnest civil liberties lawyers." The subways became breeding grounds for tuberculosis, often carried by "deinstitutionalized mental patients whose right not to take their medicine had been secured by the same attorneys." Siegel concluded that in the nation's biggest city "the breakdown of civility and authority was pervasive."

When a famous tough-on-crime prosecutor, Rudy Giuliani, became mayor of New York in 1993, he hired a police chief who had had success in restoring a sense of safety to the subway system—Bill Bratton.

The former Boston policeman arrived as head of the New York transit police system in 1990, when a record number of felonies—from outright assaults to snatching chains from passengers' necks and petty theft—made a simple train ride into a hellish venture. Bratton had graduated from a technical high school in Boston, then served during Vietnam in the Army's Military Police Corps. His first job out of the military was with the Boston police.

At thirty-two, just ten years after joining the force, he became second-in-command of the Boston police. An ambitious supervisor looking to advance further up the ranks, he developed a reputation as an attention seeker. When he boldly told a reporter he wanted the top job, the brassy display of ambition rankled his boss and got him demoted. What is clear about Bratton is that he did not fit the image of previous generations of head-busting, brass-knuckled Irish policemen. He was not willing to patiently wait for his turn to take charge according to the rules of seniority that kept the police a closed society, much like a fraternity. Instead, Bratton's ambition opened him to any good idea and any effective manager willing to be loyal to him. In particular, he became interested in the idea of using new computer technology to see where crime was being committed and to track the identity of people regularly behind crimes. The old guard of policemen bucked when Bratton suggested that crime rates could be brought down by observing crime patterns with innovative computer technology. They saw it as a threat to their old way of doing business; Bratton did not care. He saw it as a way to make a name for himself and gain promotion.

Bratton was not happy waiting in line, and his ambition to run a police force led him to leave Boston. He won the job as chief of New York's transit police and served from 1990 to 1992. During this time he first met Rudy Giuliani, the famed prosecutor who had narrowly lost a race to become mayor. In the big-city subways he put added staff behind an effort that began before he arrived to get graffiti off train cars and get the homeless out of stations. The idea was to demonstrate to the public and to the criminals that police had control of the subway system.

The theory that getting graffiti off the trains and kicking homeless people out of the stations could reduce crime had its roots in a seminal 1982 *Atlantic Monthly* magazine article by two academics, James Q. Wilson and George Kelling. The article, which set forth the "broken windows" theory of policing, made the claim that "disorder and crime are usually inextricably linked in a kind of developmental sequence. Social psychologists and police officers tend to agree that if a window in a building is broken and is left unrepaired, all the rest of the windows will soon be broken." When a community accepts small-time vandalism, they let criminals know that real crime is acceptable too. Bratton convinced his force to approach crime as an interconnected web, where misdemeanors, such as homeless people begging in the subway, are connected to bigger crimes, such as robbery. Bratton's tenure as head of the city's subway police proved the theory's success and rewarded his ambition. Crime on the subways dropped by 75 percent between 1990 and 1994.

During his time with the transit police Bratton reduced the number of police officials at headquarters, transferring more responsibility from division captains to sergeants accountable for crimes taking place in their zones. He also made his priorities clear to his team as well as to the public. His top priority was stopping robberies of subway travelers; second was discouraging people from jumping turnstiles to ride for free; and third was restoring a sense of civility and order to the subway riding experience. He wanted clear metrics for measuring the crime rate and his success at combating crime.

Bratton's success with the New York transit system landed him the job he really wanted, as head of the Boston police. He left the transit job after only two years. Two years later, the always ambitious Bratton got an even better offer. In 1994, Rudy Giuliani, the newly elected mayor of New York, asked him to run the New York City police force, the largest police department in the country.

As New York's top cop, Bratton made the crime statistics come alive with electronic, lighted maps of the city that revealed high-crime areas, the types of crime committed in various districts, and the time of day those crimes took place. The *New Yorker* headlined a 1995 story about Bratton "The CEO Cop."

Bratton later described his system as motivated by his frustration with police officers "flying blind" as they tried to fight crime. Before Bratton, cops patrolled city streets somewhat arbitrarily, responding to—but not preventing—crime. In a 1999 article in *City Journal,* Bratton and former special assistant William Andrews wrote, "The prevailing criminological wisdom held that the police couldn't do much about crime and that police strategies and tactics didn't really matter. . . . Police brass lurched from emergency to emergency, with no one looking at the overall picture." Once Bratton took charge, he and his top aides developed weekly crime reports showing "felony crime arrest data for every precinct, comparing it with the totals for the previous week and the month- and year-to-date totals. 'Compstat' was the computer-file name of this report, a contraction of 'comparison statistics.'"

With this new system Bratton instructed his command staff to compare where crime was occurring with where most police officers were stationed. "If the two didn't match up you knew you were doing something wrong," wrote Bratton and Andrews. They added, "Compstat's maps helped make sure that we were putting our resources where the problems were, and when they were happening. We could quickly assess whether new strategies and tactics worked or failed."

Bratton's statistical patterns translated into surprisingly effective policing strategies. If burglaries went up in a neighborhood, he brought in the warrant division to go after people with records for burglary who lived in the area. If there was a spike in car robberies, Bratton's police set up car registration checkpoints to make it difficult for thieves to drive away. "It's not too strong a statement to say that we reinvented police strategy in 1994," wrote Bratton and Andrews.

Bratton combined his use of data with the improved-quality-of-life standard he employed in the subways. Police precincts no longer let small offenses go without punishment. Crimes from underage drinking to street-level drug dealing and loud radios were treated with equal ferocity. Suddenly police started arresting the often drugged or homeless people who stood at red lights demanding money from car owners to wipe cars' windshields.

"In truth . . . in 1994 and 1995, the drop in New York crime accounted for more than half of the crime decline in the entire country: we weren't part of the national trend [of declining crime rates]; we drove the trend," Bratton and Andrews wrote. And they were right. Bratton's innovative approach to crime fighting became the model for modern policing.

The downside of Bratton's style was a 50 percent jump in complaints from city residents about aggressive police tactics. In poor minority communities that saw clear drops in crime, the police did not become heroes but were seen as a hostile force. The focus on minor offenses and more frequent frisking of people for drugs and weapons alienated some residents.

In a 1996 speech given at the Heritage Foundation, "Cutting Crime and Restoring Order: What America Can Learn from New York's Finest," Bratton said: "When I match the 9,000 or so complaints against the 38,000 cops who are making 300,000 arrests and issuing several million summonses, and against the millions upon millions of street encounters by police who are encouraged to get out there and take back the streets, I think that 9,000 complaints is a fair exchange."

But people did more than complain. In 1999, the first of several class action suits against the city's stop and frisk policy was filed, claiming that the procedures were unlawful and tantamount to racial profiling. Most of the people stopped, told to put their hands up, and detained— and thus shamed—were young black and Latino men. And rank-and-file police, under pressure to make their statistical maps look good with sharp declines in crime, voiced their complaints to the press about the new regime downtown, often creating friction between police and Bratton's brass in headquarters.

But Bratton's statistically proven success in cutting crime over-whelmed any critics. Politicians, business leaders, and middle-class voters applauded Bratton. He became a celebrated figure nationally, with popularity exceeding that of his boss, Mayor Giuliani. That led the mayor to grow disenchanted with Bratton's larger-than-life profile. In March 1996, just two years after becoming police commissioner, the innovative Bratton was forced out of the job.

Bratton spent the next several years doing safety and security con-sulting in the private sector, at one point working for a company hired to monitor Los Angeles's troubled police department; in 2002, six years after leaving the NYPD, he became chief of the LAPD. His intense use of statistics worked again, as crime dropped for six straight years. And he did a better job of handling the politics of police work this time around. First, he deferred to politicians more easily. And when he en-countered problems with poor and minority residents, he readily dealt with local ministers and council members. When complaints came in about police forcing suspects to get spread-eagled against walls so po-lice could frisk them, he changed the practice. An older, wiser Bratton saw it as the price for added job security and for gaining wide support for his revolutionary tactics. To gain public backing for his policing style, he put more time into increasing racial diversity and the number of women on the police force.

Unlike his previous quick exits in Boston and New York, Bratton served in L.A. for seven years, even gaining reappointment as police chief, the first time in twenty years an L.A. police chief had had his contract renewed. Bratton's innovations in policing went nationwide during this period, as his aides got top police jobs around the nation, from suburban Boston to Miami, Chicago, Baltimore, and beyond. He was a sought-after speaker on crime and addressed corporations about leadership.

A popular television show, *The Wire,* focused on the use of police wiretaps of corner pay phones, cell phones, and pagers to catch fictional drug dealers in Baltimore. The show first aired in 2002, but according to former crime reporter and creator of *The Wire* David Simon, in real life Baltimore police began employing a few basic techniques in the 1980s, such as devices that allowed them to record which numbers were frequently dialed from public phones in drug trafficking areas. The use of wiretaps and surveillance grew during the 1990s as Bratton's extensive use of the tactics in New York and later in L.A. expanded their acceptance in local and state courts.

Bratton's fame extended worldwide. Queen Elizabeth II honored him in 2009 with the title Commander of the Most Excellent Order of the British Empire. In 2011 British prime minister David Cameron tried to hire Bratton as London's police chief. That idea failed because the job required British citizenship, but Bratton became an adviser. Among other projects, he returned to a private firm that he had founded back in 1999 to do security investigations and risk assessments for corporations, and served as vice chair of an advisory group to the federal government's Department of Homeland Security. Then, in 2014, he was hired by incoming New York City mayor Bill De Blasio to serve as New York City police commissioner a second time.

In every job Bratton has pioneered expanded use of data to track patterns of crime, along with aggressive and open surveillance of city streets, automobile traffic, and entries to residential and office buildings. He has also expanded public acceptance of police watching, following, and frisking possible criminals.

In the process he has transformed modern policing. Data-driven policing and the "broken windows" theory—Bratton's two major contributions—are now standard police procedures across the United States. And Bratton's legacy goes beyond street-level policing. Any top private security force that fails to generate, gather, and analyze as much data as possible is seen as second-rate. Now police departments practice "predictive" policing by using data analysis to predict the time and location of future criminal activity. The *New York Times* reported that in 2012 New York City began using the Domain Awareness System, developed by Microsoft and the police department. It can "analyze video from the more than 3,000 police surveillance cameras across the city and comb through a variety of other databases, from license-plate readers to sensors that can pick up heightened radiation levels to arrest records."

Before Bratton, suspects had been tailed by police, been secretly photographed, and had their mail opened and phones tapped. And American courts have struggled with the need to balance personal privacy rights against the need to preserve public safety as far back as the 1800s. The fast rise in powerful, cheaper technology in the 1980s and 1990s added to the fevered increase in police tracking and surveillance of Americans.

To be sure, Bratton did not develop the techniques. He did not develop the technology. He simply used them more effectively and more successfully in fighting crime on the big stages of Boston, New York, and L.A. At every level of public safety—police, military, and federal intelligence agencies—Bratton's success is now the gold standard. His ability to convince politicians and the public of the good that comes from trusting police and federal spy agencies to conduct intense surveillance of people also created a historic shift in the previous constitutional balance between safety and privacy.

And in the aftermath of the horrific 9/11 terror attacks, Bratton's crime-fighting techniques gained further acceptance. Politicians and judges became open to allowing police, federal agents, and private security forces to be proactive in dealing with crime by extracting information from computers, email, cell phones, letters, and informants. Fear of all kinds—of being hijacked on airplanes, of being bombed, of poison gas—led the public to drop reservations about giving the government power to intrude on individual rights and liberties.

The USA Patriot Act was introduced in the House of Representatives on October 23, 2001, passed on October 24, passed by the Senate on October 25, and signed into law by President Bush on October 26.

There was limited opposition in the House, and only one senator voted against it despite provisions that seemed to directly challenge constitutional freedoms. The Patriot Act gave law enforcement the right to search a house or place of work without obtaining consent or a warrant. Following in Bratton's footsteps, the new law allowed the FBI to review a person's Internet searches, telephone records, and banking and financial transactions. Investigators could even go into public libraries and bookstores looking for lists of books a citizen had read.

The best way to prevent terrorism, Bratton argued in a 2002 interview with *Commonwealth Magazine,* is to apply "much of what we learned in dealing with the traditional crime problem in this country in the 20th century to the new paradigm of crime in the 21st." Bratton specifically pointed to "significant deficiencies we have at this time," including the lack of the sophisticated technology necessary to do the job, though he noted that "we have the capability to develop that fairly quickly." Bratton went on to say, "We had reached a tipping point in the 1970s when crime went out of control in this country and nearly overwhelmed American police forces. It wasn't until the 1990s that we were able to tip it back the other way."

Bratton also called for local police to become part of the federal effort to defeat terrorists. He pointed out that while there are only 12,000 FBI agents, there are 700,000 police officers across the country. Local police are on the streets every day, Bratton and George L. Kelling wrote, where they "communicate regularly with local residents and business owners, and are more likely to notice even subtle changes in neighborhoods they patrol. They are in a better position to know responsible leaders in the Islamic and Arabic communities and can reach out to them for information or for help in developing informants."

Bratton's idea of giving local police added authority to deal with international terrorism gained traction as the basis for getting new federal dollars flowing into city and state treasuries. Even before the terrorist attacks, Congress issued a report calling for a new federal agency to oversee all areas of "national homeland security." But it went nowhere. There has never been a national police force in the United States; the FBI helps state and local police with investigations and takes charge of crimes that cross state lines. Opposition to the idea of a national police force meant that the congressional report would simply "collect dust," reported the *Nation* after the fact in 2013. But after 9/11 opposition faded fast. Concerns from small-government conservatives and liberals worried about civil liberties protections became secondary to fear of another attack.

The first step on the path of a federal police force, created in the name of fighting terrorism, took place when President George W. Bush created a White House–based Office of Homeland Security. "The continuing threat of terrorism, the threat of mass murder on our own soil, will be met with a unified, effective response," the president said. That led the federal government in March 2003 to begin its largest reorganization since the creation of the Defense Department at the end of World War II.

Like city police forces, the federal government experienced a revolution in intelligence gathering during the twentieth century. For that we can thank the work of two men: J. Edgar Hoover, director of the FBI from 1935 to 1972, and William Donovan, director of the Office of Strategic Services (OSS), the template for today's Central Intelligence Agency (CIA) and National Security Agency (NSA).

"Today, most Americans take for granted that our country needs a federal investigative service," explains the FBI's official website. Yet the idea that the national government has the right to review a citizen's daily activities in pursuit of crime is not something that America's original Founding Fathers would have accepted. Out of fear of an intrusive federal government, the colonists approved the Bill of Rights, which outlined individual liberties that the federal government can't take away. In early America the federal government had control over resolving interstate issues, but not much else.

Yet the growing ties between the states in the early twentieth century, through business and especially the increasing network of rivers, railroads, and roads that took people across state lines, motivated President Teddy Roosevelt and Attorney General Charles Bonaparte to create in 1908 a small staff of detectives whose job would be to look into interstate bank fraud, land fraud, smuggling, bankruptcy, and illegal immigration. The FBI grew gradually during the early nineteenth century, and under J. Edgar Hoover, who became FBI director in 1932, it developed into the large, national force of crime fighters it is today.

Hoover also introduced the very controversial idea of tailing potential dissidents, especially communists during the Cold War. Hoover's domestic espionage work was matched on an international scale by the work of William "Wild Bill" Donovan, a wealthy and well-connected conservative who founded the Office of Strategic Services in 1941. The OSS was a temporary federal agency set up to organize covert missions during World War II. In 1947, as the country faced a long-term "cold war" of Soviet aggression, President Truman agreed to Donovan's proposal to create a permanent Central Intelligence Agency. Over the next half century, these two organizations, the FBI and the CIA, grew immensely, leading secret missions to assassinate warlords in far-flung nations and keeping tabs on potential Soviet spies hiding among us.

After 9/11, the immense network of government-sponsored defense agencies that had developed over the twentieth century was streamlined to fight a new enemy: global terrorism. The various parts of the government dealing with security inside the country were consolidated under the new cabinet-level Department of Homeland Security. It was not called a police force. But twenty-two previously independent agencies, from the nuclear incident response team (previously in the Department of Energy) to the people responsible for transportation security (previously a part of the Department of Transportation), began providing data and reporting to one boss.

The new Homeland Security agency used the Patriot Act to forecast likely sites for crime, advancing the use of Bratton's data-gathering techniques to prevent terrorism. Homeland Security's data collection efforts have benefited exponentially from intelligence gathered by the FBI and the NSA, including information from the Internet, the data banks of technology companies, surveillance of people, and phone company records. Section 215 of the Patriot Act allowed the federal government to get "any tangible thing" relevant to an investigation of suspected terrorists or possible acts of terrorism. Another section, 206, gave the government the right to use "John Doe" roving wiretaps. Under that provision the government did not have to name the person being wiretapped, explain the person's connection to suspected terrorist activities, or identify the place being wiretapped.

Agencies gathering information in the name of homeland security grew in number and staffing. By 2010 "some 1,271 government organizations and 1,931 private companies [were] work[ing] on programs related to counterterrorism, homeland security and intelligence in about 10,000 locations across the United States," the *Washington Post* reported. The paper said that 20 percent of those government agencies were "established or refashioned in the wake of 9/11."

The national government's use of Bratton-like data collection tactics has generated criticism outside of Congress. Some of it has come from lawyers representing people who found their names mistakenly placed on lists of those not allowed to board airplanes or targeted for warrantless searches of their homes, computers, and letters. Lawyers for those citizens cited the Constitution's Fourth Amendment protections against random search and invasion of privacy. For example, in 2004, federal agents, under the authority of the Patriot Act, secretly went into the home of an Oregon lawyer suspected of being involved with terrorists. They hid listening devices in the home. A U.S. district judge later found no probable cause to suspect that the lawyer had ties to terrorists.

"With our cellphone and Internet usage, we carry in our pockets technology that allows the government to follow our every movement," wrote Elden Rosenthal, a civil rights lawyer defending the falsely accused Oregon man. "In the name of national security we have created a secret court [the Foreign Intelligence Surveillance Act authorized creation of a court to review requests for secret warrants] and a huge spying apparatus. History tells us what can easily follow," Rosenthal added. "The government now claims: 'Don't worry, we will be careful and never use the apparatus of global monitoring to invade your rights.' . . . Americans in the future will rightly hold us responsible for casting aside the relationship between citizen and government that has been the basis of the American experiment in self-rule since the founding of our nation."

But the public fear of another attack led to further laws giving the government the right to collect personal information. In 2007 the Patriot Act was supplemented with passage of the Protect America Act. The new law allowed the government, without getting a warrant, to tap email and phone conversations between Americans and any foreign person possibly involved with terrorism. Critics, without citing

Bratton's use of similar tactics by local police, nicknamed the new law the "Police America Act" and charged that it "authorized a massive surveillance dragnet."

It was later revealed that under the Protect America Act the federal government put in place a program called the Portal for Real-time Information Sharing and Management (PRISM). With access to video, email, Skype, and files stored or transferred in the cloud by private firms, the PRISM program soon became the government's biggest net for collecting raw intelligence used to search for terror threats. But in order to find and track potential terrorists operating covertly, the program has had to collect data on people with no ties to terrorist activity whatsoever. This was Bratton's Compstat program—organized by local police to discern patterns in street crime—taken to a national level, with billions in added dollars and added manpower, and legal authority from Congress and the federal courts standing behind it.

President Obama defended the extensive secret collection of information as critical to fighting terrorism. "You can't have 100 percent security and then also have 100 percent privacy and zero inconvenience," he said. "You know, we are going to have to make some choices as a society." Thomas Friedman, a columnist for the New York Times, backed the president. Saying he worried about another terror attack, Friedman wrote: "If there were another 9/11, I fear that 99 percent of Americans would tell their members of Congress: 'Do whatever you need to do to, privacy be damned, just make sure this does not happen again.'" Friedman added that the use of data mining was better than a panicked public giving the government "a license to look at anyone, any e-mail, any phone call, anywhere, anytime."

On the other hand, a New York Times editorial condemned the Obama administration for allowing privacy rights to be crushed. The piece argued that "for years, members of Congress ignored evidence that domestic intelligence-gathering had grown beyond their control, and, even now, few seem disturbed to learn that every detail about the public's calling and texting habits now reside in a N.S.A. database."

After two young terrorists exploded a homemade bomb at the finish line of the Boston Marathon in 2013, Bratton cited the rarity of such an attack as evidence of the success of his data-driven approach to preventing street crime and halting terrorism. Displaying seeming indifference to the Founding Fathers' concerns about privacy rights, Bratton told *Forbes* magazine there might be more terror incidents if not for a "seamless web of timely, accurate, intelligence," gathered by federal and local police agencies, that allows for a "collaborative response" to any potential terror threat. "In the age of big data, the more information we have the better the analysis," said Bratton, summarizing the transformative work he began as a young, ambitious Boston policeman.

Bratton made himself into an advocate of almost unlimited use of statistical models, surveillance techniques, and the gathering of personal data about Americans by police, the federal government, and private companies. The reality he created is far from the Founding Fathers' imagined vision of America. But it is a reality for Americans today in an age when the threat of terrorism remains a part of daily life. We live with Bratton's legacy in every corner of the country, and that is why Bratton stands among our modern-day founders.

CHAPTER 5

"NO APOLOGIES, NO REGRETS"

General William Westmoreland and the Rebirth of the U.S. Military

A t football, baseball, and other sporting events these days Americans stand on command to applaud our soldiers. High-tech military jets fly over sports stadiums in ear-popping displays of American pride at being the world's undisputed sole military superpower. America spends billions on military defense, more than the world's next seven largest combat forces combined. We have nineteen aircraft carriers; China has only one. The United States has become a fortress of military marvels, armed with stealth airplanes (invisible to radar), smart bombs (able to be precisely guided to targets and even change course in flight), and drone aircrafts (remotely controlled to spy on or attack the enemy from above).

Today, the United States military is America's most trusted institution. And the most honored figures in modern American life at the start of the twenty-first century are the soldier, marine, airman, and sailor.

Who built this dominant, high-tech military machine?

Hint: it wasn't the Founding Fathers.

Once the ragtag Continental Army—an army that didn't even exist until several months into the war—won America's independence from Britain, the army disbanded and General George Washington went back to his plantation at Mount Vernon. Neither the Founding Fathers nor the American people more generally desired a powerful national standing army. To the contrary, they feared that a permanent army would become thugs and tax collectors for kings and tyrants.

In modern America, that kind of skepticism about the military is rare. Today an otherwise politically polarized American public finds common identity in its uniformed service members. And since the 1970s, the number of Americans expressing trust in the military has increased to an astounding 76 percent. Over the last fifty years, Gallup polling shows a steep loss of trust in our schools, banks, newspapers, and unions, as well as our political institutions—most of all the U.S. Congress. But as the poll numbers show, the military is respected more and more. The man or woman in uniform is honored in neighborhoods black, white, Asian, and Latino, in rich big-city neighborhoods and poor ones, and among people with a college education as well as people without a high school diploma. Questions about huge military budgets are an issue. And American public support for deploying the military in wars, from Kosovo to Iraq, is subject to political debate. It can rise or it can fall, especially when those conflicts drag on longer than predicted. But trust in the military never wavers.

The transition that led the nation to become at ease with its powerful military is primarily the work of four generals. Their fingerprints can be found all over our smart bombs, "shock and awe" strategy, and expert commando units, including the U.S. Navy SEAL team that killed al Qaeda terrorist leader Osama bin Laden. At the end of the Vietnam War, these generals took on an army suffering from racial tensions and drug abuse, as well as a public that had grown disenchanted with the military. Each in his own way, these generals restored internal order, regained the public's respect, and trained better-equipped, more-responsible soldiers able to carry out complex missions. Most of all, the new military was able to win. That success places these generals in the new founding family of people who created today's twenty-first-century America.

The leading architect of this historic project is General William Westmoreland, the man who commanded our military forces during the Vietnam War. Rebuilding the military was a personal mission for Westmoreland. After the Vietnam War, he saw himself castigated as a liar and a loser. And his military was harshly judged as dissolute in newspaper stories about the My Lai massacre and the Pentagon Papers scandal. Bestselling books, rock-and-roll songs, and Hollywood movies drew a tragic picture of the U.S. forces in Vietnam on a misguided mission against defenseless peasants and farmers.

To Westmoreland, this was an insult that cut to the pride he took in the military. A child of military men who served as far back as the Revolutionary War, Westmoreland attended the Citadel, a military college in South Carolina, before graduating at the top of his class at West Point. The man nicknamed "Westy" went on to be honored as a World War II hero, and later became the youngest major general in the history of the army. Restoring his reputation after Vietnam and halting the decline of the military's standing among the American public came together in a single mission for Westmoreland.

In 1982, Westmoreland filed a $120 million suit against CBS and journalist Mike Wallace for suggesting that he had lied about the number of enemy troops in Vietnam. CBS portrayed Westmoreland as an obsessive war hawk who had withheld crucial intelligence so that he could continue to fight what many felt was an unwinnable war. Westmoreland told reporters that the lawsuit, which he did not win, was not about "whether the war in Vietnam was right or wrong, but whether in our land a television network can rob an honorable man of his reputation." But it was also about restoring the military's good name. Because in the years following Vietnam, the U.S. military—like General Westmoreland—was seen as dishonest, dated, and pigheaded.

Three other military leaders, equally motivated by the damage done to the military's reputation by the Vietnam War, played similarly critical roles in creating today's American military—Generals Creighton Abrams, William DePuy, and Frederick C. Weyand. Together these four generals rebuilt an arm of the government broken in Vietnam and made it into the most highly respected institution in modern American life, and arguably the strongest military force the world has ever known.

Like Westmoreland, Abrams, DePuy, and Weyand were World War II veterans. They, too, saw the downfall of the military in Vietnam as their own personal crisis. "We were the evil ones; we were the clumsy ones; and we were the ones who used the big bombs, whereas the other side used persuasion and intellectual means," General DePuy recollected in an interview near the end of his career. He expressed sorrow over the way the antiwar movement and much of the press maligned Westmoreland for claiming that the United States was winning battles in Vietnam. "No one would listen to him," DePuy sadly concluded. "Only history and time will correct that."

In the wake of the unpopular war in Southeast Asia, they felt misunderstood and attacked in the press, in Congress, and on university campuses. Yet their deep identification with the glory days of the military in World War II made them determined to revive the American military at the end of their careers.

Westmoreland began the rebuilding process by going back to basics. When President Nixon ended the compulsory draft for American men in the early 1970s and switched to an all-volunteer army, Westmoreland insisted on getting good students without criminal records as cadets and recruits, and treating them as military professionals. Following Westmoreland's lead, Abrams, DePuy, and Weyand gave new shape to the military with groundbreaking strategies for managing and training the new soldiers. They created performance standards to measure their training and skill. Together, they literally rewrote the basic manual on strategies for fighting wars.

To understand the changes the four generals brought to the military, we need to look back at how the military grew before Vietnam.

During the Founding Fathers' era, the young nation didn't have enough money to afford professional soldiers. More important, as Congress declared on June 2, 1784, "standing armies in time of peace are inconsistent with the principles of republican governments, dangerous to the liberties of a free people, and generally converted into destructive engines for establishing despotism." So the army was whittled down to eighty men. And it seemed as though local militias would largely be responsible for internal order and national defense.

The idea of creating a standing army was debated by the men who signed the Constitution. Some, like Washington, argued that placing our faith in local militias was not enough. "To place any dependence upon the militia is assuredly resting upon a broken staff," he wrote in a 1776 letter to the Continental Congress. The United States needed a force "to awe the Indians, protect our Trade, prevent the encroachment of our Neighbors of Canada and the Floridas, and guard us at least from surprises," the nation's first president wrote in 1783. Anti-Federalists such as Virginia's George Mason and Patrick Henry were wary of the idea of a standing army. But the Constitution, written with the Revolutionary War and the need for defense of the nation in mind, gave Congress the right under Article 1, Section 8 to "raise and support armies"; Article 2, Section 2 named the president Commander in Chief.

After the Revolutionary War, when the men of the Continental Army returned to their local and state militias, Congress created a first regiment of U.S. soldiers under command of Josiah Harmar, a Pennsylvanian and member of the Continental Army, to fight Native American tribes. The tribes, some of which had sided with the British during the Revolutionary War, did not sign any treaties giving land rights to the Americans. In defiance of treaties between the British and the new American government to end the war, the tribes attacked colonists moving west in the late 1780s. They considered what is now Indiana, Ohio, and Kentucky as their land, sovereign Native American territory not open to white settlers.

With the help of a second regiment—men from Kentucky's militia—the new U.S. troops battled the Native American tribes to protect the settlers during the Northwest Indian War. Though the 1785–1795 conflict ended with the United States defeating the Native American forces, well over a thousand U.S. soldiers were killed, which pressured Congress for better training, supply, and control of any future fighting group sent out as a national militia. In 1792 Washington and his secretary of war, Henry Knox, created the Legion of the United States, the origin piece of what would become a standing army.

Also in 1792 Congress passed a militia act (the Calling Forth Act) to allow the president of the United States to gather militias of several states to fight "invasions from any foreign nation or Indian tribe" as well as "whenever the laws of the United States shall be opposed" by people involved in domestic rebellions. A second militia act, the Uniform Military Act of 1792, passed just days after the first, allowed state governments to draft soldiers for its regiments. This nationalized militia was used to suppress the 1794 Whiskey Rebellion, a revolt in western Pennsylvania against the federal government's right to collect excise taxes on distilled liquor. While the Whiskey Rebellion was suppressed almost entirely by militiamen, the rebellion, like the Native American wars, allowed the federal government to see the benefits of a standing army.

During the early years of the nineteenth century, the concept of a standing army slowly overtook America's tradition of local militias as the young nation battled Great Britain in the War of 1812, fought Native Americans on the western frontier, and protected American trade ships from foreign looters. The military expanded again during the Civil War, a war that saw more Americans die than in any other conflict in American history—more than 600,000 Union and Confederate soldiers lost their lives. It was the first time that U.S. forces used the railroads to transport troops and supply matériel, and the telegraph to communicate orders and intelligence. By the time of the Spanish-American War in 1898, the American navy was capable of defeating Spain so thoroughly that the peace the two countries negotiated gave the United States control over former Spanish colonies in Cuba, Puerto Rico, Guam, and the Philippines.

The army's ground forces expanded and modernized under presidents William McKinley and Theodore Roosevelt. What had been an army made up of troops billeted in forts along the western frontier to fight Native Americans transitioned to a force able to face off on European battlefields during World War I.

In 1917 the United States entered World War I, and President Wilson convinced Congress to pass a bill establishing the nation's first draft of all young men with no ability for the rich to buy themselves a pass. The new draft initially fell on men between the ages of twenty-one and thirty but was later lowered to eighteen. President Wilson justified his actions as necessary to "make the world safe for democracy." Secretary of War Elihu Root had already expanded West Point to train officers and organize a more professional military, including creating more specific career paths to retain and promote the best officers. Rear Admiral Bradley Fiske, during the same period, developed the navy into a stronger fighting force and won political support for construction of a bigger fleet located strategically for easier mobilization to protect American trade.

By 1918, more than 1 million American troops had landed in Europe. By the end of World War II, U.S. armed forces had increased to more than 12 million servicemen and -women, supported by the nation's strong industrial base. When the United States ended the war in the Pacific by dropping two atomic bombs on Japan, America emerged from the rubble of Europe and Asia as the world's sole military power.

After America's victories in World War II, the National Security Act of 1947 reorganized the military into a unified structure under the Department of Defense and created a separate Air Force. And in an unprecedented step, the 1947 act established the National Security Council and the Central Intelligence Agency to constantly monitor world affairs. Public support for the expansion of the military and intelligence agencies was nearly universal. As the postwar economy boomed, the military was celebrated for winning the fight for democracy against the Nazis, imperialists, and fascists. Tom Brokaw has termed the cohort of World War II American servicemen the "Greatest Generation." The expanded military and intelligence-gathering ability of the United States was far beyond anything the Founding Fathers envisioned. In the Cold War that followed, the United States was pitted against the other major military power of the era, the Soviet Union, in a military escalation centered around secrecy, atomic bombs, spies, and soldiers. The U.S. military established permanent bases around the world, and new agreements allowed American missiles to be positioned in countries that had been allies during the war.

The Korean War, between 1950 and 1953, was a proxy war for dominance between the United States and the Soviets. With the Soviet Union and China supporting communist North Korea and the United Nations forces, led by the United States, defending democratic forces in South Korea, the stage was set for the U.S. military to take on a new role: countering communism throughout the world. It was a far cry from the Founding Fathers' original concept of local militias. Defense spending quadrupled as the U.S. military became the "world's policeman."

Some began to question the seemingly limitless power of the military. In his 1956 book *The Power Elite,* sociologist C. Wright Mills argued that military leaders and their contractors in the business world had encouraged ever larger budgets for ever larger armed forces. But academics weren't the only ones to point to the dangers of an all-powerful military. President Eisenhower, the supreme commander of the Allied forces in World War II, was well aware of the potential downside to an unbridled military. At the end of his presidency, he gave a farewell speech to the nation voicing concerns that would have echoed those of the original Founding Fathers. "This conjunction of an immense military establishment and a large arms industry is new in the American experience," President Eisenhower cautioned. "The total influence—economic, political, even spiritual—is felt in every city, every statehouse, every office of the federal government. We recognize the imperative need for this development. Yet we must not fail to comprehend its grave implications. . . . In the councils of government, we must guard against the acquisition of unwarranted influence, whether sought or unsought, by the military-industrial complex. The potential for the disastrous rise of misplaced power exists and will persist."

The president's concerns came to life after he left office, as another war, this time in Vietnam, escalated as yet another proxy fight between the two superpowers. U.S. involvement in Vietnam stretched from 1959 to 1975. As the United States expanded its presence in Vietnam in 1964 and sought a man to command the troops, Defense Secretary Robert McNamara told President Lyndon Johnson that among American military leaders, William Westmoreland was "the best we have, without question."

Westmoreland graduated from West Point in 1936 as the top-ranked cadet. He fought in World War II as an artillery officer and was known for leaving the safety of his command posts to risk seeing the action firsthand at the front lines. By 1944, as World War II was ending, he was in charge of the 9th Infantry Division, and at the age of thirty he held the temporary rank of colonel. In his brief service as head of the 187th Airborne in the Korean War, he became a temporary brigadier general, and then a lieutenant colonel. It was a meteoric rise through the ranks. He returned to West Point as superintendent of the academy, and by 1963 he was a full lieutenant general.

When he was sent to command U.S. forces in the escalating war in Vietnam, the general's strategy was to attack the invading North Vietnamese army along World War II–style front lines, bombing them from the air and assaulting them with superior firepower on the ground. He pushed President Johnson to send more soldiers to Vietnam in a show of force intended to intimidate the enemy—both the North Vietnamese regular military and the bands of communist rebel fighters inside South Vietnam known as the Vietcong. Westmoreland's fierce, direct approach, which became known as "search and destroy," was popular with military strategists and among the political class in Washington. He was promoted to full four-star general in 1965 and named *Time* magazine's Man of the Year.

The need for overwhelming force in accordance with Westmoreland's plan led to an expanded military draft. The size of the military ballooned from under 1 million people in 1965 to over 1.5 million in 1968. U.S. forces on the ground in Vietnam peaked at 543,000 in 1969. The fast draft of new recruits and the need to prepare them to fight a jungle war far from home put pressure on the military to train them. It also strained the military's capacity to produce quality, experienced officers to lead the new troops and aircrews.

In her book *An Army Transformed*, Suzanne Nielsen explained that during the 1960s the rapid growth of the military expanded the need for commissioned and noncommissioned officers. "Promotions were accelerated and average experience levels decreased. The decision not to mobilize the reserves also interacted with the decision to give Vietnam top priority in resources . . . creating skill mismatches and personnel turbulence that . . . degraded the ability of leaders to create cohesive units—both in Vietnam and throughout the rest of the Army."

The result in Vietnam was chaos.

Richard Stewart, a military historian, writes that discipline among the soldiers broke down in Vietnam, leading to drug addiction among troops, race riots, and "even instances of 'fragging' (tossing a fragmentation grenade into the sleeping quarters or office of a superior officer or noncommissioned officer [NCO] to injure or 'warn') . . . The Army that left Vietnam and returned to America and its garrisons in Germany and Korea in the early 1970s was at low ebb of morale, discipline, and military effectiveness."

Given the sense on the home front that the war in Vietnam had been a mistake from the outset, when soldiers returned to America the public treated them with indifference and at times anger. As the war dragged on without any clear victory in sight, the glory days of World

War II, when everyone supported our soldiers' cause, seemed a distant memory.

The war itself was not going well, either. General Westmoreland's reliance on manpower, artillery, and air bombardments failed to force a surrender. Meanwhile, small-scale enemy attacks and incessant guerilla warfare tormented American troops and ultimately led to 57,000 American deaths, including a grim spike of 15,000 deaths in 1968, Westmoreland's last year in command. Despite the American fatalities, the general argued that America was winning the fight, pointing out the much higher body counts of enemy soldiers. But images of the steady arrival of flag-draped coffins holding the remains of American soldiers killed in action wore away at public and political support for the general's strategy, and the public came to believe that the war was unwinnable—or not worth winning.

As the likelihood of a quick, decisive victory faded, voices calling for a pullout of American forces increased. Walter Cronkite, the respected anchorman of the leading nightly news program, the CBS Evening News, made national news himself when he openly questioned why so many Americans had to die so far from home in a war that seemed without end. "To say that we are mired in stalemate seems the only realistic, yet unsatisfactory, conclusion," Cronkite reflected.

Political backing in the United States for the war hit a low point when communist forces managed to overrun the U.S. embassy in Saigon during the Tet offensive in January 1968. General Westmoreland's request for 200,000 more troops was met with only silence from the president and the Pentagon. Support in Washington for his consistently optimistic claims that the United States was winning the war collapsed.

President Johnson ordered Westmoreland home and assigned him to the Pentagon as the Army's chief of staff in 1968, a move that signaled the beginning of the U.S. withdrawal from Vietnam. But in an unexpected twist to what looked like a fading career, Westmoreland began resolutely working to restore the reputation of the military. The opportunity for turning the army around was afforded when Richard Nixon, during the 1968 election campaign, promised to end the draft and create an army of professionals—something the United States had not had since before World War II.

Westmoreland initially opposed ending the draft. But President·

Nixon put Westmoreland in charge of transitioning the army from a collection of draftees to a group of professional soldiers, men who were not forced to fight but who willingly devoted their lives to protecting American freedom. Nixon's choice of Westmoreland was a strategic political move. The president wanted to use the general's prestige in the military as a hard-nosed soldier and former head of West Point to counter opposition who said the transformation might degrade the quality of the military.

"The transition to an all-volunteer force was a special priority given that the Army was the service most dependent on the draft for its manpower," Nielsen wrote. "The supply of this crucial resource would be threatened by an end to draft calls in 1973 unless actions were quickly taken."

Westmoreland's own army career was perfectly in sync with the aspirations of those who wanted to be professional soldiers. Westmoreland created the Office of the Special Assistant for the Modern Volunteer Army at the Pentagon, appointed a three-star general to the office, and ordered him to accept only candidates with good academic records who were put through rigorous training and education. No longer would the army tolerate soldiers who were out of shape and who failed to respect rank. Westmoreland also wanted better training for his officers. He wanted those in charge to set high standards for those who wanted to make a career of military service. This was Westmoreland's answer to the drug problems and chaos of the draft army in Vietnam. He wanted to create a professional organization of soldiers more competent and expert than the army had ever seen.

"These changes were significant," Nielsen writes in *An Army Transformed*. "Adjustments to officer and enlisted personnel management policies decreased turbulence in the Army and facilitated the development of expertise. Changes in training philosophy and management were early precursors to the rise of performance-oriented training methods later in the decade. Finally, the most momentous change was the establishment of the NCOES [Non-Commissioned Officer Education System]. It would be difficult to overstate the importance of this reform."

Here is how Bruce Palmer Jr., the vice chief of staff of the Army at the time, described Westmoreland's vision for better leadership among unit commanders: "The key to our success and to the quality of our post-Vietnam force is the small-unit leader: the junior officer and non-commissioned officer, the people who have the closest, most direct contact with the soldier, the people who get the job done . . . The Army is people—young people—some 54 percent are under 23 years of age. . . . In the final analysis, 'face-to-face,' day-to-day leadership of these young soldiers will determine the success of our efforts to revitalize the Army and build a leaner, more professional, quality force."

Westmoreland retired from army life in 1972. He immediately went on a tour of all fifty states to speak in defense of the military, the military's record in Vietnam, and his own role in the war. "We held the line," he said at the event honoring the twentieth anniversary of the 173rd Airborne Brigade's assignment to Vietnam in 1965. "We stopped the falling dominoes [the increase of Asian nations succumbing to communist control]. It's not that we lost the war militarily. The fact is, we as a nation did not make good our commitment to the South Vietnamese." But to him, the battle hadn't ended.

"I have no apologies, no regrets," a defiant Westmoreland, who died at age ninety-one in 2005, once told the Associated Press. "I gave my very best efforts. I've been hung in effigy. I've been spat upon. You just have to let those things bounce off."

When Westmoreland retired from the military, the man selected to continue rebuilding the armed forces was the man who had taken command from Westmoreland when he left Vietnam in 1968—General Creighton Abrams.

Cigar-smoking "Colonel Abe" had been a hero as a tank commander at the Battle of the Bulge during World War II. "I'm supposed to be the best tank commander in the Army, but I have one peer—Abe Abrams. He's the world's champion," the legendary General George Patton said of Abrams after the war. During Westmoreland's first years in Vietnam, it was Abrams, as vice chief of staff for the army, who managed the army's expanded draft and put more soldiers in Vietnam. Both Abrams and Westmoreland had graduated from West Point in 1936, and both were promoted to general in 1964. Abrams arrived in Vietnam in 1967 as Westmoreland's deputy before replacing him and taking full command of U.S. forces in 1968.

Abrams shifted Westmoreland's Vietnam strategy from "search and destroy" to a new plan called "clear and hold." That strategy included more attention to training U.S. allies in the South Vietnamese military and improving life in Vietnam with better schools, more efficient farming operations, and refugee resettlement. In a famous episode, Abrams stopped a command staff meeting with a burst of profanity, marched to the front of the room, and wrote across the military chart a simple mission statement: "Protect the population."

It was a major shift from Westmoreland's command. Abrams told his field commanders: "I don't think it makes any difference how many losses [the enemy] takes ... the mistake is to think that's the central issue." For Abrams, the key was winning friends among the Vietnamese and spreading support for capitalism and democracy. Abrams put U.S. forces in a better position; nonetheless, the war continued to be seen in America as what the press referred to as a "quagmire," without end in sight. President Nixon began withdrawing troops in 1969, under a policy called "Vietnamization," in which the United States would train the South Vietnamese to protect themselves and lessen our own military presence. After Nixon signed the Paris Peace Accords in 1973, the United States committed to withdrawing all its remaining forces. Two years later the North Vietnamese defeated the South Vietnamese army and took control of Saigon.

Abrams's focus on soldiers' well-being, education, and preparedness for battle was in keeping with General Westmoreland's plan for a more professional army. Abrams advanced Westmoreland's work in developing the volunteer force by more effectively training the Army reserves. At the same time Abrams increased the number of fighting divisions in the Army from thirteen to sixteen, without adding any troops. Support for those active troops was now entrusted to the reserves, in what the military dubbed a "tooth-to-tail ratio," with the big bite of combat forces backed by a bigger tail behind them. Abrams's concept of greater reliance on the reserves was politically acceptable because the reserves had not been called on to go to Vietnam. Future wars would require that the reserves be ready to join any war effort, and bring with them local and state political support from around the country.

Abrams also made upgrading military equipment an essential part of the new military. The prospect of facing Soviet or Chinese armies, with their larger numbers of soldiers, created a need for technological superiority that multiplied the power of troops on the ground. He put a premium on intelligence gathering and communication that would allow a smaller force to act with speed, inflicting strategic strikes to cripple larger foes.

With limited resources after the expensive cost run-up of Vietnam, Abrams concentrated his drive for equipment modernization on what the military called "the Big Five"—the M1 tank (after his death called the Abrams tank), the Bradley Fighting Vehicle, the Apache attack helicopter, the Black Hawk helicopter, and the Patriot Air and Missile Defense System. "We have paid and paid and paid again in blood and sacrifice for our unpreparedness," Abrams would frequently tell military and political leaders in explaining his standards for a battle-ready, well-armed, all-volunteer Army.

Abrams died in September 1974, two years after returning from Vietnam. It was General Frederick C. Weyand, who succeeded Abrams as chief of staff, who saw Abrams's exacting strategy brought to completion.

Weyand, also responsible for resuscitating the U.S. military over the last several decades, was born in 1916 in Arbuckle, California. Weyand understood the importance of law and order from a young age. The son of the Berkeley, California, chief of police, Weyand served in the ROTC at the University of California, Berkeley, where he also got a degree in criminology. During World War II, Weyand worked in intelligence in the China-India region. He commanded a battalion during the Korean War, and during Vietnam he became a general. In 1972 Weyand became commander of the Military Assistance Command, Vietnam. In 1972 and 1973 he organized the American troops' withdrawal from Vietnam. When Weyand succeeded Abrams as army chief of staff in 1974, he focused on improving the ratio of combat to support troops, as well as sharpening troops' readiness for battle.

"One overarching commonality between the Westmoreland and Abrams and Weyand periods is that these three leaders all felt an imperative need to 'save' an Army that was in trouble," writes Nielsen. "Westmoreland placed his emphasis on personnel matters and on improving the Army's professionalism. The single greatest challenge Westmoreland tackled was the transition to an all-volunteer manpower policy. Abrams and Weyand focused on achieving stability for the Army and ensuring that it was organized to be able to handle future challenges. In combination, the efforts of these leaders were complementary in aiding the Army's recovery from the trauma associated with its rapid expansion and contraction, social problems, and other difficulties during the Vietnam War. In sum, these leaders laid groundwork for future progress."

It was these generals who created the basis for the modern American military—the most technologically capable and best-trained army in the world, with the biggest annual budget and nearly universal political and popular backing at home. One additional figure added to the fierce modern military profile of today's U.S. Army: General William DePuy, another World War II veteran who, like Westmoreland and Abrams, served in Vietnam. It was obvious to DePuy as well that the military's discipline had fallen badly during the Vietnam War. In 1966, as head of the 1st Infantry in Vietnam, he fired seven battalion commanders he considered incompetent. His actions made him a respected leader, but also a feared one, leading many to think of him as "an arrogant, unforgiving tyrant," as one writer reflects.

In an oral history published by the Army's Center of Military History, DePuy explained why he got rid of so many battalion commanders: "I'm fairly well convinced that once a man has made a bad mistake, not of judgment, but of incompetence ... and revealed ... a general weakness in command, then there is very little you can do to change him at that stage in his life."

DePuy's discontent with the leaders under his command in Vietnam became central to his work in the new military after Abrams's death. From 1973 to 1977, DePuy set the guidelines on how to organize fighting units to best make use of technology and new weaponry, approving a new Field Manual that changed the tactics the Army had used in Vietnam. Along with General Paul F. Gorman, DePuy helped put in place a new training system for soldiers that, through tests, focused less on the sheer amount of time a soldier spent in training and more on his ability to perform a given task.

"To prepare [the modern infantryman] for contemporary battle," notes one 2009 history of the U.S. Army, DePuy and his successor Gen. Donn A. Starry "evolved a comprehensive and interconnected training program that systematically developed individual and unit proficiency and then tested that competence in tough, realistic exercises." To some in the army it seemed as if they were on the verge of a revolution in training; to others it was a return to the basics of soldier training.

The heavy emphasis on training and performance testing helped to cure the military of some of its major problems in Vietnam. In a professional military, promotions went to those people who performed, period. Racial discrimination faded. More women joined the military—between 1978 and 1983 the number of women in the army rose from 53,000 to 80,000. The military began raising salaries and creating catchy advertising slogans to challenge young people to join: "Be all that you can be—in the Army."

Meanwhile, DePuy and Starry instituted changes that led, in the 2009 U.S. Army history's judgment, to a "coherent series of schools to train officers in their principal duties at each major turning point in their careers." At every level, officers received added training before advancing to take on new responsibilities as leader of a company, battery, or troop. DePuy and Starry also put more junior-level officers in troop units in anticipation of the need for quick response in the middle of high-tech, faster-paced warfare. They devised tactics for how U.S. combat forces could prevail when facing a larger fighting unit, using quick surgical strikes, communications advantages, support units, and superior technology.

Gen. Starry revised the warfare manual to put greater emphasis on support for combat troops. The AirLand Battle doctrine, developed by Gen. Starry, "aimed not only at hitting the enemy's attacking force but also striking his follow-on echelons to delay and disrupt their arrival into the main battle," writes military historian John L. Romjue. AirLand Battle doctrine depended on teamwork between air and ground forces. It was used to win the 1990–91 Persian Gulf War, and it is the precursor to changes made to respond to counterinsurgency tactics used by terrorist fighters in the Middle East after 9/11.

Today's strategically trained, technologically advanced military, which grew out of the failures of the Vietnam War, would alarm the original Founding Fathers. This professional, volunteer army is vastly different from the citizen militias that existed at the time of the American colonies. The fledgling U.S. government had no interest in sending forces overseas to battle in distant wars without authorization from the Congress.

But the sophisticated military machine created by today's new founders takes into account the new realities of the world we live in, helping the United States oust Qaddafi in Libya, battle terrorists in the mountains of Afghanistan and Pakistan, and protect South Korea and other allies. All of this is done with the acclaim and tax dollars of a highly supportive public.

The American military's might raises questions the Founding Fathers would almost surely ask: Does America really need all of this military force? Is an elite, professional military too divorced from everyday citizens and daily civilian life in the United States? And is the United States hampering its economy and financial might by putting so much of its resources into expensive high-tech jets, tanks, ships, subs, and smart bombs?

These are all legitimate questions. But the very fact that we can raise them, while safe behind the protection that our armed forces provide, is the result of the combined efforts of Westmoreland, Abrams, Weyand, and DePuy.

CHAPTER 6

IT'S THE ECONOMY, STUPID

Milton Friedman's New Math of Free Markets,
Big Business, and Small Taxes

The title of one of my favorite rock songs of the 1980s is "Money's Too Tight (to Mention)" by Simply Red. The lyrics begin: "I've been laid off from work, my rent is due / My kids all need brand-new shoes."

Sadly, that sentiment captures middle-class life in America today in the wake of the 2008 economic recession. After World War II, America enjoyed several prosperous decades that led to a growing middle class. Following the Great Recession of 2008, these successes withered away—there was a teetering-on-the-edge tone to most conversations among the middle class about money. The middle class was shrinking (and continues to shrink), and the number of people forced to live in poverty grew as manufacturing jobs with their union-scale paychecks disappeared. Most of those jobs went overseas—"outsourced" abroad, where the work would be done by cheaper workers.

Fifty years ago the three biggest private employers in the nation—General Motors, Ford, and AT&T—paid union wages with benefits. Today the biggest players in the American job market are companies that pay low wages, often without benefits, such as Walmart, McDonald's, and Yum! Brands (the owner of Pizza Hut and KFC).

The loss of good-paying, steady middle-class jobs is making Americans insecure, even anxious about their lives and the future. In

October 2008, a month after the economy hit bottom, a poll by the Associated Press found a third of the nation living in fear of losing their job and half of the people concerned with not being able to pay credit card bills or their home mortgage.

In 1971 the percentage of adults reporting that their income fit the middle-class experience reached 61 percent, according to the Pew Research Center. That number fell to 51 percent by 2011. A Cornell University study found that 65 percent of American families lived in middle-income neighborhoods in 1970. By 2009 that had plummeted to 42 percent. According to an April 2009 piece in the *New York Times,* "Anxiety, depression and stress are troubling people everywhere, many not suffering significant economic losses, but worrying they will or simply reacting to pervasive uncertainty."

Not much has changed since then. Another Pew poll in 2013 found that 54 percent of Americans felt that they had "hardly recovered" from the recession. There is fear of losing one's job, paying medical bills, affording college tuition, and saving money for retirement. Small businesses complain about the difficulty of getting a bank loan even as big corporations sit on piles of cash. Corporate executives say they fear adding new projects with new workers in a shaky economy with low consumer confidence. Consumers are worried because while the national economy grew by 18 percent between 2000 and 2011, the median household income shrank by 12.4 percent.

The roots of current tensions over money and taxes in America go back to the Founding Fathers. They lived in economically vibrant colonies. Their revolution was sparked by outrage over high taxes demanded by the king of England. In an article in the *Wall Street Journal,* historian Thomas Fleming, author of *What America Was Really Like in 1776,* writes that the colonists had "the highest per capita income in the civilized world of their time . . . [with] the lowest taxes—and they were determined to keep it that way." The Founders "concluded that the British were planning to tax the Americans into the kind of humiliation that Great Britain had inflicted on Ireland."

The American dream was born of abundance and prosperity for individuals in defiance of the king, his taxes, and government regulations on commercial trade. The Revolutionary War was fought to certify the Colonial desire for economic freedom across class lines and for "life, liberty and the pursuit of happiness." That led to a defiant streak in the American character, an attitude of risk taking by rugged individuals. Popular books and movies have portrayed America as the home of wide-open frontiers free from the fiscal restraints that the British Crown put on the original colonies.

Most of the Founding Fathers were wealthy landowners. But most people in Colonial America were part of a thriving middle class. They came to the New World looking for a better economic life based on farming, fishing, shipbuilding, and the booming transatlantic trade in cotton, sugar, and tobacco. And they did just that. They found economic security as planters, workmen, settlers moving west, merchants, skilled tailors, carpenters, tavern owners, and lawyers.

Those days are over. The economic landscape has shifted as America continues to shift manufacturing overseas and use robots to perform jobs once done by human hands. As America's upper class pass along their higher levels of education and inheritance to their children, the rich stay rich and the poor stay poor.

Republicans and Democrats campaign these days with promises of rebuilding the economy for the middle class and restoring the nation's belief that it is the land of opportunity. In a study of the world's top national economies, the United States still has the highest percentage of people (69 percent) who believe that hard work, intelligence, and skill will reap financial rewards. But the facts tell a different story. Current economic studies show far more social mobility for a talented young person trying to move up the economic ladder in Canada, Germany, Spain, Australia, and several other nations.

The United States does remain the country where people can get very rich. More of the nation's income goes to the very rich today than at any other time since the Roaring Twenties, the years before the stock market crash of 1929. Economic studies show that between 1976 and 2007, the top 1 percent of Americans—executives, medical and financial professionals, lawyers, and leaders of high-tech companies, among others—saw their pay rise from 8.9 percent to 24 percent of the nation's total income. The United States has more than twice the number of millionaires as any other nation.

Today, top college graduates pack business schools. Corporate raiders who buy companies and send jobs overseas to pump up stock values are iconic figures in modern culture, as are Wall Street brokers. Their legendary bonuses, mansions, and private jets are celebrated in movies and rap music.

Yet for most Americans, nothing could be farther from reality. In his 2012 State of the Union address, President Obama told the nation that the "defining issue of our time" is the rise of income inequality and the fear that the fabled American dream of the next generation doing better than the last is no longer true. And Americans who recognize this income inequality are angry. In fact, part of what lost Republican nominee Mitt Romney the 2012 election was a secretly recorded speech he gave to wealthy donors in which he labeled the poor, the working class, and retirees on fixed incomes the "47 percent" who are happy to live off government benefits. These people, Romney claimed, were indifferent to his call for them to "take personal responsibility and care for their lives."

Since the nation's founding, the central issue for policy makers and citizens of all political persuasions has been the proper role of government in taxing. Also of concern is how to regulate people seeking to get rich by pushing the boundaries of rules on monopolies, insider trading, and even outright fraud.

After declaring independence from Britain, the original Founding Fathers hewed to a basic economic policy that kept the government's role in the economy to a minimum, with limited taxation and small protectionist policies meant to help incubate start-up industries. With the rapid growth of big industries in the late nineteenth and early twentieth centuries, the government slowly reacted with policies to limit big monopolies and establish rights for workers as well as consumers. The Great Depression of 1929 prompted even more intervention by the U.S. government to stabilize the economy by putting people to work in jobs funded by the government.

This more activist government also began to regulate the excesses of big business. President Franklin D. Roosevelt set up bank and market regulations to ensure that a stock market crash could never occur again. And his Social Security Act, passed in 1935, created a safety net for the old and poor.

President Roosevelt's economic policies fit with the thinking of the dominant economic theorist of the first half of the twentieth century, John Maynard Keynes. Keynes favored an activist government that would keep the economy running smoothly by setting rules for financial markets and balancing spending and investment patterns. His primary goal was to achieve the political and social good of low unemployment.

But decades later, one man launched an economic counterrevolution against Keynes's theory. That economist gave intellectual backing to policies that led to today's high-risk American economy with its big rewards for big winners. It also created a worried middle class and heightened financial pain for people without the education and access to capital to launch successful businesses. That man was economist and Nobel Prize winner Milton Friedman. Friedman's economic theories have framed the last fifty years of economic debate. Although he was not an elected official or a corporate leader, Friedman is the founding father of the American economy we know today.

Ben S. Bernanke, former chair of the Federal Reserve, has said that "the direct and indirect influences of [Friedman's] thinking on contemporary monetary economics would be difficult to overstate." Alan Greenspan, another former chair of the Federal Reserve, credited Freidman with a "profound impact . . . on the American public's view" of economic markets as best left to make maximum profits for shareholders with minimal to no government interference.

Lawrence Summers, the former president of Harvard and a top economic adviser to President Obama, crowned Friedman as "the Great Liberator" and said: "Any honest Democrat will admit that we are now all Friedmanites." Friedman, he said, sold the world on the "importance of allowing free markets to operate."

Paul Krugman, the liberal *New York Times* columnist and a Nobel Prize–winning economist himself, has written that Friedman was "possibly the most brilliant communicator of economic ideas to the general public that ever lived." George Will, the conservative columnist, once described him as the "most consequential public intellectual of the twentieth century."

Friedman captured the fierce, fearless American spirit of self-reliance and independence, for better or worse, when he wrote in a famous 1970 article: "The only responsibility of companies is to make a profit." Friedman had no use for the idea of the collective good, which

he saw as the evil of state control, the kind of Eastern European socialist and communist governments his parents had fled at the start of the
twentieth century.

When Friedman died, the *Boston Globe* noted that he had helped to
shape "the intellectual climate of the twenty-first century" and "provided the theoretical underpinnings for many of the policies [lower
taxes and deregulation] put into practice in the 1980s by President Reagan and British Prime Minister Margaret Thatcher."

Friedman was a child of the Great Depression. The son of Austrian-
Hungarian immigrants, he was born in Brooklyn, New York; his parents moved to Rahway, New Jersey, when he was one. He had three
sisters. His mother operated a small dry goods shop, and his father,
in Friedman's words, "engaged in a succession of mostly unsuccessful
'jobbing' ventures—the family income was small and highly uncertain;
financial crisis was a constant companion." He graduated from high
school at age fifteen in 1928, just before the nation began its economic
free fall into the Great Depression. His father's death that year made
the impact of the coming economic problems even worse for Friedman.
Luckily, the intense, young man was awarded a scholarship to attend
Rutgers University in New Jersey. He also waited tables to help pay his
tuition. As a young man without the financial backing of a father, Friedman dreamed of a steady paycheck even as the country's economy continued to sink. He initially decided that meant becoming an actuary.
For a good math student like Friedman, calculating risk for insurance
companies offered a job with a high degree of financial security. Insurance would never go out of demand, no matter how the economy might
perform. A fast-talking New York Jew with a passion for debate, Friedman once admitted that he was prone to "talk very loud, indeed shout."
His classmates nicknamed him "Shallow," not to indicate that he was a
phony, but because he lacked the subtlety implied by the phrase "Still
waters run deep." In truth, his love of rapid-fire conversation was evidence of a deep intellect overflowing with ideas. He was drawn quickly
to political debates with professors in the economics department at
Rutgers. His mentor there, Professor Arthur Burns—a future head of
the Federal Reserve—was working on economic theories to push the
country out of the Great Depression. The idea of getting the country

out of poverty with a more vigorous economy resonated perfectly with Friedman's personal need for money.

Friedman had initially intended to become an actuary after graduating from Rutgers. But when he received a scholarship to get a master's in economics at the prestigious University of Chicago, Friedman wagered that a nation in a depression desperately needed innovative economists, and he took the offer. Along with his graduate work, Friedman worked for famous economist Henry Schultz—who would go on to found econometrics, the mathematical study of economics—and became friends with George Stigler and W. Allen Wallis, major figures in twentieth-century economics.

In the mid-1930s Friedman moved to Washington to work for the federal government. His first job, with the National Resources Committee, was to study consumer behavior. Two years later he got a position with the Bureau of Economic Research, where he studied income. That led Friedman to coauthor a book with Simon Kuznets that argued against licensing professional workers. Their theory was that licensing artificially limited the pool of people who provide important services and raised the prices of those services. Along the same line of thinking, Friedman later opposed government-imposed rent controls and minimum-wage scales for workers.

In 1940 Friedman took a short break from government service to accept a job teaching economics at the University of Wisconsin–Madison, but he returned to the Bureau of Economic Research in 1941 because of anti-Semitism at the university. From 1943 through 1945, as Americans at home and abroad used their expertise to help the war effort in any way they could, Friedman served as associate director of the Statistical Research Group of the Division of War Research at Columbia University. At Columbia, Friedman's team provided crucial statistical analysis for the production of army matériel and weapons. In 1945 Friedman worked briefly at the University of Minnesota, and then in 1946 he accepted a post at the University of Chicago, where he stayed until 1977.

During these years, and especially after World War II, Friedman began to articulate the radical economic theories for which he is now famous. The core of Freidman's thinking rejected central control of the economy by anyone, even the smartest leaders and economists and the best-intentioned government officials. "Any system which gives so much power and so much discretion to a few men that mistakes— excusable or not—can have such far-reaching effects is a bad system," Friedman wrote in his 1962 book *Capitalism and Freedom*, reflecting on the ideas that took root in his mind as he began working as an economist among bureaucrats and politicians trying to revive the crippled U.S. economy in the 1930s. "It is a bad system to believers in freedom just because it gives a few men such power without any effective check by the body politic—this is the key political argument against an 'independent' central bank.... Mistakes, excusable or not, cannot be avoided in a system which disperses responsibility yet gives a few men great power, and which thereby makes important policy actions highly dependent on accidents of personality."

Friedman's growing distaste for government control of the economy was in direct opposition to President Franklin Delano Roosevelt and his efforts to make the stock market and job market more secure— assumptions that drove government policy after the Great Depression. The prominent British economist John Maynard Keynes argued that smart government leaders acted as a buffer against boom-and-bust cycles in the financial markets—notably the "bust" of the Great Depression—with the goal of maintaining full employment. To achieve that goal, Keynes opposed balanced government budgets and low taxes. He argued for active intervention by the government, including spending money, as the secret ingredient for restoring a balanced, stable economy. "Let us be up and doing, using our idle resources to increase our wealth. With men and plant unemployed, it is ridiculous to say that we cannot afford new developments. It is precisely with these plants and these men that we shall afford them," Keynes told a group of British politicians in 1928.

Keynes observed that people irrationally hoard their money after economic failures. They take their money out of the banks, stop buying, and make what could have been a small economic recession into a full-on depression. When consumers and investors faltered, triggering an economic crisis, he encouraged government spending, even borrowing money to spend on putting people to work on building roads and bridges, in public service programs, and in other government projects in an effort to spur the economy. As people working government-sponsored jobs make money, they stop being so cautious and spend more, which creates jobs in the private sector. Once the economy has improved, government can slowly repay its debt by running a surplus (taking in more than it spends) through taxing high and spending little on programs. "Government borrowing of one kind or another is nature's remedy, so to speak," Keynes wrote in his 1931 *Economy Report,* "for preventing business losses from being, in so severe a slump . . . , so great as to bring production altogether to a standstill."

Specifically, Keynes made the case for the federal government reviving a weak economy by lowering interest rates available to people saving money in order to get those funds out of banks and savings accounts and into financial investments in businesses in order to create jobs. His thinking made him the most prominent critic of the British government's austerity program after the Great Depression.

Keynes's logic fit with U.S. policy after the Depression. President Roosevelt's New Deal put in place federal construction projects as well as job programs for artists and intellectuals. It was seen as prudent, reasonable government policy because the Depression "appeared to signal the final, inevitable collapse of an economy that had been beset for at least fifty years by overproduction and an excess of competition," according to Stanford historian David Kennedy in his book *Freedom from Fear.*

One economist who got such a government job was Milton Friedman. Friedman, who worked as an assistant in a federal survey of the nation's consumer habits, once called the New Deal a "lifesaver" for young scholars such as himself.

Despite working for the government himself as the economy struggled to produce jobs, however, the young economist did not see a role for the government in reviving the economy. He opposed the New Deal's price controls and wage standards and placed supreme trust in the free market. He opposed the Keynesian idea of the government as a primary driver of economic output during recessions and slowdowns. And he was not disposed to the government trying to create an economic safety net with Social Security and protecting workers through support for union labor rules.

Friedman saw the New Deal as a "move toward the welfare state," disguised as an effort by people of goodwill to pass laws to deal with "the defects inherent in capitalism [that] jeopardized our economic well-being and therefore reduced freedom." For all the good intentions, Friedman argued, those programs generally turned out to be failures, and on principle should always be rejected by Americans. Why? Because supporters of big government will argue that when a program isn't working, the program just needs more money or better leadership; it will never allow a program offering government entitlements or power to Washington bureaucrats to close down.

Instead, Friedman proposed a "blue-collar," "do it yourself," and "protect your own interests" approach to generating economic activity. He preferred that it be business owners and investors, along with workers and consumers, who decide where money and labor should be placed for the best chance at success. One of the few mechanisms he endorsed as a proper tool of government was to increase the money supply. That meant making sure banks had enough money to lend to people and companies.

In fact, Friedman blamed the Great Depression on the Federal Reserve's failure to increase the money supply in the aftermath of the stock market's collapse. He pointed to the Fed's decision to limit bank loans as the true cause for the slow recovery and the resulting high rates of unemployment and lines of hungry people during the Great Depression. According to Friedman, the lack of money from banks available for loans and new investment did not stabilize the economy but exacerbated the low confidence in Wall Street after the stock market failed. The short money supply limited economic expansion, he argued, and made economic recovery overly difficult.

"The Fed was largely responsible for converting what might have been a garden-variety recession, though perhaps a fairly severe one, into a major catastrophe," Friedman later wrote. "Instead of using its powers to offset the depression, it presided over a decline in the quantity of money by one-third from 1929 to 1933. . . . Far from the depression being a failure of the free-enterprise system, it was a tragic failure of government."

Friedman took a similarly skeptical view of the New Deal. He later told *Playboy* magazine: "People are imperfect. There are scarcities. Shortages. You can let things work themselves out or try to do something about them by passing a law. Of course, you know which idea is easier to sell."

Friedman's contrarian view on the New Deal and the cause of the Great Depression was just a first glimpse of his appetite for shaking up conventional economic policy. He became a champion of free markets and small government, advocating sharp limits on any regulation of business or individual choice. He identified big-government programs in the United States as leading to the same "collectivism" as socialist governments. That amounted, he said, to a threat to every American's "individual freedom." One of the only roles for government in a Friedman economy was to provide a trustworthy justice system—in other words, courts that enforce business contracts and impose compensation for damages caused by unfair competition. He supported the establishment of a police force to prevent injury to the public and to preserve overall stability and safety.

Friedman's small-government, free-market approach put him in line with the thinking of Founding Father and former president Thomas Jefferson. Jefferson favored a federal government operating under a theory often described as "a government that governs least governs best." Or, as Friedman told *Playboy* in 1973, "I think the government solution to a problem is usually as bad as the problem and very often makes the problem worse."

At every turn, Friedman's contrarian, libertarian focus was on restraining the power of the federal government, although his emphasis was on the economy.

- He opposed the Food and Drug Administration, arguing that consumers should decide which food and drugs are good.
- He opposed government price support for farmers in the belief that free markets reward good products.
- He opposed the idea that corporations had responsibilities to their community, employees, customers, and the nation. Top corporate executives are obligated only to make money for shareholders, he explained, and failure to do so made them "unwitting puppets of the intellectual forces that have been undermining the basis of a free society these past decades."

- He opposed national parks because they blocked private markets from determining the best, most productive use of land.
- He opposed rent control because it defied market values for real estate, even as part of an economic stabilization plan during World War II (a view for which other economists criticized him).
- He opposed the military draft, and called his victory on that issue one of his proudest accomplishments. "No public policy activity that I have ever engaged in has given me as much satisfaction as the All-Volunteer" panel he served on for President Nixon.
- He opposed a federal law against private businesses carrying mail, again pointing to the low cost and efficiencies that come with private markets determining how best to distribute letters and packages.
- He opposed a government monopoly on public education and supported vouchers to allow parents to decide on the best schools for their children.
- He opposed Social Security and favored privatizing the retirement income system.
- He opposed welfare, instead proposing direct payments to the poor as a "negative income tax" of limited scope. This, he argued, would do away with the need for antipoverty programs and government agencies that, to justify their existence, required a constant population of poor people to serve.
- Because of his libertarian belief in individual freedom, he opposed bans on the use of illegal recreational drugs. In 2005, he led a group of 500 economists pressuring President Bush to legalize marijuana as a benefit to the U.S. economy.
- He opposed state-run companies anywhere around the globe, even in small nations, and called for speedy privatization as key to economic growth.
- He opposed tariffs and quotas as well as fixed exchange rates for currency, citing them as blocks to free trade and free markets.

"What you want," he told *Playboy* magazine in 1973, "is a world in which individuals have a wide variety of alternatives. You want pluralism, multiplicity of choice. When you get down to small units of government, you have it. If you don't like what one town does and can't

change it, you move to another town. . . . On the whole, the formal restrictions on governmental activity should be most severe at the Federal level, less so at the state level and least of all at the local level."

The lone example of Friedman supporting a bigger role for government in the economy was during World War II. The young economist
came up with the idea of having the government withhold some taxes
as a method for boosting the flow of money needed to support the war.
He later said he regretted giving the government more power because
"the existence of withholding has made it possible for taxes to be higher
after the war than they otherwise could have been."

The *New York Times* said Friedman's opposition to Keynesian ideas
in the years of tremendous growth after World War II and his forecast that high levels of government spending would eventually result in
the devastating combination of high unemployment and high inflation
made the economic establishment dismiss him as an economic "flat-
earther." Yet "the prediction was borne out in the 1970s," the *Times*
wrote. "Mr. Friedman's analysis and prediction were regarded as a
stunning intellectual accomplishment and contributed to his earning
the Nobel for his monetary theories. He was also cited for his analyses
of consumer savings and of the causes of the Great Depression. . . . His
prestige and that of the Chicago school [of economics] soared, and his
analysis of the Depression changed the way that the Fed thought about
monetary policy."

Before he won the Nobel Prize in Economics in 1976, Friedman
had already established himself as the leading economist for America's
small-government conservatives, libertarians, and Republicans. His
rise to prominence as a public intellectual was cemented in 1962 with
the publication of his book *Capitalism and Freedom*. The book espoused a deep distrust of centralized government and gave conservatives a sound framework for their argument against high taxes and
government regulation. The book was so inflammatory and contrary
to the postwar liberal consensus that "some Keynesians successfully
lobbied to have it purged from their universities' libraries," writes historian Rick Perlstein.

Friedman accused liberal policy makers who followed Keynes's theories of attacking America's prized individual freedoms. The liberals,
he said, promoted government as the solution to every problem rather

than as an "instrument through which we can exercise our freedom." America's New Deal liberals, he wrote, had become addicted to "welfare and equality rather than freedom . . . In the name of welfare and equality, the twentieth-century liberal has come to favor a revival of the very policies of state intervention and paternalism against which classical liberalism fought."

His book *Capitalism and Freedom* led Arizona senator Barry Goldwater to make Friedman his economic adviser during the Republican's 1964 campaign for president. Goldwater cited Friedman as the source of his calls for free markets, less regulation, and low taxation. Just before the 1964 election, Friedman wrote an article titled "The Goldwater View of Economics" for the *New York Times*. He identified "freedom and opportunity" as the senator's goals. Goldwater, Friedman argued, wanted a nation where each can "pursue his own interests so long as he does not interfere with the freedom of others to do likewise." As for economic policy, he wrote, the only purpose of government is to protect the freedom and right of every citizen to make money for himself and his family.

A prominent name in the world of politics even after Goldwater's defeat, Friedman focused on the idea of a "natural rate of unemployment"— that is, that some people are always going to be unemployed in even the strongest economy. Since the Great Depression the federal government had based its economic policies on ending unemployment, or at least keeping it at a very low level. Friedman predicted that government efforts to create jobs with federal spending would lead to inflation that would consequently throw the economy into a downward spiral.

When the economy went into just such a recession in the late 1970s, Americans acknowledged that Friedman's predictions had been absolutely correct. By then he had advised Presidents Nixon and Ford— and would go on to advise President Reagan, as well as political leaders around the world, notably Britain's prime minister, Margaret Thatcher—on how to unleash economic markets by trusting the private sector to act in its own best interest.

Friedman's influence reached its crest during the Reagan presidency. Throughout Reagan's two terms Friedman served as an informal adviser as the president put in place business-friendly reforms. Though

Friedman also wanted the president to cut the size of the government—
and later admitted that Reagan failed on that account—he did com-
mend Reagan for slowing the growth of government. The Reagan
approach set the stage for significant economic growth through the
end of the twentieth century, Friedman believed. "There is no doubt in
my mind that . . . [President Reagan's] emphasis on lowering tax rates,
plus his emphasis on deregulating," transformed the economy, Friedman told PBS in a 2000 interview. "The regulations had doubled, the
number of pages in the *Federal Register* had doubled, during the Nixon
regime; they almost halved during the Reagan regime. So those actions
of Reagan unleashed the basic constructive forces of the free market
and from 1983 on, it's been almost entirely up."

Friedman died in 2006, but his ideas remain a touchstone for conservative politicians and a consistent factor in today's discussions of
the Federal Reserve's economic policies. Friedman's thinking is also
at the heart of ongoing congressional talks on budget and tax policy.
Friedman's name is a revered reference on the political right, especially
among disgruntled modern conservatives who opposed the Federal
Reserve's decision to push the economy out of recession with a policy
of "quantitative easing" designed to keep interest rates low and drive
down unemployment. Conservative critics point to Friedman to explain their opposition to the Obama administration's decision to offer
federal money to Wall Street and American car manufacturers as
bailouts. And opponents of federal stimulus spending after the 2008
stock market crisis frequently cited Friedman. When conservatives rail
against President Obama's national healthcare plan, Friedman is cited
as the economist who made the case for maximum individual choice
free of government interference.

But supporters of national healthcare have responded by criticizing Friedman's winner-take-all economic strategies as the root cause of
the 2008 recession and the high number of Americans without health
insurance. In April 2008, the *New York Times*'s Peter Goodman wrote
that the economic downturn had placed "Mr. Friedman's intellectual
legacy under fresh scrutiny." Goodman describes Friedman as the
"chief evangelist in the mission to let loose the animal instincts of the
market." Yet the depth of the recession signaled that the free market

can have a nasty, unforgiving underside—a biting edge that leads to calls for government to get back in the business of regulating the economy. "In short, the nation steeped in the thinking of a man who blamed government for the Depression now beseeches government to lift it to safety," Goodman wrote. "If Mr. Friedman . . . were still among us, he would surely be unhappy with this turn."

A *New Yorker* article in January 2010 by John Cassidy attacked Friedman and his fellow economic conservatives at the University of Chicago for providing the intellectual justification that "underpinned the deregulation of the banking system" and contributed to the recession. Cassidy described the atmosphere among Friedman's acolytes as comparable to traditional cosmologists when scientists realized how big and unwieldy the universe really was; the cosmology profession "fell into turmoil." Another critic, economist and Nobel Prize winner Paul Krugman, wrote in the *New York Review of Books* that most of the world's politically influential economic thinkers have become Friedman's acolytes, despite evidence that Friedman's policies have not spurred growth. Between 1947 and 1976 "Milton Friedman was a voice crying in the wilderness, his ideas ignored by policymakers," according to Krugman. "But the economy, for all the inefficiencies he decried, delivered dramatic improvements in the standard of living of most Americans: median real income more than doubled. By contrast, the period since 1976 has been one of increasing acceptance of Friedman's ideas . . . [and] gains in living standards have been far less robust than they were during the previous period: median real income was only about 23 percent higher in 2005 than in 1976."

Yet even as he critiqued Friedman's ideas, Krugman acknowledged Friedman's success in helping to accelerate the "great swing back toward laissez-faire policies that took place around the world beginning in the 1970s." Krugman agreed that "by any measure—protectionism versus free trade; regulation versus deregulation; wages set by collective bargaining and government minimum wages versus wages set by the market—the world has moved a long way in Friedman's direction." But by Friedman's later years, Krugman writes, the "refreshing iconoclasm of his early career hardened into a rigid defense of what had become the new orthodoxy." Krugman concluded there is now a need to fight against the dominance of Friedman's economic theories—just as there was a need, filled by Friedman, to fight against the dominance of Keynes's theories early in the twentieth century.

In a 2013 *Forbes* magazine article titled "The Origin of 'the World's Dumbest Idea': Milton Friedman," writer Steve Denning lambasted Friedman's argument for corporations' single-minded focus on making money for shareholders. Denning said the idea was taken seriously only by business executives looking for a way to put more money in their pockets. "At the time, private sector firms were starting to feel the first pressures of global competition and executives were looking around for ways to increase their returns," Denning wrote. "The idea of focusing totally on money and forgetting about any concerns for employees, customers or society seemed like a promising avenue worth exploring."

In a 1979 *BusinessWeek* article, Kenneth Mason, former head of Quaker Oats, accused Friedman of painting a "dreary and demeaning" picture of big business. Mason viewed Friedman's sole focus on profits as myopic and the equivalent of a person who ate to excess on the theory that food is required to live but failed to see there is more to life than eating.

Roger Martin, in his book *Fixing the Game,* also criticized Friedman's profits-first thinking. He tied it to corporate scandals, including Enron, and banking scandals. These "theories of shareholder value maximization and stock-based compensation have the ability to destroy our economy and rot out the core of American capitalism."

But for all the criticism of Friedman among business analysts, writers, and academics, whether they are liberals or conservatives, there is no question of the dominance of Friedman's free-market economic theories today. His winner-take-all approach has created a greater separation between rich and poor, as well as an increasingly anxious middle class. We live in a world where the rich are celebrated and the movie *Wall Street* is remembered for the powerful line "Greed is good." It has led the Supreme Court to rule that corporations are to be viewed as "people," with rights previously limited to individual citizens. It has also led to worldwide political arguments about limiting taxes, limiting government spending and debt, and limiting the size of government, particularly the social safety net of government entitlement programs, from food stamps to benefits for the unemployed and the poor. But the greatest impact of Friedman's thinking has been to clear a path for economic growth based on rewarding innovation, risk-taking investment, and higher education.

Friedman's influence extends further than the economy. In his 2011 *Age of Fracture*, Princeton historian Daniel T. Rogers writes that in the 1980s "the term 'market' that insinuated itself into more and more realms of social thought . . . stood for a way of thinking about society." He cited the increase of niche markets of the kind that are now regular features of American life, noting that they reflect unbounded personal freedom to take on narrow identities and tastes. It is evident in the growth of specialty magazines and ethnic food restaurants as well as racial, religious, generational, and gender identity groups and the websites, television cable channels, and independent movies targeted at those individual groups. One consequence is the erosion of common experiences, memories, and identity that defined America for much of the twentieth century, especially after World War II.

The cultural free market is rooted in Friedman's economic ideology. "Freedom is the major objective in relations among individuals," Friedman explained in a 1968 essay that tied his economic theory to culture. He argued that the "preservation of freedom requires limiting narrowly the role of government and placing primary reliance on private property, free markets, and voluntary arrangements."

A left-wing student once heckled Friedman as he spoke, complaining that Friedman was rationalizing selfish, greedy corporate behavior that destroyed the idea of Americans working and acting in service to the idea of greater social good. "Your objective is the same as mine—greater individual freedom," Friedman responded. "The difference is that I know how to achieve that objective and you do not."

Friedman's thinking remains central to the way American business is conducted today, and to American culture, especially the contemporary idea of freedom.

CHAPTER 7

LIBERTY AND
JUSTICE FOR ALL

Eleanor Roosevelt and the Fight
for Universal Human Rights

H ere is liberty and justice for all, twenty-first-century style.
A 2012 video posted on YouTube about a murderous African
warlord thousands of miles away in central Africa lit up social media
in the United States. Americans, most of them under twenty-five, became outraged at the man's barbaric attacks, the lack of justice for his
victims, and the absence of liberty for those left living in fear.

The young freedom fighters began emailing the video to one another and called it to the attention of their parents, their teachers, and
the White House website. Prodded by fans, TV talk show host Oprah
Winfrey and pop star Justin Bieber posted urgent messages on Twitter
urging their followers to watch the video and send money to help catch
Joseph Kony, the rebel outlaw terrorizing, raping, and killing people
while hiding in the bushes of Uganda. In just three days more than
seventy million people watched, posted messages, tweeted, sent millions of dollars, and sparked what one writer called a "worldwide man-
hunt . . . for a really bad guy."

My point? In twenty-first-century America, the notions of liberty
and justice apply worldwide. America's power to set the world's moral
compass extends further than viral YouTube videos and international
manhunts.

For instance, American thinking on human rights has changed the way people around the world view women's rights. When a fifteen-year-old Pakistani girl was shot in the head by Muslim Taliban extremists for blogging and speaking against the Taliban's prohibition on educating women, she was airlifted to England for medical care. In July 2013, only nine months after her attempted murder, she stood before the United Nations Youth Assembly to ask for their support for global public education for girls. The U.N. General Secretary introduced the young activist, Malala Yousafzai, as a powerful threat to terrorists—"a girl with a book." The following fall she spoke at Harvard University and met with President Obama.

It's easy to forget that the modern concept of personal liberty, now held as an ideal worldwide, began as an American idea. It is still relatively new. It began when Eleanor Roosevelt, the longest-serving First Lady in American history, redefined the way Americans think about liberty, justice, and equality for all. Those ideas, of course, have defined the American psyche from the days of the Founding Fathers. They animated the Colonial argument for defying King George III. When Thomas Jefferson wrote the Declaration of Independence, he made natural rights—equality, liberty, and justice for all (that is, for all property-owning Christian white men)—the very heart of his argument against the king. But he was talking about the American colonies, not the entire world. Mrs. Roosevelt took the Founding Fathers' basic concept of natural rights and elevated it to a higher level, applying these tenets not only to every U.S. citizen but also to people living far beyond America's shores.

Jefferson spoke of the "self-evident" truth of all men being equal, being granted God-given natural rights of free action, "endowed by their creator with certain unalienable rights, that among these are life, liberty and the pursuit of happiness." In fact, Jefferson began the Declaration of Independence by citing the "laws of nature" as the basis for the right of the colonies to rebel against any government power, be it a monarch, a tyrant, or a military ruler. He then made the case for rejecting British rule, and for democratic government as the natural right of men.

Jefferson was not alone in his belief in natural rights. Thomas Paine called for outright revolution, arguing that no king and no government can grant rights that come only from God. John Adams argued for rights that exist above the laws of any king, "rights, that cannot be repealed or restrained by human law—rights, derived from the great legislator of the universe." George Mason, another Revolutionary champion, also wrote about the "sacred rights of human nature." And after the Declaration was issued, Patrick Henry, first governor of Virginia and famous advocate of states' rights, called for a Bill of Rights to protect the natural or, in his words, "inalienable rights of mankind."

Two centuries later, Eleanor Roosevelt opened a new chapter in U.S. history by expanding the way Americans think about who qualifies for protection under the Founding Fathers' idea of natural rights. As First Lady from 1933 to 1945, she used the White House bully pulpit to make the case that all human beings—both men and women, Jews as well as Christians, West Virginia coal miners and Japanese internees during World War II, blacks as well as whites, refugees seeking asylum and impoverished immigrants—are born with the God-given, natural right to personal liberty.

As the head of the United Nations Commission on Human Rights in 1946, the former First Lady led a titanic political push to lift the idea of natural rights beyond U.S. borders to every form of government. She went well beyond the Declaration of Independence, beyond the Constitution and the Bill of Rights, to assert *universal rights* for all people. In that moment, Mrs. Roosevelt offered the Founding Fathers' claim of natural rights as the new baseline for judging how any government, in any place, treats the poor, political dissidents, racial and ethic minorities, women, and children. Lacking any power of enforcement, her ideals nonetheless gave new power and legitimacy to anyone speaking out about oppression anywhere in the world.

But her work in promoting universal natural rights started well before the war began. As her husband's New Deal legislation took hold and began reviving the economy after the Great Depression, Mrs. Roosevelt became an activist for workers and the rights of labor unions in the United States. Pointing to natural rights, she created expectations of the right of workers to join unions and negotiate with companies for fair wages and working conditions.

She pressed her husband, Franklin Delano Roosevelt, to encourage the government to hire women and blacks in factories gearing up for the war. She made public appeals to the president and Congress for the rights of Japanese Americans who lost their jobs, land, and liberty as a result of suspicion and bigotry in the wake of the Japanese attack on Pearl Harbor. Her efforts broke ground for women's and African Americans' rights in the United States. And her work offered the first hint that the idea of natural rights might one day be extended to gays, the disabled, and military veterans.

The stakes of Eleanor Roosevelt's work ratcheted up in the postwar era. America's triumph as a global military superpower in World War II elevated the nation to new heights of moral authority on issues of right and wrong, justice and injustice. People everywhere wanted clear moral rules on how to treat each other in the aftermath of the horrific human rights abuses committed by the Nazis, fascists, and imperialists. It was the key, everyone felt, to preventing future wars. As one of the first U.S. delegates to the newly created United Nations, Mrs. Roosevelt began exporting the American concept of natural rights. Before her work on the U.N.'s Universal Declaration of Human Rights, the world had never heard an argument for global action to protect all people because they have God-given, natural rights. And no one had made the case that international action to defend those natural rights superseded claims of any sovereign government to set its own rules and do as it pleased with its citizens within its own borders.

Not everyone approved of Eleanor Roosevelt's push for global human rights. American critics derided her as an unrealistic dreamer, irritating scold, and self-righteous know-it-all. Some said Roosevelt did not know her place and was a troublemaker and a socialist. People gossiped about her close friendships with other women. Even after she chaired the committee drafting the declaration and helped win approval for it worldwide, President Eisenhower attempted to undercut her achievements by commenting that opponents of the declaration were helping to "save the U.S. from Eleanor Roosevelt." Despite all the criticism, Eleanor Roosevelt successfully reinvented the way people think about human rights. The roots of her work are in the brilliant but narrow assertion of rights first articulated by America's Founding Fathers. Mrs. Roosevelt took that idea to a new level, a blossoming tree of liberty for the world.

Even with the lofty assertions of natural rights made by America's

Founding Fathers—all of whom were wealthy white men—human rights weren't a reality in America during the eighteenth century and much of the nineteenth. Early American women, who lived under the authority of their husbands, didn't get the right to vote until 1920, and even then they were second-class citizens when it came to holding jobs and political office. Though African Americans were given their freedom at the end of the Civil War, well into the twentieth century many blacks were barred from voting, living in certain places, attending certain schools, and holding many jobs. Children belonged to their parents and had no individual rights of their own. And homosexuality, when it was even recognized, was a forbidden act practiced by deviants and criminals. Yet on the Founders' sturdy, if skeletal, frame of natural rights, Mrs. Roosevelt fleshed out a new American sensibility, extending human rights to all.

City, state, and federal laws reflect this new standard. Mrs. Roosevelt's standards have been confirmed in court rulings over civil rights, fair housing, education, job discrimination, and more. We feel her legacy in the tolerant and sensitive way that Americans from different cultures treat one another on a daily basis. Laws and court rulings supporting the gay marriage movement are part of Mrs. Roosevelt's legacy. So, too, are a woman's right to legal abortion and contraception and black America's success in overturning the laws of segregation—not to mention legal protections for the mentally ill, protections for the rights of prisoners and refugees, and laws providing shelter and care for the homeless. A transformation so far-reaching, so complete, so unyielding in its power to persuade is hard to quantify or define. It is like talking about a world without electricity or airplanes. There was a world before those inventions, but the way we think and live as a result of those changes is so vast that the former world seems unimaginable. Mrs. Roosevelt created an equally vast change in the American mindset, one that transformed the way much of the world thinks about basic human rights. Her success in reforming how Americans think about and treat each other—coupled with the way she transformed America from just another nation into the world's moral compass—makes her one of the new founders of today's America.

In polls, Mrs. Roosevelt is ranked as the most admired woman of the twentieth century. She is the only First Lady to be honored with her own statue at a national presidential memorial—the memorial to her husband, FDR. Her life-size statue has a prim and proper feel to it. She stands alone in a long coat with the symbol of the United Nations on the wall behind her head. Cut in stone on the wall next to her statue is a quote by her husband, FDR: "The structure of world peace cannot be the work of one man, or one party, or one nation. . . . It must be a peace which rests on the cooperative effort of the whole world."

She is also honored with a statue in New York City; here she is casually resting against a rock, looking into the distance, as if in thought. Her words on the power of natural rights are carved into granite: "Where, after all, do universal human rights begin? In small places, close to home . . . Such are the places where every man, woman and child seeks equal justice, equal opportunity, equal dignity."

At her memorial service in 1962, the first state funeral for a First Lady, Presidents Kennedy, Eisenhower, and Truman as well as Vice President Lyndon Johnson and the chief justice of the United States, Earl Warren, came to honor her. Truman called her the "First Lady of the world." Adlai Stevenson, the former Democratic presidential candidate, described the impact of her life work in this way: "She would rather light candles than curse the darkness, and her glow has warmed the world." Speaking at another memorial service for Mrs. Roosevelt held later that month, Stevenson asked, "What other single human being has touched and transformed the existence of so many others?"

More than forty years later, Secretary of State Hillary Clinton, speaking at the State Department's 2010 Eleanor Roosevelt Human Rights Award ceremony, described the twenty-first century's global struggle against injustice as a flower whose seeds were planted by Mrs. Roosevelt. A former First Lady herself, Clinton harnessed Mrs. Roosevelt's ethical legacy when she began her speech by recognizing the people "being persecuted, jailed, or tortured today." For Clinton, what Roosevelt and the others who wrote the Universal Declaration succeeded at was to take the idea of human rights beyond the confines of laws and beyond political differences—to, as Clinton put it, establish the principle of "equal rights for every man, woman and child; freedom from want and fear . . . we must speak out when people are not free to vote or practice their religion; when girls are trafficked or married against their will; when boys are forced to become child soldiers." And, Clinton notes, Mrs. Roosevelt was able to do all this in clear, plain speech: "The language of a document intended to be universal had to be so clear that anyone could understand it. And if you read, as I do, international treaties and agreements—you know that the fact Eleanor succeeded was nothing short of a miracle."

Before Eleanor Roosevelt, human rights violations were often ignored as a problem beyond remedy because of social traditions and local laws in other countries, other cultures. The concept of universal natural rights did not exist. Journalists usually ignored human rights violations as harsh, sad realities. But part of Mrs. Roosevelt's genius was the ability to show Americans and the global community that human rights were truths that extended deeper even than local laws and social traditions.

In the words of a PBS documentary film on Mrs. Roosevelt, "History and personal events combined to propel Eleanor from the rigid confines of Victorian femininity to the center stage of twentieth-century political activism." Born in October 1884 to a wealthy political family that included an uncle who later became president, Theodore Roosevelt, young Eleanor was wounded early on by the death of her parents. Her mother, Anna Hall Roosevelt, died of diphtheria when Eleanor was eight, and her father, Elliott Bulloch Roosevelt, suffering from serious alcoholism, tried to commit suicide by jumping out of a window, and died of a seizure soon after. Eleanor was only ten.

Even when she was alive, Anna Hall Roosevelt was never much of a mother to young Eleanor. Eleanor's mother made it known that she regretted that her daughter lacked the grace and beauty expected by the "high society" in which the Roosevelts moved. Her father was more loving, but alcoholism clouded his relationships. The result was an insecure girl starved for affection, sent to live with a grandmother who, when Eleanor was only fifteen, packed her off to a girls' boarding school in England. At the boarding school, however, she became a standout under the tutelage of a strong headmistress, who made Eleanor her personal assistant and took her on her travels throughout Europe.

She was called back to the United States by her relatives three years later, and introduced as a debutante. Her formal education ended there;

she never went to college. Yet even though she was a society girl from a good family, her peers viewed her as a socially inept orphan. The pressure of society life, she later recalled, was so great that it left her near "nervous collapse." Eleanor Roosevelt was a woman of her era. As PBS's *American Experience* described her in a video documentary, she was no radical leading protests for change: "For most of her early life, Eleanor was dependent on and deferential to the wills and demands of those around her."

Based on her all-girls boarding school experience, she began to create her own society among women. New York City at the time was a rough place, with a growing number of factories attracting working-class and poor people to the city's crammed tenements and violent neighborhoods. In her twenties she worked with New York's Junior League, a group of society women, in the city's infamous Lower East Side slums, including the Rivington Street settlement house for immigrants.

She attracted few men until a chance meeting with her distant cousin Franklin D. Roosevelt on a first-class train ride to upstate New York in 1902. Two years older than she, Franklin was attracted to her intellect and independence. They began trading letters, later began dating, and married in 1905.

Their marriage was troubled from the beginning, however, because of the opposition of Franklin's mother, Sara Delano Roosevelt. She did not consider Eleanor an appropriate match for her son. After Franklin proposed to Eleanor, his mother convinced him to join her on a cruise, where she spent the entire trip trying to persuade him to call off the engagement. He refused, and he and Eleanor were married, with President Theodore Roosevelt giving away the bride. The young couple lived in a New York City townhouse connected to the house next door— where Franklin's mother lived. Even as Eleanor gave birth to six children, Sara remained the dominant figure in the family. "Your mother only bore you; I am more your mother than your mother is," Sara once told her grandson James.

When Franklin became assistant secretary of the navy in 1913, the family moved to Washington, D.C. By her own admission, Mrs. Roosevelt found motherhood stressful. The exciting world of D.C. politics then became a means to escape the family life that never seemed to fulfill her. In a nation preparing to enter a major world war, experiencing a massive industrial buildup, and coming to terms with a nascent labor movement, there was a whole lot to be excited about. Eleanor emerged as a power player in Democratic Party politics and the labor movement.

Her problems with family life became more acute in 1918 when she found out her husband was having an affair with her social secretary. Franklin Roosevelt's political advisers and even his mother told the rising political star he could not divorce Eleanor without sacrificing his political future. Three years later their faltering marriage took another turn when Franklin was diagnosed with polio. His legs paralyzed, he was largely confined to a wheelchair.

Despite their personal struggles, Eleanor took over Franklin's care and encouraged him to stay in politics; their marriage evolved into a political partnership. She campaigned by his side when he was the Democratic vice presidential candidate on a losing Democratic ticket in 1920. That year American women gained the right to vote, further elevating Mrs. Roosevelt as a leading voice in the party. She was particularly known for her ability to organize and rally Democratic women. Her work paid off in 1928 when her husband was elected governor of New York.

As the governor's wife, Eleanor became his public stand-in, traveling the state to look at crisis situations and reporting back to him as a political ally who had his complete trust. She began appearing as a surrogate for him at political meetings, negotiating disputes inside his administration. She was frequently featured as her husband's voice at public events, expanding his ties to labor unions as she advocated for workers' right to organize, minimum wage, and child labor laws.

The Roosevelts' political partnership became even more important when FDR was elected president in 1933. She became a high-level political actor with a vision of government standing up for the natural rights of all Americans, including those who were politically weak: women, children, uneducated factory workers, refugees seeking safety in the United States from oppression in their native lands. In fact, she became the most activist First Lady the nation had ever seen. In an era when women were still barred from many professions, Eleanor Roosevelt dared to attend important political meetings in the White House; she held her own press conferences, barring male journalists in order to pressure newspapers to hire more women as reporters; she gave around 1,400 speeches as First Lady and wrote a widely syndicated newspaper column. A 1933 *New Yorker* political cartoon showed a man wearing a coal miner's hard hat looking out of the dark shaft as he said to another miner: "For gosh sakes, here comes Mrs. Roosevelt!"

Her brash actions led some to call her the most controversial First Lady in history. "No first lady before her had ever wielded such power," wrote author John Sears. As fascism spread through Europe in the years leading up to World War II, Eleanor petitioned her husband to allow persecuted groups to immigrate to the United States more easily. Mrs. Roosevelt also cared about the plight of African Americans. During the war, she advocated for the creation of the Fair Employment Practices Committee, established by FDR's 1941 Executive Order mandating the integration of the defense industry.

Her best-known project began in 1933: a federally funded community in Arthurdale, West Virginia, with housing for low-income mine workers, some of whom had been fired for trying to bring unions into the mines. Mrs. Roosevelt wanted blacks to be part of the community, but the mostly white miners insisted on keeping the town all white and all Christian. Critics condemned the entire project as a "communist plot." Even some fellow Democrats publicly worried that the government was doing the work of private builders by establishing a town, with Mrs. Roosevelt setting standards for everything from heating to room size in the new development. Federal support for the project faded and funding ended in 1941. But Mrs. Roosevelt never lost her passion for Arthurdale as an example of innovative government policy improving the lives of hardworking people.

Her support for equal rights for black Americans also broke new ground in Washington. When African American opera singer Marian Anderson was banned from singing at Constitution Hall in 1939 by the Daughters of the American Revolution, Mrs. Roosevelt stepped in and had the federal government open the steps of the Lincoln Memorial for a special concert featuring the singer. She won the hearts of black Americans by supporting congressional passage of a law banning lynching, then a great fear in the lives of southern black people. When she visited the training camp of the all-black Tuskegee Airmen, the nation's first black air combat unit, and took an hour-long flight with a black pilot,

Mrs. Roosevelt further inspired blacks, who had previously been largely Republican voters, to begin moving into the ranks of the Democrats.

Even in matters of policies directly tied to the war, Mrs. Roosevelt did not shy away from making her voice heard. She argued with her husband over the internment of Japanese Americans. She advocated for greater immigration of children from Europe and for Jewish refugees. She went to England in 1942 to visit American troops, and in 1943 she went to see the troops in the South Pacific.

President Roosevelt died in April 1945, ending Eleanor Roosevelt's time in the White House. After serving as the longest-tenured First Lady in history over her husband's three terms in office, Mrs. Roosevelt returned home to Hyde Park, New York, to set up the nation's first presidential library and museum.

President Harry S. Truman, FDR's successor, saw her potential as a powerful political ally. She was an icon among American women, union members, and African Americans. She was also the widow of the president who led America out of the Great Depression and to victory in World War II. While she resisted any suggestion of running for political office, Truman surprised her by offering to make her the U.S. delegate to the newly created United Nations.

"When President Harry Truman appointed Eleanor Roosevelt to the first [U.N.] General Assembly delegation, which met in London on October 24, 1945, she concentrated on human rights, believing that without justice and liberty there could be no peace; without a 'Magna Carta for the world' economic development would remain a cruel and greedy business," wrote Blanche Wiesen Cook in the magazine *Peace and Freedom*. She took to the work with a personal passion, frequently citing her late husband's vision for a world council dedicated to preventing future world wars. She spoke about empowering people, enshrining God-given individual rights as inviolable by birth. She saw individual rights as the way to prevent another Holocaust or act of genocide.

The presence of the politically powerful former First Lady added credibility to the nascent United Nations. She was a worldwide figure at a critical historical moment in history, as America assumed a mantle of power and authority it had never had before. At the first gathering of the U.N. General Assembly, Mrs. Roosevelt charged the Soviets with mistreating World War II war refugees. "The Soviet Union and its allies insisted that the refugees return to their countries of origin; the Western nations believed they should be allowed to settle elsewhere if they so wished," wrote John Sears in describing Mrs. Roosevelt's rise as an international stateswoman. Eleanor Roosevelt "debated this issue first in committee, then in the General Assembly with Andrei Vyshinsky, the tough Soviet delegate," Sears wrote. "[Her] success in this debate established her reputation as a strong and able diplomat."

Mrs. Roosevelt's renown and her political connections in the United States and internationally led to her election in 1947 as the first chair of the United Nations Commission on Human Rights. The commission was asked to create a Universal Declaration of Human Rights that included political and civil rights and social and economic rights. "As chairman of the Human Rights Commission, Eleanor Roosevelt provided the leadership that kept the project moving, the political influence that held the State Department on board, and the personal attentions that made each member of the Commission feel respected," wrote Harvard professor Mary Ann Glendon.

Mrs. Roosevelt stood out on a panel that included many other strong, politically able international leaders, while managing ideas on what should be in the declaration from some of the world's best-known writers and thinkers, including Mahatma Gandhi and Aldous Huxley. Jay Winter of Yale University wrote that while "the idea of human rights is present in one form or another in every major religious or philosophical tradition . . . [t]his cosmopolitan consensus is what gave the Universal Declaration of Human Rights its standing as a landmark in international affairs."

But Mrs. Roosevelt had to deal with concerns not just international but American as well, especially at the State Department. Undersecretary Robert Lovett, the second-highest-ranking official at State, opposed the idea of any declaration on human rights. On a practical level, he argued that a human rights declaration conflicted with America's more immediate priorities, specifically its military and economic goals worldwide. The State Department tried to limit the principles of the declaration to civil and political rights along the lines of the Bill of Rights. Mrs. Roosevelt persisted in pressing for American support for both economic and social rights as part of the international covenant of individual rights to be included in the declaration. Mrs. Roosevelt also anticipated opposition from white Southern democrats, whose segregationist policies contradicted the principles laid out in the Universal Declaration.

One line of argument among the segregationists was that America's enemies might exploit racial trouble in the United States by citing them as evidence of American hypocrisy. And the most often heard critique of her ideas was that the declaration was simply an empty vessel because it could not be enforced—it was, at best, a utopian dream.

But Eleanor Roosevelt proved herself to be a shrewd strategist. She accepted the fact that the declaration was not a binding document. Instead, Mrs. Roosevelt tightly crafted the declaration as an assertion of common principles and goals in service to the ideal of human rights. No sanctions existed for any nation that chose to stray from those goals. But Mrs. Roosevelt's strategy left violators risking exposure to the rest of the world as human rights outlaws. Mrs. Roosevelt's previous political battles in Washington led her to see the value in loudly trumpeting new ideals and visions that no government, including the United States, could prevent its people from hearing and holding up as a standard of behavior.

On December 10, 1948, the U.N. General Assembly adopted the Universal Declaration of Human Rights. News accounts heralded it as the first expression of a common standard for treatment of all people. Still, the attacks against the declaration continued. It became a target for derision from political cynics who labeled it a fantasy. What they missed, however, is that the declaration tapped into our basic human aspiration, after two world wars, for peace and the simple, honest, and fair treatment of people everywhere.

The declaration's preamble begins: "Whereas recognition of the inherent dignity and of the equal and inalienable rights of all members of the human family is the foundation of freedom, justice and peace in the world; whereas disregard and contempt for human rights have resulted in barbarous acts which have outraged the conscience of mankind." Picking up the pledge that Mrs. Roosevelt's late husband, FDR, had given during his 1941 State of the Union Address, also known as the "Four Freedoms Speech," the declaration called for a world "in which human beings shall enjoy freedom of speech and belief and freedom from fear and want."

The Founding Fathers' determination to stand up for their political rights as a function of their human rights can be seen in the declaration, too. The third paragraph of the preamble speaks of the "essential" protection for all offered by the "rule of law," so that people will not be compelled to use violence and organize for war as "rebellion against tyranny and oppression." In fact, the Founding Fathers' belief in natural rights is evident from the very first sentence of the declaration's Article 1: "All human beings are born free and equal in dignity and rights." In line with the ideas of the Founding Fathers and Enlightenment philosophers such as Kant and Rousseau, it asserts that all human beings are "endowed with reason and conscience and should act towards one another in a spirit of brotherhood."

But with the declaration's Article 2, Mrs. Roosevelt and the commission went far beyond the Founding Fathers' Declaration of Independence: "Everyone is entitled to all the rights and freedoms set forth in this Declaration, without distinction of any kind, such as race, colour, sex, language, religion, political or other opinion, national or social origin, property, birth or other status." The natural rights espoused by the Founding Fathers had been transformed into human rights for all.

The declaration went on to say these rights and privileges for all people extended beyond sovereign lines of any nation and any form of government. Even within a nation's borders, Mrs. Roosevelt's panel said, "arbitrary arrest" of political opponents was in violation of basic rights. In addition, "everyone has the right to work ... and to protection against unemployment," as well as "rest and leisure," "equal pay for equal work," and help from government in the form of entitlement aid if they cannot earn enough to provide their family with "an existence worthy of human dignity."

Speaking to the U.N. General Assembly the day before its members voted on whether to approve the declaration, Ms. Roosevelt asked the world delegates to think in terms of America's Founding Fathers and others who had set identified standards for equal rights. "This declaration may well become the international Magna Carta of all men everywhere," she said. "We hope its proclamation by the General Assembly will be an event comparable to . . . the adoption of the Bill of Rights by the people of the United States, and the adoption of comparable declarations at different times in other countries."

Forty-eight countries, including the United States, voted to approve the Universal Declaration the next day. Only eight nations, including the countries of the Soviet bloc, South Africa, and Saudi Arabia, abstained. Today, more than 160 nations have adopted the Universal Declaration of Human Rights.

Professor Robert B. Tapp, writing in the magazine *The Humanist,* later called the Universal Declaration of Human Rights a "pioneer" document that was "not only ahead of its time but remains ahead of most of the 193 nations now comprising the UN." In fact, the United Nations has subsequently adopted further declarations to amplify the rights of children, the disabled, women, and refugees.

By any measure, the conception of human rights spelled out in the declaration is far more extensive than anything that came before it. In her book on the declaration, Mary Ann Glendon summed it up as a "bold new course for human rights," with unprecedented connection between previous ideas of natural rights and new ideas of human rights "linked to social security, balanced by responsibilities, grounded in respect for equal human dignity, and guarded by the rule of law."

Yet many U.S. lawmakers were reluctant to support future U.N. agreements. In April 1953, Secretary of State John Foster Dulles told the Senate Judiciary Committee that the Eisenhower administration would not support the U.N. covenants then being drafted because the U.N.'s provisions might limit America's dealings with other countries. Indeed, the United States did not sign on to the U.N.'s Covenant on Economic, Social and Cultural Rights (ICESCR) and its Covenant on Civil and Political Rights (ICCPR) until 1977—more than ten years after they were adopted by the U.N. General Assembly.

Even after its adoption by the U.N., the declaration and Mrs. Roosevelt faced continual criticism. Domestic political critics attacked Mrs. Roosevelt as a loose cannon. Her legacy of support for unions and the civil rights of black Americans had led to a four-thousand-page-long FBI file. She attracted the enmity of extreme conservatives in the Republican Party, including Senator Joe McCarthy, who made no secret

of his distaste for what he considered her push toward communist principles and entitlements for all—he and others viewed the declaration
as potentially a cover for communist governments that might provide
education or healthcare but ignore any right to political free speech.

But Mrs. Roosevelt, once an insecure society debutante, by now
had gained skills and confidence that allowed her to respond to criticism of both the United Nations and her Declaration of Human Rights.
When Senator McCarthy began his infamous witchhunt to oust supposed communists working in the U.S. government, Mrs. Roosevelt,
in keeping with the Universal Declaration of Human Rights, gave a
speech in 1950 before the American Democratic Action organization
where she claimed that "The day I'm afraid to sit down with people I do
not know because five years from now someone will say five of those
people were Communists and therefore you are a Communist—that
will be a very bad day." Two years later, Mrs. Roosevelt continued her
defense of the U.N.: "Without the United Nations our country would
walk alone, ruled by fear instead of confidence and hope," she said at
the 1952 Democratic National Convention in Chicago. "To weaken or
hamstring the United Nations now, through lack of faith and lack of
vision, would be to condemn ourselves to endless struggle for survival
in a jungle world."

As a result of Eleanor Roosevelt's fight, the declaration has become a new standard of natural rights and human rights around the
world, consistently cited by human rights groups in response to any
government abuse of people. It is also referred to in new agreements,
including those on eliminating racism, ending discrimination against
women, and upholding the rights of children. New organizations such
as Human Rights Watch and Amnesty International, as well as new
charities, have expressly made it their mission to act on the rights articulated in the declaration.

In "Eleanor Roosevelt and the Universal Declaration of Human
Rights," John Sears writes that the declaration has become "the cornerstone of the modern human rights movement ... Most significantly, perhaps, it has inspired and given authority to numerous
non-governmental human rights groups in their efforts to bring public
pressure to bear on governments that violate the human rights of their
own citizens."

Mrs. Roosevelt stands alone as the American who ushered her country into its role as worldwide leader on human rights, a concept that has taken flight over the last half of the twentieth century and continues as a goal of the twenty-first century. Her vision has given shape and inspiration to human rights efforts around the world that once were dismissed as fantastic, unrealistic idealism.

CHAPTER 8

THE BRIDGE AND TUNNEL CROWD

Robert Moses, William Levitt,
and the American City

The first Founding Fathers, for the most part, were "country boys." In Colonial days, fewer than 10 percent of Americans lived in cities; 90 percent of the American people and most of the Founding Fathers lived on farms, rarely going to the city at all. A lack of good roads and hotels and the threat of hostile Indians left most people to rely on their family and far-flung neighbors for support. American Colonial life in the late 1700s required self-reliance, the only companionship at night that of the stars.

Today the reverse is true—80 percent of Americans, roughly 250 million bodies, live in large cities or their surrounding metropolitan areas. The suburbs are a phenomenon the Founding Fathers never could have imagined. The vast majority of us get in a car and drive ourselves to work, often on crowded interstate roads and highways. Half of the nation lives in cities with more than half a million people. At night the city lights are so bright it can be hard to see stars.

When the original colonists first laid anchor in what would eventually become the Eastern seaboard of the United States, they faced hundreds of miles of thick, seemingly impenetrable forest. Today the heart of the geographic area once occupied by the thirteen American colonies is a five-hundred-mile stretch of urban life running from Boston to Washington, D.C., with close to fifty million people.

Our twenty-first-century megalopolis might as well be the planet Mars to the Founding Fathers. The biggest city in Colonial America was Philadelphia, the center of politics and culture. With thirty thousand people, it was America's largest city by population. (In contemporary America, Colonial Philadelphia wouldn't come anywhere close to making it into the list of the 100 most populated cities in the country.) Cities existed during the Colonial period only as endpoints for commerce; goods moved from creeks and rivers to ocean ports in Boston, New York, Philadelphia, and Charleston, South Carolina. Those cities welcomed ships loaded with sugar and molasses from the West Indies as well as European goods such as mirrors, paper, and linens from across the Atlantic. Lumber, furs, rice, and tobacco from the thirteen colonies were exported to Europe.

Today, the East Coast cities that have replaced the original colonies are still major forces in the nation's economy. But a completely different set of businesses dominates major metropolitan economic life. The East Coast is the center of finance, banking, advertising, medical care, fashion, and media. Major interstate highways and high-speed railroads facilitate travel between cities, and bustling airports located in or near these cities serve as hubs for travel to the rest of the country as well as internationally.

The transformation of America's cities began in the mid–nineteenth century as the economy shifted from agriculture to industries such as steel and textiles, which required central locations near shipping ports for their factories, as well as a nearby population of available workers. In the twentieth century those older, industrial cities, with their tenements, smokestack manufacturing, and busy downtown shopping districts, changed again: office buildings came to symbolize the heart of the new American city.

The look and feel of living in twenty-first-century America can perhaps best be traced to the work of two men, Robert Moses and William Levitt. Neither was an architect or an engineer; neither studied sociology or urban planning. Moses studied political science, and Levitt majored in English and math before dropping out of college.

But Moses, representing public interests, and Levitt, working for private profit, are the modern-day founders of much of the way American communities are formed in the twenty-first century. Their work left a lasting imprint on our city streets, suburban cul-de-sacs, and the houses and apartment buildings that Americans call home. Their influence is evident in the traffic jams we encounter during rush hour and the racially segregated schools that are a common feature of modern American life.

When Robert Moses was born in 1888, the gritty urban landscape was packed with a mix of poor and working-class workers and their families, as well as lots of newly arrived immigrants from Europe. Upper-class merchants, shopkeepers, and emerging industrialists filled out the landscape. Some blacks, just decades after the Emancipation Proclamation and the end of slavery, had begun the great exodus to the North for a new life away from the slave plantations and the rigid segregation of the southern states. Life and politics in the American cities at the end of the 1800s was full of corruption and patronage, as well as racial and ethnic divisions.

The young Robert Moses wanted to reform city and state government to improve living conditions in New York. Born in New Haven, Connecticut, to wealthy German Jewish parents who made their money in real estate and department stores, Moses and his family moved to Manhattan, just off the gilded prosperity of Park Avenue, when Robert was nine. He got his bachelor's degree at Yale University, went to Oxford University to receive another bachelor's degree and a master's, and then got a doctorate in political science at Columbia University. His upper-class background gave him a distaste for the crass, criminal undercurrent of much of city government. He wanted to reform it.

When he began working in New York City government, his goal was to use good, sensible city planning ideas to defeat the tribal political powers and the wealthy landowners and industrialists who ruled New York City life. Thanks to lax zoning laws and sticky-fingered politicians, businessmen located their factories wherever they pleased. Moses wanted to refashion the city in a way that would create happier, better living conditions.

Nearly, sixty years later, in his bestselling and Pulitzer-winning book *The Power Broker,* author Robert Caro cast Moses as a bullying maniac and one of American history's greatest villains for destroying New York City neighborhoods. Villain or hero, it was Moses who paved the way for the major civic centers, parks, beaches, bridges, tunnels, and parkways of today—inventions that are the basis of contemporary suburban life. The iconic skyscrapers and superhighways that define America in cities today are the products of his mind.

Caro describes Moses as a man who bulldozed through New York's middle-class neighborhoods to create new highways and who ignored the urban poor except to warehouse them in dangerous, out-of-the-way public housing developments. Without ever winning an election, Moses received political appointments that gave him unrivaled authority and control of huge sums of public money. A modern Machiavelli, he managed to control public money and local and state politicians so completely that he answered to no one, and listened to none, as he became an autonomous force sculpting the new America.

That may be true. But Moses also left behind a record of substantial accomplishment. He built 150,000 apartment units and houses, 13 bridges, nearly 700 playgrounds, and close to 500 miles of parkways. During his career as an official for both New York State and New York City, from the 1920s until he died in 1981, he put his imprint on the design of nearly every kind of construction project built with government money in New York, and inspired similar urban development nationwide.

For better or worse, he steered public money away from subways and other forms of mass transit to build broad avenues, bridges, and parkways for automobiles. He skillfully used—some say manipulated—zoning regulations to put in place his grand vision of the best use of public dollars to create public space. And with public money as a whip, he reined in private development to fit his vision of the public good. In one celebrated case, his refusal to reconsider a land use decision on a lot in downtown Brooklyn led to the Brooklyn Dodgers baseball team leaving the city for the West Coast.

To picture Moses at the height of his power, imagine the man as a mythic giant straddling the nation's richest, most influential city, New York. His hand moved buildings and bridges and parks like toys as he redesigned the modern American city. His ability to control construction projects in New York City and the state shaped nearly every type of public infrastructure, from roads, bridges, and dams to art museums, public housing, beaches, playgrounds, schools, and hospitals. He transformed a Queens' ash dump into beautiful park grounds for the 1964 World's Fair and cleared land for Manhattan's Lincoln Center for the Performing Arts, home of the New York Philharmonic, the New York City Ballet, and the Metropolitan Opera. It was Moses who gained control of the land and attracted the private funding necessary to bring the United Nations headquarters to New York.

His transition from idealistic reformer to power broker began in defeat. The city's newly elected mayor in 1914, John Purroy Mitchel, promised to end government corruption; he chose Robert Moses, fresh out of graduate school, to take charge of rebuilding the city's civil service system. The energetic Moses devised a new system for hiring and evaluating city workers; if they failed to pass the new standards, he wanted them fired. The entrenched political powers that ruled New York City saw him as a threat.

"So great a nuisance did he make of himself that in 1918 Tammany Hall decided it had to crush him," Caro wrote. And it did so with efficiency. When Mayor Mitchel did not win reelection in 1917, Moses lost his government job as well. "At the age of thirty, with [his proposals to end patronage] being used as scrap paper, the Central Park shelters and great highways [that he dreamed of building] unbuilt, Robert Moses, Phi Beta Kappa at Yale, honors man at Oxford, lover of the Good, the True and the Beautiful, was out of work and, with a wife and two small daughters to support, was standing on a line in the Cleveland, Ohio, city hall applying for a minor municipal job—a job which, incidentally, he didn't get."

Moses eventually found work with a commission studying the best way to consolidate and reform state government. New York state's government was fragmented, corrupt, and run by local powers. Moses's energy and skill at writing laws to centralize control of the state government gained the trust of New York governor Al Smith. Still in his thirties, Moses became a master of working the bureaucracy and playing the political game to get Smith's projects done.

"When the curtain rose on the next act of Moses' life, idealism was gone from the stage," Caro concluded. "In its place was an understanding that ideas—dreams—were useless without power to transform them into reality. Moses spent the rest of his life amassing power, bringing to the task imagination, iron will and determination."

He became skilled at finding pools of money for public projects, including raking in federal money from President Roosevelt's New Deal. Moses's success in landing federal grants from the New Deal continued throughout World War II and after the war. The nation was especially ripe for commercial and residential development in the boom years of economic growth after World War II.

Two economic factors helped to magnify Moses's influence. First, the mass production of affordable cars, beginning in the 1920s, forced changes in the design of city streets. Second, in the 1930s the federal government incentivized the banking industry to issue more long-term mortgages at fixed rates, which created new demand for housing construction. These changes conspired to open the urban landscape.

But the biggest factor that allowed Moses to impose his vision on the future tenor of American cities was an unprecedented shuffling and relocation of the American people. After the 1929 Great Depression, the population of American cities grew rapidly as people came to America's urban centers looking for work.

"During the 1930s many people abandoned regions fraught with economic and environmental problems for new places that were thought to offer better opportunities and living conditions," according to a 2004 report on early-twentieth-century cities by the U.S. Geological Survey. "Others who had been involved in the armed services were exposed to parts of the country that had greater appeal as future places of residence than their former communities."

Using his ties to Governor Smith, Moses became president of the State Parks Commission for Long Island and chairman of the New York State Council of Parks, building a political base out of sight and control of the New York State legislature and his enemies in the New York City political machine and the unions controlling city hall.

But he still had his eyes on reforming New York City politics. The growth of the city led to more sweatshop factories, more tenement slums, and more crime. Infamous for its chaotic, corrupt use of public space, New York and its politicians proved unable to impose order on placement of roads and basic infrastructure such as sewers.

In 1934, after a failed run for governor, New York City mayor Fiorello La Guardia consolidated control of all the parks in the city's five boroughs and named Moses the commissioner of the Department of Parks for New York City. That same year Moses was appointed chairman of the Triborough Bridge Authority, which, under Moses's leadership, merged with the New York City Tunnel Authority in 1946 to become the Triborough Bridge and Tunnel Authority. Suddenly he had influence over approving the biggest development projects in the city, as well as the leverage to shape smaller public works projects.

His political power continued to grow as he gained control of federal funds for construction projects. One of every seven dollars from President Roosevelt's Works Progress Administration went to building projects in New York City. Moses also controlled the steady flow of cash from tolls paid to use the bridges and tunnels. The Triborough Bridge, connecting Manhattan with the Bronx and Queens, opened in 1936. He used the money the bridge generated in tolls to sell bonds that, in turn, allowed him to pay back the federal government for its loan that financed the project.

And that was in addition to the influence he had as chairman of the New York State Council of Parks. According to a history of the New York City parks, Moses assembled "an enormous park design and construction team . . . 1,800 designers and engineers drawing up plans for the expansion, rehabilitation and modernization of New York's parks. An additional 3,900 construction supervisors oversaw the work of an army of Parks Department relief workers—70,000 strong in 1934—all paid by the federal government."

Over the next thirty years Moses was unchallenged in deciding on the contours of the urban landscape, beginning with placement of bridges that are the central arteries to the life of New York City, including the Throgs Neck Bridge, the Henry Hudson Bridge, and the Verrazano-Narrows Bridge.

The center of Moses's universe was the island of Manhattan. The industrialists in the city's business towers and the wealthy living along the beautiful boulevards, including Park Avenue near his parents' residence on 46th Street, were the people he knew and socialized with. He won favor with the *New York Times* editorial boards for many of his projects as part of "urban renewal," a call to revive the city for its upper-income residents.

Moses made strengthening the city as a regional center for business and major cultural institutions his priority, even if he sacrificed areas of the city where the working class and poor lived. To achieve his goals he built new roads, expressways, and tunnels. He wanted well-off Manhattan residents to have easy access by car to parks, beaches, and recreation centers in Brooklyn and Long Island. As a result, a lot of people were left without money or influence, trapped in tenements or public housing, or forced to move out of the city altogether.

Caro argued there was a racial component to Moses's high-handed, cavalier attitude toward the poor. "More significant even than the number of the dispossessed were their characteristics: a disproportionate share of them were black, Puerto Rican—and poor," he wrote. "And the housing he built to replace the housing he tore down was, to an overwhelming extent, not housing for the poor, but for the rich. . . . When he built housing for poor people, he built housing bleak, sterile, cheap. . . . And he built it in locations that contributed to the ghettoization of the city, dividing up the city by color and income." To Caro, Moses served the narrow interests of Manhattan's prosperous white population.

Joan Marans Dim, describing the impact of Moses's work in *Barron's* in 2012, wrote that he "cared not a whit for the working stiffs, who didn't need or couldn't afford an automobile." And the record of budget decisions made by Moses supports the idea that his focus was so targeted on cars that he starved public transportation projects. "In 1929, when the Second Avenue Subway was proposed, Moses wasn't keen on it," Dim wrote. "In 1942 and again in 1954, when the city attempted to build that line, Moses prevented funds he controlled from being allocated to the project, preferring instead to spend them on building expressways between his bridges through densely populated neighborhoods in the Bronx and Brooklyn."

Moses's concept of the city as a place to be enjoyed by moneyed people who could speed into and out of it in their cars while living in expensive city neighborhoods with fashionable stores at a remove from working-class and poor people is the reality of most American cities in the twenty-first century. "Neither an architect, a planner, a lawyer, or even a politician (he was never elected to public office), Moses was," in Dim's eyes, "a zealot who built a city for automobiles and those who could afford automobiles."

In Moses's vision of urban life, middle-class employees were encouraged to live outside the city; highways would bring them in for their jobs. It was an idea that cemented the supremacy of the car in modern America. Driving was seen not just as a leisure activity but as a necessity for every person who worked.

"By building his highways, Moses flooded the city with cars," Caro wrote. "By systematically starving the subways and the suburban commuter railroads, he swelled that flood to city-destroying dimensions . . . he insured that that flood would continue for generations if not centuries." Moses responded to Caro's criticism by saying he faced the reality that "we live in a motorized civilization," and that he only tried to guide how the automobile changed the shape of the city for the best of all its residents.

Moses's most prominent critic was a Greenwich Village community activist named Jane Jacobs. Jacobs literally took to the streets, opposing Moses's plan for a highway, the Lower Manhattan Expressway, that would have cut her neighborhood in half and, in her opinion, degraded the look, feel, and intimacy of the community. To her, the high-minded talk about "urban renewal" and "urban renaissance" took on sinister tones as euphemisms for the destruction of the city's affordable, safe neighborhoods for middle- and working-class people. She became the public face of opposition to neighborhoods being carved up to fulfill Moses's vision of a better city. Her opposition to Moses's highway ended with her being sent to jail.

Jacobs got the attention of news reporters, politicians, and city planners. Over time her theories about sustaining urban neighborhoods gained a large following, especially among urban planners. And during a thirty-year period in the middle of the twentieth century Moses stayed clear of the briar patch of politics that included Jacobs, as well as other neighborhood activists and special interests.

While Jane Jacobs was able to stand up to Moses for middle-class city residents, there was no equally prominent voice among the poor. Moses's public housing projects—large, ugly towers in isolated parts of town—often felt like jails. They invited institutionalized squalor, poverty, and violence. Moses later responded to critics who charged him with racism and hostility to the poor by saying: "I raise my stein to the builder who can remove ghettos without removing people as I hail the chef who can make omelets without breaking eggs."

Moses's work and its legacy has survived—warts and all—because he had the power to create a model for urban planning that was replicated nationwide. Moses and his staff became consultants on hundreds of urban reclamation projects across the country and around the world. His vision is evident in how most cities in the United States function today. That includes the emphasis on highways and cars, but also in the construction of parks within the city and the development of large parks and beaches outside it, and for his special consideration of public spaces such as concert halls, museums, and ballparks. His disregard for the impact of his ideas on the poor, as well as his love affair with the automobile, was emulated widely.

"Some say Moses was wrong to build for the car," wrote Harvard economist Edward Glaeser in 2007. "Some say the city should have bet exclusively on public transportation that would better serve the poor. But those critics ignore the millions of people who fled the older cities that weren't car friendly. Every one of the 10 largest cities in the country in 1950—except for Los Angeles and, miraculously, New York—lost at least one-fifth of its population between 1950 and today. Moses's bridges and highways helped to keep some drivers living and working in New York. Those middle-class drivers helped New York to survive and grow."

Moses's greatest accomplishment, in retrospect, may have been his ability to get things done, despite city and state politics that often suffocated projects under mountains of red tape, endless meetings, votes, and institutional inertia. He opened the door for development of suburban housing to complement his vision of high-priced residences and commercial office towers in the city.

IN THE YEARS after World War II, the man who pioneered the look and feel of suburban housing to complement Moses's vision of high-priced city apartments, condominiums, and townhouses was another New Yorker, William Levitt.

In his *New York Times* obituary, Levitt, who died in 1994, was credited with exerting a "powerful influence on the shape of postwar America." That power came from setting the mold for suburban American life. By the end of the twentieth century American suburbs were home to about half of the U.S. population. Jon C. Teaford, a Purdue historian, crowned Levitt and his family as the inspiration for thousands of local developers throughout the United States who during the second half of the twentieth century built "scores of houses along the suburban fringes."

The development and explosion of the suburban "fringes"—an explosion that William Levitt helped bring about—was the result of several interlocking factors in postwar America: most important, a new system of roads pumping cars in and out of the city. The parkways—highways that prohibited trucks, innovated by Robert Moses—paved the way and supported automobile makers, oil and gas companies, tire dealers, and roadside diners. As the federal government built larger roads—expressways, highways, beltways, and interstate superhighways—the blacktop permanently transformed the landscape of the nation and accelerated the emigration of people from rural areas to the city, and from the city to the suburbs. The creation of this national network of roads for cars and trucks in the twentieth century was "the largest and most expensive public works project ever undertaken," reads one history of urban sprawl.

The government investment in the interstate highway system is rooted in the 1956 Federal Highway Act, passed in the post–World War II economic expansion. As mass production made cars affordable, the Eisenhower administration, with the support of unions, the auto industry, and the oil industry, pushed the legislation through Congress to improve on the hodgepodge of small roads built in the 1920s. Previously distant townships outside New York now fell within a reasonable travel time for people working in the city, who desperately needed reasonably priced housing that was unavailable in the city.

It was Levitt who was the first to build middle-class residential communities off the exits of the parkways and highways. The company

William Levitt's father, Abraham, established built custom-made houses for the rich on Long Island. The Levitt family got their initial experience with mass-produced housing in 1941 when they won a contract with the Navy to build houses for defense workers in Norfolk, Virginia.

Levitt and his sons devised new building techniques in Norfolk. In an era when most construction companies built three to four houses a year, the Levitts organized assembly-line housing construction that, they hoped, would build 750 housing units a year. They used previously assembled walls and roofs. Instead of hiring carpenters, plumbers, and other craftsmen to build a single house, he put together twenty-seven teams of workers. Each team specialized in one specific area of construction. The new approach was a stunning and profitable success. "By the end of the war," recounts New York magazine, "Levitt & Sons had built close to 2,500 structures for the government."

In 1944 the thirty-six-year-old Bill Levitt left the family to join the war effort as a Navy lieutenant. As part of the Navy's construction battalion, or Seabees, he was put in charge of 260 men for a construction project in Hawaii. According to legend, during his time in Hawaii the young Levitt asked his fellow soldiers about their plans after the war. The young men said they wanted the American dream—to start a family and one day buy a house. As recounted in New York magazine: "It was then, as the transports filled with home-going doughboys, that he sent the telegram to his father that was overheard and repeated until it became a Long Island legend: Look for land."

Abraham Levitt found a several-thousand-acre stretch of Long Island potato farms, and in 1947 began construction of the nation's first major suburban bedroom community. William returned home to handle zoning issues, government relations, and labor deals for the $50 million investment. Each house had a first floor with two bedrooms, a kitchen, and a living room. The unfinished attics were designed as open spaces that each family could individualize. The entire house was 750 square feet, and set on a lot that was sixty feet wide and a hundred feet long.

Those small houses in Levittown answered widespread prayers. At the time there was a nationwide housing shortage for the surge of married couples starting families after the war. The situation was acute in

New York, with its high rents and cramped apartments. With the new roads being put in place by the state and federal government, it became possible for anyone with a car to drive the twenty-five miles from Manhattan to the affordable housing in Levittown. The federal government lent a hand by offering veterans low-interest loans for home buying, while giving banks guarantees on the money loaned for construction costs.

"Levitt's houses were so cheap (but still reasonably sturdy) that bus drivers, music teachers and boilermakers could afford them," *Time* magazine wrote. The houses sold for about $8,000 each, with the Levitts making a $1,000 profit on the sale.

In 1950 Bill Levitt appeared on the cover of *Time* magazine as their "Man of the Year." Levitt claimed to have written 1,400 contracts in a single day. By 1951 Levitt had built a total of 17,447 houses. News stories crowned Levitt the "king of suburbia." After completing Levittown he went on to build suburban housing in New Jersey, Pennsylvania, Maryland, Virginia, Florida, Puerto Rico, and beyond, even building suburbs outside of Paris, France.

Levitt's greatest influence was in the example he set for other developers, who followed his trailblazing approach and built suburbs outside of every American city. As middle-class residents emptied out of the cities, the Levitt model for suburban life expanded to meet their needs. The iconic image of a suburban house, with a barbeque grill and a driveway, became a widely accepted standard of the American middle-class dream.

Demand for Levittown-style suburban life picked up speed in the 1950s and 1960s as the boiling stew of racial and ethnic mixing in the cities heated up and previous demarcations of race and class began to break down with the 1954 Supreme Court *Brown vs. the Board of Education* ruling against racially segregated schools. In the 1960s, as the national civil rights movement for racial equality led to new laws against segregation, many big cities erupted in race riots. Protests against the Vietnam War and the rise of a youth counterculture, as well as high rates of drug use and crime, also marred city life. That friction made the suburbs even more attractive to the growing American middle class, in search of quiet and safety far removed from the urban turmoil. One particular incentive behind the move to the suburbs was the deep concern among white families over racial tensions at newly integrated public schools—particularly the controversial practice of busing children from racially segregated neighborhoods to racially balanced schools.

Just as Robert Moses made no excuses for herding poor blacks into institutional, high-rise public housing separate from the city's core, William Levitt made no apology for selling suburban homes to a white-only clientele. He claimed whites would not buy the houses if they had to live with blacks. In fact, the Levittown contracts excluded all but white people—"members of the Caucasian race"—from living in the development.

As he told a *Saturday Evening Post* reporter in 1954: "If we sell one house to a Negro family, then 90 to 95 percent of our white customers will not buy into the community. That is their attitude, not ours. . . . We can solve a housing problem, or we can try to solve a racial problem, but we cannot combine the two." To prove he was acting solely in response to the profit motive, Levitt reminded critics that when his Jewish family built homes for the wealthy in the 1930s, they refused to sell to Jews. As was the case with African American families, selling homes to Jews would be bad for business. The suburbs slowly began to integrate during the 1980s and 1990s, as immigrants and a growing black middle class began settling in suburbs instead of the cities. But wealthier suburban areas remained overwhelmingly white. In addition to criticism of their racial exclusivity, the suburbs became a target of derision for lacking the dynamic energy of city life with its entrepreneurs, artists, and business community. As the writer Rich Cohen wrote in a 2013 article about Bill Levitt, his suburban idyll was "denounced for its bland sterility: little houses, little people, little dreams . . . [Levitt] became associated with the worst sins of modern culture . . . homogeneity, intolerance."

Bestselling authors, including John Updike and John Cheever, created dark stories of suburban life. Updike's best-known character, Harry "Rabbit" Angstrom, was a middle-aged suburbanite struggling to find his true identity by escaping the bland conformity of suburban life. Social critics pointed out the rise of even bigger, more expensive suburban houses farther out from the city, dubbing them "McMansions." The contempt fit with long-standing complaints about the homogeneity of suburban strip malls. There were a chorus of complaints about suburban conformity, alienation, a raft of bored teenagers, and all the "desperate housewives" and "Stepford wives" gulping Prozac and martinis.

A 1998 *Time* magazine article titled "Suburban Legend William Levitt" described Levittown as having become a "living glimpse of the ticky-tacky future." Author Richard Lacayo, who grew up in Levittown, wrote, "As Levittown matured, suburbia itself began to look like humanity at room temperature, a place where the true countryside was denatured, while the true civilization of the cities collapsed into strip malls and dinner theater."

Land use experts raised concerns about the proliferation of roads, sewers, schools, and strip malls that wiped out the previously natural landscape. But others justified the development as necessary for suburban development. The new suburbs were also criticized for promoting the waste of gasoline and other sources of energy. The efficiency of a single downtown area that offers a range of stores to a range of shoppers in nearby neighborhoods, accessible by public transit, is not possible in the suburbs. As suburbs stretch farther from nearby cities, shoppers drive their cars to come into the city or to the massive, enclosed, and sterile suburban shopping malls. The suburban areas of northeastern cities have now extended so far out that their edges border the suburbs of the next city, creating one large megalopolis.

Design critics, environmentalists, and architects share a disdain for the suburbs. At a 2005 conference, James Howard Kunstler described the rise of the suburbs as "the greatest misallocation of resources in the history of the world." Kunstler also wrote a book critical of Levitt-inspired suburbanization, called *The Geography of Nowhere*. Suburban development took middle-class taxpayers out of the cities, making it difficult for cities to fund schools or care for the disproportionate number of poor people who remained behind.

But Kunstler and other critics have had little impact on today's new geography. The combination of highways, cars, and more housing for less money continues to attract Americans. Meanwhile, crime rates, troubled schools, and racial tensions provided an incentive for people with families to leave the cities. That said, census data early in the twenty-first century show a reversal of the trend: more people are now moving into cities, and fewer are leaving for the suburbs. In keeping with Robert Moses's vision, the people moving into the city now are better educated, more affluent, and white, creating a wave of what is called "gentrification," while increasing numbers of lower-middle-class people, including minorities, are moving out to fill the aging tier of inner suburbs constructed by Levitt and his imitators half a century ago.

Today's divide between city and suburbs, of course, is a universe away from the divisions between urban and rural and between North and South that existed in the American colonies at the time of the original Founding Fathers. While there are many forces at work that have helped to create the new American social fabric, many of the sharpest economic, political, and social debates can be traced to the vision and work of Robert Moses and William Levitt. For better or for worse, it was Moses and Levitt, and those who followed and imitated them, who have created the landscape of today's cities and suburbs, which is central to the way we live.

CHAPTER 9

"KEEP THE BOYS HAPPY"

George Meany, Labor Unions,
and the Rise of the Middle Class

The Founding Fathers lived in a world of craftsmen, apprentices, indentured servants—and slaves. In fact, as I noted earlier, some of the Founding Fathers owned slaves.

Colonial America took a dim view of labor unions. Under British common law, workers who formed unions to demand better pay in the 1700s faced criminal charges of conspiracy and illegal restraint of fair trade; newspapers of the time described them as being guilty of "insolence." When a Savannah, Georgia, carpentry union went on strike in 1746, the union members were not applauded for standing up for workers' rights. Rather, they were fined under British law.

That said, the basic rhythms of everyday twenty-first-century American life are the result of labor union contracts. It was the unions that put in place the five-day workweek and the two-day weekend. Unions persuaded politicians to pass a minimum-wage law, institute unemployment benefits, and ban child labor. The eight-hour day, lunch breaks, retirement benefits, and paid vacations all came to life as terms of agreement between business and labor unions.

Unions were behind the birth of the nation's social safety net. During FDR's New Deal of the 1930s they pushed for Social Security. During

LBJ's Great Society of the 1960s they backed the creation of Medicare, as well as workplace safety standards.

The man at the center of shaping what it is like to work in America today was a stumpy, bald, cigar-chomping Irish plumber from the tough streets of the Bronx, George Meany. From the 1930s to the 1970s, Meany, with his intimidating, steely stare and blunt manner of talking, had enough economic and political muscle to go toe to toe with corporate titans and powerful presidents, from Franklin Roosevelt to Richard Nixon. As head of the American Federation of Labor–Congress of Industrial Organizations (AFL-CIO), he had the final say on labor negotiations coast to coast. His gut opinions set the tone for blue-collar voters on critical cultural fights from race relations to the Vietnam War.

In 1979, four months before Meany died, President Carter held a Labor Day picnic at the White House, where he told the crowd: "There are three things that a President always has in mind, you know—national security, always present; the Congress, always present; President George Meany, that's the third one." The nation has seen labor leaders come and go since Meany, but none of them measured up to that standard. Even before Meany died, labor unions had started their long, accelerating decline. The balanced foundation he tried to hold together between capital and labor has been coming apart. The defining concern for workers in twenty-first-century America is the growing income gap between the average worker and his or her corporate bosses. Workers are so anxious about falling behind in an era of corporate downsizing and outsourcing that they are often scared to join a union. A July 2011 study featured in the *American Sociological Review* found that with the union decline in power and membership since the late 1970s—the end of Meany's reign—the nation's private sector wage inequality has grown by 40 percent.

Today union membership continues to sink, causing a dramatic drop in the once fabled political power of organized labor. Even with public opinion polls showing more than 70 percent of Americans supporting a minimum wage increase, unions are too weak to pressure Congress to pass such legislation. And generally unions don't have public opinion on their side in trying to force companies to bargain on union contracts. The companies face little backlash from consumers for spurning unions. General Motors, once the nation's biggest employer, used to enter fierce negotiations with the United Auto Workers (UAW) to avoid a strike. Today the nation's biggest employer, Walmart, makes a defiant show of opposing unions and refuses to negotiate with them.

The troubled state of American unions was on vivid display in Chattanooga, Tennessee, in 2014. The UAW, one of the nation's biggest unions, tried to organize a Volkswagen manufacturing plant and lost, even though the company did not try to block the unionization campaign. One worker told the *New York Times* he voted against joining the union because he blamed excessively generous union contracts, rather than bad management or inferior cars, for undermining domestic carmakers. "Look at what happened to the auto manufacturers in Detroit and how they struggled. They all shared one huge factor: the U.A.W.," said Mike Jarvis, who worked for three years without a union at the Volkswagen plant. He worried that any change might cause the company to move out of the state and leave him unemployed. "If you look at how the U.A.W.'s membership has plunged, that shows they're doing a lot wrong."

Conservative politicians proudly led the fight to defeat union organizers in Chattanooga. A generation earlier they would have feared tangling with the politically powerful American labor unions. But in 2014 Republican politicians openly defied the unions. At rallies they reminded Chattanooga's workers of the region's loss of blue-collar manufacturing jobs, due in part to the rise of free trade in the 1970s, '80s, and '90s, when the owners of textile mills, toy factories, T-shirt factories, and tire makers with strong unions outsourced their production to China and other locales overseas with no unions and lower labor costs. Blue-collar unemployment in the area rose dramatically, and for many workers those jobs have never come back. The nation's 2008 recession and the subsequent spike in unemployment intensified the fear of job losses.

This surge of outsourcing has been accompanied by major geographic shifts within the United States. In the early twentieth century, the nation's biggest auto and steel manufacturers primarily built their factories in the urban North. These plants became heavily unionized around midcentury. But times have changed. Today only 45 percent of cars sold in the United States are made by American carmakers based in the North. Those manufacturers are in competition with foreign-run companies, including Volkswagen, Mercedes-Benz, BMW, Honda, and Toyota, which build about 30 percent of their American-made cars at plants in the southern United States. Just like the Volkswagen plant in Chattanooga, these factories are located in states whose conservative majorities have never taken kindly to unions. Thus their workers are often not unionized. Today American union membership is the lowest it has been in seventy years.

The nation's unionized workforce hit a peak in 1954, when nearly 35 percent of American workers belonged to a union. As recently as 1983, 20 percent of the nation's workers remained in unions. In 2012 union membership fell to 11 percent nationally. Today America has a lower percentage of union workers than many other developed countries, including Germany (27 percent), Canada (27 percent), and Finland (70 percent). Today only 6.7 percent of American workers employed by for-profit companies belong to unions. A third of government workers (35 percent) are in unions.

With unions in steady decline, Tennessee's conservative anti-labor politicians led a political-style campaign to defeat union organizing at the Volkswagen plant. Like big business, they had no fear of a backlash from the American public. Republican governor Bill Haslam forecast that the state would lose jobs again if workers approved a union. He claimed that automobile parts companies would not locate in the area if workers joined the union. The Republican majority in the legislature opposed having a union at the plant as well. A GOP state senator threatened that unless workers rejected the union, the legislature was not likely to approve tax breaks for Volkswagen as a financial incentive to add production of a sports utility vehicle to its operation and bring more jobs to the area.

One of Tennessee's Republican U.S. senators claimed that a unionized workforce diminished chances of Volkswagen creating jobs in the area by expanding operations at the plant. He also insisted it would lead to lower living standards for employees. He ignored the fact that Volkswagen's employees in Chattanooga earn $9 an hour less than comparable senior workers at U.S. car companies, and less than workers at other factories opened by foreign car manufacturers in the United States.

Conservative talk radio delighted in trumpeting the anti-union campaign, vilifying the union drive as the work of out-of-step liberals—

"they've never met a payroll"—and corrupt union bosses. The union-bashing dominated conservative radio hour after hour. A conservative lobbying group from Washington put up billboards asking employees if Chattanooga wanted to be the next Detroit, a crime-ridden city that fell into bankruptcy.

What happened at the Volkswagen factory is a window into the work world in early-twenty-first-century America. Despite the fact that union workers earn more than non-union workers ($943 in median weekly income for unionized workers versus $742 for non-unionized) and have more job security, there is a strong move away from unions. Polls show that in 2009, as unemployment rose in the months following the economic meltdown, public approval of labor unions dropped under 50 percent for the first time. A 2011 Gallup poll found Americans more likely to use negative language than positive language to describe unions. And Republicans were overwhelmingly negative, with 58 percent condemning unions, compared to only 19 percent of Democrats. Gallup found that for the first time, a clear majority of Americans, 55 percent, believe unions will be even weaker in the future.

This tide of political and public opposition to labor unions has increasingly pulled apart the world built by George Meany. For most of the twentieth century, Meany succeeded in expanding the American middle class, built on a foundation of good-paying jobs with benefits for working people, mostly white men with only a high school education. Meany's motto was to do everything possible to "keep the boys happy." Now those same workers are willing to ditch the union if it means getting a job, any job.

As manufacturing factories left the United States in search of cheap labor, the American economy continued to grow, but it left blue-collar workers behind. The growth sectors for the economy, from high technology to pharmaceuticals, rewarded highly educated workers. Meanwhile, the 2008 recession further reduced the number of workers in construction as well as state, local, and federal government. As the middle class began to shrink, so did labor unions.

In comparison, today the top 10 percent of American income earners take in 50 percent of all the money earned in the nation, with the top 0.1 percent claiming 10 percent of all income. And that does not include wealth increases from stocks, bonds, real estate, and other capital gains. The 0.1 percent now has a bigger share of U.S. income than the entire top 5 percent of the U.S. economy did in the 1980s. Between 1978 and 2011, the average worker saw a 5.7 percent increase in annual pay; top executives got an increase of 726.7 percent.

In 2014 the *New York Times* reported, "The American middle class, long the most affluent in the world, has lost that distinction. While the wealthiest Americans are outpacing many of their global peers, a *New York Times* analysis shows that across the lower- and middle-income tiers, citizens of other advanced countries have received considerably larger raises over the last three decades. . . . [M]ost American families are paying a steep price for high and rising income inequality."

In George Meany's lifetime, that newspaper story and the numbers behind it would have translated into political leverage for new contract demands. He had public support to insist on more for his union members, including improved wages and benefits for all workers, as a counter to economic inequality. Even at the end of Meany's twenty-four years as president of the AFL-CIO, he was able to win in contract negotiations, because of his political connections and his singular focus on better pay and benefits packages for his members.

As union membership falls today, conservatives and liberals caricature Meany as an Archie Bunker character, a blowhard supporter of the Vietnam War, someone who didn't appreciate the women's rights movement. He is remembered for his failure to endorse Democrat George McGovern over Richard Nixon in 1972, a decision that inspired many union members who usually voted Democratic to shift their political support to the right in the 1980s—a bloc of voters that came to be called "Reagan Democrats." In 1981 President Reagan, once a union leader for the Screen Actors Guild, would devastate unions by firing air traffic controllers for striking, making a show of the weakness of their union—and organized labor lacked the capacity to punch back.

On immigration and race, too, Meany lacked vision. He had no feel for the social justice of Cesar Chavez's effort to organize migrant farm workers. He was an opponent of the black-led March on Washington for Jobs and Freedom that featured Martin Luther King Jr.'s "I Have A Dream" speech.

But for decades Meany helped to set the framework for twenty-first-century middle-class employment in America. Polls consistently find the number one political issue for Americans is the call for good middle-class jobs, with strong benefits. In other words, people want more of those "old school," Meany-style union jobs.

GEORGE MEANY WAS a workingman virtually from his birth in 1894. He dropped out of high school at age sixteen to become a plumber's apprentice. He got his journeyman's certificate and joined the plumbers' union in 1917. During his years working as a plumber, American labor unions were frequently denounced as organizations of violent thugs with ties to communists and the Russian Revolution.

Irishmen like the young George Meany dominated the local plumbing union. Not only was Meany's father a plumber, but so were his grandfather, Lawrence Meany, and his two uncles. Meany's grandfather had arrived in New York at the end of the Irish famine of 1845–1852. Desperate to escape starvation, many Irish boarded overcrowded, poorly provisioned boats called "coffin ships," headed for America and the promise of paying jobs and a better future. The numbers of Irish immigrants grew as demand rose in the United States for cheap labor—men willing to cut trees, work in lumber mills, build canals, dig sewers, and lay rails for trains.

Meany's grandparents were barely twenty when they arrived in New York. The Irish were the poorest of the white people immigrating to the new nation. They lived in crowded streets and back alleys known as shantytowns. Poorly educated and working for low wages, they faced outright contempt from the established English and German Protestant families who occupied America's elite business and political class of the mid-1800s. Signs reading "No Irish Need Apply" became commonplace. The Irish newcomers were regularly caricatured in newspapers as drunks given to brawls, and mindless followers of the Catholic Church. The established Protestants, usually of British origin—the upper class of the era—didn't even call their Irish workers and servants by their given names, using insulting epithets such as "Paddy" and "Biddy" to their faces.

The Irish did not accept their status as second-class citizens without protest. In 1863 President Lincoln instituted a draft of men to fight in the Civil War—a move that hit the working-class Irish particularly hard, as the upper class could afford to pay a fine or buy their way out of the draft. At the same time, they developed increasing resentment toward the newly emancipated blacks, seeing them as competition for jobs. In July of that year Irishmen tore through New York in a series of protests that came to be known as the Draft Riots, in which at least 120 people were killed, including several blacks who were lynched.

But George Meany's grandfather did not let the tensions and the violence stop him from doing an honest day's work. Meany's grandfather held several jobs at once—he was able to fix any pipe or sewer line, but he was also willing to hammer nails. His ability to get regular work gave him special status within the Irish community, able to speak up for unskilled Irishmen desperate for a job. As skilled workers began to organize after the Civil War, beginning with cigar makers and shoemakers, George Meany's grandfather became a leader among Irish workers, organizing to keep up the price of their labor by limiting the number of newcomers to the plumbing trade.

Born in 1864, George Meany's father, Michael Meany, had a simple aim as he raised his sons, John and George: to keep any job he had while getting more work and higher pay. It was not complicated, and it was not political; he was looking out for himself. He eventually rose to become head of the local plumbers' union, a key part of the New York City Central Labor Council. Michael Meany dragged his son George into meetings of what was locally called "the organ-i-zation." Local 463 was one of the largest chapters of the United Association of Journeymen and Apprentices of the Plumbing and Pipe Fitting Industry. Many of the local's meetings took place at the Meanys' house on 133rd Street in the Port Morris section of the Bronx. It was a neighborhood where all the Irish families attended one big church, St. Luke's Parish, the heart of Roman Catholic Port Morris. The neighborhood had a number of small houses owned by the better-off families of plumbers, mechanics, and construction workers, such as the Meany family. But most of the neighborhood was made up of tenement apartments filled with Irish families struggling to find work.

George played catcher on his school baseball team in Port Morris, and later played on a semi-pro team. But in 1916, when George was twenty-one, his father, Michael, died of a heart attack. And a year later, Michael's older brother John enlisted in the army, leaving George—

who had started working as a plumber when he was sixteen—to support his mother and six younger brothers and sisters.

Unlike some other members of the labor movement, Meany wanted nothing to do with socialist talk about uniting workers of the world. He and the other Irish just wanted more plumbing jobs and bigger paydays. In the wake of his father's death, the men in the union local found the young George Meany more than capable of keeping a close eye on union records and business deals. By the time he was twenty-eight Meany won election as Local 463's business manager.

Historian Robert Zieger called Meany a "consummate union functionary—shrewd, articulate, honest, and always respectful of the labor movement's protocols and rituals of deference and influence." He was also prized for his knowledge of union rules that protected members' jobs.

Soon union work became a full-time job for Meany. Handling union dues sent him to job sites to check on the number of workers and their assignments and to enforce the lines of responsibility as spelled out in contracts. His most important job was to lay down the law to employers about hiring people outside the union. At local unions around the state Meany became a well-known face, and he was a strong voice in the New York City Building Trades Council. He broke new ground when he won a court injunction to stop builders from locking out workers. Up to that point, the unions had viewed the courts as a tool of the business owners. His innovative strategy made a big impression with the older leaders. Meany showed up at fundraisers, dinners, and parades, and helped the council to develop ties to politicians in city hall and in Albany, the capital of New York State.

In 1934, at the age of forty, Meany was elected president of the New York State Federation of Labor, the biggest state federation within the AFL, according to Zieger. He was the leader of 800,000 union members in New York and a bold, brash player in the increasingly powerful national American Federation of Labor (AFL).

As head of the New York labor federation, Meany created a new public image for union leaders. Older union organizers tended to keep their business private and talked only to reporters from papers affiliated with the union. Meany broke with that tradition. He held press conferences. He endorsed politicians. He made campaign donations to state politicians in place of bribes. In Albany, he became well known for his no-nonsense "I'm a workingman" style of testimony before the state legislature. His political influence with the governor, Democrat Herbert Lehman, and the Democratic majority in the legislature resulted in Meany winning passage of seventy-two bills, including the nation's first unemployment insurance law. He pushed workmen's compensation laws from his perch in New York, helping them become a reality across the nation. Meany also supported New York's Jewish Labor Committee in its efforts to help trade union members get out of Nazi Germany, building Meany's political influence and contacts across the union movement. He gave his political backing to another FDR supporter, Fiorello La Guardia, the Republican mayor of New York. With unemployment still high after the Great Depression, he dared to threaten a strike for high wages for skilled workers in New Deal jobs—and he won. He helped to start the American Labor Party in 1936, to bring the left wing of the labor movement into FDR's reelection campaign.

His success in Albany was reported in New York's newspapers, which led to Meany developing a national reputation as a politically deft labor leader. That plus his connections to the president led to a job with the union's national office in Washington, where he continued to rise, winning the job of national secretary-treasurer in 1939, becoming the second-highest official in the union behind AFL president William Green. The aging Green was a steady but dull leader. Meany soon became the energetic face of the AFL when he won a seat on President Roosevelt's National War Labor Board, setting wages for workers in shipping, railroads, auto manufacturing, and airlines. He threatened to quit at one point over the issue of workers being allowed wage hikes during the war, and again he won. The board's goal was to keep labor peace in domestic industries and prevent any disruption of supplies to the military.

Meany's reputation was enhanced by the fact that he was a plumber's kid who made good. In the tradition of his grandfather and his father, his focus was on getting more work and better pay for his union members, and nothing more. He stayed loyal to the low-profile Green, and he never crossed the line into controversial arguments over social justice or attacked the rich. Meany refused to use threats or violence to get his way, an approach that set him apart from previous public images of violent, communist-infiltrated unions. In newspaper stories he was the all-American, "good guy" union boss, the alternative to the thuggish image of most first-generation union bosses in the age of industrialization. And he had continued to produce bigger paychecks for union members.

In order to appreciate the impact George Meany had on organized labor, it is crucial first to understand the history of labor in the United States, as well as the exciting decades during which Meany climbed to the top of the AFL. Fear of unions in the United States began in the first half of the 1800s, as large numbers of American workers left farms to find work in booming cities along the Atlantic seaboard. The courts saw labor organizations as a threat to public safety, bent on extorting higher pay from legitimate businessmen. In 1806, for example, a Philadelphia court ruled that an organization of shoemakers' attempt to raise their wages was conspiratorial and, in the jury's own words, "unnatural." According to historian Lance Compa, "the idea of collective bargaining as a criminal conspiracy persisted for much of the nineteenth century." In 1842 in Massachusetts, the state courts ruled that workers had the right to form unions as long as they did not engage in threats or violence against employers. The National Trades' Union was formed in five East Coast cities in 1834 but soon failed. In 1866 the National Labor Union (NLU) was created as a trade group of construction workers and skilled craftsmen, including stonecutters. The NLU stayed out of trouble with the courts and big business by disavowing strikes. In exchange they got the government and business leaders to agree to keep out Chinese laborers.

In 1866 the NLU passed a resolution calling for an eight-hour workday. In 1867 an organization of workers took shape, representing fifty thousand shoemakers in the Northeast—the Order of Knights of St. Crispin. To avoid trouble with the courts, the Knights took care not to call themselves a union; their name suggested a fraternity or religious organization. They made it clear their goal was to slow the entry of new workers into the shoemaking business in order to protect the current workforce by keeping demand high for experienced shoemakers. And in 1868 Congress passed a law limiting the workday to eight hours for all federal employees. But as American industry grew in the late 1800s, organized, peaceful strikes by construction workers, coal miners, and railroad workers demanding higher wages became increasingly accepted by the federal courts.

The first nationwide union came to life in the 1870s. Called the Knights of Labor, it represented an innovative approach to unions because it welcomed a range of workers, from farmers and cigar makers to railroad workers and coal miners. Railroad travel helped with organizing. The railroad workers became great examples of the benefits of union organizing, because they had wage scales and insurance benefits. In 1882 the Knights, at the insistence of a group of carpenters, helped celebrate the first Labor Day, which became an official federal holiday in 1894.

But newspapers regularly stoked fears of unions as fronts for European socialists. Every instance of violence by workers was held up in papers controlled by big business as evidence that unions remained corrupt and thuggish. This tarnished image remained fixed in the American mind when Meany took the reins fifty years later.

The specific charge of socialist influences took root in 1894 with a strike led by the American Railway Union and its president, Eugene V. Debs, against the Pullman Company, a major manufacturer of railroad cars. During the strike, 125,000 members of the American Railway Union in twenty-seven states refused to show up for their jobs. In Chicago the railroad system was completely shut down, which effectively ended all passenger and freight transportation in the western United States. This potential crisis prompted President Grover Cleveland to send federal troops to Chicago, where the strike was centered, to end the action. The strikers rioted when the federal troops arrived. In the government's attempt to end the strike, thirty railroad workers died and another fifty-seven were seriously hurt. President Cleveland justified his actions by arguing that a railroad strike interfered with mail delivery. The federal government filed an injunction to halt the railroad strike on the Sherman Anti-Trust Act and the Commerce Clause of the Constitution.

Eugene Debs's political fight with a government that ruled against unions led him to run for president as a socialist in 1900. He received close to 100,000 votes, convincing him to run in consecutive presidential elections at the top of the socialist ticket. In 1912 he received close to a million votes, losing to Woodrow Wilson. Debs later was sent to jail under the Espionage Act of 1917 for opposing World War I. In the speech that got him jailed, Debs excoriated industry owners for being "wrapped up in the American flag" and "shout[ing] their claim from the housetops that they are the only patriots." He called for workers to "be free men instead of industrial slaves."

Another prominent union leader, William "Big Bill" Haywood, openly defended the use of sabotage and violence against mine owners in the western states, and was elected to the executive committee of the Socialist Party. He fled to Russia after being convicted for encouraging strikes that undermined the war effort.

The radical left-wing flavor brought to the labor movement by Debs and Haywood hurt the Knights of Labor. Labor was dealt a significant blow during the 1886 Haymarket Riot—a Chicago rally incited by the murder of two McCormick Harvesting Machine Company workers during a strike. During a rally the following day, a bomb was thrown. Seven police officers and four civilians were killed. Eight anarchists were convicted of starting the rally: four of them received the death penalty. The labor movement—and the Knights of Labor in particular—came to be associated with violence and anarchy in the public eye.

Vilified in the press, the Knights of Labor dissolved, and many of its members joined a new group, the Federation of Organized Trades and Labor Unions, led by the leader of the cigar makers union, Samuel Gompers, a Jewish immigrant from London. By 1886 Gompers's group had grown into the American Federation of Labor. Gompers, who led the AFL until 1924, is widely acknowledged as the father of modern American labor. He grew the AFL's membership into the millions and set a model for George Meany. He presented his union as an all-American, patriotic group, free of socialist ideology; the union sought only the best for hardworking Americans. (The AFL often excluded blacks, Chinese, and women before such bias was an issue.)

It was Gompers's job to defend labor against those who believed that union organizing was an illegal conspiracy against business. In 1908 the U.S. Supreme Court ruled that a boycott of hats made in a non-union factory was illegal restraint of trade. The union's image improved, however, in the wake of a tragedy in New York. A massive fire in 1911 at a lower Manhattan factory, home of the Triangle Shirtwaist Company, killed almost 150 workers; the workers could not escape because their bosses kept the doors and windows locked to prevent theft. The deaths stirred national support for union protections for workers. National protests rose again during a 1914 strike by Colorado miners working for John D. Rockefeller, in which state militiamen and company guards set fire to tents occupied by strikers, killing the workers, women, and children. When President Wilson put Gompers on the Council of National Defense during World War I to solidify labor support for the war, Gompers used his position to gain favor with Congress and the president.

Two years earlier, Congress acted to protect workers by passing the Clayton Act, establishing that "the labor of a human being is not a commodity." Gompers called it the "Magna Carta" of American labor rights because the Clayton Act legalized strikes and boycotts. Previously, big industry had been able to defeat the unions by getting the courts to rule that strikes violated anti-trust law. With the new laws in place, the AFL's membership grew to 2.5 million by 1917, even as the National Association of Manufacturers pushed back by publicly arguing that the union movement was tied to European communists and "un-American" activities.

The public image of unions took another battering as the result of a strike by the United Mine Workers in 1919 in which the federal government charged the union with undermining the military effort in World War I. The owners of the mines charged that the union was under the control of communists, and the strike collapsed. That same year, an organization of Boston policemen called the Boston Social Club demanded higher pay and asked the AFL to recognize them as an affiliate. When over a thousand Massachusetts policemen did not go to work, Massachusetts governor and future president Calvin Coolidge ruled the police had no right to strike, and called in the state militia. Coolidge, a lawyer who had worked for banks before he was elected governor, became a star in the national Republican Party for defying AFL president Samuel Gompers when he declared: "There is no right to strike against the public safety by anybody, anywhere, anytime."

Through the 1920s, as Meany was rising as a union leader in New

York City, union activism fell into further disrepute. Business groups called them a threat to national unity and a platform for leftist European radical thinking. One sign of the dominance of big business in national affairs was that Coolidge, a favorite of banking and business interests, was made the GOP's vice presidential nominee on the ticket headed by Warren G. Harding. When President Harding died of a heart attack in 1923, Coolidge became president. Gompers died the following year and was replaced by William Green, who held to a philosophy of unions promoting themselves as partners to big industry. His lack of militancy cleared the way for the new, pro-business president to capture the historical moment of big money's influence on national affairs, when Coolidge famously said: "The chief business of the American people is business." He made Andrew Mellon, a multimillionaire, his treasury secretary and won Congress's support for strong cuts in taxes on the theory that more money in the hands of successful business leaders was the best path to higher investment, industrial expansion, and more jobs for workers. In 1928, Coolidge's secretary of commerce, Herbert Hoover, who became a multimillionaire in the mining business, ran for the White House and won a landslide victory for the Republicans and big business. Hoover was renowned for proclaiming: "If a man has not made a million dollars by the time he is forty, he is not worth much."

Meany, then in his early thirties, was nowhere close to being a millionaire. He was, however, getting a priceless education in how to successfully work with politicians in the city and state. New York was the center of the nation's union activism, and unions there had more political influence among politicians than anywhere else in the nation.

In Hoover's first year as president, he emphasized his business background by launching an "Efficiency Movement" to cut the size of government and make the government more accommodating of public-private ventures in support of big business. But when the stock market crashed later that year, ushering in the Great Depression, unemployment skyrocketed. Hoover responded by raising taxes on the rich. He also started a series of government-supported public works projects, such as construction of the Boulder (later Hoover) Dam, to try to get Americans back to work. Hoover deported Mexican citizens from the United States and pressured business leaders to keep up their employees' wages and not take advantage of high unemployment as an excuse to pay American workers low wages.

As the Depression gripped the nation, Meany, then with the New York Building Trades Council, took the lead in gathering support among New York's unions to push for congressional approval of the 1931 Davis-Bacon Act. The act called for builders to pay plumbers and other construction workers "local prevailing rates" for wages on federal worksites. That included any local and state government construction job that had federal subsidies. It was a critical win in efforts to keep out cheaper workers willing to move in temporarily to win construction jobs. Meany was still taking care of his "boys" in the union.

The next year, with the Great Depression choking jobs and unions out of the economy, President Hoover signed the Norris–La Guardia Act, which made it illegal for employers to force workers to sign contracts that banned unions from their job sites.

Despite Hoover's efforts, unemployment hit 25 percent by 1932 and workers continued to flee unions, unable to pay union dues and hungry for any job, unionized or not. The newly elected president, Democrat Franklin Delano Roosevelt, followed up by passing the National Industrial Recovery Act in 1933, giving workers the right to collective bargaining as members of labor unions. When the Supreme Court ruled the act to be unconstitutional, the Democrats in Congress responded with a 1935 bill, the National Labor Relations Act. The bill, nicknamed the Wagner Act for New York's Senator Robert F. Wagner, gave labor unions protection from court injunctions by establishing their right to negotiate for workers. In 1938 the Congress gave labor another victory with passage of the Fair Labor Standards Act, which set minimum wage standards for the first time and established a forty-hour, five-day workweek. Union membership rebounded, and strikes in New York and nationally took place in record numbers.

The positive image of unions helping struggling workers out of the Great Depression brought George Meany national attention as a defender of the union cause. Big business, however, looked for ways to push back. In 1947 the National Association of Manufacturers and other big business lobbyists got Congress to pass the Taft-Hartley Act, intended to restrain the growth of unions. The act limited unions from supporting each other with industry-wide strikes and allowed the federal government to halt any strike considered a threat to national safety. The law also opened the door to "right-to work" legislation that gave employers the right to hire people who didn't belong to unions. The legislatures of Southern states, in particular, passed right-to-work laws, and Meany sometimes found himself on the losing side.

Meany kept his political friends in Washington happy by frequently calling on American workers to be patriots and support the president. He proudly rallied behind the war effort and the fight against the Nazi and Japanese regimes during World War II. As the war ended, he made news again as the leader of the AFL's boycott against the World Federation of Trade Unions because it welcomed communist workers from the Soviet Union.

Inside the labor movement, Meany's refusal to expand his vision beyond protecting skilled workers, including plumbers, electricians, and tailors, led to a split. More political and left-wing labor organizers wanted to organize all workers in major industries, from farm workers to people in the steel industry, from automobile workers to textile mill workers, into one union, regardless of their job. The different approaches resulted in the creation of two American houses of union activity. One was the long-established AFL, still holding under Meany to its tradition of representing skilled workers. The second group, called the Congress of Industrial Organizations (CIO), came together under John L. Lewis in 1935 after passage of the Wagner Act gave unions new legal protection against conspiracy charges. Unlike the AFL, the CIO's approach was to organize employees across an entire industry, regardless of what kind of job they had, skilled or unskilled.

In 1947 Meany battled Lewis over federal laws requiring union leaders to sign a pledge that they had no ties to communists. Lewis refused and accused other labor leaders who did sign of being willing to "grovel on their bellies." At the AFL's convention, Meany responded that refusing to sign meant a loss of focus on advancing workers' rights. He pointed a finger at Lewis for allowing men with ties to communist groups to work in his union, at the sacrifice of the larger union movement's true goal of providing better jobs and pay for workers. Meany's speech was a sensation among the delegates, who did not expect anyone to go head-to-head with Lewis, a famed orator, much less eclipse his message.

In 1952, when AFL president William Green died, Meany officially succeeded him, though he had been AFL leader in all but name for several years already. A few weeks earlier the head of the CIO, Phillip Murray, died, and his successor, Walter Reuther, head of the United Auto Workers, who had worked with Meany to minimize strikes during the war, began to work on bringing the two unions together. In 1955 they merged the two houses of labor into one group, the AFL-CIO. Meany, as the head of the AFL, which had more members, became head of the new group. Their combined political stature and legitimacy led to a wave of new organizing among workers who previously had never joined unions, including government employees. Meany's picture appeared on the cover of *Time* magazine. By 1960 he had succeeded in bringing a third of American workers into the union movement, a record level of union membership in the United States. Meany's high political standing was evident when he traveled overseas with a fellow Irish American, President John F. Kennedy. Meany stood behind the president at the Berlin Wall in 1963 as Kennedy gave his famous call for a united Germany with the words "Ich bin ein Berliner."

"The merger of the AFL and CIO, reuniting the house of labor, was the accomplishment I take the most pride in," Meany later said. But Meany and Walter Reuther had a major falling-out that led the UAW to abandon the merged AFL-CIO. Reuther's strong sense of social mission was at odds with Meany's singular focus on more jobs and money for workers. Reuther famously said the UAW was not limited to concern about one more "nickel in the pay envelope."

Reuther, an admirer of Eugene V. Debs and the socialists in the union movement, was critical of Meany's strong anti-communist rhetoric and lack of attention to bringing more people into the union movement by "organizing the unorganized." He wanted to reach out to new groups, like Cesar Chavez's United Farm Workers, and he strongly backed the black civil rights movement. Meany was slow to embrace those efforts at social justice, including the movements for women's rights and gay rights, as union business. The Vietnam War deepened the split, as Meany became bellicose in his support of the flawed U.S. policy. Meany saw the policy as a fight against communism, while Reuther viewed the AFL-CIO's defense of President Johnson's war policy as "intemperate, hysterical and jingoistic." By 1968 Reuther had resigned his post at the AFL-CIO, and his union, the UAW, stopped paying dues. Meany suspended the UAW, and for fourteen years the UAW operated as an independent union, before returning to the AFL-CIO. But Reuther died in a plane crash in 1970, leaving Meany unchallenged as the guiding force of organized labor in America.

After Reuther's death, no labor leader challenged Meany, pushed him to speak out for the poor, or faulted his lack of attention to organizing more workers. When Meany retired in 1979, only a quarter of non–farm workers had a union card. Twenty-four years earlier, a third of the nation's non–farm workers had belonged to a union.

"Meany was so hostile to the new liberalism emerging in the 1960s that he withheld AFL-CIO backing from the 1972 presidential bid of Democrat George McGovern, a Vietnam dove," wrote labor historian Nelson Lichtenstein in his book *State of the Union: A Century of American Labor.* "Meany and others in the AFL-CIO high command excoriated anti-war demonstrators, ignored the rise of a new feminist sensibility, and ridiculed gay demands for dignity and civil rights." To Lichtenstein the union movement found itself limited by the culturally conservative views of older leaders like Meany with their exclusive focus on the white working-class men who had been the backbone of the union movement earlier in the century.

The old Irish American plumber from the Bronx saw the black civil rights movement, the people marching in the streets to protest the Vietnam War, and the political unrest among college students as far from the "pork chop" focus of unions on better jobs and better pay for people who go to work every day to pay the bills. "Workers are not blind to the imperfections and injustices of the system," he was quoted as saying in the *Christian Science Monitor,* "but they are deaf to the cries of those who would wreck the best system of government yet devised by man in the vain hope that something better might replace it."

As a result of Meany's hard resistance to cultural and political change in the country, unions lost touch with the energy of the times and never developed the imagination required to see a role in a new, more white-collar economy. They missed the opportunity to change and grow, to pick up new members as more women came into the workforce, as more blacks got an education and aspired to better jobs in the civil rights era, as a new wave of nonwhite immigrants, especially Latinos, came into the country. As the economy shifted away from jobs in industry and manufacturing to more jobs in the service industry and high technology, the unions stumbled in their struggle to organize workers in these sectors. And the legacy of the golden days, collective bargaining for workers and generous pension packages, was derided for making companies less competitive in a global economy. Big pension obligations for retired public school teachers as well as police and other public employees are blamed for draining state and local governments of money they need to operate right now.

Today the weakness of unions in the United States is as much a part of Meany's legacy as the accomplishments of unions over the years. Even among liberals and Democrats, traditional support for the union label has frayed. Meany recognized that his "boys," the white men who started the union movement, had become less willing to fight for the union over the years. "We no longer march on the streets, we no longer have the sitdown strikes, and labor to some extent has become middle class," his *New York Times* obituary quoted him as having said. "In other words, when you have no property, you don't have anything, you have nothing to lose by these radical actions. But when you become a person who has a home and has property, to some extent you become conservative. And I would say to that extent, labor has become conservative."

Financial donations by unions to Democrats remain the heart of labor's political power. But labor donations have lost impact as they have been dwarfed in number and size by the flood of money from political action committees operated by big business and funded with money from individual magnates. The nation's courts have opened the door to almost limitless political contributions from the rich on the grounds that it is part of their right to free political speech.

For all of Meany's and the Labor Movement's accomplishments in giving workers a better, safer working environment, shorter hours, weekends off, better benefits, more pay, and greater access to the middle class, they also created the framework for business dominance of the American economy in the twenty-first century. Meany, like Gompers at the start of the last century, chose to avoid an aggressive union push into creating a separate political party of union activists. They won impressive contracts that created the world-famous mid-twentieth-century model of social mobility and stability known as the American middle class. But Meany and the AFL did not pursue union ownership of major factories, and they did not focus on increasing union membership. It was Meany and the AFL who established a framework for an unapologetic brand of low-tax, low-regulation business that today has rejected unions, to the point that less than 10 percent of private sector workers now belong to a union. The foundation of American capitalism still includes unions, of course, but the current economy celebrates and rewards venture capitalists and corporate leaders as our current economic winners.

CHAPTER 10

ONE NATION UNDER GOD

Billy Graham and the
Power of the Christian Right

Forty percent of Republicans tell pollsters they go to church weekly. On the other hand, 53 percent of Democrats tell Gallup and other pollsters they rarely or never go to church.

The presence of church-going GOP voters as the heart of today's Republican Party emerged with the rise of the Christian right's identity as a pillar of conservative politics. GOP opposition to abortion, contraception, gay marriage, and pornography are bright lines of division in today's polarized politics. Every one of those issues comes from the Christian conservative political agenda.

Those divisive issues have taken flight in American politics over the last fifty years as religious conservatives have demanded more influence over American culture, judges, and politicians. Their goal is to defend church doctrine and cultural traditions in the face of the rising secular liberal politics of single women, racial minorities, and gays. The leaders behind this phenomenon remain household names—Billy Graham, Jerry Falwell, Pat Robertson, and James Dobson.

To me, Billy Graham stands above the others. Graham blazed a new path in politics by winning friends among the rich and influential and getting politicians to recognize the power of appealing to the religious community for their vote. He also awakened evangelicals to the enormous clout they had in picking which politicians to bless with their friendship and votes. President George H. W. Bush crowned him with the title "America's Pastor." Graham took the mix of politics and religion mainstream, lighting the way for other religious leaders to follow.

Graham's life was changed when he was a teenager by a controversial preacher named Mordecai Ham. Born in 1918, Graham grew up on a quiet, out-of-the-way North Carolina dairy farm on the rural outskirts of what was then a very small city, Charlotte. Ham held a revival there after years of struggling through the Great Depression as a traveling salesman. His shouting, stomping, preaching, and tears at the controversial revival jolted, scared, and unsettled the sixteen-year-old Graham, making him suddenly aware of the possibility of a larger life beyond the farm, and beyond the hardscrabble isolation of the South.

But Graham wanted something grander and more meaningful than the schlock of a traveling tent show. He wanted to expose people to Christianity's inspiring power beyond mere Sunday church services. He saw himself leading people to a larger purpose. He wanted to stir people in small towns and rural communities like his own North Carolina town. Graham saw his future as a faith leader able to call on Christians to hold the cross high every day, not just in church on Sunday—to shape the world.

"I was spellbound," Graham wrote in his autobiography, *Just as I Am,* describing the experience of being a teenager inside Ham's tent revival. The book's title came from the signature phrase Graham used to invite people at his revivals to come forward and commit to a Christian life. "In some indefinable way, he was getting through to me. I was hearing another voice . . . the voice of the Holy Spirit," Graham wrote about watching Ham. Graham described walking to the front of one of Ham's tent revivals to commit himself to Christ as a moment prompted less by the Holy Spirit than by his own decision to lead a more purposeful life. "No bells went off inside me," he recalled. "No signs flashed . . . No physical palpitations made me tremble. I wondered . . . if I was a hypocrite, not to be weeping or something. I simply felt at peace. Quiet, not delirious. Happy and peaceful."

Graham, raised by his mother as a Presbyterian, decided after Ham's revival to become a preacher and a Southern Baptist. He attended fundamentalist Baptist and evangelical colleges. By 1947 he began preaching at his own tent revivals. His almost instant success in attracting crowds and press coverage led him to quickly become sought after as a spiritual guide to celebrities, the powerful, and then a line of U.S. presidents.

Religious leaders have emerged in every era of American history. What sets Graham and the modern religious right wing apart is their lasting influence. After World War II the religious right found a new place as leaders in the nation's fight against what they saw as godless communists. They resisted challenges to the status quo of race relations from black civil rights activists and their liberal Jewish supporters; they took pride in defying women's rights groups promoting abortion rights, birth control, and sexual liberation. They helped create the "Moral Majority," the unprecedented conservative revolution that anointed President Reagan in 1980 and ended the postwar "Liberal Consensus." This movement was made up of white evangelical southern Christians who wanted to see their values reflected in the nation's government, its laws, and its culture. The Christian Right has set the terms for the last forty years of debates over contraception, abortion, and school curricula. It has led the fight against violent and sexually explicit content in movies and video games. On a more local level, the new political clout held by the evangelicals motivated President Reagan to proclaim 1983 the "Year of the Bible."

Writing in *USA Today*, Susan Page reported that prior to the 1972 election, churchgoers split their vote between Democrats and Republicans. They did not vote differently from people who stayed away from church. If anything, they were less likely to go to the polls. "But after the tumultuous 1960s, President Nixon appealed to the traditionalist views of the nation's 'silent majority,'" Page wrote. "A significant gap, 10 percentage points, opened in the 1972 election."

Much of the gap resulted from President Nixon's success in using a religion-based appeal to attract white southerners. Since the Civil War and their defeat at the hands of the Union Army and a Republican president, white southerners had voted for Democrats. In the wake of the Great Depression, FDR's New Deal programs kept Democrats in control of the South.

Republican Richard Nixon changed that pattern by forming an

alliance with Graham and aiming a direct appeal at Graham's older white church-going voters concentrated in the South and Midwest. Those voters—many of whom disapproved of the 1964 Civil Rights Act, ending legal racial segregation—wanted to keep the world they knew. They did not want the rapid societal change of the 1950s and 1960s that included the Supreme Court–ordered school integration, the civil rights movement, and the rising political power of black people, as well as the social unrest brought on by protests against the Vietnam War, recreational drug use, and a women's movement that championed sexual liberation and the increasing use of birth control pills.

Church leaders and President Nixon found a powerful point of agreement in their opposition to abortion, which became a key wedge issue for Nixon to win over older white Democrats concerned about the "culture war" that they saw eroding family values, respect for the church, and community traditions.

By the 2000 election almost thirty years later, 58 percent of the Americans who regularly attended religious services voted for President Bush, while Gore received only 40 percent. A Gallup poll in 2004 found 87 percent of people who went to church once a week identified themselves as "conservative" or "moderate," while 74 percent of people who never went to church identified themselves as "moderate" or "liberal."

"White conservative evangelical churches have become across the South the organizational engine for the Republican party the way labor unions became the organizational engine for the Democratic Party in the industrial heartland in the 1930s," political scientist Mark Silk told *USA Today.*

The importance of religion in capturing votes became glaring in the 2012 presidential election. Seventy-nine percent of white evangelical Protestants voted for Republican Mitt Romney's losing presidential campaign. Seventy percent of people without any religious affiliation voted for President Barack Obama. The heavy Republican tilt among evangelical Christians has led to a certain amount of blowback from critics, who argue the evangelicals have put politics ahead of the faith message. Large percentages of young people with no ties to churches tell pollsters they now label all Christians as opponents of gay rights and "too political." In the poll, Christians are seen by them as too often at "war" with America's changing demographics, culture, and politics. According to sociologist James Davison Hunter in his book *To Change the World,* American church leaders have dug trenches to resist change through alliance with conservative Republican politics. On the other hand, social scientists Robert Putnam and David Campbell have found a rise in the number of people with no church affiliation: "There's been a kind of a quiet backlash among young people against this politicization of religion," Putnam, author of *American Grace: How Religion Divides and Unites Us,* told NPR. "And as a result, young liberal-minded people have often ended up avoiding religion because they associate it with conservative Republicanism."

In fact, many of America's proudest moments of progressive social change are rooted in organized religion. For example, Jane Addams's Settlement House Movement and Martin Luther King's March on Washington were both based on religious principles and identified with the left wing of American politics. Yet the success of the evangelicals, with their conservative political agenda, has erased memories in contemporary culture of the religious elements of these progressive movements. This is in addition to the mainstream cultural backlash in which many Americans view the evangelicals' approach to gay rights, abortion, and racial integration as out of touch with contemporary life.

That has led to more Americans staying away from organized religion. In 2012, the Pew Research Center reported: "The number of Americans who do not identify with any religion continues to grow at a rapid pace. One-fifth of the U.S. public—and a third of adults under 30—are religiously unaffiliated today, the highest percentages ever in Pew Research Center polling." Most of those "unaffiliated" (68 percent) told Pew they still believe in God, and 37 percent said they are "spiritual" but not "religious." "Overwhelmingly, they think that religious organizations are too concerned with money and power, too focused on rules and too involved in politics," Pew reported.

The *National Journal* in 2014 quoted Trevin Wax, thirty-three, an employee of the Southern Baptist Convention, as saying young people now see church-based political activism as "problematic when it falls prey to partisanship and is co-opted by the various agendas of different political parties. Partisanship robs the church of its prophetic voice."

Despite this backlash against mixing religion with politics,

Americans remain more likely to practice religion than people in other Western industrialized nations. The Pew Research Center consistently finds that close to 60 percent of Americans report "religion is very important in their lives," compared to 17 percent of British residents, 13 percent of French people, 21 percent of Germans, and 22 percent of the Spanish. And church attendance in the United States is higher; about 40 percent of Americans report that they go to church regularly. Actual diaries of weekend activities show a more modest 26 percent of Americans going to church. Even so, that is still far higher than the 10 percent in Britain and 15 percent in France.

"Why do Americans . . . feel the need to overreport their religious attendance?" wrote Shankar Vedantam, a statistician with *Slate,* the online magazine. Vedantam suggests that answering questions about their religion for Americans is "like asking them whether they are good people, or asking whether they are patriots." Reviewing a statistical portrait of Americans and public expressions of faith, Vedantam offers a historical view of politics and religion in America: "You could say that religiosity for Americans is tied to their identity in a way it is not for the Germans, the French, and the British. . . . Historians will point to the European roots of North American colonization. Many European settlers came to the New World in search of religious freedom."

Putnam and Campbell argue that religion in the new century is behind much of the self-sorting, groupthink behavior that undergirds the partisanship in current American politics. "People often glean political information from interaction with friends, family, and neighbors," they write in *American Grace.* "People whose social networks are rooted in a religious congregation or community are more likely to receive religiously infused signals about many areas of interest, politics included." Putnam and Campbell conclude that "religious socializing 'explains' roughly half of the connection between religiosity and partisanship" and that "among those who have a dense religious social network, religiosity is tightly connected to Republican affiliation."

The rise of the Tea Party wing of the GOP in 2010, with its opposition to a national healthcare plan and call for small government with balanced budgets, now gets far more media attention than activities of the religious right. But the Tea Party operates at the fringes of the GOP. The mainline Republican Party is still under control of an array of preachers, strategists, and business leaders. They use conservative white Christian churches to build today's grassroots conservative movement. But the relationship to Tea Party politics remains uncertain.

When Indiana governor Mitch Daniels considered a run for president in 2012 and suggested the GOP leave religious and social issues to the side while focusing on the Tea Party priorities of smaller government and balanced budgets, his campaign immediately fell flat. Meanwhile, touchstone issues for evangelicals, such as public prayer, Christmas symbols in public places, and teaching creationism as an alternative to scientifically based understandings of human evolution, continue to stir the passions of the Republican base.

The most powerful and enduring issue for the Republican base precedes Tea Party priorities: opposition to abortion. It is the center of gravity for the religious right. Abortion emerged as a flashpoint in the debates over the national healthcare plan, known widely as "Obamacare." Anti-abortion activists have used Tea Party victories to push for laws to narrow the options for women seeking abortion.

Rolling Stone magazine reported that Michigan's Republican majority state legislature voted without debate to "ban abortion coverage, even in cases of rape or incest, from virtually every health-insurance policy issued in the state." *Rolling Stone* went on to identify twenty-four states with some form of ban on abortion coverage in insurance policies sold through health insurance exchanges. "Since 2010, when the Tea Party–fueled GOP seized control of 11 state legislatures—bringing the total number of Republican-controlled states to 26—conservative lawmakers in 30 states have passed 205 anti-abortion restrictions, more than in the previous decade," according to the magazine.

An essential part of the social conservative argument at the start of the twenty-first century is to link Christianity to the Founding Fathers' vision of America. Politicians appealing to the church community frequently defend their policy proposals as being in line with the Christian tradition of the original Founders. Their critics—people seeking to separate government policy from church doctrine—contend the Founding Fathers consciously avoided any intermingling of religion and government policy. God, Jesus, and other deities, they argue, do not appear in the Constitution or the Bill of Rights.

The impassioned desire to claim the support of the original Founding

Fathers obscures the reality of the Founding Fathers' work, which carefully tailored constitutional government to provide protections for religious beliefs. They made this a principle of American democracy, while opposing the establishment of any national religion.

"The Founders struggled to find a balance between ensuring religious freedom and honoring the important place of religion in American society," wrote Matthew Harris and Thomas Kidd in the introduction to their book *The Founding Fathers and the Debate over Religion in Revolutionary America: A History in Documents*. Harris and Kidd describe a Colonial America filled with churches. While the best-known of the Founders "were not overtly traditional Christians," they wrote, "they lived in a heavily Protestant Christian society and took many Christian rituals and assumptions for granted."

Most historians argue that the Founding Fathers' beliefs were shaped by Deism. Franklin, Jefferson, Madison, Washington, and Adams did not believe in Jesus as the Son of God, even though they went to church and celebrated Christian holidays. Deists believe God created the world and gave human beings reason, memory, the capacity for teamwork, and mercy. Modern Deists define God as a "universal creative force," not given to human behavior such as loving some and punishing others. The Deists refute the idea that God recognizes any "individuals and organized religions" through "special divine revelation." None of them publicly criticized Christianity, but in their writings and deliberations over the founding principles for governing the new nation, they "emphasized freedom of conscience, liberty of thought, and religious equality, and they favored morality over dogma, good deeds over pious words, and reason over revelation as the surest way to understand the world."

In the last half century, however, American politicians, including presidents, have made regular references to the Christian roots of the nation. President Reagan was explicit in saying, "America was founded by people who believed that God was their rock of safety." If so, God and Christian principles are not in evidence as guiding forces in the Declaration of Independence, Constitution, or Bill of Rights.

James Madison, one of the principal authors of the Constitution, wrote in an April 1774 letter, before independence, about "religious bondage," which "shackles and debilitates the mind and unfits it for every noble enterprise." Ethan Allen, a Founding Father who battled the British, wrote bluntly, "I am no Christian." And President John Adams signed a treaty that read: "The government of the United States is not, in any sense, founded on the Christian religion." That sentiment fit with the writing of journalist and Founding Father Thomas Paine. In *Age of Reason* he asserted that he had no faith in the "creed professed by the Jewish church, by the Roman church, by the Greek church, by the Turkish church, by the Protestant church, nor by any church that I know of . . . Each of those churches accuse the other of unbelief; and for my own part, I disbelieve them all." Paine added that all "national institutions of churches . . . appear to me no other than human inventions, set up to terrify and enslave mankind, and monopolize power and profit."

Part of the King of England's charter for the colony of Virginia in 1624 was that the Anglican Church, Britain's official church, be named the colony's official church. That included taxing colonists to financially support the state church. In the late 1700s, as demand for independence grew in the colonies, so did protests against state support of the Anglicans. The Baptists, Methodists, and other Protestant churches, largely attended by working-class colonists, took offense that the political elite pushed for public dollars to be used to support the Anglican Church. In 1784 Patrick Henry introduced a bill to the Anglican-dominated Virginia legislature that argued in support of public tax dollars going to their churches because religion was beneficial to good public behavior. Madison defeated the bill and later wrote to Jefferson that he envisioned future fights over similar efforts at "making laws for the human mind."

When Ben Franklin was asked if Jesus was the Son of God, he admitted to "doubts as to his divinity." He joked that he didn't feel the need to study the issue because as an old man he expected to die soon and have the "opportunity of knowing the truth with less trouble." Thomas Jefferson, author of the Declaration of Independence, was another Founding Father who distanced himself from the church. His critics attacked him by calling him an atheist. As president, Jefferson famously wrote that the U.S. government was founded with a "wall of separation" between church and state.

Jefferson's skepticism extended to taking a razor to the Bible. He cut out all mention of miracles and mystical acts, from virgin birth to resurrection, as hyperbole not worthy of a guidebook on morals, just behavior, and common sense.

To be sure, Jefferson did not disdain religion. As a writer, leader, and president, Jefferson tried to eliminate religion from public life simply to keep it from dictating public policy. Jon Meacham, the author of a book on how the Founders viewed religion and politics titled *American Gospel: God, the Founding Fathers and the Making of a Nation*, describes Jefferson as seeing religion and politics as threads in the fabric of human experience. "What Jefferson was doing when he wrote the letter that brought the phrase 'wall of separation,' he was talking about church and state, not religion and politics," Meacham said in an NPR interview. Jefferson "very well understood that while church and state can be separate, by and large, religion and politics are inextricably intertwined because politics is about people and religion is one of the factors among many that drives people." Jefferson, who clearly believed in God, once wrote, "I tremble" at the possibility that "God is just." Similarly, Franklin told the Constitutional Convention, "The longer I live, the more convincing proofs I see of this truth—that God governs in the affairs of men."

The true history of religion in America is often at odds with the legend. For example, it is historically inaccurate to suggest that the Founding Fathers supported religious freedom and the separation between church and state solely for the best interests of American democracy. Oftentimes, calls for a secular government were simply means of discriminating against religions that the Protestant Founders and their progeny didn't like: namely Catholicism and Judaism. In the words of religious historian Tracy Fessenden, "The representation of religious freedom as freedom from rather than freedom for Catholics in America has long been a fixture of American republicanism." In *Common Sense,* Thomas Paine calls monarchy a "Popery of government." The phrase "religious dogma" was used interchangeably with Catholicism. According to Fessenden, there was a perception that Catholics, in their support of popes and kings, might also support the slave system. Fessenden wrote, "Protestant abolitionists who saw Catholicism as inherently despotic [thought that Catholics were] natural allies of the slave [trade.]" In 1843, a Jewish spokesperson from Philadelphia claimed that the city's public schools "took special pains to warp the mind and to implant the peculiar tenets of Christianity clandestinely [by using prayers] in which the name of a mediator is invoked [and supporting the study of the New Testament] as an authority equal if not superior to the received word of God."

The Founders' embrace of religion, even with its sometimes discriminatory intent, proved to have lasting impact. Abe Lincoln, a Baptist, picked up on the theme of religion in American politics in the mid-1800s as the nation fought the Civil War. After an early Union Army victory in an 1862 battle against the Confederates he told his cabinet, "God has decided this question in favor of the slaves." Three years later, speaking at his second inaugural as the war continued, Lincoln contemplated the almighty's "own purposes" in wanting an end to slavery even as the war continued. Lincoln's speech included a prayer for the end of the war. But he said that no matter how long the conflict continued, "it must be said 'the judgments of the Lord are true and righteous altogether.'"

The first president to have a stand-alone prayer at his inaugural was Dwight Eisenhower, in 1953. In 1954, Eisenhower signed a bill allowing the words "Under God" to become part of the Pledge of Allegiance, and in 1956 he signed another one that made "In God We Trust" the national motto. Over the next ten years, the words "In God We Trust" were placed on all newly printed American money. The focus on faith emerged in 1949, at the start of the Cold War between the United States and the Soviet Union, when the Soviets exploded a nuclear device to prove they were equal in military power with the United States, raising questions about the end of the world. It also opened debate about good versus evil, often in the guise of democracy versus communism.

Americans differentiated themselves from the Soviets by claiming God for their side and portraying themselves as defenders of God-given liberties and rights. Politicians and preachers began combining patriotism and love of God to establish their superiority to "godless communists" in the Soviet Union. Eisenhower made a show of attending church and used his speeches to urge Americans to go to church. He told Americans, "Our form of government has no sense unless it is founded in a deeply felt religious faith."

The utility of religion as a campaign tool has its roots in the 1930s. Father Charles Coughlin, a Catholic, reached millions with his weekly radio show. As the country's economy scraped along after the Great Depression, Father Coughlin, a supporter of Franklin Roosevelt, gave voice to populist anger at bankers as he called for "social justice" for working people. In fact, he published a newspaper called *Social Justice*, spoke against socialism, and was strident in his opposition to communism. Father Coughlin's populism made him a vocal supporter of Roosevelt's New Deal. He came up with the phrase "The New Deal is Christ's deal." At one congressional hearing on communist activity in the United States he said: "God is directing President Roosevelt." But by 1934, Father Coughlin had lost confidence in Roosevelt, seeing him as favoring big industry and Wall Street over out-of-work Americans. He opposed Roosevelt's increased focus on stopping German aggression in Europe, and accused the president of championing "international socialism." Coughlin's broadcasts became anti-Semitic, and once America entered World War II, the nation's support for the war effort led audiences to abandon him. But his use of radio and his newspaper demonstrated the powerful appeal of a political message coming from a religious figure.

After World War II, the marriage of politics and religion faced opposition from the Supreme Court. In a 1948 case, the justices ruled 8–1 that it was unconstitutional for public schools to allow religious groups into schools to teach religious doctrine. The Court's decision to keep government-run schools separate from church school—*McCollum v. Board of Education of Champaign, Ill.*—was written by Justice Hugo Black. In his opinion, Justice Black cited President Jefferson's language about the "wall of separation between church and state." He wrote that the First Amendment, as established by the Founding Fathers, "rests upon the premise that both religion and government can best work to achieve their lofty aims if each is left free from the other within its respective spheres." But the Court could not ban the mix of religion and politics.

As World War II ended, Cold War rhetoric about "godless communists" opened the door for evangelical ministers to claim both the flag of Christian faith and the flag of the United States. In the decades to follow, rock and roll, sex in movies, and the civil rights movement prompted fear of loss of traditional culture and respect for religious teachings. The fear ran especially deep among fundamentalist Christians, who were concentrated in southern states. Religious leaders emerged as the ideal figures to give voice to those anxieties over change at home and fear of the enemy abroad. These religious leaders drew large audiences. And the millions listening to them attracted politicians seeking to build a voting bloc out of those conservative evangelical Christians seeking to have their values reflected in the nation's laws, government policies, and court rulings.

In the last half of the twentieth century these ministers rallied their followers to enter politics as Christian soldiers fighting in the name of Christian values against communism, abortion, and gay rights. The fundamentalist preachers rejected scientific theories of evolution and called for schools to teach that God created the world known to them in seven days—the biblical theory of creationism. They called for Christian prayer to be accepted in schools and at political events.

The political foundation established by the best of those evangelical ministers has shaped the twenty-first-century Republican Party. They are the Mount Rushmore of the religious right. Great preachers such as Billy Graham and Jerry Falwell catered to the scriptural concerns of the religious right, as well as their political worries. Pat Robertson and James Dobson built financial empires by capitalizing on the desire among evangelicals to find like-minded people on television, on radio, and in elected office. What sets the religious right apart is its lasting permanence. It succeeded by insisting on a place at the table in political debate, and by shaping mainstream American values in ways few other movements—religious or secular—achieved. The religious right continues to define the nation's political discourse to this day.

The ministers who took the lead in the movement succeeded by giving voice to those who felt alienated by the rapid social and political changes in the nation after World War II. They delighted in scoffing at the leading newspapers and universities, labeling them as out-of-touch liberal elites and charging them with ignoring the concerns of the average working family. And the most powerful of those ministers, the man who gave shape to mixing politics and Christianity, is Rev. Billy Graham.

Graham has always claimed that he is a man of the gospel, not a political leader. But the large following he built with his revival meetings, the respect and trust generated by his sermons, and the attention he got from newspapers made him a valued friend for any politician. He served as a spiritual adviser to every president in the second half of the twentieth century. His success in gaining access to the highest levels of American power revealed the possibilities for the evangelical right to demand that government policies and law reflect fundamentalist Christian values.

"Graham rose to success in the God-fearing years of the early Cold War," CNN's Molly Worthen wrote in an article titled "How Billy Graham Became an American Icon." As Graham was holding the first of his revival meetings in 1949, Worthen notes, President Truman was appealing to voters by declaring: "The basic source of our strength as a nation is spiritual . . . Religious faith and religious work must be our reliance as we strive to fulfill our destiny in the world."

Graham called his revival meetings "crusades," in the tradition of early Christians who battled to raise the holy cross in Jerusalem. Beginning with a nightly "crusade" in a Los Angeles parking lot in 1949, Graham was scheduled to preach for three weeks. Newspaper stories about the handsome preacher attracted large crowds, and Graham stayed on for eight weeks.

Graham was a preaching sensation. He would call on people in the audience to come forward and take a Bible booklet, confess their sins, and accept Jesus. As he made the call a choir sang "Just as I Am." He often quoted the words of a rich man who turned away from money after finding true wealth in Christ, dedicating himself to spreading the Christian message as a missionary: "No reserves, no retreat, no regrets."

Standing over six feet tall, with flowing, wavy blond hair and a calm, comforting presence, Graham was described by *Time* magazine as "Gabriel in a gabardine suit." He attracted big, curious audiences around the nation. But the place to see Graham in action was in the South, among white Protestant fundamentalists moved to passionate displays of tears and hallelujahs. He became a media star in the 1950s, the same era in which Congress added the words "under God" to the Pledge of Allegiance. At one point in the 1950s he was offered $1 million a year to appear on NBC television, but he turned it down to continue preaching at revivals.

Graham's sermons contained "just the right mix of patriotism and reproof. He urged Americans to stand strong against 'godless communism' but also criticized American hubris," according to Worthen. At a time of sharp splits among Christian denominations Graham's celebrity transcended theological divisions. He attracted people of all races, rich and poor, anyone curious about their faith, pushing his appeal beyond the Southern Baptist fundamentalist beliefs that made up the core of the evangelicals.

"His crusades mobilized hundreds of volunteers from local churches—not just evangelical churches, but liberal Protestant and Roman Catholic parishes as well," according to Worthen. Graham's biggest benefactor, beyond the world of evangelicals, was one of the nation's largest newspaper publishers, William Randolph Heart. Reporters for the conservative nationwide chain of Hearst papers were under orders from Hearst to "puff Graham." The publisher never met Graham, but he saw marketing gold in Graham as a good-looking, appealing religious figure able to attract readers to buy his newspapers. And Hearst liked Graham's ability to combine the uplift of religion with politics at a time when the possibility of a nuclear war created an ominous, dark global landscape. Hearst also found the preacher's sermons useful support for his papers' conservative Republican editorial stand against communism. In his book *Billy Graham and the Rise of the Republican South,* historian Steven Miller wrote, "Graham became a religious media phenomenon to a degree unseen in North American soil since the eighteenth-century peregrinations of English evangelist George Whitefield." Whitefield was a renowned Anglican preacher famous in Great Britain and the colonies for his "fire-and-brimstone" sermons during the Great Awakening, an era of Protestant religious fervor during the early eighteenth century.

On June 26, 1950, one day after the Korean War began, Graham telegrammed President Truman, telling the President that South Korea had "more Christians . . . per capita than any part of the world" and that we needed "total mobilization to meet the communist threat." "Graham infused America's anticommunist struggle with an underpinning of evangelical theology," according to Daniel K. Williams's book *God's Own Party: The Making of the Christian Right.* "Fighting communism was a religious duty, and the American government was engaged in the work of the Lord when it opposed the Soviet Union," Williams wrote in describing Graham's message to people attending his revivals. "The 'American way of life' was therefore the Christian way of life, and a threat to one was a threat to the other."

Williams quotes Graham as telling a 1950 revival that "Soviet Russia may well be the instrument in the hands of God to bring America to her knees in judgment. God may well do it today unless America repents of her sins of immorality, drunkenness, and rebellion against God."

President Truman had been suspicious of Graham, telling his biographers that Graham was "one of those counterfeits" whose interest was only in getting his name in the paper. But Eisenhower, a Republican, found Graham to be genuine. Graham became so close to President Eisenhower that Graham convinced him to join the Presbyterian Church and to be baptized. That made President Eisenhower, according to reports, the "first and only president to be baptized while in office."

Beginning with Truman, Graham met with every president, including President Obama. His relationship and his private counsel varied with the man in the White House. But presidents have always found political advantage in publicizing their time and their talks with Graham. At the very least a visit with Graham signaled to evangelicals that the president, regardless of his religious practices or lack of church attendance, respected the views of Graham and his flock.

The political wisdom of meeting with Graham was evident in JFK's willingness to talk with Graham and have news photographers in the White House record the moment. Graham had engineered anti-Catholic attacks during Kennedy's 1960 campaign, and Kennedy had had to overcome suspicions that any Catholic's loyalty was to the Pope and not to the Constitution. Still, once he won the election, Kennedy decided it was better not to hold a grudge: a visit with Graham offered the new president legitimacy with southern Democrats, specifically evangelicals.

After President Kennedy's assassination, Graham became a regular presence in the Johnson White House. The President even had Graham come and kneel at his bedside to pray with him. Johnson was the first occupant of the White House to attend one of Graham's revival meetings. "I almost used the White House as a hotel when Johnson was

President," Graham told a biographer. "He was always trying to keep me there. He just wouldn't let me leave."

Graham was in the White House on Johnson's last day as president and he stayed for the first day of his successor, President Nixon, another political friend. Graham led worship for President Nixon at the White House, and Nixon became the first president to give a speech at an evangelical revival.

Jon Meacham, in *American Gospel,* described the benefit to politicians, whether they were Democrats or Republicans, of associating with Graham: "From Eisenhower on, politicians who were seen with Graham were invested with a kind of religious aura, and Graham apparently never met a famous person he did not like. It is easy—too easy—to be cynical about Graham, to consign him to the role of pastor to the powerful. His decades of ministry, however, show him to have been at once a maker and a mirror of the nation's public religion, from Cold War millennialism to the suburban sunniness of the conservative counterculture in the sixties and seventies."

Author Steven Miller writes that religious scholars saw Graham in the 1950s, '60s, and '70s as a "conduit through which flowed much of the zeitgeist of the latter half of the twentieth century." But unlike the combative, fire-and-brimstone tone of several of his predecessors and successors in the pulpits of the evangelical Right, Graham was seen by the American public as a "beacon of stability and graciousness," according to Miller. Graham never damned sinners in the tradition of fundamentalist preachers. He never claimed to possess mystical spirits with the ability to scare anyone. There was no $10 bottle of holy water being sold as people walked out of the tent. And mainstream denominations welcomed him in their churches as a visiting preacher and even sponsored some of his crusades. They believed he brought people to their pews as much as into the ranks of evangelicals.

Although Graham was evangelical, as Worthen points out in her CNN article, "he abandoned the strict fundamentalism of his youth for a less doctrinaire theology." Graham also straddled the political fence by maintaining public relationships with Democrats as well as Republicans. No political party objected to his emphasis on strong families. He drew praise from both parties for opposing communism. In that era his opposition to homosexuality and gay marriage did not set off political fights. He did a political tap dance around the civil rights movement. While he bailed civil rights leader Dr. Martin Luther King Jr. out of jail, he rarely challenged southern segregation in public, and did not march with King.

But Graham's above-the-political-fray image was damaged when a tape recording surfaced of a conversation he had had with President Nixon. Graham supported Nixon's lament of Jews running the media. And it was hard not to notice his close ties to Nixon as Republicans transformed the white Protestant South from mostly Democratic to mostly Republican. He served as a reassuring figure as Republicans mixed politics and religion to appeal to evangelicals and church-going white Protestants and Catholics. He remained a smiling, gentle, Christian face, an implicit endorsement for Nixon and other Republican politicians who made a show of their desire to preserve social traditions and patriotic customs in the face of liberals calling for change. Graham never ran for office, never organized a political group, and denied being a political leader for Republicans in the South. But there is no question of the enormous role he played in the rise of American conservative politics.

Despite some slips of the tongue over his years in public life, Graham succeeded in dodging charges that he was a right-wing partisan clothed in religious garb. He created legitimacy in the middle of the twentieth century for the open exercise of religious influence on the president, Congress, and the media. That shift allowed three other men of the cloth to demand that their religious values be imposed on politics, judicial rulings, and public policy, and they had less reservation than Graham about mixing politics and religion. In some cases, they had no reservations whatsoever.

Two of those men were evangelicals inspired by Graham's success on radio and television in the early 1950s. In 1956 Rev. Jerry Falwell, then only twenty-two years old, began broadcasting the *Old-Time Gospel Hour.* Right away Falwell developed a television following by voicing support for a literal, fundamentalist view of the Bible as God's word. Unlike Graham, he did not avoid public conservative stands on politics. He used his show, based in segregated Virginia, to support opposition to racial integration in schools. He was a leading voice behind "massive resistance" by white southerners to mixing children of different races after the Supreme Court's 1954 *Brown* decision called for public schools to be integrated. In 1967 he founded Lynchburg Christian Academy, a segregationist private school, to help white families avoid integration. "If Chief Justice [Earl] Warren and his associates had known God's word and had desired to do the Lord's will, I am quite confident that the 1954 decision would never had been made," Falwell said. "The facilities should be separate. When God has drawn a line of distinction, we should not attempt to cross that line." Regular guests on his television show included segregationist political leaders like Georgia governor Lester Maddox and Alabama governor George Wallace.

Falwell also attacked communism, abortion, and gay rights as contrary to the biblical word of God. By the late 1970s he started a political lobbying group, the Moral Majority, to support fundamentalist Christian stands of public policy. In 1980 the Moral Majority proved key to delivering votes from the southern religious right wing to Ronald Reagan.

"Television made me a kind of instant celebrity," Falwell later wrote of the start of the *Old-Time Gospel Hour*. "People were fascinated that they could see me [on television during the morning] and hear me preach that same night in person."

Rev. Pat Robertson, too, followed Graham's media model to build an evangelical empire, and he was even more political than Falwell. The son of Absalom Willis Robertson, a former U.S. congressman and U.S. senator from Virginia, Robertson worked as a volunteer at Graham's 1957 New York City crusade. He had graduated from Yale Law School two years earlier. But Robertson failed to pass the New York bar exam, so he shifted his focus to religion and became a close follower of Graham. In 1959 he graduated from New York Theological Seminary with a master's of divinity. His immediate goal was to start a television network to carry evangelical preaching.

He went home to Virginia and identified a small television station with limited broadcast range around Portsmouth as within his financial reach. By 1961 the Christian Broadcasting Network (CBN) was carrying Robertson's image and his evangelical message. In 1966 the success of CBN led Robertson to begin hosting a show that soon had a national audience, *The 700 Club*.

According to the show's website, *The 700 Club* was named in honor of a pledge campaign Robertson led in 1963. He asked seven hundred viewers to agree to give $10 a month to help keep the network on the air. "Wherever 'The 700 Club' airs," according to CBN's website, "lives are touched by the program's testimonies, teachings and ministry . . . On average, more than 11,000 people call CBN's toll-free prayer line each day, while others e-mail CBN.com with their requests for prayer and spiritual help."

A biography of Robertson by David E. Harrell Jr. describes Billy Graham as an early and constant supporter of CBN and *The 700 Club*. "Every charismatic knew that the occasion" when Graham blessed the new CBN headquarters building, Harrell wrote, "was laden with symbolic significance as the leader of American evangelicalism praised Robertson's ministry."

In 1965 Jim Bakker, another evangelical minister, began a show on CBN with his wife, Tammy Faye. That show's brand of charismatic evangelism was described in Robertson's biography as a sensational fundraising vehicle. Rev. Jim Bakker was "one of the most gifted fundraisers in modern religious history," with "a shameless willingness to expose his feelings and his financial needs to the public . . . and emotional personality that swings moment by moment from flights of rapture to fits of despair and weeping."

By 1977 Robertson's success allowed him to buy a cable television station able to broadcast *The 700 Club* and other evangelical shows across the nation. The same year he started an evangelical university in the same facility he used to broadcast CBN.

Like Falwell, Robertson was a major supporter of Ronald Reagan's 1980 presidential campaign. Incumbent President Jimmy Carter, a Democrat, charged Falwell with buying "$10 million in commercials on southern radio and TV to brand me as a traitor to the South and no longer a Christian."

Robertson ran for the Republican nomination for president himself in 1988. He told reporters the nation needed a more conservative leader to change the Supreme Court's stand on abortion by appointing more conservatives in line with Christian convictions. He extended the evangelical position to fiscal issues as well, saying it was right to "take a meat ax to the federal budget."

"Robertson seemed to be an ideal candidate to challenge the party's 'country club' establishment on behalf of evangelicals," wrote Daniel Williams in his book on the Christian right. "He was a wealthy business owner and a senator's son. He was telegenic and personable. . . . Even as he publicly professed nonpartisanship, Robertson engaged in a variety of political efforts that largely escaped media scrutiny. He used his Freedom Council to lobby for the rights of Christians to assert their faith in the public sphere, and he employed three hundred lawyers to defend Christians in religious liberty cases throughout the country."

While Robertson and Falwell engaged in direct political campaigning, Graham remained intent on his crusades and evangelism. After Reagan's 1980 victory, Graham distanced himself from Falwell with critical remarks in a letter to Falwell that was released to the press. Graham cautioned Falwell about "sermonizing" about politics while losing touch with the gospel. The goal of a minister, Graham made clear, was to bring people into the church, not the voting booth.

By then, however, it was too late for Graham to rein in his acolytes. Graham's success in building his brand through radio, television, newspaper columns, and live events had become a model for Robertson and Falwell, and their turn as television broadcasters led them directly into political messaging and organizing. Both men took it even further by leveraging their celebrity to start private schools as they played on evangelical resentment about attitudes toward the religious right at public schools and top universities. Falwell's Liberty University is, according to the *Washington Post,* the "largest Christian university in the world"; Robertson started Regent University.

These men also took steps to organize political power. Falwell's opposition to the liberal consensus in American politics, coupled with his disdain for the perceived godlessness of American culture, led him to join forces with Christian activist Paul Weyrich to form the Moral Majority, which they used as a political lobbying arm to fight abortion, oppose the Equal Rights Amendment, and defend school prayer. They also fought for their rights to start private, segregated schools. The Moral Majority continued to grow in the 1980s as the newly powerful voice of evangelicals in politics, issuing position statements, offering support for candidates, and always standing for ending abortion, opposition to homosexuality, and favoring "traditional" and conservative positions on public policy.

After Robertson's 1988 presidential campaign, the Christian Coalition was created out of the list of evangelicals who gave money to Robertson's campaign for the White House. The coalition reached the peak of its power in the 1990s with voter guides it sent into evangelical churches. In 1999 the group lost its tax-exempt claim as a religious organization because of its steady support for Republican candidates.

The Moral Majority and the Christian Coalition never did get Billy Graham's endorsement. He pulled away from the Moral Majority by saying, "I'm for morality but morality goes beyond sex to human freedom and social justice. . . . Evangelists cannot be closely identified with any particular party or person." And while Graham never repudiated Falwell or Robertson, he clearly stated in interviews that religious leaders need to be able to "preach to all people, right and left."

Graham continued to thrive over the decades, with large revivals and efforts to unify Christians across denominations. He spoke after the Oklahoma City bombing in 1995, and after the attacks on September 11, 2001, he was selected to lead a prayer service at Washington National Cathedral. In the meantime, Robertson and Falwell furthered their stature as the voice of the religious political right with a stream of controversial comments made through their media and political empires.

Falwell, for example, strongly condemned homosexuals. "Gay folks would just as soon kill you as look at you," he told one audience. He suggested that a character named Tinky Winky on a children's television show was secretly being used to promote acceptance of homosexuality among young people.

Robertson wrote a book titled *The New World Order* in which, his critics charged, he "propagated theories about a worldwide Jewish conspiracy." He called for the assassination of Venezuelan president Hugo Chavez. He once suggested that detonating a nuclear bomb at the U.S. State Department might serve to change its sinful policies. He suggested that Israeli leader Ariel Sharon had had a stroke as punishment from God.

The Falwell-Robertson approach of mixing religion, politics, and mass media combined to create a major political storm after the 9/11 attacks. Speaking on Robertson's *700 Club,* Falwell blamed the terror attacks that killed nearly three thousand people on "pagans and the abortionists and the feminists and the gays and the lesbians ... the ACLU, People for the American Way, all of them who have tried to secularize America." He concluded that the attacks were "probably deserved." Robertson's reply to Falwell's commentary? "I totally concur." Robertson followed up in 2005 by blaming Hurricane Katrina on the nation's policy of legal abortion and said the hurricane and 9/11 could be a sign of God's anger at America.

The trailblazing Graham-Falwell-Robertson push in the late twentieth century to energize the Republican Party with the religious passion of the evangelicals opened the door to political influence for a man who was not a religious leader. James Dobson had a psychology doctorate from the University of Southern California and worked as a professor of child psychology at the University of Southern California School of Medicine. After writing a bestselling 1977 book on the importance of strict parenting, including physically punishing children by spanking them, Dobson became a sensation among evangelicals. He followed up with books aimed at church audiences in which he counseled men to take command of women and families. He advised women to follow their men at a time when the women's movement was advocating liberation. Later he promoted treatment programs promising that homosexuality could be "cured."

In 1977 Dobson created an organization called Focus on the Family. The group was intended to promote Dobson and his radio show with a target audience of evangelicals. That led him to brand the group as a "global Christian ministry dedicated to helping families thrive." Initially Dobson stayed away from politics. But in 1983 he created the Washington, D.C.–based Family Research Council to act as a lobbying group for conservative family principles in the capital.

The Family Research Council became the Washington think tank, lobbying operation, and political guide for Christian evangelicals. Gary Bauer, selected by Dobson to run the Washington operation, ran for the Republican nomination for president in 2000. By 2004 Dobson was openly campaigning for the Republican nominee, incumbent President George W. Bush. In 2008 Dobson backed former Arkansas governor Mike Huckabee, a fellow evangelical. In 2012 he supported another evangelical candidate, former Pennsylvania senator Rick San-torum. His anger at President Obama defined him. "Could the Ameri-can people actually give this radical narcissist four more years at the helm," Dobson wrote during the campaign, "after his having wrecked the economy, undermined religious liberty, weakened the institution of the family, surrounded himself with Marxists and leftist czars, turned his back on Israel, virtually bankrupt our nation, forced recipients of health insurance to support abortion, declared himself to favor same-sex marriage, and weakened our armed forces[?]."

The confrontational power of Dobson's writing and the ongo-ing influence of the Family Research Council among Republicans in Congress remain hallmarks of the evangelical imprint on American politics today. But while attacks steeped in Christian ideology excited evangelicals and right-wing Tea Party members, it also moved evan-gelicals farther right in terms of mainstream politics. Obama was re-elected in 2012 with more than 50 percent of the vote.

To those on the left, mixing religion and politics has been unsuc-cessful. "As we look back on more than a quarter century of political engagement by the religious right, two things now appear obvious," Jon-athan Merritt wrote in the *Atlantic* magazine. "First, partisan religion is killing American Christianity. The American church is declining by nearly every data point. Christians are exerting less influence over the culture than even a few years ago, organized religion no longer garners the respect of the masses, and two in three young non-Christians claim they perceive the Christian church as 'too political.' Church attendance is declining, and the percentage of Americans claiming no religious affiliation is rising. . . .

"Second, we learned that partisan Christianity cannot effectively change our culture," Merritt continued. "When the religious right formed, conservative Christians were energized around restricting abortion and same-sex marriage, reducing the size of government, and protecting religious freedom. More than a quarter century later . . . [l]ittle progress has been made despite their best efforts, and an in-creasing number of individuals now recognize the religious right strat-egy has largely been a failure."

The modern Republican Party, however, continues to embrace the look and language of the evangelical movement, and now controls the majority of governorships and state legislators and both houses of Congress. The Republican Party platform remains strongly opposed to abortion. Even as gay marriage has become accepted in American politics and culture, the GOP's leading politicians remain silent on the issue out of fear of alienating the evangelicals in their base. And the most reliable Republican voters are still closely identified by their regular church attendance and viewership of right-wing media, including evangelical programs.

Tea Party activists have picked up some of the evangelicals' energy, focusing on opposition to the president's healthcare reform program, to big government, and to entitlements for the poor, while continuing opposition to abortion and gay rights. However, some commentators point out that their overwhelmingly white, older constituency, at a time when the nation is becoming younger and more racially diverse, may make it harder for evangelicals and conservative Republicans to regain the White House.

Today Billy Graham is elderly and rarely makes public appearances. Falwell died in 2007, and the energy behind his Moral Majority has largely disappeared. Robertson's Christian Coalition has faded, too. He still appears on the *700 Club*, but his apocalyptic predictions have made him more of a fringe player in today's politics. Dobson's Family Research Council remains a fixture in Washington circles, but Dobson speaks to a niche audience with declining political relevance.

Nonetheless, Billy Graham and his protégés have changed American politics and the Republican Party. They have sharpened the partisan divide over religion today, and made religion a potent force in American politics.

CHAPTER 11

GIRLS TO WOMEN
TO YOUR BOSS

Betty Friedan and American Feminism

My wife has a master's degree. So did her mother. My daughter is a prominent corporate lawyer. My sister is a lawyer specializing in international law. Her daughter is a medical doctor. My daughter-in-law is a doctor as well. My sister-in-law ran a winning state campaign that helped to elect President Obama. Her daughter is a corporate lawyer with a major law firm. My other sister-in-law helps to manage the nation's federal housing policy. And her daughter has a master's degree and designs cities.

The Founding Fathers did not know any women like the ones I deal with daily. When Washington, Jefferson, Adams, and their band of revolutionaries wrote the Declaration of Independence in 1776, they asserted an inspiring idea, but limited it only to men. The signature idea—that all men are "created equal" and that they are "endowed by their creator with unalienable rights"—simply ignored women.

Abigail Adams, wife of Founding Father John Adams, did ask her husband to "remember the ladies ... [if] attention is not paid to the ladies we are determined to foment a rebellion, and will not hold ourselves bound by any laws in which we have no voice or representation." But the letter to her husband and his fellow Founding Fathers was put aside, and Mrs. Adams and women of her generation did not follow through on her threat of a women's rebellion. The all-male authors of the Declaration held to their view that no woman was their peer or entitled to equal rights, even highly educated, take-charge women like Abigail Adams. And, by the way, all but one of my female family members that I've listed above are black; it is even less likely that the original Founding Fathers dealt with highly accomplished black women.

After the Civil War, and nearly a hundred years after the Declaration of Independence was written, a new generation of American men expanded the reach of citizens' rights. With the Fourteenth Amendment to the Constitution they gave equal rights to black men—former slaves. Yet that generation of American politicians went further than the Founding Fathers on restricting women's rights. They wrote women out of any claim to equality by expressly limiting expansion of rights to "male citizens." The Fifteenth Amendment giving black men the right to vote also specifically excluded women, no matter what their color.

It was not until 1920, more than half a century later, that women won the right to vote. That one bold step advanced the idea of equality beyond the limited male-dominated vision of American equality.

But American women continued to push for equality of opportunity, beginning in the 1960s. And that's the orbit for the high-flying women in my family. Historians label the era as the "second wave" of feminism, to signal the progress made after women gained the right to vote. Today, we can see that progress everywhere we look.

Women in the twenty-first century make up half of the nation's workforce. They are more than half of the country's professionals and managers. Today American women make up about 25.1 percent of the S&P 500 executive officials and managers. Women sit in 19 percent of the board seats for Fortune 500 companies. Twenty percent of the U.S. Senate is female, as is 19 percent of the House. Women hold three of nine seats on the Supreme Court. In the last fifty years there have been more than two dozen women governors. A woman heads the nation's financial controls as chair of the Federal Reserve. Women are 2.7 percent of the nation's combat troops, 7 percent of the generals, and more than 14 percent of active-duty military. And in December 2015 the Pentagon announced that women are eligible to join combat units. "They'll be able to drive tanks, fire mortars—they'll be able to serve as army rangers, green berets, navy SEALs, marine corps infantry, Air

Force parajumpers, and everything else that was previously open only to men." With that step, 220,000 military positions previously limited to men became available to American women. Also in 2015, women for the first time qualified to join the army rangers, an elite infantry combat unit. American women have also faced down the nation's enemies as secretary of state, secretary of Homeland Security, and national security adviser to the president.

But possibly more important than any one statistic is the way twenty-first-century Americans treat women as a class. It is no longer culturally acceptable to define women in terms of their beauty, youth, and fertility. Instead, Americans are coming to judge women much in the way men are judged, by paying attention to their intellect, character, and personality—aspects of their person that can't be reduced to physical characteristics. Though it's hard to quantify this paradigm shift, it's a change that has transformed the way we talk, think, feel, and act on a daily basis.

Who created this twenty-first-century world of high-performing American women, a world that is so distant from the Founding Fathers' eighteenth-century limitations? Who created the world in which we no longer believe that one sex is essentially better than the other?

To my eyes, there is one revolutionary who stands above all others: Betty Friedan. As the *New York Times* put it in its 2006 obituary, Friedan "ignited the contemporary women's movement in 1963 and as a result permanently transformed the social fabric of the United States." The *Times* went on to describe her as the "suburban housewife who started a revolution . . . [that led to] sweeping, tumultuous and continuing social transformation."

She created enormous social change without government authority or an official title. She never ran for elected office. Unlike others who advanced equal rights, she did not make pushing new laws through Congress her central issue. The critical change she achieved was cultural and economic. The absence of an official title or platform makes Freidan exceptional even among her peers. Using only the powers of argument and persuasion and her personal example as a woman willing to speak her mind, she enacted revolutionary change, uprooting American culture. The revolution she sparked permanently realigned the workforce in the world's biggest economy and changed relations between men and women, and consequently family life, in America. The lightning bolt she used to spark this world-changing fire was a book titled *The Feminine Mystique.* "With its impassioned yet clear-eyed analysis of the issues that affected women's lives in the decades after World War II—including enforced domesticity, limited career prospects and ... the campaign for legalized abortion—*The Feminine Mystique* is widely regarded as one of the most influential nonfiction books of the 20th century," the *Times* wrote. Other folks tell a different story. According to the online conservative magazine *Human Events,* *The Feminine Mystique* is the seventh "most harmful book of the 19th and 20th centuries."

Friedan's book gave voice to deeply pent-up furies among women—furies formerly covered up by the idea of the "happy housewife." Once revealed and articulated, that energy gave rise to new roles for women, new ways for girls to think about being a woman, and new possibilities for women to shape America's social landscape and culture. Is it possible the furies of repressed women would have been released without Friedan? Hard to say. Yet the simple truth is that they did not emerge before her book.

A century earlier, in 1848, American women used the language of the original Founding Fathers to point out that equal rights should apply to all, including women. In a "Declaration of Sentiments," authored at a women's convention at Seneca Falls, New York, the organizers, namely one activist named Elizabeth Cady Stanton, wrote about the "laws of nature and nature's God," in language that literally mimicked and even expanded on the Declaration of Independence: "We hold these truths to be self-evident: that all men and women are created equal."

Over a century later Friedan stirred the same pot, but this time American society was ready to listen. And Friedan's message remade American life so completely that the nation today would be unrecognizable to the original Founding Fathers and to all those who lived in America before Friedan. Gloria Steinem, a far more politically involved activist in the women's rights movement, once credited Friedan with opening the eyes of middle-class American women to their second-class status and bringing those women into the promise of "all men are created equal." "It really is a revolution," Steinem said in a 1971 speech to the National Women's Political Caucus, a group she and other well-known women, including Friedan, founded. "Sex and race, because they are easy and visible differences, have been the primary ways of organizing human beings into superior and inferior groups and into the cheap labor on which this system still depends." Steinem added that the goal of the women's rights revolution was "a society in which there will be no roles other than those chosen or those earned—we are really talking about humanism."

I knew Friedan as the writer in the office next door when we both had writing fellowships at an academic center in Washington in the 1990s. She was over seventy at the time. But her fame, wit, and demanding personality gave her an intimidating presence. At first glance she looked like a character out of a scary children's book: she was short, with a big head of thick, wild gray hair. Her face had the tired look of a perpetual cynic, with her mouth set in a snarky grimace. But she was quick-witted and funny and given to winking a hooded eye at me when people came by to fawn over her and tell her how she changed their lives or their mothers' lives. A newspaper writer described her during this period as having the "broad features of a woman the French might describe as une jolie-laide, which refers to a magnificent kind of ugliness that can be attractive, even beautiful."

She was a friend to me, but by her own admission, as she once said: "I've always been a bad-tempered bitch—some people say I have mellowed some. I don't know." Germaine Greer, a younger feminist writer, described her as a diva. On a trip with Friedan, Greer found her easily offended and "breathless with outrage if she did not get the deference she thought she deserved." Greer found her behavior "tiresome," but conceded that Friedan had reason to insist on respect. "Women don't get the respect they deserve unless they are wielding male-shaped power; if they represent women they will be called 'love' and expected to clear up after themselves," Greer wrote. "Betty wanted to change that forever."

Friedan's former husband offered similar testimony about his famously temperamental, difficult wife. Said Carl Friedan, "It took a driven, super aggressive, egocentric, almost lunatic dynamo to rock the world the way she did." Confirming what Greer and others said about the tension involved in dealing with Betty Friedan, he added: "Unfortunately, she was that same person [aggressive and egocentric] at home, where that kind of conduct does not work. She simply never understood this."

There was far more to Friedan than her rough personality. But firing the first shot in the women's revolution led to intense personal scrutiny of every aspect of her life. People repeatedly questioned her motivation for upsetting what many still consider the idyllic picture of American family life in the post–World War II years. That world, captured in 1950s TV shows like *Father Knows Best* and *Leave It to Beaver* featured stay-at-home housewives as happy homemakers who found their fulfillment in taking care of their husbands and children.

What made Friedan so irate that she wanted to upset relations between men and women, some asked. Was she an abused wife? In a memoir published in 2000, she claimed that her husband punched her in the face, leaving her with a black eye. Later she denied her husband had struck her, and declared she was "no passive victim of a wife-beater." She explained simply that "we fought a lot and he was bigger than me." They finally divorced after twenty-two years of marriage; her husband once said her criticism of him was part of her anger at "the whole male gender." In another interview he said bluntly that his former wife "hates men." But Friedan herself later wrote in one book that "random hatred of men" was "dangerous and diversionary," and alienated people from the serious work of achieving equal rights for women at school and at work. She said men and women have a common cause in fighting for equal rights for all in public policies, from the price of health insurance to property division in divorce cases.

Some critics dismissed her as a lesbian. Friedan made it clear that she was not. The mother of three children, she described herself as a mainstream woman who wanted the feminist movement to stand for equal opportunity in education and jobs. But her refusal to elevate gay rights to the top of the feminist agenda eventually caused some feminists to distance themselves from her.

Did she come from a troubled, broken family? Again, no. Her parents, who lived in Peoria, Illinois, remained together. Her father, a Russian Jewish immigrant, owned a jewelry store. Her college-educated mother, Miriam Goldstein, of Hungarian Jewish heritage, was editor of the women's page of the local paper. Her mother had to quit writing to fulfill societal expectations that a good mother stayed home to raise a family. Friedan later told interviewers she did not want to repeat her mother's mistakes. But as a child the young Friedan grew up in a secure and strong family.

Was she shunned by the boys in high school? Friedan said her "adolescence was quite miserable ... because there was anti-Semitism in Peoria." She could not get into any of her high school's sororities and by her own account spent a lot of time reading sad poetry. But she had boyfriends at college and in graduate school, including a young physicist who she claimed envied her academic success and persuaded her to turn down a fellowship and remain in graduate school so she could be close to him. She met her husband, Carl, soon after moving to New York, and was married at age twenty-six.

One critic, in an essay called "Feminism's Dirty Secret," argued that Friedan's feminist thinking grew out of her association with Marxists seeking to destroy the capitalist system. She did have far-left, Marxist friends as a psychology student at Smith College and at the University of California at Berkeley. That was also true when she moved to New York's Greenwich Village, where she worked for nine years at left-wing labor union newspapers. While writing for those newspapers, she was critical of the efforts by the House Un-American Activities Committee to label union activists as communists. But her writings during her college years and later strongly opposed fascism and authoritarian governments.

Some claimed her real focus was legalizing abortion. But Friedan defied attempts to define the source of her call for women's liberation by a single issue. In her late seventies, long after the *Roe v. Wade* Supreme Court decision legalizing abortion in the United States, she wrote that she remained "uneasy about the movement's narrow focus on abortion, as if it were the single, all-important issue for women when it's not." She once asked, "Why don't we join forces with all who have true reverence for life, including Catholics who oppose abortion, and fight for the choice to have children?"

But more than any one motivating force from her personal life was the general feeling of hopelessness that Friedan sensed in herself and the women around her. In 1957, Friedan—then a housewife and an occasional journalist—took a survey of two hundred women who had graduated from Smith College with her fifteen years earlier. She asked the women to tell of their experiences since graduating and to explain how they felt about how their lives had turned out thus far. The women recounted being adrift in their lives, unhappy in their marriages, made to feel guilty for their children's problems, and all the while drinking and taking tranquilizers to get through their bored suburban lives. The divorced women told of feeling that their lives had ended. The mothers' schedule of suburban shopping, taking the kids to soccer, church socials, and having dinner ready for their husbands frequently left them bored, listless, feeling what Friedan described as a "nameless, aching dissatisfaction."

Friedan, with her training in psychology and news reporting, sensed there was something going on among her friends and in her own life—a nagging discontent with playing the role of the good wife with children in a suburban fantasy. After the results of her 1957 survey at the Smith reunion revealed to her that she was one of many women unhappy with the life being sold to them, Friedan sent a similar questionnaire to Radcliffe women. She got the same discontented responses. That led her to begin writing about her findings in articles. Despite being a published writer in top women's magazines, from *McCall's* to *Ladies' Home Journal* to *Redbook,* her articles about unhappy suburban women got rejected wherever she submitted them.

"It offended the editors of the women's magazines," she told a PBS interviewer. "So after I had about four versions of it turned down, I said, 'Hey, what's going on here?' Because I had never had an article turned down. And I realized that what I was saying was threatening, somehow, to the editors of these women's magazines. That it threatened the very world they were trying to paint, what I then called the 'feminine mystique.' And I would have to write it as a book, because I wasn't going to get it in a magazine. And the rest is history."

Three years after doing her survey Friedan managed to get one small, watered-down account of her survey of smart, discontented women into *Good Housekeeping* in September 1960. It was titled "Women Are People Too!" By then Friedan was more than halfway done with her book. She did her writing in between raising two young boys and a girl, all under the age of thirteen, in a Victorian house. Her husband spent his days as a Madison Avenue advertising executive. As she put it, "I loved my kids and I loved my house and I loved a lot of things about my life in the 1950s."

But she felt a lack of personal fulfillment. And the survey of other college-educated women affirmed her own feeling of emptiness, wasting away as an affluent suburban housewife and not achieving the goals she, a summa cum laude college graduate, had set for herself almost twenty years earlier at Smith College and at Berkeley. That sense of personal drift, along with her skills as a writer, her studies in psychology, and her restless, penetrating intellect all came together in her book.

The generation of educated American women Friedan surveyed lived in a time of economic boom and suburban growth after the nation's triumph in World War II. It was far different from the world for American women earlier in the century. After the Great Depression, as the nation struggled to regain its economic balance, businesses openly discriminated against women job applicants. Employers showed a clear preference for hiring men on the theory that men supported families. Even stereotypical jobs for women, such as teachers and librarians, showed evidence of bias, giving preference to hiring single women—so-called spinsters—on the assumption that single women did not have a man to support them. With the start of World War II, more jobs opened to women as able-bodied men went into the military. Women began working in construction, running farms, and working in factories that supplied the war effort. There was even a women's professional baseball league, as chronicled in the movie *A League of Their Own.*

After the war ended in 1945 those jobs were once again given to men, and top-level jobs as executives, lawyers, professors, and doctors became the exclusive domain of men. The return of men from the military to civilian life also prompted a boom in marriage, with women staying home to take care of their children. The jobs that did exist for women were at lower pay levels in the growing service industry—as secretaries and clerks, salespeople in retail stores, waitresses in restaurants, and maids in hotels. Women enrolled in college in higher numbers in the postwar era, but for many of these women, college was seen as a place to meet upper-class men with good future earning potential and, as the joke goes, earn their "Mrs." degree.

Friedan generally fit the postwar model for women. Within three years of finishing graduate school she was married, and five years later, pregnant with her second child, she was let go from her job as a newspaper reporter. That is when she began freelancing for women's magazines. To the editors of the magazines, a happy woman was a woman who delighted in being a good mate, a good mother, and a good housekeeper. The book that best captured the zeitgeist in terms of women was the big bestseller *Sex and the Single Girl* by Helen Gurley Brown. Published in 1962, it featured smart, pretty women on the hunt for the man with the biggest paycheck.

Friedan's book was published a year later. In the preface she described her journey to the insight that led to the book: "Gradually, without seeing it clearly for quite a while, I came to realize that something is very wrong with the way American women are trying to live their lives today," she wrote. "I sensed it first as a question mark in my own life, as a wife and mother of three small children, half-guiltily . . . almost in spite of myself, using my abilities and education in work that took me away from home."

In the early pages of the book she gives a description of "the nameless, aching dissatisfaction" afflicting her and other educated women of her generation, a condition she called the "problem that has no name." "The problem lay buried, unspoken, for many years in the minds of American women," Friedan wrote. "It was a strange stirring, a sense of dissatisfaction, a yearning that women suffered in the middle of the twentieth century in the United States. Each suburban wife struggled with it alone. As she made the beds, shopped for groceries, matched slipcover material, ate peanut butter sandwiches with her children, chauffeured Cub Scouts and Brownies, lay beside her husband at night—she was afraid to ask even of herself the silent question—'Is this all?'"

Friedan wrote that American culture—the women's magazines, the movies, the music, and bias in classified job advertising—all pulled women into this limited, stifling role. "Experts told them how to catch a man and keep him, how to breastfeed children and handle their toilet training, how to cope with sibling rivalry and adolescent rebellion; how to buy a dishwasher, bake bread, cook gourmet snails." At one point Friedan referred to women as captives of a "comfortable concentration camp."

According to Friedan, women, weighed down by social expectations found themselves pushed into narrow definitions of success, and similarly narrow definitions of what it means to be truly feminine. This was what Friedan later labeled as "the feminine mystique." She said the mystique didn't come from women but was created by men and used to deny women the opportunity to explore the world freely, to use their talents outside being mothers and housekeepers. To be sure, many of the women Friedan interviewed were frustrated with their powerlessness. And many of the women did realize that something was wrong. But they were told that any such problems were a result of flaws in themselves. The power of Friedan's *Feminine Mystique* is that it broke away from that kind of thinking. The problems of American women were not based on their failure to conform, but that they were being asked to conform to an unjust system.

"In the fifteen years after World War II, this mystique of feminine fulfillment became the cherished and self-perpetuating core of contemporary American culture," Friedan wrote. But she argued that women are capable of more complex, interesting lives.

The Feminine Mystique became an instant, massive bestseller, with sales of more than 3 million copies. Excerpts from the book appeared in two major women's magazines, *McCall's* and *Ladies' Home Journal*, reaching thirty-six million readers. Friedan became a frequent guest on television talk shows to discuss her hotly debated book. One of the most often cited passages described women as caught up in someone else's dream and living a nightmare: "Millions of women lived their lives in the image of those pretty pictures of the American suburban housewife, kissing their husbands goodbye in front of the picture window, depositing their stationwagonsful of children at school, and smiling as they ran the new electric waxer over the spotless kitchen floor." Friedan wrote. "Their only dream was to be perfect wives and mothers; their highest ambition to have five children and a beautiful house, their only fight to get and keep their husbands . . . they wanted the men to make the major decisions. They gloried in their role as women, and wrote proudly on the census blank: 'Occupation: Housewife.'"

The book's cultural impact was immediate. Friedan later told an interviewer that "it was quite fantastic, the effect it had—it was like I put into words what a lot of women had been feeling and thinking, that they were freaks and they were the only ones." She gave public voice to private discontents that allowed American women to be freed, liberated from shame of not happily fitting into the magazine stories of the perfect housewife. Just as important, she allowed women to see behind the beautiful curtains on the house next door and realize that they had a sister next door, a female neighbor whom society had put in the same limiting, claustrophobic box. Other women did not like their limited lives, either, and Friedan's book gave permission to say it, to stand up for themselves and assert that there is more than one way to be a successful woman.

A writer for the *New Yorker* wrote that the political power of the book was in its shining light on the common "belief that women are biologically destined to be domestic and subordinate" and exposing it as "just a construct," used to justify discrimination against women who try to move past that box.

The book's popular success opened women readers to new conversations about their lives. It led to debate about how often women faced bias in applying for a job, and led to the end of classified employment ads in newspapers that segregated jobs for men from jobs for women. It also led to new awareness of the "glass ceiling" facing women trying to move up the corporate ranks. In public life there was a sudden rush of discussion about the law and women, including how to be sure gender bias did not hurt women in court cases dealing with divorce, child custody, and division of property. These intense discussions of gender equality were totally new to postwar America. So, too, was the idea of putting discrimination against women on the same level as discrimination against black Americans. None of this had ever taken place before Friedan's book.

The cultural image of women also shifted permanently. The editors of women's magazines began to pursue a new ideal image for the modern woman as capable and able to make decisions without a man, able to be both sexy and a mother, a boss and a worker, without losing the capacity to raise children or love a partner. Psychological judgments about women shifted, too, as Friedan's book challenged Freudian concepts of women as suffering from "penis envy" that led them to be inferior and subservient to men. As a matter of history, there is a bright starting line for the world of increasing numbers of independent, self-sufficient, educated women in twenty-first-century America.

That starting line comes into view with publication of *The Feminine Mystique.*

The year after her book came out, the Presidential Commission on the Status of Women called for greater attention to equal rights for women. But the pamphlet the commission produced had nowhere near the number of readers as Friedan's lively, controversial book. The presidential document fit into the debate as support for Friedan's book, an afterword to the main work. The social stir caused by debate over *The Feminine Mystique* led to talk about the need for something never previously heard about before—a women's liberation movement. That soon led to the creation of the National Organization for Women (which Friedan co-founded in 1966) as well as other women's groups inside political organizations to support women candidates for elected office. Those new organizations provided a platform for debates over the propriety of men's clubs and all-male schools. Questioning the accepted wisdom of men as separate and superior to women, the book sparked the creation of women's groups in unions and in schools, as well as leading to departments of women's studies in colleges.

The waves of social change generated by the book led a New York literary club to list it in 1976 in the top ranks of "books as troublemakers." The club said *The Feminine Mystique* was a good example of a book that permanently shifted the society in which it was published. Among the other books selected for the honor were works by the astronomer Galileo, who first argued the earth was not the center of the universe, and Karl Marx, who argued for communism as a governing political and economic principle.

In 1999, more than thirty-five years after it was published, an essay in the *Atlantic Monthly* described *The Feminine Mystique* as "one of the most powerful works of popular nonfiction written in America . . . launching the contemporary feminist movement."

In 2011, well after Friedan's death, a *New Yorker* essay claimed Friedan's book transformed American thinking about women. "It is easy now to explain what was wrong with that existence"—living the limited life of a housewife when a woman wants to do more—"but it was not so easy to explain it when Friedan was writing her book," wrote literary critic Louis Menand. "Apart from the Nineteenth Amendment, which gave women the right to vote, there were no laws against gender discrimination as such. The word 'sexism,' in its current meaning, did not exist. The most brilliant thing about Friedan's very brilliant book was her decision to call what was wrong with the lives of apparently comfortable and economically secure women 'the problem that has no name'—and then to give it a name."

Menand concluded that Friedan's book marks a line in American history, dividing "the sixties from the fifties as the day from the night."

In 1967, Betty Friedan and the National Organization for Women adopted a Bill of Rights for Women. That document is the source of numerous twenty-first-century concepts that have redefined how women are treated in law and public policy. Karen DeCrow, a women's rights activist writing in an article published in the year 2000, describes the Bill of Rights for Women as the root of so many changes that came to reality in the years that followed: "The 1967 NOW Bill of Rights include: Paid maternity leave; federally mandated child-care facilities; a tax deduction of full home and childcare expenses for working parents; the elimination of sex discrimination in admittance to academic institutions and job training equal to men for women on welfare and in poverty programs. Healthcare, education, the needs of the elderly, childcare, tax relief for parents . . . It was the feminist movement that moved them to the center of every national party platform. Our persistence showed that it is not just women and children who need clean air to breathe and it is not only women who grow old and require prescription medication."

Friedan pushed that agenda as the president of NOW, and organized a march called the Women's Strike for Equality in 1970, fifty years after American women won the right to vote. The suburban housewife and bestselling author had become a political activist able to organize and lead a parade of several thousand people down New York City's Fifth Avenue. Friedan described it as "probably the high point of my life."

She was a founder of the National Women's Political Caucus, along with fellow activists Gloria Steinem, Bella Abzug, and Shirley Chisholm. The political caucus's motto called for women to "make policy, not coffee." The group's effort led the Democratic Party in 1976 to agree that half of all delegates to its presidential nominating conventions must be women. Forty years after the book was published, Friedan's prominence helped to get the New York State legislature to pass laws protecting legal abortion. Friedan also became a director of the First Women's Bank and Trust, an effort to confront the once common banking practice of different and higher standards for women seeking business or mortgage loans.

New York Times writer Janet Maslin wrote a tribute to Friedan and her book in 2013. "I have a photograph of myself with Betty Friedan," she wrote. "We were together on a radio show. I was there because I was a critic for the *Times* and I arrived at the *Times* because of opportunities her book created. I wish I had known how much I owed her."

That debt is the respect due to the woman who reshaped the nation we live in today.

CHAPTER 12

THE POWER
OF DIPLOMACY

Henry Kissinger, Richard Nixon,
and the Opening of China

Even to his critics, Henry Kissinger is the major intellectual force in American foreign policy in the last half of the twentieth century. But in the rough-and-tumble of American politics, he is also lambasted as "shifty" and "manipulative."

Those in China, America's primary rival for global and economic power in the twenty-first century, have no such qualms: they respect him for his role in creating today's China. Kissinger was a key visionary in moving China from international isolation to a modern global economic superpower.

At a 2008 banquet inside the Forbidden City, the ancient Chinese capital in Beijing, Kissinger was one of several guests of honor from around the world celebrating China's role as host of the Summer Olympics. It was a major milestone in the country's rise to power on the world stage.

Among the other guests that evening was former President George H. W. Bush, who had been the second U.S. liaison to China in 1974. At the time of the banquet, the older Bush was also the father of the incumbent U.S. president, George W. Bush. But the Chinese hosts gave the former president far less attention than Kissinger, a man who had not held a major government position in over thirty years. The Chinese political, business, and media elite buzzed around him, whispering requests for meetings with the former secretary of state, presidential adviser, and businessman. They laughed at his jokes, offered business cards, and angled for pictures with him.

I attended the dinner as a guest of the China-U.S. Exchange Foundation and China Heritage Fund. When eighty-five-year-old Kissinger gave a toast, the entire audience quieted. They were well aware of the key role Kissinger had played in turning America's focus away from the Cold War and the nuclear threat posed by the Soviet Union. With Kissinger at the steering wheel, America had paved the way to today's booming Chinese economy, while limiting Soviet power and influence, as China became a potent U.S. ally in the game of world dominance.

With China entering the world stage, the military contest between the United States and the Soviets took a backseat to financial and manufacturing deals cut between the United States and China. China became the world's second-largest economic force and a nation with wide-ranging U.S. economic interests, from holding U.S. Treasury bonds to building manufacturing factories for steel and T-shirts to becoming a force in the world of technology. Today China is the biggest foreign holder of U.S. debt.

Speaking that night at the dinner in the Forbidden City before the opening ceremony for the Olympics, Kissinger told the audience that seeing China host the Olympics left him emotional and nostalgic. Looking back to 1971, when he had first come to China as a secret envoy from President Nixon, Kissinger said that the isolated, economically underdeveloped China of the time, with most of its population living in the countryside in poverty, had existed less than thirty-six years ago, but was a universe away from the economic strength and rapidly growing middle class in modern China. As he finished, the room of wealthy, powerful, and influential Chinese and their American guests rose to their feet to applaud Kissinger.

AMERICA'S INTRICATE RELATIONSHIP with China— and with several distant global powers—would have perplexed our original Founding Fathers. In his Farewell address after two terms as president, George Washington set the American ship of state on course to avoid reliance on other countries. Washington cautioned the first generation of Americans to remain a "sovereign" nation, protective of controlling its own affairs and within its rights to fight off interference from Britain, France, or any other country making claims on U.S. political or business affairs.

"Observe good faith and justice towards all nations; cultivate peace and harmony with all," Washington wrote in the address, published in several newspapers. In pursuing independence from all nations, Washington wrote, "nothing is more essential than that permanent, inveterate antipathies against particular nations and passionate attachments for others should be excluded; and that, in place of them, just and amicable feelings towards all should be cultivated." He cautioned that "habitual hatred, or an habitual fondness" risked having the new nation become a "slave to its animosity or to its affection, either of which is sufficient to lead it astray from its duty and its interest."

Washington later added that favoring one nation over another is "particularly alarming to the truly enlightened and independent Patriot" because it opens the door to foreign nations tampering "with domestic factions, to practice the art of seduction, to mislead public opinion, to influence or awe the public councils."

The first president's emphasis on complete independence for the new nation led him to issue the Proclamation of Neutrality, signaling to American citizens as well as world powers that the United States would not take sides in a war in Europe. The Congress agreed and approved the proclamation as the Neutrality Act of 1794.

But President Washington made no effort to be uniform in his approach to world affairs, such as the fight between the British and the French. President Washington simply wanted to protect American interests and not serve any other nation. Nonetheless, arguments over foreign policy led to the nation's first political divide. Thomas Jefferson, the nation's first secretary of state, wanted the United States to practice free trade and maintain particularly strong relations with the French, who had supported the colonists during the American Revolution. But Alexander Hamilton, the first treasury secretary, wanted to fuel America's economy by erecting tariffs against foreign goods. Unlike Jefferson, he supported Britain rather than France.

Washington feared the political division over foreign policy between

Hamilton and Jefferson might harm the young nation's stability. It was one of the factors that helped create the nation's first rival political parties. Washington opposed the split, fearing that preoccupation with foreign affairs would lead to feuds far removed from American independence and halt the growth of the former colonies into a functioning union.

In the end, Washington's approach based on neutrality in foreign affairs had lasting effect. A second war with the British, the Northwest Indian War, broke out over British support for Indians attacking American settlers in the territory that became Ohio, Indiana, and Michigan. The ten-year-long war ended with the United States able to control lands that became the midwestern part of the country. In 1795, President Washington signed the Jay Treaty, which required Great Britain to give up its forts in the old American Northwest. The same desire to stop foreign interference in U.S. affairs was later evident in President Jefferson's Louisiana Purchase of 1803. The land Jefferson purchased allowed the new nation to eliminate French power over U.S. commercial interests at the port of Louisiana and push American settlers west of the Mississippi River.

Washington's policy of neutrality in service to American growth and financial stability also played a role in the Monroe Doctrine of 1823, which committed the United States to stay out of conflicts between European powers, as well as European colonies that had already been set up in the Western Hemisphere. But the doctrine also warned that European nations were not allowed to colonize any new territory in the Western Hemisphere. "The American continents," concluded President James Monroe, "are henceforth not to be considered as subjects for future colonization by any European powers." By the middle of the 1800s the United States had claimed Texas from Mexico, and in 1848 it gained control of the western land that became New Mexico, Arizona, California, Utah, and Nevada, as well as sections of present-day Wyoming and Colorado.

The first large U.S. military entry into world affairs beyond its contiguous borders came with the Spanish-American War in 1898. The war lasted ten weeks and won the United States control of Caribbean and Pacific countries colonized by Spain, including Puerto Rico, Guam, and the Philippines. The United States also held temporary control of Cuba as it began to flex its influence as a global power for the first time.

By 1904 President Theodore Roosevelt had created a corollary to the Monroe Doctrine. He asserted the right of the United States to protect its interests by barring European efforts at new colonization and economic control in Latin America and the Western Hemisphere.

The United States reluctantly began to assert itself as a global political power in 1917 when President Woodrow Wilson committed U.S. forces to join Britain and its allies in World War I against Germany. The alliance of U.S., British, Italian, and French forces defeated Germany in 1918. Afterward President Wilson supported creation of the League of Nations, where international disputes could be settled. He envisioned America as a light or beacon to the world illuminating the beneficent power of democracy and a global commitment to respect the sovereignty of all nations.

But Wilson's political foes in Congress were concerned that the United States avoid being trapped by feuds and alliances in Europe. It was yet another reprise of President Washington's concerns expressed 130 years before. Congress did not want to be forced under treaty to defend some distant nation, and President Wilson could not convince Congress to sign on. The United States signed only specific, individual treaties, again principally for protection of its trade.

During this period of American political isolation, the county enforced strict immigration quotas as well. Fear of left-wing European ideology, from communism to socialism, led to Justice Department crackdowns on labor unions and political groups critical of American big business and the tremendous wealth of the early-twentieth-century industrialists. This period extended until the onset of World War II, when President Roosevelt began assisting the British and French in their fight against the Nazis. The war expanded to the Italian fascists, and finally the Japanese imperialists. It was only in the wake of the attack on Pearl Harbor in December of 1941 that Roosevelt convinced Congress to declare war against Germany and Japan, and join the war effort.

The Allied victory over Germany and Japan in 1945 elevated the United States to the status of a superpower, both economically and militarily. Isolationism no longer was an option for America when so much of Europe and Japan needed to be rebuilt. Congress approved the creation of the United Nations. American and Soviet nuclear power set the parameters for a new hierarchy of global power, setting off a Cold War for dominance between the two post–World War II superpowers. The United States agreed to major international treaties, such as the North American Treaty Organization, which committed the United States to military defense of Western Europe against the Soviets. It was the nation's first major military agreement to use its forces to defend other countries in an effort to stop the Soviets from spreading communist ideology.

George F. Kennan, America's foreign policy architect of the period, advanced a policy of U.S. "containment" of Soviet ideology and power in order to avoid direct conflict. But smaller, "proxy" wars, such as those in Korea, Iran, and Vietnam, became a regular feature on the world stage. The United States competed with the Soviets over the number, size, and range of nuclear weapons and ballistic missiles, to be the first to send a spaceship to orbit the globe, and later to reach the moon and dominate the new world of space exploration.

The dark threat wrapped in this Cold War between the Soviet Union and the United States was fear of another possible global war—World War III. For people who had lived through the horrors of World War II, the Cold War was often viewed as a thin veil that separated global political stability from the nightmare of an apocalyptic nuclear confrontation. This was the mindset of a German Jewish immigrant to the United States named Henry Kissinger.

Kissinger was born in 1923. During his childhood, the Nazis rose to power, and the young Kissinger saw his father lose his teaching position because he was a Jew. Kissinger's family fled Germany when Kissinger was fifteen, but thirteen of his relatives died in the Holocaust, so he knew what tyranny felt like. But Kissinger's childhood also made him skeptical of popular democracy. Watching the Nazis use grassroots support and mobs to overthrow the weak Weimar Republic and take control of Germany, Kissinger learned to respect leaders who knew, when necessary, how to lead through secrecy and manipulation rather than consensus and popular approval.

Relocated in New York, Kissinger attended Manhattan's George Washington High School, where he was designated a child with a "foreign language handicap." The young immigrant switched to night school so he could work at a shaving brush company during the day to help his family pay bills. Arriving in New York during the Great Depression, Kissinger's English-speaking father could not get a job. It took him two years to obtain a low-paying job as a bookkeeper at a factory owned by a German friend.

After graduating from high school, Henry went on to study at the City College of New York, where he pursued a degree in accounting before being drafted into the army after the U.S. entered World War II and sent to basic training in South Carolina and Louisiana. His strong performance on military aptitude tests and his ability to speak German made Kissinger a standout recruit. But what really distinguished him was his capacity to make friends with men in power; he became a protégé of Fritz Kraemer, a fellow German expatriate working for the Army.

Kraemer recommended Kissinger to top army officers as an extraordinary talent. That led to Kissinger's appointment as personal translator to an army general in Germany. When the war ended, the twenty-one-year-old Kissinger was assigned to be the U.S. administrator for Krefeld, a German town of two hundred thousand people. Later he served as head of the U.S. Counterintelligence Corps in the smaller but strategically key city of Bensheim.

Young Kissinger's intelligence and his knowledge of the way his fellow Germans looked at the world led to a legendary story: he quickly managed the difficult task of capturing and jailing large numbers of former Gestapo officers by advertising job openings for people with "police experience." Kissinger handled the men who answered the ad with masterful deceit. "I asked him what he had been doing and he said 'Staats Polizei' [state police]," Kissinger said. "So I locked him up." Having captured one Gestapo agent, Kissinger persuaded the man to "prove his good faith" by helping Kissinger to find other Gestapo agents. And the fellow did just that, as did other former Nazi agents as they fell into Kissinger's hands. "I locked up more Gestapo than the entire rest of the U.S. Army," Kissinger boasted.

He also proved adept at getting the German civilian government back up and running, by hosting social events to bring war-weary communities back together. His success and ongoing relationship with Fritz Kraemer led to Kissinger's transfer in 1946 to the U.S. European Command Intelligence School in Germany. Kraemer helped to start the school for the army and brought the twenty-three-year-old Kissinger in to teach classes on how to root out the remains of Nazi rule and discuss the best approach to reviving democratic institutions in Germany.

The young Jewish immigrant's rise in the U.S. military and return to Germany as a power broker was nothing short of spectacular. Nevertheless, Kissinger had his detractors. His army superiors found him "a problem person," at times manipulative, secretive, arrogant, and liable to be defiant of military rank. For example, he refused to turn in lesson plans for approval to his superior officer before teaching classes at the European Central Command, and he defied orders by keeping a dog in his office. Kissinger's taste in tall blond German women also led to gossip and grousing. In a country struggling with postwar recovery, the poor Jewish boy from the Bronx took delight in conspicuous high living, leading to jealousy among fellow officers. In one German town he claimed a large villa as his house and drove around in a showy Mercedes sedan confiscated from a Nazi businessman.

After the war, his success in the military and a scholarship under the G.I. Bill helped Kissinger gain admission to Harvard in 1947, the foremost university in the country in terms of studying public policy, government, and politics. It was a far cry from studying accounting at New York's City College. At Harvard, Kissinger became a government and philosophy major. He developed close ties to professors working with U.S. State Department officials in Washington on postwar foreign policy and managing the Cold War in the early 1950s. Kissinger thrived in Harvard's heady academic setting and stayed on to earn both his undergraduate and doctoral degrees. When he was offered a teaching position at the school, he accepted.

His behavior at Harvard was hardly happy-go-lucky. One biographer described Kissinger during this period as secretive, conspiratorial, insecure, and arrogant, despite his success in the military and his academic achievements at Harvard. In part Kissinger's reaction may have been the result of the insecurity he felt as an outsider. Harvard had only recently begun to open its doors to Jews. A Harvard colleague said that Kissinger had "the brooding melancholy of a man who has experienced tragedy as a child."

His 383-page undergraduate thesis argued that all history amounts to a philosophical contest between determinism and free will, along the lines of the World War II battles between totalitarian regimes and democratic governments. Kissinger favored strong leaders of democratic governments capable of managing the passions of populist movements by providing what he called "transcendent leadership." (The long academic work became famous for prompting Harvard to create the so-called Kissinger rule, limiting senior theses to less than 150 pages.)

Kissinger's doctoral dissertation, which he wrote while remaining at Harvard to receive his master's and his doctorate even after earning his bachelor's degree, revealed his preference for centralized government with a clear hierarchy. He showered praise on two masters of 1800s European diplomacy, Robert Stewart, better known as Viscount Castlereagh, the British foreign secretary, and Klemens von Metternich, foreign minister of Austria, who created alliances among European powers to defeat Napoleon and give political stability to Europe by restraining military coups and popular democratic movements that threatened Europe's existing political powers. While writing his doctoral dissertation, Kissinger worked with Harvard's Department of Government to create "Cold War networks." The idea, in keeping with his academic work, was to use diplomatic alliances to stop the spread of anarchy and political instability in favor of central government—even to the point of backing tyrannical leaders, as long as they could enforce world peace. At every turn, Kissinger seemed intent on thwarting the power of populist movements such as the Nazi socialist groups that had taken over Germany and ruined the lives of so many.

As a young professor, Kissinger was asked by the famous historian and Harvard professor Arthur Schlesinger to comment on a paper Schlesinger had written on President Eisenhower's promise to use "massive retaliation" in any military fight with the Soviets. Kissinger's response to Schlesinger became the basis of his first major publication, an essay in the April 1955 edition of *Foreign Affairs* magazine.

Kissinger argued for an alternative to an all-out nuclear war, calling for the United States to engage in limited conventional fights or "little wars" with its rival superpower.

The welcome response to the article's approach to preventing warfare in the nuclear era led to a job offer for Kissinger at the Council on Foreign Relations in New York. It also became the basis for his first book, published in 1957, *Nuclear Weapons and Foreign Policy,* which made some bestseller lists.

Kissinger's reputation as a Harvard foreign policy superstar opened doors to powerful political patrons. New York governor Nelson Rockefeller turned to the young Harvard academic for advice on foreign affairs. Kissinger also began advising President Eisenhower's foreign policy team. But along with all the accolades, he developed a reputation for arrogance. After hearing that a foreign policy speech he wrote for Rockefeller was being edited, he told one of the governor's assistants: "When Nelson buys a Picasso, he doesn't hire four housepainters to improve it." Nonetheless, Kissinger remained close to Rockefeller as "Rocky" ran for the GOP's 1960 presidential nomination.

Meanwhile, his work at Harvard led to ties with Democrats as well, most notably Harvard's favorite son, Massachusetts senator John F. Kennedy, who won the presidency in 1960. After the new president read an admiring review of Kissinger's book on nuclear weapons, he got the head of his National Security Council, McGeorge Bundy, Kissinger's former Harvard dean, to officially name Kissinger as a White House adviser. But Bundy did not take well to Kissinger's dismissive view of the day-to-day political work on foreign affairs taking place in Washington. According to one biographer, Bundy quickly became "fed up with Kissinger's habit of swooping into Washington for a day or two and critiquing projects that other aides had been wrestling with full-time." President Kennedy lost his fascination with Kissinger, too. Biographer Walter Isaacson wrote that in the Kennedy White House Kissinger "was a character out of Wagner trying to play in Camelot." One Kennedy aide described Kissinger as "pompous and long-winded," while the Kennedy staff put a premium on people who were "polished, glib, fast-talking."

His lack of success with the Kennedy staff did not slow Kissinger's rise in academic and global political circles. He was already a star guest

speaker before elite international groups debating global affairs. Top
foundations around the world awarded him grants to travel and study.
During his graduate school and early professional years he co-founded
the Center for International Affairs, while directing the Harvard International Seminar and later the Harvard Defense Studies Program,
all with financial backing from Harvard, but also with grants from the
Central Intelligence Agency, the State Department, and foundations
concerned with preventing nuclear war by promoting global political
dialogue. Kissinger's International Seminar program, a summer school
program at Harvard, attracted young intellectuals from around the
world, including the future prime ministers of Japan, Belgium, and
Turkey. Kissinger had succeeded in placing himself at the crossroads
of the highest levels of intellectual and political life. In every case his
calling card was his bestselling book and his work at Harvard on the
critical issue of how to slow the proliferation of nuclear bombs. His
expertise was increasingly in demand as the world focused on how to
avoid the post–World War II nightmare of the United States and the
Soviet Union pushing the launch codes to ignite mutual nuclear destruction.

The original Founding Fathers would have been baffled by the
twentieth-century tangle of global military and economic relationships, as well as America's leading role as one of the world's two major
nuclear superpowers. It is exactly what President Washington warned
the young nation against in his Farewell Address, assisted by Alexander
Hamilton and James Madison, when he urged "as little political connection as possible" with other countries. The original Founders' principal concern was protecting American sovereignty against potential
interference from Britain and European powers of their day.

But it was the very complexity of America's post–World War II Cold
War confrontations, from the Korean War to the Cuban missile crisis
and Vietnam, that drew top Republicans and Democrats to Kissinger.
In a world where the United States was one of two superpowers, isolation and neutrality were not options.

"Many Baby Boomers, who lived through the Cold War but who
have no personal memory of World War II, artificially separate these
two conflicts," Robert D. Kaplan wrote in the *Atlantic* in 2013 in defense
of Kissinger's brand of American statesmanship. "But for Kissinger, a

Holocaust refugee and U.S. Army intelligence officer in occupied Germany . . . the Cold War was a continuation of the Second World War. . . . People forget what Eastern Europe was like during the Cold War . . . the combination of secret-police terror and regime-induced poverty gave the impression of a vast, dimly lit prison yard. What kept the prison yard from expanding was mainly the projection of American power, in the form of military divisions armed with nuclear weapons . . . [T]he men who planned Armageddon, far from being the Dr. Strangeloves satirized by Hollywood, were precisely the people who kept the peace." For Kaplan, that strategy was epitomized by Kissinger.

Kissinger held no formal title in the Kennedy or Johnson administrations. At best he was an outside adviser—and an irritating one at that. In 1965, for example, the U.S. ambassador to South Vietnam, Henry Cabot Lodge Jr., invited Kissinger to visit South Vietnam as a consultant. When Kissinger returned to the United States, he broke diplomatic protocol by sitting down with reporters and offering harsh critical comments about corruption in the South Vietnamese government. His comments damaged delicate U.S. dealings with the South Vietnamese leaders and infuriated President Johnson.

Nonetheless, by 1967 Kissinger had made himself indispensable to LBJ's efforts to end the war and bring more than 550,000 American troops home. At a Paris foreign policy conference Kissinger developed ties to a French intellectual with access to Ho Chi Minh, the North Vietnam leader. Though Kissinger's 1967 attempt to end the war failed due to North Vietnam's reluctance to agree to peace talks and Johnson's reluctance to stop bombing Vietnam, Kissinger's secret channel to North Vietnam won him the respect of Johnson's advisers. Even after his official role in the peace talks concluded, historian Robert Dallek writes, "Kissinger would have access in 1968 to inside information about a new Johnson peace initiative." Kissinger was at the center of the discussions that failed when the North Vietnamese decided on a show of increased military strength, via the Tet offensive of 1968, that prolonged the war.

This intimate knowledge of the Johnson administration's negotiations with Vietnam proved invaluable to Kissinger as peace talks between Johnson and the North Vietnamese resumed in 1968. In *The Price of Power: Kissinger in the Nixon White House,* journalist Seymour

Hersh writes that Kissinger shared details of the talks with Richard Nixon, who was running for the presidency. Kissinger's leaks led Nixon's campaign to tell the South Vietnamese that, if elected, he would not follow the terms of the agreements currently being hammered out between Johnson and the North Vietnamese. Thus the South Vietnamese should not accept any agreement that the Americans and North Vietnamese proposed to them. At the same time, Kissinger also corresponded with Vice President Hubert Humphrey in an effort to hedge his bets and win a post in the next administration regardless of which party won the White House. One of Humphrey's aides recalls that Kissinger was a "both-sides-of-the-street kind of guy."

In that storm of politics and war, Hersh argues that Kissinger's back-door offers of information undermined the Johnson administration's efforts to achieve a peace accord.

Kissinger was openly supportive of Rockefeller's campaign for the 1968 GOP nomination as the party's presidential nominee. He told friends that Nixon is "a disaster . . . fortunately he can't be elected—or the whole country would be a disaster." Nonetheless when Nixon defeated Rockefeller and went on to win the November election, Kissinger got a call from Nixon's top staff. Kissinger realized that the newly elected president held no grudge from the campaign and there might be a path for him to return to power in Washington. Both men wanted to streamline the foreign policy decision-making process by centralizing key decisions inside the White House. Finding common ground on their need for tighter control of U.S. foreign policy, Kissinger changed his attitude toward Nixon and accepted the new president's offer to become his national security adviser.

Time described Kissinger's relationship with the new president as "improbable." The Harvard professor's ties to academic elites, top newspaper columnists, and high society in Boston, New York, and Washington grated on Nixon's nerves. The Republican son of a California grocer, Nixon never felt accepted by that high-flying crowd. And Nixon held some bias against Jews. As a result, President Nixon's relationship with his new national security adviser was a constant tug-of-war. John Ehrlichman, the president's chief of staff, is quoted as hearing Nixon "talk about Jewish traitors, and the Eastern Jewish Establishment—Jews at Harvard." Ehrlichman claimed Nixon toyed with Kissinger, ranting about Jews in front of the Jewish immigrant. "And Henry would respond: 'Well, Mr. President, there are Jews and then there are Jews.'" It was a sly, evasive response that reflected the anger and mutual disdain in their relationship, as well as the priority Kissinger placed on preserving his relationship and power in the Nixon White House.

One critic described the relationship as a mix of "secretive loners who worked together in a conspiratorial manner but . . . often spoke disparagingly of each other." Isaacson quotes Kissinger as calling his boss, the president, "our drunken friend" and the "meatball mind," while Nixon is reported to have suggested to his top aides that they get Kissinger to agree to see a psychiatrist.

But Nixon relied on Kissinger for policy advice as well as gossip. Isaacson reported that "by the end of their first summer Kissinger and Nixon were no longer communicating by memos; instead, they were spending hours in rambling conversations . . . ranging from grand strategic concepts to petty biases about various leaders . . . along the way [Nixon] would cast a few aspersions on the State Department or engage in some bureaucratic gossiping." Kissinger used his close relationship with the president to diminish Secretary of State William P. Rogers and limit the State Department's power. They kept Congress and the press in the dark about their actions. They secretly used the CIA to support a coup in Chile. Nixon and Kissinger covertly launched a bombing campaign in Cambodia in 1969 to weaken supply routes from China through Laos and Cambodia to the North Vietnamese military.

Kissinger and Nixon favored back-channel talks with leaders of other nations to public diplomacy. "Kissinger rejected a moralistic approach to the Soviet Union based on anti-communist ideology," according to a PBS documentary. A realist, he recognized Russia as a rival superpower, and sought to achieve a global balance of power by pursuing areas of cooperation with Moscow, a policy known as détente.

The shift from containment of the Soviet Union's influence and the spread of communism to détente was a major shift in U.S. foreign policy. Until then the American military, American politicians, and Cold War conflicts had focused on defeating the Russians as the way to end the challenge to U.S. security and democratic values. Isaacson's biography credits Kissinger with genius in his "ability to see the relationships between different events and to conceptualize patterns." One of those new patterns was how to use U.S. power to end the Vietnam War.

The survivor of Nazi extremism had no patience for drawn-out policy debates with congressional committees. He consulted and socialized with an earlier generation of so-called diplomatic wise men at the State Department. But he could be petty in protecting his power from bureaucratic rivals, and he sometimes exploded in tantrums. To his critics Kissinger's manner was arrogant, even disdainful, and seemed to hold contempt for a democratic society's willingness to engage in long debate. What was clear to both fans and critics was that Kissinger was a very powerful and influential man set on turning the page on a U.S. foreign policy based on Cold War conflict.

His harsh life experience as a child in Nazi Germany seemed to strengthen Kissinger's conviction that he knew the best path forward in terms of diplomacy—what some called his realpolitik, or practical view of the use of power. To Kissinger, realpolitik included diplomatic, economic, and military power—whatever would allow him to make his way through the jungle of raw threats to U.S. interests around the world. Given his own personal demons, he was intent on halting persecution by any populist or extremist groups in order to prevent a third world war.

To that end he preferred to work on his solitary mission under the cloak of secrecy, using the interest he and the president shared in keeping U.S. foreign policy under the White House's control. He put his sculptor's hand and his personal mark on international relations for the final years of the twentieth century and the start of the twenty-first.

Kissinger was the first to see a triangle of competing interests among the United States, China, and Russia, a new global chess board he thought he could manipulate to benefit the Americans. Opening the door for China as an ally bolstered America's diplomatic positions and its power. Kissinger calculated that two world powers positioned against the Soviet Union were better than a one-on-one, U.S.-Russia conflict. But no American president had negotiated with China since it fell to communism in 1949. This was unexplored and dangerous new territory for American foreign affairs and America's identity as a world power.

Despite having engineered a U.S.-China alliance, Kissinger was initially skeptical about how quickly President Nixon could win over the Chinese. He thought it could take years. One problem was that Nixon was best known to the Chinese as a Republican Cold War conservative from his days as President Eisenhower's vice president. The Chinese had long derided Nixon as a "gangster" for advocating aggressive U.S. military intervention against communists.

Three months into the Nixon administration, in March 1970, Kissinger found an opportunity to speed up the U.S. embrace of China. Tensions between Russia and China escalated when the Russians threatened to bomb the northern city of Lanzhou in China, in a dispute over border territory. Kissinger realized the Chinese thought the United States supported Russia, or at least did not care if Russia acted against Lanzhou. Kissinger saw an opportunity to privately let the Chinese know the United States opposed the attack and was willing to share strategic military information in the event of any military conflict with Russia. Kissinger hoped the secret gesture might lead to more talks. But in China, the Americans' long-standing military and economic support for Taiwan as an independent nation overshadowed any show of friendship.

So for the time being, the United States continued to send small but effective messages to China. And China reciprocated. In September 1970, the president told *Time* magazine that he'd be excited to go to China one of these days. In response, Mao Zedong told *Life* magazine that he "would be happy to talk to [Nixon], either as a tourist or as president." Then, in August 1969, Nixon set up a secret Pakistani communication to China through which he told China that the United States would like to improve their relationship. In response, in December 1970, Chinese Premier Chou Enlai used the Pakistani channel to write to Kissinger: "In order to discuss the subject of the vacation of Chinese territories called Taiwan, a special envoy of President Nixon's will be most welcome in Peking." In response, Kissinger and Nixon told Premier Chou that although the "meeting in Peking would not be limited only to the Taiwan question . . . [W]ith respect to the U.S. military presence on Taiwan . . . the policy of the United States Government is to reduce its military presence in the region of East Asia and the Pacific as tensions in this region decrease."

Two years into the Nixon administration, in April 1971, the Chinese surprised Nixon with a gesture of political embrace. They invited the U.S. ping-pong team to extend its visit to Japan by stopping in China. Spiro Agnew, the vice president and a strong anti-communist, condemned the trip as a Chinese "propaganda" trick, but he was quickly told to shut up. The president praised the ping-pong diplomacy. Years later Kissinger recalled to PBS's Charlie Rose that from the very start of the Nixon presidency, in 1969, he was surprised to discover that Nixon "had come [to] similar conclusions . . . that the United States needed an alternative vision of world order than simply the cold war."

In June 1971, two months after the U.S. ping-pong team visited China, the Chinese government sent another surprising message to the president. Kissinger recalls walking into the Lincoln Sitting Room, off the Oval Office, to read the message to Nixon. Nixon later re-created the scene for reporters, saying Kissinger's voice was trembling as he spoke. "Mr. President," Kissinger said, "this is the most important communication that has come to an American president since the end of World War II." It was an invitation for the president to visit China. Later Kissinger recalled telling Nixon that the message was the start of a "diplomatic revolution."

Nixon immediately celebrated. "I went down and found some old brandy that somebody had given me right after the inauguration," he said later in describing the scene. "Never been opened. Courvoisier, one of the better Courvoisiers."

It was left to Kissinger to keep the visit secret even as he made arrangements with the Chinese for the historic visit. Secretary of State William Rogers was not briefed on the trip. Nixon invited him to the president's home in San Clemente, California, that July, at the exact time of Kissinger's trip through Asia with scheduled stops in Vietnam, India, Thailand, and Pakistan.

During Kissinger's public visit to Pakistan in July, reporters covering the trip and the White House staff were told Kissinger had become ill from the long trip and withering heat of the subcontinent. He was going to the mountains to rest. Instead, a secret plan, organized under the code name "Marco Polo," was put into place. A body double was put in Kissinger's car as his motorcade snaked along for several hours to reach the cool mountain heights. Kissinger himself, disguised in a black hat, sunglasses, and dark raincoat, made a clandestine dash in a private car to a Pakistani military airport, from which he would fly to China.

In China, Kissinger met with Chinese premier Chou Enlai to seal the terms of a possible Nixon visit. But once Kissinger sat down with the premier, it became obvious there would be no visit if the United States refused to withdraw its support of Taiwan and offer communist China recognition as the only Chinese government. During that visit, the Taiwan problem was left unresolved.

The talks, which lasted for seventeen hours over two days, accelerated as the two men discussed the war in Vietnam, with Chou Enlai calling for U.S. withdrawal and Kissinger asking for China to help with negotiations. Kissinger suggested that a speedy end to the war was tied to U.S. pressure on Taiwan to resolve its differences with the Chinese. He also said resolution of the China-Taiwan stand-off was a necessary stepping-stone for the United States to support admission of the People's Republic of China to the United Nations.

The surprisingly easy tone of the conversations seemed to make the idea of the Nixon trip inevitable. They agreed on a date, February 1972. But Chou Enlai wanted their joint statement to indicate the trip was taking place at the request of President Nixon. Kissinger wanted it to indicate China was inviting the president to make the trip and omit any mention of their talks over Taiwan. After a full night of debate over the wording and help from their aides, the announcement was set.

At the White House, before television cameras on July 15, 1971, President Nixon read the prepared statement: "The announcement I shall now read is being issued simultaneously in Peking and in the United States," he said. "Knowing of President Nixon's expressed desire to visit the People's Republic of China, Premier Chou Enlai, on behalf of the government of the People's Republic of China, has extended an invitation to President Nixon to visit China. . . . President Nixon has accepted the invitation with pleasure." Nixon said the summit would "seek the normalization of relations between the countries and also to exchange views on questions of concern to the two sides."

In his official report to the president on the planning trip he had made to China, Kissinger concluded: "We have laid the groundwork . . . for you and Mao to turn a page in history." That fall Kissinger made another trip to China to finalize details of the upcoming high-level visit. During this October visit, Kissinger and Chou coauthored a communiqué articulating that the United States would agree to view Taiwan as an internal issue for the Chinese and acknowledged that China, including Taiwan, was one nation. According to Isaacson, "Nothing was said . . . about which of the opposing Chinese governments should govern both the mainland and Taiwan. That decision was left to the Chinese, but with the American understanding that it would not be the result of force."

The reaction to the presidential trip was political thunder. The idea of Nixon going to China silenced the Democrats. They considered him a hard-line, law-and order conservative, leader of the "silent majority," fixed in his Cold War thinking, and stridently anti-Communist. On the political right there was talk of treachery and even treason. Internationally, the Russians grew alarmed at the prospect of this new political alliance. Less than a week later the Russians invited Nixon to visit Moscow for renewed talks on limiting the size of nuclear arsenals; less than a year later the United States and Russia signed their first Strategic Arms Limitation Treaty.

Meanwhile, Taiwan's government claimed the United States had abandoned their friendship. A critical newspaper column, written after Nixon's trip, concluded that the Chinese had outsmarted Nixon and Kissinger. The headline on the piece said it all: "They Got Taiwan—We Got Eggrolls."

President Nixon asked California's governor, Ronald Reagan, to travel to Taiwan to reassure Taiwanese leader Chiang Kai-shek. Reagan, who later was elected president at least partly because of his advocacy of a strong military, wrote in a letter to a friend that he was no fan of Chinese communists and considered them "a bunch of murdering bums." But he added, in an echo of Kissinger's logic, that as long as "Russia is still the head man on the other side, we need a little elbow room."

News of Kissinger's success in arranging the China trip made him an instant media star. PBS's *American Experience* documentary on Nixon's trip to China later described the man with the thick German accent and plodding, grim manner as suddenly achieving "unprecedented international celebrity." His picture appeared on the cover of

Time magazine, and he and Nixon were named "Men of the Year" in 1972. The Gallup Poll rated him as the most admired man in the nation. President Nixon was thrilled with Kissinger's success in arranging the trip to China but tried to stop him from doing interviews with the *New York Times* and the *Washington Post* as well as the major television networks. Kissinger ignored the ban and had twenty-four meetings with journalists in the next month. And in Nixon's crazy relationship with Kissinger, the president's response to his defiant adviser was to send him a memo asking Kissinger to tell reporters that Nixon was "cool. Unflappable . . . A tough bold strong leader . . . A man who knows Asia."

Nixon's visit to China was a media sensation. His touring, the gala dinners, and announcements were carried on national television. The opening banquet of the two delegations was presented on morning news shows in the United States. The photograph of Nixon shaking hands with Mao made the front page of every major newspaper. Kissinger was involved with five meetings with Chairman Mao during the trip and later wrote in his memoir: "My children speak of the 'vibes' of popular recording artists to which, I must confess, I am totally immune. But Mao emanated vibrations of strength and power and will."

Kissinger's successful diplomacy with China echoed the success of one of the original Founding Fathers, Ben Franklin. It was Franklin's travels to France that first gave the United States credibility and standing as a nation deserving of support in its fight for independence from Britain. Kissinger's brand of one-man diplomacy similarly expanded the international standing of the United States as the leading nation on the world stage in maintaining world peace.

The new world born from Kissinger's vision placed a priority on global economic prosperity based on capitalism. Military confrontation to stop the spread of communism now took a backseat to agreements to expand economic growth. China's embrace of the United States as an ally left the Russians behind the times and at a disadvantage as increased economic power translated into greater military capability by both the United States and China, dwarfing Russian firepower. Russia realized it could not keep pace with the growing U.S. economy, and looked to sign pacts to limit U.S. and Soviet nuclear arsenals.

"And by the 1980s there was a curious new slogan in communist Beijing: 'To get rich is glorious,'" said the narrator of a 2000 PBS documentary titled *Nixon's China Game,* which highlighted the success of ending China's global isolation by preaching the gospel of capitalism.

Just months after the China trip, the Nixon White House began to implode with the Watergate scandal that ultimately led to the president's resignation. Kissinger became an even larger figure in national life, helping to maintain a steady White House while Nixon was preoccupied with the scandal. Kissinger was never tied to the scandal. To the contrary, he provided increasingly rare good news for the Nixon White House in 1973 when he won the Nobel Peace Prize for his diplomatic efforts to end the Vietnam War. He also steered a Middle East peace deal between Israel and Egypt when he replaced William Rogers as secretary of state while keeping his role in the White House as the president's national security adviser. Kissinger had become the king of American foreign policy.

Even as he dealt with foreign policy, Kissinger remained close to Nixon. Stories later emerged of Nixon drinking and getting on his knees with Kissinger to pray together in the Oval Office. In the end, Richard Nixon became the first president to resign from the nation's highest office. When Vice President Gerald Ford replaced him, Kissinger stayed on as the nation's guiding hand on foreign policy in both the White House and the State Department. The downside to his unquestioned power was that Kissinger's skill as a political infighter muted any contrary views.

In the press, Kissinger's every foreign policy move was dissected by his critics. Among Kissinger's more questionable policies was backing Middle East dictators who favored U.S. policy, such as the shah of Iran. The United States supported efforts at a military coup of Chile's elected president, and Kissinger's policy of détente with the Russians, in the eyes of his critics, led to Soviet appeasement. While the critics swarmed, Kissinger's defenders responded that his secret deals with powerful but corrupt world leaders was evidence of his genius in protecting U.S. interests and the stability of the global marketplace.

The 1976 election of Democrat Jimmy Carter—who defeated President Ford—marked the end of Kissinger's official leadership of U.S. foreign policy. But Kissinger continued to advise major American corporations doing business overseas, as well as multinational companies based outside the United States. In 1979, when the shah of Iran was overthrown, Kissinger helped him find a temporary home in Mexico. When the shah was diagnosed with terminal cancer it was Kissinger, working with David Rockefeller, the chairman of Chase Bank, who brought the longtime U.S. ally to the United States for treatment. Some critics went so far as to argue that Kissinger's actions angered the shah's opponents in Iran and helped to provoke the attack on the U.S. embassy in Iran that resulted in fifty-two Americans being held hostage for 444 days.

When Ronald Reagan defeated Jimmy Carter, Kissinger tried to regain his power and influence with the new president. But Reagan felt Kissinger's willingness to negotiate with the Russians was contrary to his hard-line opposition to Russia. That left Kissinger to operate outside of government. But his influence continued to be felt. From his offices in New York and Washington, Kissinger became an adviser to governments around the globe. He created his own team of foreign policy experts, including future secretary of state Lawrence Eagleburger, national security adviser Brent Scowcroft, and Bill Richardson, who served as ambassador to the United Nations. His corporate clients included global firms such as Coca-Cola, American Express, and the insurance firm American International Group (AIG). Kissinger helped the Atlantic Richfield Company (ARCO) sell oil that it found in China. He helped Heinz sell baby food in China. He helped AIG get the first foreign license to sell insurance in China. He started a company called China Ventures to invest $75 million in Chinese companies, although the effort failed due to political unrest in China after the 1989 riots in Tiananmen Square. After Tiananmen Square, Kissinger used his still-prominent voice in the American media to urge the United States not to take any action against the Chinese government. "China remains too important for America's national security to risk the relationship on the emotions of the moment," Kissinger wrote in a newspaper column. His words had an effect. President George H. W. Bush imposed economic sanctions on the Chinese as punishment, but they lasted only briefly and the relationship between the countries continued to grow.

If we look back over the last forty years of the twentieth century and the start of the new century, Kissinger stands out as the leading hand setting new parameters for U.S. foreign policy. Just as the United States broke away from a narrow definition of national interests to stop European colonization in the Western Hemisphere and protect its trade routes in the late 1800s, Kissinger rewrote American foreign policy at the end of the twentieth century.

Kissinger believed, according to Robert D. Kaplan in a piece titled "In Defense of Henry Kissinger," "that in difficult, uncertain times—times like the 1960s and '70s in America, when the nation's vulnerabilities appeared to outweigh its opportunities—the preservation of the status quo should constitute the highest morality." Kissinger's work in bringing the United States into alliance with the Chinese, according to Kaplan, was a great "humanitarian gesture" because it put "China in a position to devote itself to peaceful economic development: China's economic rise, facilitated by [Chinese premier] Deng Xiaoping, would lift much of Asia out of poverty. And as more than 1 billion people in the Far East saw a dramatic improvement in living standards, personal freedom effloresced."

To Kaplan and other Kissinger supporters, the German immigrant who fled the oppression of Nazi Germany and rose to power in America is to be applauded for doing an exceptional job of diplomacy under threat of nuclear war and the Cold War. Walter Isaacson, in his biography of Kissinger, reached a similar conclusion. Isaacson wrote that he remained uneasy with Kissinger's willingness to ignore bad behavior in the world and even encourage bad actors if they benefited U.S. foreign policy interests. But, he argued, the "structure of peace" created by Kissinger—his realpolitik triangulation of U.S., Chinese, and American power—puts him "atop the pantheon of modern American statesmen."

CHAPTER 13

ONE-THIRD OF A NATION

Pat Moynihan and the War on Poverty

The debate on how to help the town drunk, the beggar, the widow, the orphan child, and the wounded soldier is older than the Declaration of Independence.

Here is how Founding Father Ben Franklin wrote on "management of the poor" in November 1766: "I think the best way of doing good to the poor, is not making them easy in poverty, but leading or driving them out of it. In my youth, I travelled much, and I observed in different countries, that the more public provisions were made for the poor, the less they provided for themselves, and of course became poorer."

A more compassionate proposal came from another original Founding Father, journalist Thomas Paine. He called for property and estate taxes to be used to support the elderly, the "lame and the blind," as well as a stipend of fifteen pounds sterling—roughly $1,200 in today's dollars after converted to American dollars and adjusted for inflation—to all Americans on their twenty-first birthday to help them get started at business and become self-supporting. Published in 1797, the pamphlet, titled "Agrarian Justice," was an American take on the poor laws established by the British in the 1600s. The poor laws required parents to feed their children, and adult children to support their parents. It allowed beggars to be beaten and stoned for refusing to take jobs in public workhouses. But people judged to be truly needy—"the deserving poor," including widows, the disabled, and orphans, as opposed to able-bodied citizens who just didn't want to work and were considered lazy—qualified for handouts from local churches, funded by local taxes.

In the American colonies, local government was the last line of defense for the poor. The needy first went to family members and their churches. Next they turned to the generosity of rich landowners. By the mid–seventeenth century, as populations increased and poverty became a more acute problem, local taxes did pay for families to take orphans, the elderly, the handicapped, and the sick into their homes. But the Puritan work ethic of Colonial America convinced town leaders of their civic responsibility to compel poor but healthy people, called "sturdy beggars," to work. The poor could get work, food, and a bed as indentured servants—people legally bound to work for an employer until the term of their contract ended and they could try again to support themselves.

The new nation's Founding Fathers did not offer money from the national treasury to be given to the poor—either the "sturdy beggars" or the deserving poor. The idea of an unemployment check, much less a modern welfare check, would baffle the most charitable of the Founding Fathers. But of course the Founding Fathers lived before the many widowed wives and wounded soldiers of the Civil War. They lived before the end of slavery created economic havoc for the nation's black population. They knew nothing about big factories and the shift of American workers from farmlands to the cities. In Colonial America the average American barely lived beyond his fiftieth birthday, far from today's average life span into one's late seventies.

As a result of changes like these, the government in the 1930s created a social safety net to provide assistance for impoverished children, to train the poor for jobs, and to provide money for people who lost their jobs due to a corporate or economic downturn. And no one shaped the modern social net more than Daniel Patrick Moynihan.

As a child, Moynihan personally experienced the economic struggle caused by a father who drank too much, a mother who divorced (twice), and bouts of family poverty. But Moynihan's drive to succeed and the education he received helped to pull him out of poverty. He relied on that life experience to design the nation's federal policy for helping to get people out of poverty in the twenty-first century. Moynihan's approach reframed the national debate on poverty. He offered advice on dealing with the poor to four presidents. As a member of the U.S. Senate for twenty-four years, he continued to be a leading political voice on poverty. Despite charges ranging from arrogance to racism, his attention to the breakdown of American family life, especially among black Americans, forced a national political conversation on the social factors that complicate today's policies for getting the poor of all colors out of poverty. His voluminous work, preserved in sociological reports, academic studies, books, speeches, and policy recommendations, and even his silence on the 1996 welfare reform had tremendous impact on the way Americans talk about poverty today.

For better or worse Moynihan took America's long debate over the roots of poverty and squeezed the choices into two boxes: is poverty the harsh result of the system—capitalism's winners and losers, class advantage, and racial privilege—or is it the result of personal failure to accept responsibility for bad choices that lead to family breakdown, financial upheaval, and children becoming accustomed to living off welfare and repeating the cycle as they become adults?

Before Moynihan, the federal government played a limited role in fighting poverty, beginning with benefits for veterans of the American Revolution and the Civil War. The poor continued to rely on church groups and charities.

In 1912, the federal government created the U.S. Children's Bureau, a government agency that provided research on the status of American children, particularly infant mortality and child labor. Then, in 1921, the Sheppard-Towner Act allotted federal funds for the creation of roughly three thousand child and maternal health centers in forty-five states. But for the most part, the federal government played little to no role in social welfare. America's Puritan work ethic and national identity as a country founded by independent, self-sufficient citizens allowed only for local and private efforts to help the "deserving poor" or people caught up in a temporary spell of misfortune.

Then came the Great Depression, with unemployment rates of 25 percent. With most of the nation in fear of falling into poverty, the federal government began using tax dollars to help the states provide money to the unemployed, to single mothers and their children, and to people with physical handicaps. The government created Social Security, a federal retirement program supported with taxes on employers and employees to provide income for those over the age of sixty-five to supplement their savings

Moynihan changed that framework. After World War II and a period of steady economic growth, Moynihan decided to tackle poverty by making efforts to keep families together and provide incentives for people to prefer work as opposed to taking a government check.

Moynihan was born in Tulsa, Oklahoma, into a stable, middle-class family in a middle-class neighborhood. His father was a newspaper reporter with some college education at Notre Dame. His mother worked as a nurse. His father moved the family to New York when he received a very good job as a public relations man with RKO Pictures, a thriving film production company. As his dad's income grew, Pat's family moved to suburban New Jersey and Long Island and the comforts of a middle-class life outside New York City. So as a child, Moynihan had a positive male role model, and understood the benefits of education, ambition, and success. Then his world started to crumble. His father, a heavy drinker who loved to gamble and visit prostitutes, left the family, and while Pat later found out that his father had moved to San Jose, California, he never saw him again. Without their father's income, Moynihan's family found themselves on hard times. Pat's mother moved her children in and out of cheap, cramped, low-end rental apartments in the city.

"If Pat Moynihan grew up in real poverty at times, the trauma was not the usual story of a working-class family that never had a chance," wrote biographer Godfrey Hodgson. "It was the more complex predicament of a middle-class family whose status and prospects were dramatically affected when the father left home."

Historian James T. Patterson, in his book *Freedom Is Not Enough,* concluded, "Though his father's flight pitched him into the dismal world of Manhattan tenements, Pat's middle-class background had given him memories and aspirations that differed greatly from those of other shoeshine boys—some of them black—he encountered in Times Square," where Moynihan also worked shining shoes for a time. Moynihan's luck shifted again when his mother remarried and the family moved to a big house in suburban Westchester County. The marriage lasted only a few years, however, and Pat, his mother, Margaret, and his siblings soon found themselves back in the rough-and-tumble of the city. Pat attended a predominantly Italian, Puerto Rican, and black high school, Benjamin Franklin High. During summer vacation, he worked as a day laborer on the docks in Manhattan. His job as a stevedore was to unload goods from freight cars to be packed on ships. Moynihan picked up the nickname "Young Blood" because he was tough, took no crap, and had a strong back.

Pat's mother insisted her children stay in school, talked with their teachers about their progress, and set clear goals for grades and earning money from after-school jobs. When short on money for rent and other necessities, she put a bowl on the kitchen table. Everyone had to put his or her earnings in the bowl to be used as needed. Her love, the discipline she imposed, and the expectations she set for her family reinforced their basic values of dedication, hard work, and understanding what a dollar was worth. For example, Pat and his brother, Mike, would buy the early editions of newspapers in bulk and sell them in bars, sometimes faking fights to gain the attention and sympathy of the bar's patrons.

After getting good grades in high school, Pat went on to college at City College of New York and later Tufts University in Massachusetts. In between he spent time in the Navy. Later he did graduate study overseas as a Fulbright Scholar at the London School of Economics. Moynihan had expertly climbed the ladder of upward mobility, and escaping poverty was later to become the consuming focus of Moynihan's life.

"His travails as a boy also left him with very mixed feelings about life on welfare," wrote James Patterson. "Though he thought that public assistance programs were absolutely necessary, he often complained that the U.S. welfare system was ill designed, poorly funded, and stigmatizing, and argued that it badly needed reform." The lessons Moynihan took from his firsthand experience with poverty became the basis of his policy work and his thinking on poverty and what the best path out of poverty in modern America would be.

The way out begins with having someone who loves you when you are a child and makes an effort to spend time with you in those early, formative years. Staying in school is key. Living in a racially mixed, middle-class neighborhood is a big plus, as are not getting married until you have a secure job and not having a child until you have a steady paycheck. The U.S. Census Bureau suggests that people who follow those guidelines have almost no statistical chance of living in poverty in modern America.

It's a formula that worked for me. I grew up as a poor immigrant black child thirty years after Moynihan. My older brother, sister, and I were under the care of our mother during the 1950s and much of the 1960s. She worked sewing dresses in a factory that most people would call a sweatshop. We managed to get into government-subsidized housing in a working-class neighborhood. My father did not immigrate to the United States for several years. But with a close, loving family, I never felt poor. My mom's schooling ended at fourth grade, but she set high expectations for our work in school, and my sister, brother, and I all went to college. Like Moynihan, I always believed it was possible to succeed. I believed in the American dream.

But while I followed a proven path up the economic ladder, it is also true that lots of people have fallen off the ladder. Since the late 1960s the poverty rate in the United States has remained basically unchanged, around 15 percent of the population. As the *Washington Post* reported in 2014, economic studies confirm that "children growing up in America today are just as likely—no more, no less—to climb the economic ladder as children born more than a half-century ago."

What has changed between the middle of the last century and the start of this one is a widening gap between rich and poor. The middle class, too, is under pressure because of stagnant wages. The top 1 percent of Americans took in 9 percent of all income in 1976; in 2010 they claimed 24 percent. Alan Dunn, writing in *Forbes* magazine in 2012, said America at the start of the new century stands apart from most of the nation's history in that the top 1 percent "control 43 percent of the wealth in the nation; the next 4 percent control an additional 29 percent." He adds: "It's historically common for a powerful minority to control a majority of finances, but Americans haven't seen a disparity this wide since before the Great Depression—and it keeps growing."

So while the odds of moving up the ladder of economic opportunity are about the same as they were in the 1960s, the economic and social distance between rich and poor is far wider. That gulf creates more stigma and greater isolation for today's poor. It also puts more pressure on the middle-class worker to avoid falling behind. The Pew Research Center reported in 2014 that 57 percent of poor Americans were between eighteen and sixty-four years old, in what Pew called "their prime working years." Fifty years ago only 41 percent of people in their prime working years lived in poverty.

Now, there has been some success. For most of American history the poorest people have been the elderly, especially old women. Pew reports that as recently as 1966 "28.5 percent of Americans ages 65 and over were poor; by 2012 just 9.1 percent [were]. . . . Researchers generally credit this steep drop to Social Security, particularly the expansion and inflation-indexing of benefits during the 1970s." As the number of elderly people in poverty fell, the number of children in poverty rose. Children of all colors now dominate the ranks of the poor. That awful reality is tied to the increase in children born to single mothers and the rise in divorce. In the 1960s the majority of poor children lived in two-parent families. Today more than half of those poor children live in single-parent families. In the 2010 census, the overall percentage of American children under age eighteen living in poverty reached 22 percent.

The high poverty rate among children—even with the decline in poverty among the elderly—is the prime reason that the United States now has about 46 million people living in poverty. According to the U.S. Census Bureau, that is almost the largest number of Americans living in poverty since President Johnson began his "War on Poverty" in the 1960s. As a result, the national debate over poverty and welfare is very different from what it was fifty years ago. And thinking about how to help the poor is light-years from the private charity of Colonial American life.

The current debate about income inequality is fueled by today's gilded lifestyle of the so-called 1 percent. The flashy displays of wealth— luxury cars, private jets, second and third homes, high-end dining—by the upper class is seen by some as a taunt. It is far from the daily grind of the middle class and even further from the reality known to poor people. According to President Obama, the resulting income inequality, class envy, and breakdown of the American dream of young people believing they can do better than their parents is "the defining challenge of our time." And the man who framed that challenge for the early twenty-first century is Patrick Moynihan.

Moynihan's outside-the-box approach to poverty was born as a political sensation in 1964 when President Johnson asked his Council of Economic Advisers to begin a "War on Poverty." Even today politicians, policy makers, academics, and journalists still celebrate or condemn Johnson's war on poverty as the genesis of modern American thinking on the subject.

Moynihan's public work on poverty began with a fifty-page report for Secretary of Labor Willard Wirtz on the high poverty rate among black Americans. Wirtz called the summary of Moynihan's report "nine pages of dynamite about the Negro situation." When the summary reached the White House, President Johnson was so impressed by Moynihan's work that he asked Moynihan to help him turn it into a speech. The official, bureaucratic title of the Labor Department document "The Negro Family: The Case for National Action" (though most people just called it the "Moynihan Report") hid its true power. But by whatever name, the paper shaped future debate on government policy in dealing with poverty.

By studying black families, Moynihan explained, he was simply trying to figure out why certain people have better success in escaping poverty and why others fail. The reason he chose to look at the black community was that he felt the struggles of black Americans could be boiled down to root causes and serve as a model for effective antipoverty strategies everywhere. Black America, the nation's poorest racial group, the people with the highest unemployment rate, was the figurative canary in the mine of poverty for Moynihan. If he could find out why black families were having trouble and fix it, the nation would be able to end poverty in every other community. With the right kind of government intervention, he believed, the problems could be uprooted, creating new opportunities that would allow the community to flourish.

Moynihan's poverty report was heavily influenced by an earlier report he had prepared, "One-Third of a Nation." The initial impetus for his report came from a military study showing that a substantial number of draftees failed the mental and physical exams administered before they could be inducted. The army report led him to apply the same standards to young people about to enter the U.S. job market. More than a year before the Moynihan Report was published, Pat concluded that a third of these American men (of all races, but mostly whites) not only would fail the military's exams but also would be unqualified for civilian jobs. Moynihan's paper proposed that the federal government offer men who could not qualify to join the army the job training, medical help, and education needed for them to get ahead in the civilian job market. President Johnson responded to Moynihan's analysis by ordering testing of the nation's young men. That testing found that 26 percent of the nation's eighteen-year-olds could not pass a test required to graduate from the seventh grade.

This remarkable ability to diagnose social contagions would serve Moynihan well as he confronted America's unique racial situation. Beginning with the 1954 *Brown* decision by the Supreme Court ordering desegregation of public schools, the movement for racial equality led to a new civil rights law, a new voting rights law, and the federal enforcement of those laws. Moynihan viewed those changes as having little capacity to remedy poverty among black people. He wanted to bring blacks into the mainstream job market. Labor Department research had found a link between unemployment and family stability. In black America, the statistics indicated, a quarter of black urban marriages ended in divorce, a quarter of black children were born to unwed mothers, and a majority of black children at some point in their youth had to be supported by public welfare. Children without fathers performed poorly on standardized tests, were more likely to become juvenile delinquents, ended up incarcerated at higher rates, and were more likely to become unemployed as adults.

"The Negro family in the urban ghettoes is crumbling," he wrote in the Moynihan Report. The report was groundbreaking in that it looked beyond race to explain the cause of economic failure for so many black people. "A middle-class group [of blacks] has managed to save itself, but for vast numbers of the unskilled, poorly educated city working class, the fabric of conventional social relationships has all but disintegrated. . . . So long as this situation persists, the cycle of poverty and disadvantage will continue to repeat itself."

How did Moynihan propose to fix that problem? "The policy of the United States is to bring the Negro American to full and equal sharing in the responsibilities and rewards of citizenship," Moynihan wrote in his famous report. "To this end, the programs of the Federal government bearing on this objective shall be designed to have the effect, directly or indirectly, of enhancing the stability and resources of the Negro American family."

The diagnosis of the problem as the broken black family structure stood out from any previous approach to ending poverty. It also stood out from most of the report's sterile bureaucratic language. As the report drilled into the "tangle of pathology" within the black community, the picture it drew of family breakdown, failed parents, and the absence of responsible men with jobs able to support families created anger. Moynihan was charged with insensitivity for saying black America had become a "matriarchal structure." His report tracked the black male unemployment rate and found that—with the exception of periods during World War II and the Korean War—it had been at "disaster levels."

The result, Moynihan concluded, is a society of women struggling to raise children without men. As a result, the black population was "so out of line with the rest of American society [that it] seriously retards the progress of the group as a whole, and imposes a crushing burden on the Negro male and, in consequence, on a great many Negro women as well."

One troubling result of this dysfunction, Moynihan wrote, was a culture of bad behavior that had been ignored and allowed to fester by government neglect as well as by church and civil rights groups. They all preferred to excuse bad behavior—from out-of-wedlock births to drinking and crime—by pointing to the history of slavery, discrimination against blacks, and lack of economic opportunity. Moynihan advised a new approach: he proposed stopping the excuses and finding ways to put black men in jobs. It was high unemployment rates, he argued, that put black families at a higher risk of falling into poverty and then getting trapped in a destructive cycle of repeating bad habits that led to more unemployment and more social problems from generation to generation. The problem of single mothers, crime, and all the rest that led to high poverty in black America could only be solved, in Moynihan's analysis, by a coordinated approach or "general strategy."

The report was a game-changer. It tossed into doubt generations of American policy on the poor. Until then the government's approach to poverty had been to put the poor in institutions, from orphanages to shelters and insane asylums. Liberals' approach to poverty called for more compassion and understanding and put blacks in a different category from the other poor because of the nation's history of slavery. Conservatives regarded the problems of poor blacks as separate from the problems of poor white people because they were the racial minority; to many of them, family breakdown was a personal failing, due to laziness, a lack of moral fiber, immorality, and reckless behavior, not a rallying cry for government action.

Moynihan's report opened the door to the argument that the problems of poverty and unemployment were rooted in common problems of broken families, poor education and training. The report was short on specific policy ideas, however. Nearing the end of the report, Moynihan wrote, "The object of this study has been to define a problem, rather than propose solutions to it." That being said, Moynihan told readers "a national effort towards problems of Negro Americans must be directed towards the question of family structure. The object should be to strengthen the Negro family so as to enable it to raise and support its members. . . . After that, how this group of Americans chooses to run its affairs, take advantage of its opportunities, or fail to do so, is none of the nation's business." Outside of the report, Moynihan discussed ideas such as having the government offer federal jobs and military positions to black people. He also considered the prospect of giving poor black families government allowances. The report also sided with the idea that black families might have a better chance for success if families were smaller. To that end he supported giving black women easier access to birth control.

President Johnson praised the report and made it the basis for a speech he gave at historically black Howard University in the spring of 1965. "You do not wipe away the scars of centuries by saying: Now you are free to go where you want . . . [E]qual opportunity is essential but not enough," the president told graduates, in a refrain straight from the Moynihan Report.

The Johnson White House used the report to explain the outbreak of black rioting in big cities that summer. The president and his top domestic advisers saw it as sympathetic to the social problems and economic needs that undermine life in poor neighborhoods, especially poor black neighborhoods.

But the press tore the Moynihan Report to shreds. *Wall Street Journal* reporters Robert Novak and Rowland Evans summarized Moynihan's work as a condemnation of the black family. The writers left out important information, making it seem as if Moynihan was arguing that black families were essentially flawed and immature. Civil rights leaders protested loudly that the Labor Department had given Moynihan a platform for calling blacks worthless people.

The reaction among black leaders surprised Moynihan. He had suspected that his recommendation that government take affirmative action to train poor black people for jobs, give them preference in admission to the military, and even provide allowances to black families might upset southern whites; he feared they might see the plan as racial compensation for slavery. Godfrey Hodgson, in his biography of Moynihan, concluded, "There is a special irony about this: So far from wanting to 'blame the victim,' as his liberal critics later accused him of doing, [Moynihan] was prepared to go beyond New Deal tradition to the extent of actively intervening to compensate for the previous neglect of black people."

But when the report was made public, the charges of racism came from civil rights groups, the press, and white liberals, leading the administration to retreat from the study and the man who wrote it. The Johnson administration feared losing influence over the potentially explosive politics inside black America by damaging ties to mainstream groups in the civil rights movement, such as the NAACP and the Urban League. In the face of national rioting, the White House feared the report would anger black radicals and lead to even more violence, as well as encourage a white conservative backlash that would result in votes for Republicans who labeled rioting as "black crime" and promised to crack down on it.

Not yet forty, Moynihan quit the Labor Department. He ran for New York City council president and lost. Afterward, he went back to academia, teaching at Wesleyan and then at Harvard, where he ran a program on urban studies. Despite being an outcast in Washington, many academics acclaimed Moynihan for his work. According to biographer Doug Schoen, the demand for his articles, speeches, and advice made him a celebrated public intellectual. Conservatives rallied to Moynihan as a hero for refusing to be intimidated by critics in the civil rights movement who called him a racist. Within a year of leaving Washington, Schoen wrote, Moynihan was much in demand.

Moynihan used his new platform to become a celebrated critic of the White House's top domestic program, the "War on Poverty." He felt it was pumping money into politicians' pockets by creating new poverty programs instead of giving money and jobs to the poor. Moynihan remained convinced that the nub of poverty was lack of work for men. Any meaningful welfare program, in Moynihan's view, had to prepare people to succeed in the workplace and give them a job. All the new poverty agencies being created by the administration were a waste of time and money, he thought.

"Moynihan worried that the War on Poverty . . . was foundering because the money was being spent on elites in the field rather than on the poor themselves," wrote Steven Weisman, summarizing Moynihan's thoughts from a collection of personal letters. Historian James T. Patterson similarly points to "Moynihan's reservations about hastily assembled government programs . . . he repeatedly pointed out flaws in Johnson's highly touted War on Poverty." Moynihan felt the War on Poverty ignored differences among the poor, such as the distinctions between the problems of poor whites in rural Appalachia and poor blacks in big cities. "As an Irish Catholic from polyglot New York City, he was especially mindful of the enduring power of religious, ethnic, and racial identifications," Patterson wrote; "the powerful cultural attachments of people, he believed, must always be considered before reformers jumped in to better their world."

In his new life outside government, Moynihan helped to author a report on education reform. The purpose of the study was to look at the impact of inadequate school facilities on student performance in poor neighborhoods. But Moynihan lent his support to a conclusion that student achievement between the most modern and the most outdated schools was not as significant as the difference between student achievement in children coming from families with high unemployment as opposed to children whose parents had good jobs with stable incomes. This prognosis strengthened the argument made in the

Moynihan Report, which had already linked the poor performance of African American children to their parents' increasing divorce rates. His policy solution, once again, was job training for the poor and full employment. Welfare fit into his thinking only as income maintenance for people preparing to take a job, and for their children.

At two famous speeches given to Harvard's Phi Beta Kappa chapter and the Americans for Democratic Action, both largely liberal groups, Moynihan moved farther away from Democrats and political liberalism. He argued that the federal government did not hold the solution to all poverty and racial problems. He strongly rejected charges of racism aimed at his calls for attention to strong families and getting people jobs. And he condemned the far left, most of all the loud anti–Vietnam protesters and black radicals, claiming that their calls for revolution did nothing to help solve national problems.

Conservative Republicans took to Moynihan. Liberals condemned him as having abandoned liberalism to become a neoconservative. When Richard Nixon was elected in 1968, he appointed Moynihan as the administration's assistant for urban affairs, with a portfolio that included welfare, education, and crime. The Nixon White House delighted in Moynihan as their daring and defiant "idea man." And his first big idea for President Nixon was a Family Assistance Plan. Moynihan proposed that all American families be guaranteed a base income of $1,600 that year. If they earned less than $1,600, they would be given government money through a negative income tax, to bring them up to the $1,600 level. Moynihan made the case for the plan as a good way to reward families that stuck together. He also noted that under FAP it was impossible to take in more money from welfare than from a real job. In addition, he backed jobs programs to help the poor move beyond the $1,600 level. Moynihan celebrated the plan as a color-blind approach to poverty to unite blacks and whites. But the Democratic Senate voted down the proposal, 49–21.

Earlier in 1970, Moynihan sent a private memo to President Nixon on how to handle persistent high rates of poverty and crime among black Americans. The report began on a high note. Moynihan reported that black American incomes were up as the number of black people graduating from college increased, and they qualified for more jobs beyond just manual labor. But despite the 1965 voting rights bill and increased school integration following the Supreme Court's 1954 *Brown* decision, Moynihan pointed to the statistical reality that black people were disproportionately poor. He described a black child's prospects as difficult due to a number of social, educational, as well as economic hurdles.

That led him to the bad news. First he noted that the number of female-headed households had drastically increased. Without men bringing home a paycheck, black families earned less money than white families. Second, Moynihan pointed to statistics showing that a quarter of black children were now being born to single mothers. The lack of fathers, he implied, led to a third troubling reality: young black people were increasingly engaged in antisocial behaviors such as muggings, robberies, and setting fires. White liberals, Moynihan claimed, excused such bad behavior by young blacks by pointing to the history of slavery, inequality, and discrimination against blacks. The result, he said, was that black criminals were seen as political rebels and lionized by the left.

In order to counter this troubling trend, Moynihan proposed that the president stop talking about social and racial injustice and begin a period of "benign neglect." "We may need a period," he counseled President Nixon, "in which Negro progress continues and racial rhetoric fades. The administration can help bring this about by paying close attention to such progress . . . while seeking to avoid situations in which extremists of either race are given opportunities for martyrdom, heroics, histrionics, or whatever." The administration's only public attention to the black community, he continued, should go to black people with jobs, those in the middle and working classes who wanted nothing to do with the Black Panthers and other radicals but held political views in the middle of the road. Moynihan said it was time for the president to reward the "silent black majority." He advised the administration to remain faithful to the cause of equal rights and doing away with ghettos of racial isolation.

The president and his top aides gave the memo admiring reviews. But when the memo was leaked to the press it immediately became the subject of a page-one story in the *New York Times* and a raft of incendiary newspaper columns and magazine stories depicting the report as racist. Moynihan's earlier attention to the breakdown of the black family made him a ripe target for a new round of criticism. His refusal to view problems in the black community as primarily tied to racial oppression set off another firestorm of left-wing criticism that this time raised suspicion of Moynihan's motives across the political spectrum. To ordinary Americans it sounded as if the Nixon White House wanted to neglect a group of people who had a history of slavery, who had just suffered through riots in their neighborhoods, and who had high rates of poverty.

Moynihan left the Nixon administration in 1971 to resume teaching at Harvard. But Moynihan was still in touch with the president, who made him the U.S. representative to the United Nations Social, Humanitarian and Cultural Affairs Committee, where Moynihan made news again by taking a strong anti-communist stand against claims that there was more social equality in the Soviet Union than the United States. He loudly pointed out that poor people were not allowed to speak out about political oppression and lack of economic opportunity under totalitarian regimes.

Four years later, in 1975, President Ford appointed Moynihan as his ambassador to the United Nations. The next year he ran for the U.S. Senate from the state of New York and won. He became a leader on the Senate Finance Committee calling attention to the financial problems of big cities in New York State, including New York City, as well as the growing financial pain for the state because of large welfare and Medicare costs. The first-term senator worked with President Ronald Reagan to pass a finance package to keep Social Security on a sound financial base by cutting some benefits and raising taxes. He also worked with Republicans as a champion of tax reform to reduce the federal deficit. Moynihan attracted conservative support with proposals to end loopholes that allowed big corporations and the rich to evade taxes, while tax rates on the middle class kept climbing. In 1986 Moynihan joined with President Reagan to win passage of a tax reform bill that lowered tax rates for the rich but also eliminated some tax loopholes for the upper class while keeping taxes low on the working class.

In 1988 Moynihan got the president to sign a welfare reform bill that changed the core purpose of welfare, shifting the emphasis from sustaining people in poverty to getting people out of poverty. The new bill did not increase welfare payments. But it also did not cut benefits, even as Reagan and Republicans in Congress engaged in headline attacks on "welfare bums" and "welfare queens" riding in Cadillacs. Moynihan was public in his complaints about Reagan's attention to cutting taxes for the rich to boost the economy—known as "supply-side economics"—while proposing cuts to federal programs for the poor, especially poor children.

Since the 1960s, the number of single mothers among all racial groups had grown, putting more children in poverty. Moynihan tied the troubling trend to high unemployment among blue-collar men in manufacturing and construction. Unemployed fathers were not marrying their partners or supporting their children. Moynihan's solution was the same one he had offered twenty years earlier: create more jobs. The one difference in his thinking was that he wanted more jobs for women, too. The percentage of women in the workforce had jumped since the 1960s as the social stigma put on working mothers faded. Moynihan saw that as a new opening for improving social welfare.

President Reagan and Senator Moynihan crossed party lines to support a bill that required "mandatory education, training, and work requirements" for men and women receiving welfare money. Critics on the left labeled it a "new kind of slavery," according to one Moynihan biography, because it forced poor people to work in jobs they might not want. But Moynihan sold the new system as an innovative step to create bipartisan support for a plan to halt poverty. Republicans voted for it because the money to aid poor people was now time-limited, a temporary support while the poor prepared to help themselves. Enough Democrats got on board to get it through Congress. Senator Bob Packwood, the longtime Democratic dean of financial legislation in the Senate, supported the Moynihan welfare reform deal: "There's no guarantee that this bill will resolve the crisis facing our welfare system," Packwood said. "But there's one certainty, and that's that the present system does not work and cannot work. And but for Pat Moynihan, we would not be trying to fix it at all."

In February 1987, as the bill was making its way through Congress, Moynihan told a *New York Times* interviewer that the nature of American poverty had changed over the years. The poor were not "one undifferentiated mass of people." Offering different policies to remedy different types of poverty was key to Moynihan. He called attention to the need for a policy to help "about a quarter of mothers who receive Aid to Families with Dependent Children . . . for less than one year." He described them as "self-sustaining, capable people who have had a sudden divorce or separation," and predicted "they'll get their lives put back together and we won't see them again."

He was less optimistic about another quarter of the population "who are unmarried and in real trouble and go on welfare very young. If you don't get hold of those people very quickly and work very hard and put a lot of resources into them, you have a spoiled life. And their children have fairly chancy prospects."

When they did pass, Moynihan felt the 1988 reforms were a start on smart, targeted use of public dollars to get the poor out of poverty and into jobs without punishing the most vulnerable of the poor, children. But when Republicans took control of Congress in 1994, another welfare reform movement took hold that included cutting benefits for the poor, including people in job training or school as well as children. Newt Gingrich, the Republican Speaker of the House, proclaimed that even after the Reagan reforms, the federal welfare program still motivated the poor to rely on checks from the government and to get more aid by having children out of wedlock. Moynihan protested—he had never envisioned welfare reform that did not attend to poor children. He was particularly angry when President Clinton, a Democrat, proved willing to go along with the GOP idea of limiting payments to poor children as a political response to losing the House of Representative to Republicans in the 1994 election. "Just how many millions of infants we will put to the sword is not yet clear," Moynihan said in October 1995, before citing a federal estimate that more than 4 million children could lose benefits. "Those involved will take this disgrace to their graves. The children alone are innocent."

Moynihan, the man who shaped American policy for dealing with poverty in the latter part of the twentieth century, chose to be a bystander in the political negotiations between the president and the conservatives. Jacob Heilbrunn, in an article in the *American Prospect*, later quoted one of the senator's top aides as saying Moynihan had concluded that if he proposed a "serious alternative" with "painful compromises," he would lose, because the conservatives would want still more cuts, and liberals would blame him for any cuts. "Why even dirty your hands," he explained. Moynihan was among twenty-one Senate Democrats who voted against the Personal Responsibility and Work Opportunity Reconciliation Act as it passed the Senate in August 1996. President Clinton famously stated that the bill will "end welfare as we know it."

A *Washington Post* news story on the signing of the bill described it as forever changing America's approach to poverty. "The bill ends the long-standing cash assistance known as Aid to Families with Dependent Children, abolishing an entitlement created 61 years ago that guarantees any eligible poor person can receive aid," the *Post* reported. The plan also reversed more than a century of increased federal responsibility for dealing with the poor. Under the Clinton plan, the states and local government got lump-sum payments from the federal government, but the states set the terms for who qualified for welfare. The federal government did require that welfare recipients get a job within two years of going on welfare and limited lifetime assistance to five years. The government also required that in the next six years, by 2002, half of the adults getting welfare would be working or off the welfare rolls.

Even without Moynihan's direct involvement in the 1996 welfare reform bill, the legislation was simply the latest version of his work in the 1960s and 1970s, reinventing the American approach to helping poor people get out of poverty. The bill was born of his ideas, based on the conclusions of his often controversial reports, and tied to his personal history of childhood tumult caused by an absent father.

The roots of the Clinton-Gingrich plan can be found in the original idea expressed in the work Moynihan did in 1964, "One-Third of a Nation." That is when Moynihan came up with the idea that the best way to end poverty was to make it government policy to educate and give job training to citizens who could not find or hold a job. It was the 1965 Moynihan Report that turned government policy to the business of giving the poor—beginning with the crumbling black family— incentive to hold families together. That included tougher enforcement of child support payments and day care grants to allow women to be both mothers and workers. The 1996 plan walked down the path Moynihan had first blazed in connecting poverty and unemployment to unstable families, and it was the flower of seeds planted in Moynihan's 1970 work on the Family Assistance Plan, which proposed guaranteed incomes and negative income taxes to incentivize people to go to work instead of relying on welfare.

"In the 16 years since President Clinton and Congress overhauled the nation's welfare system, the number of people receiving cash assistance has fallen by two-thirds," CNN Money reported in 2012. "And public spending on the program has dropped by more than half." The CNN story noted that critics argue the plan "does not adequately support the poor, particularly in tough economic times." But Moynihan's idea was never to "support the poor" so much as to put them to work. In the explosive debate over the history of disadvantage leading to high rates of black poverty, it was Moynihan who proved to be a prophet. He called attention to the "tangle of pathology" that trapped a disproportionately high number of black people in poverty.

Welfare and poverty programs have shifted, too. At the start of the twenty-first century the national policy debate on helping today's poor is focused on how to get the poor out of poverty by targeting the root causes of poverty—something Moynihan would have advocated. The goal is to get them into the workforce. With more limits on eligibility for public assistance payments since the mid-1990s, the number of people on welfare has significantly decreased.

But with a major economic recession in 2008, there are also more programs to feed the poor. And there are more homeless shelters. A federal program provides cell phones so the poor can stay in touch as they apply for jobs. There are more people qualifying for government healthcare under Medicaid. The biggest social program of recent vintage, the Affordable Care Act, provides low-cost healthcare plans to people with no private insurance. These social safety net programs now also include tax credit to help poor parents support children, and the Earned Income Tax Credit to increase pay for low-income workers and give them incentive to continue working instead of going on welfare.

"Such programs . . . kept some 41 million people out of poverty in calendar year 2012," the Center for Budget and Policy Priorities estimated. "Without any government income assistance, either from safety net programs or other income supports like Social Security, the poverty rate would have been 29.1 percent in 2012, nearly double the actual 16 percent."

The faces of the poor have changed, too. The percentage of Hispanics in poverty is now about equal to the percentage of blacks in poverty. That is a major change with a big impact, since Hispanics now are a larger percentage of the population than blacks—17 percent to 13 percent. According to the Pew Research Center, "more than half of the 22 million person increase in official poverty between 1972 [when the census first measured Hispanic poverty] and 2012 was among Hispanics." And according to the 2010 census, 38 percent of black children under the age of eighteen and 32 percent of Hispanic children under eighteen remain in poverty. That is far higher than the 13 percent of Asian American children and 17 percent of white children in poverty.

Despite these economic, demographic, and cultural shifts among America's poor people, Moynihan's emphasis on pushing poor parents into jobs remains the distinctive center of the modern American approach to ending poverty. When Moynihan died in 2003, *Time* magazine wrote that Americans like politicians who are "average thinkers with average ideas." The magazine said the nation should be "comforted" rather than "threatened" by the presence of great thinkers in Washington. "As Moynihan proved over the course of nearly 40 years in government, great minds are well used in the messy and essential arena of public service."

CHAPTER 14

EQUAL PROTECTION UNDER THE LAW

Harry Hay, Barry Goldwater, and Gay Rights

Here's an eye-opening fantasy: The first generation of Founding Fathers travel across time to attend President Obama's second inaugural speech at the U.S. Capitol. The first black president begins by celebrating the "exceptional" and enduring American loyalty to an idea the original Founders "articulated in a declaration made more than two centuries ago: we hold these truths to be self-evident, that all men are created equal."

The Founders hear themselves described by the president as "the patriots of 1776" who fought the "tyranny of a king" and trusted "each generation to keep safe our founding creed." Standing before the Capitol on this crisp January day, Obama says the idea of equality for all is "the star that guides us still; just as it guided our forebears through Seneca Falls [women's voting rights] and Selma [racial equality] and Stonewall . . . Our journey is not complete until our gay brothers and sisters are treated like anyone else under the law—for if we are truly created equal, then surely the love we commit to one another must be equal as well."

At that point the Founding Fathers' heads might be spinning in bewilderment. Who are America's "gay brothers and sisters"? The word "gay" was not used to refer to people with same-sex desires until the

1920s. When it is explained as a modern synonym for "homosexual," they continue staring in confusion. They do not know the word "homosexual"—a late-1800s invention—either. Finally they are told the president is talking about men who engage in "sodomy," "buggery," and "that infamous crime against nature."

As commander of the Continental Army, Washington expelled one of his lieutenants, Frederick Enslin, for having sex with another man. Enslin was literally "drummed out of camp . . . by all the drummers and fifers in the Army never to return," according to Washington's secretary. Washington reportedly viewed Enslin's behavior with "abhorrence and detestation."

President Jefferson, the author of the Declaration of Independence, is also baffled by the idea of protecting homosexual rights. Jefferson thought he expressed some compassion for men who had sex with other men by arguing in 1778 for them to be merely castrated, at a time when Virginia's standard penalty for people engaged in sodomy was execution. Jefferson's fellow Virginians turned down his idea of a lighter penalty as too liberal.

How did a nation created by men who viewed same-sex behavior with "abhorrence" become a nation in which the president honors gay people as continuing the work of the nation's Founding Fathers? How did America of 1776 become a nation in 2016 where any picture of a rainbow signals gay pride and where gay people, thanks to a 5–4 Supreme Court decision, have the legal right to marry?

Anyone explaining the radical change since the first Founders would lead them to two Americans, in particular, and one gay riot. The first of the two Americans is Harry Hay, an English immigrant who moved to the United States in 1917, and created the first major U.S. gay rights group in 1951. Hay sparked "the radical beginning of a continuous history of gay political organization in the United States," according to historian John D'Emilio.

The second American is none other than Barry Goldwater, the Arizona Republican and 1964 GOP presidential nominee known as "Mr. Conservative." Late in his life, Goldwater loudly advocated for equal rights for gays, arguing that conservative reverence of the Constitution and its guarantees of personal liberty include the right to make a personal choice about sexual preferences. He famously said, "Politics has no business in the bedroom"—words creating an opening that became a seismic cultural divide and finally a canyon of doubt about social conservative and religious opposition to equal rights for gays.

And the riot? The riot took place in New York City in 1969 when gay men and women began fighting with police who raided a Greenwich Village gay bar. The police demanded identification and then began using their hands to forcibly check whether people were men or women, and arresting men dressed as women. According to a history of Stonewall published in 2014 by a U.S. Air Force base in Massachusetts commemorating the gay liberation movement, and then picked up by the U.S. Federal News Service, as the police began beating one woman she shouted to her friends in the bar: "Why don't you guys do something?" Though eyewitnesses disagree as to whether this woman or someone else sparked the events that followed, a crowd of hundreds soon began to battle police, and the police "were driven away that night, but returned each night following to try and take back the venue and street . . . The riots lasted six days." The Stonewall riot, named after the bar, "turned out to be the birth of a movement," according to the *Washington Examiner*. The paper noted that "on the one-year anniversary [of the riots] the first gay pride parades were held in cities around the country." Andrew Kopkind, writing for the *Nation*, described the event as "a transformative moment of liberation, not only for homosexuals, who were the street fighters, but for the entire sexual culture, which broke out of confinement that night as surely as gay people emerged from the closet."

But it was Harry Hay who first opened the conversation. In 1948 Hay tried to organize a group of homosexual men to support the presidential campaign of the Progressive Party nominee Henry Wallace. Hay saw the potential for the Progressive Party to add a gay rights plan to their platform. Hay's group was tentatively named Bachelors for Wallace, and later referred to as Bachelors Anonymous—whose name drew on the confidentiality of Alcoholics Anonymous. Unfortunately for Hay, he never signed up members or held a meeting. There was too much risk of being fired or sent to jail for most gay people to sign their name to a check for a gay rights group or attend a rally that identified their sexual orientation. But that initial, small organizing effort led Hay to write a declaration, or "The Call," for homosexuals to begin political organizing beyond the presidential campaign to promote their interests. He wanted a political agenda "devoted to the protection and improvement of Society's Androgynous Minority."

"The Call" began circulating as a defiant declaration that men who preferred sex with men deserved to be treated as a respected minority group. Much of the thinking was based on Hay's experience with the Communist Party. An actor and screenwriter, he joined the U.S. Communist Party in 1934. The group strongly disapproved of homosexuals, claiming they were evidence of the bourgeois excess in a capitalistic society still struggling with the Great Depression. To fit in with the communists Hay married a fellow female party member and eventually adopted two girls. But he later said sexual experiences with other boys, beginning at age nine, led him to constantly have extramarital affairs with men. He had been having sex with men at Stanford, where he studied political science and history, before dropping out due to illness. He went to live with his parents in Los Angeles and worked various jobs in the film industry. The work brought him into leftist union activities. By 1937 he was known to the FBI as a leading communist in Los Angeles and he openly taught classes on Marxism while participating in public protests against the threat to Russia posed by Nazi Germany's rise in Europe. Hollywood, he discovered, also had an active if secret homosexual scene.

In 1950, two years after first typing and circulating "The Call," Hay found financial support for the idea of a political organization of gay men from a lover, Hollywood costume designer Rudy Gernreich.

"First, 'The Call' took two years for Harry to circulate [and] for one single other person [to] agree to come to a meeting," said Hay biographer Stuart Timmons in a 2002 NPR interview. "And after he found that single other person in July of 1950, it took several more months for the two of them, talking to hundreds and hundreds of gay men in Los Angeles, and lesbians, to find five other people with which to have a meeting. They had that meeting in November of 1950, and officially formed [the organization later known as] the Mattachine Society."

The name "Mattachine" came from a secret society of men in medieval France who danced through the streets in colorful costumes and masks, performing mocking skits about the powerful French king and royal court. In a 1976 interview with historian Jonathan Ned Katz, Hay described how this medieval group "received the brunt of a given lord's vicious retaliation. So we took the name Mattachine because we felt that we 1950s gays were also a masked people, unknown and anonymous, who might become engaged in morale building and helping ourselves and others . . . to move toward redress and change."

Fear of being publicly ridiculed, blackballed from jobs, losing professional licenses as doctors and stockbrokers, and being prosecuted led the men to originally call the group the "Society of Fools."

Initially, Hay and Gernreich joined with three other men in Los Angeles to discuss organizing along the lines of communist activists. Hay wanted a visible, defiant, proud group willing to publicly defend the rights of homosexuals. He believed that homosexuals in the United States had many of the unifying traits that Joseph Stalin used to characterize a "nation" in his famous 1913 text *Marxism and the National Question:* a common psychology, language, and culture.

In California, the fear of gay persecution was very real. In 1949 Earl Warren, California's governor, pushed the legislature to increase jail time for sodomy and made loitering around a public toilet—an occasional meeting place for socially alienated homosexuals—into a criminal act. Historian David Carter notes in a book on the history of gay rights that "at California's Atascadero State Hospital, known soon after its opening as 'Dachau for Queers,' men convicted of consensual sodomy were, as authorized by a 1941 law, given electrical and pharmacological shock therapy, castrated and lobotomized."

Facing that threatening political reality, Hay remained a solitary, defiant driving force for gay rights, the political agitator and angry heart behind the organizing drive. "Harry was a very aggressive and annoying person," said Jon Marans, who wrote a play about the early days of the Mattachine Society called *The Temperamentals.* "The only reason the Mattachine Society ever happened was because he fell in love with Rudy Gernreich," according to Marans. "Rudy was the opposite of Harry. He could charm the pants off anybody. He had that delicious quality about him and everybody liked being around him."

Hay took an unprecedented step when he testified at a hearing on charges of police brutality against the Hispanic community in Los Angeles. Homosexuals had a long history of being harassed by the police. Hay did not speak as a homosexual. He appeared as a community activist charging that the police were too quick to use violence; they were, he claimed, a group of thugs with badges acting without regard for the rights of citizens. Two years later, in 1952, one of the Mattachine Society's founding members, Dale Jennings, was arrested for "lewd" behavior in a city park. At that point Hay and the other members of the group saw the opportunity to make a political statement about the rights of gay people. They hired a radical lawyer to defend Jennings on the grounds that he was a homosexual and his public display of affection for another man did not amount to lewd behavior.

The defense was explosive; it had never been argued that homosexual behavior was normal behavior. In post–World War II America the police equated any show of same-sex interest with lewd behavior; most of the public saw it as immoral. In preparation for the Jennings trial, the Mattachines, seeking to maintain the secrecy of their society, created a front group, the Citizens Committee to Outlaw Entrapment, through their newly established nonprofit organization the Mattachine Foundation. The L.A. newspapers, recognizing the society as a group of homosexuals, refused to write stories about the organization. Hay was infuriated and went back to his typewriter to write a series of flyers that the Mattachines circulated at gay beaches, at gay bars, and among gays working in Hollywood. Hay was not coy in these pamphlets. These pamphlets said that the trial was a violation of the constitutional rights of homosexual men as citizens of the United States. The trial lasted for ten days. When the jury got stuck in a deadlock over whether Jennings should be acquitted, the prosecutor, frustrated that such a trivial case was costing so much time and money, asked the judge to throw away the case.

The surprising victory made the Mattachines a sudden sensation in the small, whispered world of homosexuals. Gay men suddenly wanted to be a part of the group. Mattachine discussion groups attracting dozens of men popped up around Southern California. The Mattachine Foundation, the group's nonprofit organization, received financial backing from pastors and professors, and sent letters to political candidates urging them to speak against gay harassment.

The Mattachines also started a magazine, the nation's first gay publication, called *ONE*. The magazine later made national news when the U.S. Post Office confiscated an issue that featured a bawdy poem satirizing a British sex scandal. In response, the Mattachines went to court to dispute the post office claim that the magazine contained "obscenity." The appeal failed when the court ruled that only the Mattachines regarded the material as not obscene because "their own social or moral standards are far below those of the general community." It would take repeated appeals until the Supreme Court ruled in 1958 that the magazine had the First Amendment right to publish the poem. Despite the initial legal defeat, the Mattachines' reputation for activism grew among gays.

In April 1953 a hundred men gathered for the first national gay rights meeting in the United States. In California alone, the Mattachine Society now had two thousand members. Yet Hay's leadership became an issue when, a month before the meeting, L.A. journalist Paul V. Coates revealed that the Mattachines' lawyer, Fred M. Snyder, had been "an unfriendly witness at the [House] Un-American Activities hearings." The implication was that the Mattachines were a communist organization, especially considering the fact that Harry Hay, its founder, was a member of the Communist Party. The people newly attracted to the group had no particular loyalty to Hay, nor did the newcomers like the Marxist and conspiratorial feel of the organization. While the Mattachines' founders hoped gays would band together to form an insular fraternity, a "homosexual minority," the newcomers wanted to fight for public acceptance and integration into mainstream society. Thus Hay was pressured to resign. After his departure, the group changed its constitution to require members to state their loyalty to the United States, and it was no longer active in politics. Instead the new leadership called for apolitical, mainstream acceptance of gays.

Hay did not fight being pushed out. He thought he could start a new, more militant gay group. But again he was hamstrung by his history of working with the Communist Party. Hay was called before a panel of the House Un-American Activities Committee in 1955 looking into Communist Party subversion in California. The usually combative Hay was boxed in by his concern that he would hurt the Communist Party if his homosexuality was used to discredit him. The Cold War with Russia and the fear of nuclear attack created an anti-communist fervor that dominated American politics during the 1950s. Playing on the term "Red Scare" in reference to rampant fear of communist infiltration, some commentators dubbed the combination of homophobia and anti-communism as "The Lavender Scare." J. Edgar Hoover's FBI hunted gays on the theory that people with a secret sex life were vulnerable to being blackmailed by communists. President Eisenhower authorized the firing of gay federal employees as a security risk, and the State Department made a public show of firing gay employees. A rough draft of the 1952 McCarran Walter Act actually blocked "homosexuals and sex perverts" from entering the United States. Though the final bill used the word "psychopathic personalities" instead of "homosexuals," the Senate Judiciary Committee noted that the "change of nomenclature is not to be construed in any way as modifying the intent to exclude all aliens who are sexual deviates."

An appearance before congressional investigators held significant risk for Hay, the communists, and the Mattachine Society. So he refused to testify. It was a potentially explosive situation, but Congress defused it when it decided not to call him. "The committee [ultimately] considered him insignificant and he was dismissed," according to the Associated Press.

Bereft at having cut his ties to the Mattachine Society, and no longer involved with the Communist Party, Hay invested his energy into becoming a flamboyant gay figure doing bookstore lectures on homosexuality. Reflecting the growing cultural rebellion of the late 1950s and '60s, he began wearing skirts and women's jewelry in public because "I never again wanted to be mistaken for a hetero." He went through several gay relationships before falling in love with a gay man who manufactured kaleidoscopes, and helped to run his factory. At one point he tried to pull together a social group of gay men—still arguing that homosexuals should stand together as a minority group deserving of rights—but it never took hold. Later he tried to rally support for allowing gays to enlist in the military. His argument was probably influenced by the fact that five thousand soldiers and four thousand sailors were forced out of the ranks on Section 8 discharges during World War II. Those men lost rights to the generous benefits given returning veterans under the G.I. Bill, including help with education, mortgages, and medical care. Even with a booming economy, employers who saw their military record began asking uncomfortable questions. But Hay again failed to gain traction for this new movement. Even among gays, it was a hard sell to suggest the military world was ready to embrace gays.

Gay life in the United States grew even as gay political activism stalled. The first lesbian organization, the Daughters of Bilitis, was formed in 1955. At first a purely social network, the group began holding book club meetings and soon became public as a political voice for lesbians, particularly on the issue of child custody. Women who left their husbands for women regularly lost custody of their children, as judges viewed their sexual behavior as immoral, creating an unfit environment for raising children.

Academic work on human sexuality in the postwar period opened the way for increased acceptance of homosexuality. In 1948 sex researcher Alfred Kinsey published a study that found "37 percent of all males had some form of homosexual contact between their teen years and old age; 50 percent of males who remained single until the age of 35 had overt homosexual experience to orgasm." The Kinsey Report shifted psychiatric views on homosexual behavior. If more than a third of men had some homosexual activity in their life, psychiatrists reasoned, perhaps homosexuality was better classified as a phase, a point in the sexual experience of a good number of American men, than as a perversion.

American culture also shifted. Gay magazines, under the category of "beefcake" or weight-lifting magazines, began to circulate more freely. Once confiscated by the post office as pornography, magazines in the sports category found a legally protected niche even as they continued to feature pictures of muscular men wearing tight, bulging briefs. The magazines affirmed the gay life by including letters of support for men who admired men. One letter writer said bluntly: "I know I am not alone in my beliefs." Another wrote: "You know you are doing a wonderful job in uniting young men from all over the world who share a common interest." Containing ads for gay clubs, gay-themed movies, and clothing, these publications also helped create a new gay "consumer culture" in the United States, writes historian Michael Bronski, citing an argument made by historian David K. Johnson. A magazine for lesbians, titled *Vice Versa*, had been circulated in California since 1947.

Major metropolitan areas saw a surge in gay bars, restaurants, bookstores, and nightclubs that featured cross-dressing dancers and singers. The scene became part of the growing counterculture. Early-twentieth-century anti-gay civic groups that encouraged police to crack down on men loitering in public restrooms as well as men dressing in women's clothes all seemed distant, oppressive artifacts of American history, far out of sync with the sexual liberation of the 1960s. Nightclub operators cut deals with police, and the bribes allowed a renaissance of gay public life.

The "down-low" payoffs between gays and the police, of course, could not stop all the raids. Some police did not take the bribes; some wanted more money. Criminals, including Mafia gangs, found operating the clubs a quick route to blackmailing gay businessmen for a steady stream of money. The haunting fear of being uncovered or "outed" kept most gay life relegated to an illicit, edgy subculture.

Then, on June 28, 1969, the gay subculture erupted in a riot. In the heat of that summer night, at about 1:20 a.m., the police raided the Stonewall Inn, a well-known gay bar in Manhattan's Greenwich Village. News reports described it as a "known mafia-run underground bar." The club's closed door opened only to people known to the muscular security men looking through the peephole. The police targeted the bar that night because of complaints from a Wall Street stock-trading house that its gay stock traders were being blackmailed after visiting Stonewall, possibly by mobsters hired by rival Wall Street firms. But the people in the bar did not know that. The cross-dressers, lesbians, after-work suit-and-tie crowd, preppy guys in tight tennis shorts, and tough guys in leather, saw the eight policemen entering and turning up the lights as one more humiliation.

Later investigations confirmed that individual cops extorting bribes from gays—sometimes after pressuring them to perform sex acts—was a leading cause of police corruption in the city. And it was not taking place just in New York City. In 1969 most states considered consensual gay sex a major crime. During the 1950s, more than two hundred arrests were made per month in Philadelphia on morals charges that resulted in names being printed in the newspaper, loss of jobs, and public ridicule. In New Jersey, half of the people in jail for sex crimes at the time were gays prosecuted for consensual homosexual acts. In

Indiana, a quarter of the people designated as sexual psychopaths had been arrested for consensual sodomy among adults. In Ohio, being arrested and charged with a gay sex crime often meant jail time and being forced to take heavy doses of antidepressants.

The official reason listed on the warrant for police action at Stonewall was to halt the sale of alcohol without a license. It began as a "routine raid," writes Michael Bronski. But this time the bar's patrons were fed up with the manhandling, discrimination, and shame. In the words of one activist whose story historian Martin Duberman tells in a book called *Stonewall*: "You could feel the electricity going through people" as they collected on the street. "You could actually feel it. People were getting really, really pissed." Accounts differ as to what in particular caused things to escalate from there. But it is clear that as insults were thrown and objects were hurled at the police, the mob grew angrier and more energized. It was such pandemonium that, at one point, the cops were forced to take cover inside the bar. In need of reinforcements, they called in the Tactical Patrol Force, a special squad created to help subdue urban and antiwar protests.

The *New York Times* reported the next day that police threw two hundred people out of the Stonewall Inn, and as the raid was in progress, another two hundred people arrived on the scene to fight with the gays against the police. The paper described the scene as a "rampage."

The Associated Press later reported that one Stonewall customer, Raymond Castro, described the people being rousted from the bar and the crowd outside as a mix. "It wasn't just gays," he told the wire service. "It wasn't just white gays. You had straight people sympathetic to gays. People of the arts. You had people who had had enough (of the police). You had Latinos, you had blacks, you had whites, Chinese, you had everything. It was a melting pot. Young, old. Fems, butches."

The weekend of rioting by gay people stretched into the next week. It was a shock to the public even in an era of race riots, violent protests against the Vietnam War, and the assassinations of Martin Luther King Jr., John F. Kennedy, and Robert F. Kennedy. Gay people had never shown such open contempt and anger at the social rules and the laws that confined them, requiring them to acquiesce to life in hidden places.

"Michael Fader, a club patron, was present that night and later recalled, 'We felt that we had freedom at last, or freedom to at least show that we demanded freedom,'" the Massachusetts Air Force base reported. "'We weren't going to be walking meekly in the night and letting them shove us around—it's like standing your ground for the first time and in a really strong way, and that's what caught the police by surprise. There was something in the air, freedom a long time overdue ... [T]he bottom line was we weren't going to go away. And we didn't.'"

Martin Duberman, in his book *Cures: A Gay Man's Odyssey,* wrote that Stonewall marked the beginning of a new era in gay rights. "And almost immediately after the Stonewall riot, a movement did emerge, substantially different from the one that had preceded it." Suddenly civil rights protests and antiwar protests included people demanding gay rights, too. Only a month after the riot a national, proudly gay civil rights group suddenly appeared—the Gay Liberation Front. It published a newspaper called *Come Out!* The paper editorialized for bars to end rules against homosexuals holding hands and kissing. It also led to gays taking their fight to a new level by publicly challenging the Catholic Church for its use of the Bible to legitimize the condemnation of gay life. Other gay rights groups—some with more or less confrontational styles—emerged in the next few years. The new and very public groups included the Gay Activists Alliance, the National Gay and Lesbian Task Force, and the Human Rights Campaign.

Andrew Kopkind, a liberal commentator writing in the *Nation,* described the surge of activism as the result of a convergence of a "most magical" series of political and cultural shifts triggered by Stonewall. "Somewhere in the existential depths of that brawl of screaming transvestites," Kopkind wrote, "were all the freedom rides, the anti-war marches, the sit-ins, the smoke-ins, the be-ins, the consciousness-raising, the bra-burning, the levitation of the Pentagon ... the years of gay men and lesbians locking themselves inside windowless, unnamed bars; writing dangerous, anonymous novels and articles; lying about their identity to their families, their bosses, the military; suffering silently when they were found out; hiding and seeking and winking at each other ... It's absolutely astonishing to think that on one early summer's night in New York that world ended, and a new one began."

Almost immediately after Stonewall new language and a new attitude about homosexuality entered into American newspapers and political debate. One of the most enduring changes caused by the riot was the rise of the term "gay pride." One year after the riot the first gay pride parades took place in New York, as well as Los Angeles, San Francisco, and Chicago. The Gay Liberation Front, the first of the activist groups formed after Stonewall, was poorly organized and lasted only until 1972. But the Gay Activists Alliance proved to have staying power by focusing on the specific challenge of getting rid of laws against homosexual behavior. That goal fit with the shifting perception of homosexuals from perverts to an oppressed group now standing up for their rights. Everyday Americans got to see gays as strong men rather than scared people living in the dark and demeaned as "pansies" for remaining silent in the face of insults and discrimination. The Alliance became well known for conducting "zaps," noisy demonstrations by gays drawing political and media attention to bias against gays, such as the sign outside a Los Angeles bar that said: "Faggots Keep Out." They held a "zap" against the officials of the New York City Marriage License Bureau for refusing to grant marriage licenses to gay couples.

Five years after Stonewall the first openly gay person was elected to a state legislature: Elaine Noble in Massachusetts. Seven years after Stonewall the Carter administration invited a delegation of gay activists to the White House to discuss the conflict between constitutional guarantees of equal rights and bias against gays in the military, bias in immigration law, and abuse of gays in federal prisons. By 1979 thirty-five states, including New York, California, Illinois, and other states with major gay populations, had reacted to political pressure from gays by decriminalizing consensual sodomy.

The medical community's psychiatric assessment of homosexuality also began a public shift. The earlier consensus among medical experts was that gays suffered from a "neurotic condition," a disease that caused people to engage in "pathological" behavior. That diagnosis, deeply stigmatizing, was now subject to debate. The National Institute of Mental Health issued a report in 1969 that said homosexuality was not a disease but a social issue. That fit with the Kinsey Report's finding that a third of men had homosexual experiences during their lifetime. Such a high percentage gave support to the position that gay behavior was not fairly described as aberrant or deviant sexual activity. The steady shift in medical opinion on homosexual behavior reached a crescendo in 1974, when the American Psychiatric Association removed homosexuality from its list of mental illnesses.

The national conversation about accepting gays as citizens with constitutional rights and protections got a collateral boost with the advance of birth control after the Food and Drug Administration approved the birth control pill in the 1960s. Previously, critics of homosexuality argued that same-sex activity was corrupt and immoral because it was only about personal pleasure and lacked the potential to create life. The widespread use of the birth control pill by the 1970s weakened the argument that sex for pure pleasure and with no tie to reproduction was wrong. So, too, did the decline in marriage among heterosexuals, as more people preferred to live together before or maintain a relationship outside of marriage.

The rapid strides made by gay activists in the 1970s led to a backlash from the church and social conservatives. The Roman Catholic Church, the Southern Baptist Convention, and black Baptist churches lent support to what the press described as a movement to support "traditional family values." They stood against sex education in school as inappropriate, arguing that it was best done by parents. They also opposed the increasing number of people living together without marrying. But their major fight was to stop abortion and condemn homosexuality as contrary to Christianity and God's word in the Bible.

The movement found a charismatic leader in a former Miss America, the well-known singer Anita Bryant. She became the face of the anti-gay movement when she testified in opposition to a bill banning employment discrimination in the Miami–Dade County area on the basis of sexual orientation. When she spoke at a public hearing in 1977 she was joined by hundreds of supporters, including priests, who carried signs reading "God Says No!" and "Don't Legitimate Immorality for Dade County." Her effort failed, as the new law banning employment bias took effect. But she continued to fight with a national campaign called "Save Our Children." She argued that "as a mother I know that homosexuals cannot biologically reproduce children; therefore they must recruit our children." Bryant pushed for a public referendum that led the county to change its position and allow employers to once again cite gay sexual behavior as a legal basis for refusing to hire gays.

She did not stop in Florida but traveled around the country preaching the evils of gay rights. She succeeded in repealing gay rights laws through voter referenda stirred by her grassroots appeal in places such as St. Paul, Minnesota, and Eugene, Oregon.

But in 1978 Bryant's crusade in the name of protecting the heterosexual family began to come apart when in an interview she made confused comments about people performing homosexual acts not being homosexuals. "Look, what I'm saying is that people experiment . . . it doesn't mean they are practicing homosexuals for life." She described her own difficult marriage, and when it came to sex between men and women it became evident that she lacked clear standards for what was normal behavior. Even if Bryant's husband asked her to do something she disagreed with, Bryant said: "Biblically I would submit, yes." The interviewer concluded that Bryant is "a confection of contradictions: pristine nun and gamy tease . . . Independent spirit, cowering wife . . . She is a demonstrably intelligent woman who stays steadfastly ignorant."

The interview fueled a backlash that hurt her financially. Bryant's main income came from her work as the pretty, happy, singing face of television advertising for the Florida Citrus Commission. When gay activists began a national boycott of orange juice, it posed a direct threat to her biggest paycheck. Instead of Screwdrivers, a mixed drink made of vodka and orange juice, gay bars served a drink called the "Anita Bryant," made with vodka and apple juice. As sales dropped, the orange juice companies ended their contract with her. She took more criticism, this time from allies opposed to homosexuality, when her marriage ended in divorce shortly after the interview. That turned religious fundamentalists against her because they opposed divorce. As Bryant's public image became strained, her once confident stand against gay life faltered. Other social conservative and religious groups stepped in to continue the anti-gay effort, notably the high-profile television personality Rev. Jerry Falwell and his Moral Majority.

In a country founded by Puritans who shushed any talk of sex, especially same-sex activity, the emerging, defiant gay insistence on equal rights under law forced an intense ideological split. It sparked a cultural and sociological debate that made its way to the cover of major magazines, onto television news programs, and into political campaigns—

"Should gays be allowed to join the military?" and "Do you favor equal rights for gays?" Meanwhile, as conservative politicians did their best to put gay people back in the closet, gay men were creating a new public culture based on the idea that they no longer had to hide their desires. They called it Bathhouse Culture—in Ancient Greece and Rome, bathhouses were social centers where straight men bathed, socialized, and conducted business. But in the 1920s and 1930s, America saw its first bathhouses gain a reputation as places where gay men could secretly have sex with one another. As consensual sodomy laws began to loosen in the 1970s, gay bathhouses became common in major American cities as settings for anonymous sex. Some of them were famous places, such as the Everard Baths in Manhattan, the Ritch Street Health Club in San Francisco, and the Compound in L.A. The clubs were located in out-of-the-way neighborhoods, tucked behind black metal doors, featuring bars, as well as saunas and private party spaces, where gay men could socialize, dance, parade, and have sex with each other. It was not uncommon for a bathhouse patron to have anonymous sex with three people per visit, according to David Barlow, a professor of psychology at Boston University.

To some conservative critics, the newly brazen gay culture confirmed negative stereotypes of gays as sexually out-of-control and lacking morals. But that's not how gay leaders understood what was going on. They refused to apologize. Instead, they spoke of gay pride after years of having been forced to hide their sexuality. According to Samuel Delaney, a gay African American novelist and cultural critic, the bathhouses taught him that "there was a population—not of individual homosexuals . . . not of hundreds, not of thousands, but rather of millions of gay men, and that history had, actively and already, created for us whole galleries of institutions, good and bad, to accommodate our sex." He felt a "sense of political power."

But then, suddenly, the party ended when, in the early 1980s, gay men around the country started to catch this strange, unheard-of disease that would eventually be called AIDS. Over the next thirty years a half million people would die of the disease that was a toxic combination of cancer, pneumonia, and a weak immune system. Labeled HIV-AIDS in 1982, the disease was mostly found in the gay community.

The nasty politics of the debate over acceptance of gays as deserving of constitutional rights led some critics to derisively call the illness "The Gay Plague." They tied the spread of AIDS to promiscuity among gays, such as public acceptance of the popular bathhouses, where anonymous men went to have sex with strangers.

"AIDS is nature's retribution for violating the laws of nature," said Patrick Buchanan, the popular conservative columnist and former aide to President Nixon, on his syndicated radio show in advance of his run for the GOP presidential nomination in 1992. With comparable ferocity, Jerry Falwell said, "AIDS is not just God's punishment for homosexuals. It is God's punishment for the society that tolerates homosexuals." In 1984 the American Family Association, a fundamentalist Christian nonprofit, sent a letter to its members explaining that "since AIDS is transmitted primarily by perverse homosexuals, your name on my national petition to quarantine all homosexual establishments is crucial to your family's health and security." Several states followed the advice of these conservative leaders and organizations, passing laws forbidding people with the disease from buying insurance, purchasing homes, or attending school.

To gay leaders it seemed that more than the far right was turning their backs on them; the whole country was afraid of AIDS and shunned gays as the group most associated with the disease. Massive cuts to the federal budget in the 1980s sliced funding for the Centers for Disease Control and Prevention just as it was trying to cope with AIDS. President Reagan did not mention the word "AIDS" until 1987. So when gay activists protested in the 1980s, they were fighting for more than equality and recognition. They were fighting for their lives. The new group ACT UP (AIDS Coalition to Unleash Power) typified this new style of protest. They pressured the federal government to fund more research into a cure for AIDS with protests at the Food and Drug Administration headquarters in Washington, D.C., and later on, the White House. Many of the protesters had been diagnosed with AIDS; they had nothing left to lose, so they went for shock value. In December 1989 an estimated 4,500 people demonstrated outside of St. Patrick's Cathedral in New York to protest Cardinal John O'Connor's stand against the government providing condoms as protection against

AIDS. They had some success: by the late 1980s the surgeon general's office had published and distributed over a hundred million copies of a pamphlet called "Understanding AIDS."

The deaths of so many people, both gays and people who got the disease by sharing needles, via blood transfusions, or through heterosexual sex with an infected person, led to widespread grief and sympathy from people outside the gay community. Popular culture began to reflect the power of the emotional pain felt by families and friends of people with the disease, whether they were gay or not. A Pulitzer Prize–winning play about the torment caused by AIDS, *Angels in America* by Tony Kushner, made its debut in 1992. A year later, two of Hollywood's biggest stars, Tom Hanks and Denzel Washington, appeared in a hit movie, *Philadelphia,* about a courageous gay lawyer who goes to court to fight being fired from his firm because he is suffering with AIDS.

As American culture began to shift toward accepting openly gay people, one towering pillar of opposition to legal protections for gay rights remained in the alliance of the political and religious right. Political conservatives and religious fundamentalists often lumped gay rights, abortion rights, drug use, pornography, and premarital sex together, claiming that these behaviors were the consequence of liberal excess and were harming the nation. They derided gays as a threat to family life, to children, and to the moral strength needed to defend America's democratic ideals.

But a Herculean effort to topple the opposition to gay rights came from a surprising source. Barry Goldwater, a former Arizona senator, a well-known conservative, and former GOP nominee in 1964, began speaking out for gay rights. His fierce support made national news. Part of his motivation appeared to be that his grandson and a grandniece were gay. His grandson was also HIV positive. But that did not lessen the stunning political impact of Goldwater's decision to become a battering ram for gay rights, clearing the way for conservatives to embrace gay rights by publicly facing down the movement's right-wing opposition.

No one questioned Goldwater's conservative credentials. He was the same defiant Republican who had opposed President Franklin Roosevelt's New Deal as a threat to free market capitalism. Elected to the U.S. Senate in 1952, Goldwater even criticized President Eisenhower, a fellow Republican, as an elitist for failing to uphold conservative principles because he had expanded Social Security, built the federal interstate highway system, and pumped up the size of government with higher federal spending. Goldwater was the Western conservative lion who deified the East Coast business-class Republicans, roaring into political battle against labor unions and big-government Democrats in Washington. He defiantly supported right-to-work laws intended to limit the power of union organizers, and led a sensational Senate investigation of top union leader Walter Reuther.

Throughout his political career, Goldwater opposed people he called "powercrats" who thought they knew what was best for every American and who wanted every American indebted to big government. Goldwater identified the roots of his conservative vision for America in Thomas Jefferson's advocacy for smaller, limited government that deferred to the rights of individual citizens. He opposed the 1964 Civil Rights Act to increase enforcement of constitutional rights for black Americans, claiming it led to government interference in the personal decisions of individual citizens. Though he lost badly to President Johnson in the 1964 election, most historians view Goldwater's campaign as the beginning of the modern conservative movement. He was the first Republican to win the Deep South and its large working-class white population since Reconstruction. In 1980, Ronald Reagan relied on that base to carry him to the White House. So it was a political stunner that Goldwater had a different take on gay rights.

Goldwater's political coming-out in support of gay rights began in the early 1990s. After speaking in favor of a 1992 Phoenix, Arizona, gay-rights ordinance, he announced that he favored full rights for gays in the military. Goldwater, a pilot who had served with the Army Air Corps in World War II and founded the Arizona Air National Guard, denounced the military's "don't ask, don't tell" policy, put into place by President Clinton as a compromise that allowed gays to serve as long as they did not disclose that they were gay. Goldwater said that Clinton's political compromise lacked relevance to the real issue: the legal right of capable, willing citizens of any sexual orientation to do any job, including jobs in the military. "Having spent 37 years of my life in the military as a reservist, and never having met a gay in all that time, and never having even talked about it all those years, I just thought 'Why the hell shouldn't they serve? They're American citizens,'" Goldwater told the *Washington Post* in 1994. In a 1993 letter to the paper, Goldwater wrote that "You don't need to be 'straight' to die for your country. You just need to shoot straight."

In a 1994 newspaper column the senator wrote: "It is time America realized that there is no gay exemption in the right to 'Life, Liberty and the Pursuit of Happiness' in the Declaration of Independence." Looking to the nation's past in support of giving full citizenship rights to gays, he was quoted in a 1995 magazine as asking: "Are gays a new phenomenon in the Nineties? Do you think none existed in the Forties, Fifties, Sixties? There have been gay people in the military since the Pilgrims landed. There were probably some gay Indians on the shore waiting to greet them."

Speaking to the U.S. Senate in support of his brand of Republican politics years before he began supporting gay rights, the senator described himself as a man who "spent quite a number of years carrying the flag of the 'Old Conservatism.'" Then he scolded the religious right for taking positions based on "religious issues" that "have little or nothing to do with conservative . . . politics."

"Being a conservative in America traditionally has meant that one holds a deep, abiding respect for the Constitution," he explained to the Senate. "We conservatives believe sincerely in the integrity of the Constitution. We treasure the freedoms that document protects. . . . By maintaining the separation of church and state, the United States has avoided the intolerance which has so divided the rest of the world with religious wars . . . Can any of us refute the wisdom of Madison and the other framers?"

Goldwater later told an interviewer he had always supported equal rights for gays and "I haven't changed my outlook at all." As for his fellow conservatives in the religious right basing their opposition to gay rights on their personal interpretation of the Bible, Goldwater found the argument weak.

"You don't have to agree with it [gay sexual behavior]," Goldwater told the *Post* in his 1994 interview, "but they have a constitutional right to be gay. And that's what brings me into it." He explained that as a lifelong conservative, he believed the government had no legal basis to inhibit the personal liberty implicit in sexual preferences. To Goldwater it was a matter of the individual's right as a citizen with no regard for religious principles. He later said flatly, "Politics has no business in the bedroom . . . and that goes for pursuit of a career in the military, the corporate world, or even the White House."

When he returned to Phoenix, the senator opposed a proposed city council law that would have allowed local businesses to discriminate on the basis of sexual orientation by refusing to hire gays. And Goldwater took his fight for gay rights beyond interviews when he became honorary co-chair of Americans Against Discrimination. The Human Rights Campaign Fund created the group, whose goal was to pass federal legislation protecting homosexuals from job discrimination.

Goldwater's stand for gay rights was the first crack in the foundation of right-wing opposition to gay rights. The *Miami Herald,* in a 1994 editorial, mirrored Goldwater's libertarian stand for individual rights. On the twenty-fifth anniversary of the Stonewall riot, the Florida paper described that event as "the equivalent of the Boston Tea Party" and as an affirmation for every "fed-up human being weary of defending their privacy against the organized wrath of a puritanical state." The *Herald*'s support for protecting the constitutional rights of gay people seemed to accept Goldwater's libertarian logic: equal rights for homosexuals was important to "every snooped-on, preached-at, hectored, harassed and vilified American who in any way ruffles the finishing-school sensibilities of the powerful. In post-Stonewall America, the government may not decide with whom you can dance—you cannot be told whom to love."

Goldwater died in 1998 at the age of eighty-nine. But his example lived on, as leading Republican figures from Vice President Dick Cheney to Senator Rob Portman (R.-Ohio) have followed in his footsteps to become advocates of gay rights. Both said they have gay children, and both have stood up to support equal legal rights and protections for homosexuals.

By 2013 the Supreme Court seemed to pick up on Goldwater's thinking about gay rights. The Court ruled that constitutional protections for equal rights in the Fifth Amendment must apply to all Americans, including gays, and it struck down a federal law, the 1996 Defense of Marriage Act, that denied federal benefits to same-sex couples. To refuse such benefits to any American, including gays, Justice Anthony

Kennedy wrote, would be a "deprivation of the liberty" promised to all Americans by the original Founding Fathers and would undermine the idea of a nation of law that promises equal rights to all.

As of 2010, when the military repealed its 1994 "Don't Ask, Don't Tell" policy, a *Washington Post*/ABC News poll reported that almost 80 percent of Americans supported the idea of homosexuals being able to serve openly in the military. Goldwater's position on gay rights also reflected the American public's experience. "In 1999, only 39 percent of Americans said they had a friend, family member or colleague who was gay," wrote Gabriel Arana in *Salon* in 2014. "Today that number has jumped to over 70 percent. Once you know a gay person, support for gay rights becomes a foregone conclusion." And in 2015 the Supreme Court ruled by a 5–4 majority that same-sex couples have the right to marry, regardless of the state they live in.

From Harry Hay to the riot at New York's Stonewall Inn, from Barry Goldwater's brand of politically conservative support for gay rights to the Supreme Court's 2015 ruling on same-sex marriage, America's twenty-first-century attitude toward human sexual behavior is now well past the bounds of law, culture, and religion known to the original Founding Fathers. Perhaps their heads would spin to see what has come to be in the nation they founded long ago. But I believe they would recognize the spark of the revolution they set in motion: people seeking freedom and individual rights.

The Stonewall rioters and other gay rights activists changed the nation by fighting for independence and liberty. At the Stonewall Inn there may not have been a George Washington, but the bar patrons who fought against police to assert their rights set in motion a similar revolution.

CHAPTER 15

BACK TO THE FUTURE

Ronald Reagan, Ed Meese,
and the Remaking of the Judicial System

President Reagan loved the Founding Fathers.

America is best, he often said, when it gets back to basics, back to the Founders' vision, back to their original constitutional framework. In Reagan's most famous speech, given in 1964 in support of GOP presidential candidate Barry Goldwater, he asked Americans if "we still know the freedoms that were intended for us by the Founding Fathers." He asked if today's citizens wanted to "abandon the American revolution" and the Founding Fathers by giving power to control life to "a little intellectual elite in a far-distant capitol" who say they "can plan our lives for us better than we can plan them ourselves."

The most concrete expression of Reagan's belief in the Founding Fathers was his opposition to "activist" federal judges who moved away from "constitutional vigor," a strict application of the law as written in the Constitution. Like President Jefferson, President Reagan wanted to limit the powers of the courts by having judges strictly adhere to the exact language of the Constitution. Jefferson even started a political party based, in part, on calls to limit U.S. courts to issuing decisions only within a strict interpretation of the Constitution.

President Reagan frequently called out the names of several of the original Founding Fathers to rally patriotic feelings. He spoke of their willingness to fight a revolution to declare their independence of big government control. As a reporter, I saw him bring audiences nation-wide to their feet when he spoke about the Founders' belief in America's exceptional role as a "shining city on a hill," with fiercely protected individual rights set in stone by the Constitution. The day before he won the presidential election in 1980 Reagan made two major pledges to his supporters: to cut taxes, and to return America to "the standards of decency and excellence envisioned by the Founding Fathers."

So it was no surprise to me when President Reagan alluded to the Founding Fathers near the start of an exclusive 1984 interview with me and two other journalists, saying he felt a "growing hunger in our land for what I called a spiritual revival . . . people with a belief in themselves and in our country, a belief in our institutions."

At the end of the interview I tried to push the president off his well-practiced answers to political questions by presenting him with a question that would have made no sense to the original Founding Fathers. I asked him if there was any role for the federal government "to bring about equality between the races." The Founding Fathers had no concept of the federal government playing a role in limiting racial discrimination, because blacks in Colonial times were slaves. The Supreme Court, in the 1896 case *Plessy v. Ferguson,* ruled that the Constitution allowed for "separate but equal" treatment of blacks and whites. They found nothing in the Constitution to stop the government from treating blacks differently than whites, even as an inferior class of citizens. The Founding Fathers knew nothing about the Thirteenth Amendment (ending slavery), the Fourteenth Amendment (giving equal rights to all citizens, including blacks), or the Fifteenth Amendment (giving black men the right to vote). They had no idea about the civil rights laws of the 1960s.

President Reagan pushed right back at me, the smile on his face indicating that he welcomed the question. He said he'd lived longer than me and that he "sometimes wonder[ed] if some of you who are younger realize how far we have come, how totally different this country is than what it was then." He reminded me that when he was a sportscaster "blacks were not allowed to play in any of those games." One glance at sports on television today, he said, shows that "it's all been changed."

He went on to say it was impossible to "ever totally erase, anyplace in the world among human beings, bigotry and prejudice." So people, he said, without mentioning any role for government, have to "be alert" that "we don't fall back into any of the other patterns."

I pushed the president one more time, raising a question aimed at his tax cuts for corporations and the wealthy. Critics derided his policy as "trickle-down economics." I wanted to know what he might say about whether his economic policy was hurting young black women, one of the poorest groups of citizens in America. The question went beyond tax policy because President Reagan wanted private business to have the freedom to hire the best people without fear of government oversight based on racial or gender equality.

Here is how I put the question: If "Ronald Reagan was a young black woman, in Dixon, Illinois, today [where Reagan grew up], trying to make it in America . . . do you think that young black woman would prosper" under the president's tax and economic policies?

Reagan did not miss a beat. He responded: "Much of what we've done in our economic recovery has been more beneficial at the bottom of the economic ladder." Then he told me a story about a black woman in Chicago, just ninety miles from Dixon, who "today runs a tremendously successful multimillion-dollar advertising agency." He said reduced taxes led to lower unemployment for all, and childcare tax deductions helped working women. "I think there is greater opportunity for young people today in the country than there's been for a long, long time," he said, referring to an earlier time, before the New Deal and the beginnings of big government, when low taxes and a small federal government gave Americans wide latitude to pursue life, liberty, and happiness.

Two hundred years of changing realities in the nation did not deter the president from his conviction that the greatest opportunity for all Americans at all times is achieved when the government goes back to basics, beginning with limiting itself to its constitutional responsibilities. The "Reagan Revolution" brought conservative values and politics to new heights in American life—from cracking down on federal spending to opposition to unions and abortion rights.

But the most enduring and divisive element of the Reagan Revolution has proved to be his imprint on the federal judiciary. President Reagan's attachment to the Constitution was most evident in his selection of judges. He successfully changed the direction of legal thinking with his emphasis on judges who stuck closely to the Constitution. He wanted his Justice Department to limit its law enforcement powers to the explicit dictates of the Constitution. He wanted federal agencies limited in their regulation of business.

The man the president put in charge of bringing the courts back to the Constitution and the intent of the original Founding Fathers was Ed Meese, Reagan's longtime friend and the president's attorney general. When a reporter once questioned Meese's motives over an issue, the president responded: "If Ed Meese is not a good man, there are no good men." Meese made his legacy by putting conservative judges in place to fulfill President Reagan's conservative vision for the courts. Meese's efforts increased the political tension that continues to define the incredibly high political stakes around nominations, confirmations, and opinions coming from the nation's sharply polarized courts, including the Supreme Court.

Meese's guiding principle was President Reagan's open political condemnation of courts dominated by liberal, activist judges who gave rights and privileges to criminal convicts (by, for example, attempting to ban the death penalty) and to racial minorities (through upholding affirmative action) that were not found in the Constitution. Reagan's lament about activist judges went back to the 1960s and the conservative political crusade of 1964 GOP presidential nominee Barry Goldwater. Goldwater opposed the 1964 Civil Rights Act as unconstitutional interference in a citizen's right to freely associate and do business with people of his or her own choosing. He lost the presidential campaign, but his message took root in southern states still dealing with the Supreme Court's 1954 school desegregation ruling, *Brown vs. Board of Education.*

At the 1968 Republican convention, Richard Nixon, the party's nominee, declared that he wanted "men on the Supreme Court who are strict constitutionalists, men that interpret the law and don't try to make the law." Giving voice to conservative complaints about the Supreme Court's decision to allow racial integration of schools, Nixon said the high court is not "qualified to be a local school district and to make the decisions as your local school board." He also complained that the Supreme Court had been finding new rights for criminals and "seriously hamstringing the peace forces in our society and strengthening the criminal forces."

As governor of California and later as president, Ronald Reagan echoed Nixon's condemnation of judges who strayed from strict application of the law, particularly in sentencing criminals. Voters responded with loud applause anytime he voiced anger at judges who found new rights and privileges in the Constitution. He charged those judges with using the Constitution as a mere outline to prop up their interpretation of how the law should be shaped to fit their personal opinions and shifting views of what was right and wrong. Working from President Reagan's directive to rein in the judiciary, Attorney General Meese selected strict constructionist nominees for court openings. Meese and Reagan put more judicial appointees on the federal courts than any subsequent president over the next thirty years. Many of those judges eventually rose to become chief judges on most of the nation's federal circuit courts.

"They became the first judges in more than a half-century to say the Second Amendment protects an individual's right to own guns," wrote *USA Today*'s Joan Biskupic in a 2008 article headlined "Reagan's Influence Lives on in U.S. Courts." She added: "They took the lead in ruling against affirmative action and other race-conscious policies. And they upheld bans on an abortion procedure called 'partial-birth' before it reached the Supreme Court."

Biskupic claimed Reagan and Meese had broken with "the prior White House pattern of accepting senators' preferences for appeal court seats." Instead the Reagan team "put in place a sophisticated screening of candidates run by Department of Justice and White House lawyers." And all of their nominees had to fit into Reagan and Meese's plan for a court system with judges who believed in a strict reading of the Constitution as the basis for all decisions. Biskupic concluded that the Reagan administration's judicial selections are now among America's most powerful judges, setting the direction of the law at every level of the federal courts—district courts, appeals courts, and the Supreme Court of the United States.

Meese held to a clear standard: he wanted people who subscribed to the conservative political premise that the only legitimate function of the judiciary was to issue limited, constitutional-based rulings. One of

President Reagan's young conservative aides in the White House counsel's office, John Roberts, became chief justice of the Supreme Court. Another Reagan political appointee, Clarence Thomas, was head of the U.S. Equal Employment Opportunity Commission and was later appointed to the Supreme Court. Anthony Kennedy, the conservative swing vote, and Antonin Scalia, the nation's preeminent and voluble voice of strict constructionism, were appointed by Reagan and remain on the Court. "They became the legal vanguard of the Reagan agenda to lessen federal control—and protections—in American life," Biskupic wrote.

Legal scholar Paul Brest popularized the term "originalism" in 1980, the year Reagan became president. In an essay titled "The Misconceived Quest for the Original Understanding," Brest wrote that originalism in judicial rulings "accords binding authority to the text of the Constitution or the intentions of its adopters." In his fight against judges who saw the Constitution as a flexible "living document," Meese adopted Brest's terminology and intellectual framework as a tool to get judges to stick to the law as written by Congress. A law-and-order conservative, he wanted to stop judges from creating novel interpretations of constitutional law to create new rights and privileges for criminals, but his logic extended to limiting new legal protections for minorities, gays, women, the disabled, and other special classes of citizens. Meese looked for justices who limited themselves to searching out the intentions of the original framers of the Constitution as it was written in 1787, as well as to understand the intent of the people who wrote subsequent amendments to the Constitution.

Two decades after President Reagan left office, the proper role of the federal judiciary is still hotly debated. Should judges base their rulings on the notion of a flexible "living Constitution," or should they be strict constructionists, hewing narrowly to the words and intent of the original document?

As a result of that fierce clash of legal ideologies, the opinions of conservative judges appointed by President Reagan now "routinely draw national attention," Biskupic wrote. In 2008, when Biskupic was writing, Reagan's appointees continued to dominate the legal landscape. "Eight [Reagan-selected judges] are the chief judges of their circuit courts and in key positions on the U.S. judiciary's policymaking committee. Many are superstars of the conservative movement, appearing as speakers at meetings of the arch-conservative Federalist Society and, in past years, landing on GOP presidents' short lists for Supreme Court appointments."

Meese, the master builder who followed Reagan's design for installing those conservative judges as the cornerstones of the federal court system, was born in Oakland in 1931, in the aftershock of the Great Depression. He grew up in a middle-class home; his father worked in county government, as a court clerk, treasurer, and Alameda County's tax collector. At the age of ten Meese published his own local newspaper called the *Weekly Herald*. During his childhood Meese also earned money as a paperboy, drugstore clerk, and maintenance worker in the county park system. He was best known as the star of the Oakland High School debate team and valedictorian of the class of 1949. He later described the Oakland of his youth as "very nice," "small," and with "lots of civic spirit." By the time he left for college at Yale University after World War II, his hometown was rapidly changing, with more blacks and Latinos coming in as the economy grew after the war. The new arrivals' presence was amplified as they quickly gained power in left-leaning unions that represented workers at the docks. There was an increase in racial tension as the older, conservative white establishment was prodded by the newcomers' liberal, civil rights movement approach to local politics.

Meese later told the *Christian Science Monitor* that he had thought he was a liberal when he went east to attend Yale, but his experience at school led him to realize he was a conservative. He explained that Yale held a recruiting event to enlist new students in college political groups. "The only party whose principles I felt really comfortable with was the conservative party—that's how I learned I was a conservative," he said. "From a philosophical standpoint, the conservative's belief in the worth of the individual, in liberty and freedom and the free-market system, are the principle values that would mark me as a conservative."

The scholarship student from Oakland became president of the Yale political union, as well as heading the university's debate society. Meese then returned home to California to go to Boalt Hall law school at the University of California at Berkeley. In the middle of his law school education he left to join the army for two years, serving as an artillery

officer, before returning to earn his law degree in 1958. After gradua-
tion he took a job as deputy district attorney for Oakland. He quickly
became a star with the older established white political class in the city
when he took a hard stand against the Free Speech Movement. In December 1964, Meese famously advised Edmund "Pat" Brown, governor of California, to order police to charge into a university building
and arrest student protesters. Overall, he successfully prosecuted over
seven hundred Berkeley students for their role in the riots protesting
the Vietnam War.

His work in the DA's office in Oakland led him to become a voice for
police and sheriff's departments across the state, as well as for prosecu-
tors, as they pushed the state government for better pay for police and
longer sentences for criminals.

Meese's work as a strong advocate for law enforcement in Sacra-
mento, the state capital, led to a job interview with Governor-elect
Reagan in 1966. The new governor, who was from the small town of
Dixon, Illinois, a community of eight thousand, shared Meese's view
of the importance of preserving American traditions against the rush
of criticism of the current political establishment. Reagan hired him on
the spot, making Meese his legal affairs secretary, the liaison between
the new governor and state courts, the attorney general's office, and
associations of California lawyers. His top responsibility was screening
nominees for judgeships on state courts.

Meese worked closely with the new governor to develop a system
for screening and appointing state judges who shared Reagan's political
belief in strong law and order enforcement and punishment, including
the death penalty. Meese later said that before Reagan, the state had a lot
of "hacks" sitting on the state bench who did not consistently back police efforts to punish criminal behavior to the full extent possible under
state law. Meese found like-minded senior judges, newspaper editors,
and bar association officials and recruited them for panels to identify
candidates for judgeships. Meese further earned Governor Reagan's
trust by presiding over the clemency hearing of Aaron Mitchell, a black
man who had killed a cop. Whether to give Mitchell the death penalty
was the toughest decision Reagan ever had to make, a former Reagan
staff member told biographer Lou Cannon. Against mass resistance
to the death penalty in California, Meese convinced Reagan to keep

Mitchell's death sentence. President Reagan "appreciated how Meese had stood firm in the face of other advisers who had recommended clemency," wrote Meese's biographer Lee Edwards.

Meese's success in these various endeavors, including his aid in remodeling the state courts for Governor Reagan, led Reagan to appoint him his chief of staff from 1969 to 1974. One of his first recommendations as chief of staff was for the governor to escalate the police response to student antiwar protests at Berkeley. The confrontations between police and students made national news and raised Governor Reagan's national stature among political conservatives. It was key to advancing Reagan's efforts to win the GOP nomination for president beginning in 1976. When Reagan ran again in 1980, Meese was chief of staff for the governor's presidential campaign, and then led Reagan's presidential transition team. During his years working for the Reagan administration, Meese would never lose his early focus on strengthening a conservative approach to law enforcement by backing judges who imposed sentences for convicted criminals to the full extent of the law. Now working for the president, Meese put the same conservative thinking into taming activism in the federal courts, beginning with careful selection of judicial nominees.

"President Reagan was a great believer in the Founders' wisdom and in the uniqueness of the Constitution," Meese later told an interviewer. "So one of the things President Reagan was very keen on when he came into the presidency was to appoint constitutionally faithful judges. President Reagan was very much concerned about judicial activism, which occurs when judges substitute their own political ideas, partisan views or policy preferences for what the Constitution actually says, what the law is and what the statutes actually read. President Reagan was interested in appointing those kinds of judges who would, in fact, apply the law rather than try to usurp certain functions of the legislature and make the law."

In the White House, now serving as counselor to the president, Meese had unequaled stature as the new president's closest, most trusted aide. His immediate interest was to find conservative judicial nominees for the federal courts.

In the late 1960s, before Meese had climbed up to the national stage, the country had a preview of the storm surrounding efforts to pack the

Supreme Court with conservatives. Chief Justice Earl Warren, under attack for the activism of his court, tried to prevent Republicans from picking his successor in 1968 by resigning while President Johnson, who had decided not to seek reelection, was still in office. But LBJ's nominee, Abe Fortas, came under attack and withdrew, and Johnson did not have time to name another nominee. The next president was a Republican, Richard Nixon, who successfully nominated Warren Burger as chief justice. Senate Democrats, however, blocked Nixon when he nominated two strong conservatives for seats on the Court, Clement Haynsworth and G. Harold Carswell. Nixon, in a nationwide speech in 1971, made his thinking on selecting judges clear when he said the best judge is one who understands "the duty of a judge to interpret the Constitution and not to place himself above the Constitution or outside the Constitution."

During Reagan's first term, Meese picked up on Nixon's conservative complaint about liberal, activist judges and the federal courts. Along with Jim Baker and Mike Deaver, Meese was one of the three highest-ranking members of Reagan's team. They were called the "Big Three." But as the only one of the Big Three who also served on the cabinet, Meese had a "special, elevated position," according to the *Christian Science Monitor*. He oversaw all the cabinet departments, acting as the president's primary link to government agencies and boards, and serving as a member of the National Security Council and, later on, as head of Reagan's Domestic Policy Council. In the second term, Reagan made him attorney general. In both administrations Meese focused on putting conservative people and policies in place to advance the Reagan Revolution. Meese said in an interview, "It wasn't really until Ronald Reagan came along that someone wanted to halt the expansion of government and restore it to its constitutional basis." With his law enforcement background, he made it his express priority to stop the federal courts from advancing a liberal agenda on a range of issues: an end to the death penalty, legal abortion, racial goals and timetables aimed at achieving equality, and laws that limited big business's power in terms of controlling the environment and its natural resources.

But it was as attorney general that Meese's power to neutralize liberal judges reached its apex. In July 1985 Meese gave a speech to the American Bar Association, intending "to lay down a marker on what the jurisprudence of the administration would be in terms of constitutional issues." Meese called for all judges to limit their actions to being "faithful guardians of the Constitution," and challenged them to "resist any political effort to depart from the literal provisions of the Constitution." He insisted that "the original intention of those who framed [the Constitution] would be the judicial standard in giving effect to the Constitution."

Meese cast this approach as key to protecting the federal courts from "the charge of being either too conservative or too liberal." Basing court rulings solely on "explication of original intention would produce defensible principles of government that would not be tainted by ideological predilection," he said.

"The Constitution is the fundamental will of the people," Meese told the ABA; "that is why it is the fundamental law. To allow the courts to govern simply what it views at the time as fair and decent, is a scheme of government no longer popular; the idea of democracy has suffered. The permanence of the Constitution has been weakened. A Constitution that is viewed as only what the judges say it is, is no longer a Constitution in a true sense. Those who framed the Constitution chose their words carefully; they debated at great length the minutest points. The language they chose meant something. It is incumbent on the Court to determine what that meaning was."

Meese's pointed speech made front-page news across the nation. It sparked heated debate among judges and lawyers. But the argument went beyond the law, speaking to larger debates over politics and culture. Meese and the president came under attack for trying to undermine decisions opposed by conservatives, specifically the Warren Court's 1954 ruling in favor of school desegregation and later rulings giving protections to people facing the death penalty as well as making abortion legal. Supreme Court justice William Brennan responded to Meese with a charged speech in which he implied that Meese was a fraud and that originalism was nothing more than "arrogance cloaked as humility."

Justice Brennan, who was appointed by President Eisenhower, a Republican, but who was considered a famous liberal on the Court for his rulings, said that contrary to Meese's assertion, any contemporary judge facing twentieth-century legal conflicts cannot reasonably and properly claim to know how the Founding Fathers might apply the Constitution to modern problems. In fact, it is "arrogant" to assume to know how the framers would respond to contemporary issues. This is, in part, because "the Framers themselves did not agree about the application or meaning of particular constitutional provisions, and hid their differences in cloaks of generality."

We "current Justices read the Constitution in the only way we can," Justice Brennan said, "as twentieth century Americans. We look to the history of the time of framing and to the intervening history of inter-pretation. But the ultimate question must be: What do the words of the text mean in our time? For the genius of the Constitution rests not in any static meaning it might have had in a world that is dead and gone, but in the adaptability of its great principles to cope with current prob-lems and current needs."

The debate pitted conservative preference for limiting the reach of judicial decisions by tying them to the words of the Constitution against liberal support for the Warren Court and legal thinkers who described the Constitution as a living document capable of adapting to changing times. The fiery debate continues with new combatants to this day; constant new flare-ups exacerbate the deep divide among liberals and conservatives. It rages in political split decisions in the nation's federal courts. And the heat goes beyond legal circles. It is a regular feature of the national political scene with its harsh, polarized rhetoric, conservative Republicans versus liberal Democrats. The acri-mony is prominent in congressional hearings for any nominee to the Supreme Court—most famously in the failed nomination of conserva-tive Robert Bork. And the bitter histrionics now find their way into many Supreme Court arguments, with a conservative majority, most of them adherents of strict constitutional construction, dominating the Supreme Court today.

The result is that the federal courts now are a political football, tar-gets for criticism on both sides of the political spectrum. Long gone is any pretense that the courts are supposed to be neutral ground for in-dependent rulings that deliver justice to conflicting parties; no longer is the Supreme Court viewed by the press or the public as "nine wise men" and the height of independent, erudite national legal deliberation. Now the justices are viewed, to quote Linda Greenhouse of the *New York*

Times, as "politicians in robes." A breaking point for public trust in the high court came in 2000 when the conservative majority, in a total fracture from the Court's liberals, essentially decided the presidential election in favor of the Republican candidate, George W. Bush, by halting a recount vote in Florida that might have tipped the state's twenty-five electoral votes to Democrat Al Gore.

The twenty-first-century angst over the politicization of the courts has precedent in arguments among the original Founding Fathers. At the Constitutional Convention, thirty-five of the fifty-five delegates were lawyers or judges, or had some form of legal training. In the public debate over the Constitution, supporters of a strong centralized federal government downplayed the power of the Supreme Court to overwhelm the Congress and the president with the power to interpret the meaning of the Constitution.

Alexander Hamilton, writing in *The Federalist Papers,* described the federal judiciary as lacking "the sword" or the power of the army as commanded by the president. The courts had to rely on the support of the president as commander in chief if there was a need to force public compliance with any ruling. And Hamilton also noted that judges lacked "the purse," that is, the budgetary authority to fund any program. Congress controls the budget, he said, and Congress also stands apart from the courts in being able to write and rewrite legislation to override any objection from the courts. He described the judiciary as having the least "capacity to annoy or injure" of the three branches of the federal government. The court's sole point of authority, by Hamilton's measure, was to protect "the power of the people" in the Constitution against any legislative statute that violated their constitutional rights.

But even in that role the courts had limited power, according to Hamilton. The judiciary's right to rule on the constitutionality of any act of Congress, he wrote, "only supposes that the power of the people is superior to both [legislative and judicial power]." The courts simply serve as a balance to the power of the other branches in a constitutional system of checks and balances, he said.

But less than twenty years later the strength of the federal courts became clear. In the 1803 case *Marbury v. Madison,* John Marshall, the fourth chief justice of the high court, wrote that the federal courts alone have constitutional power to decide the meaning of any law and to what extent it violated the Constitution. "It is emphatically the duty of the Judicial Department to say what the law is," according to the decision. "Those who apply the rule to particular cases must, of necessity . . . interpret that rule. If two laws conflict with each other, the courts must decide on the operation of each." Chief Justice Marshall, a proponent of a strong national government, dismissed the possibility of any disagreement. Marshall's ruling was shaped by the *Federalist Papers,* in which Hamilton wrote that it was not logical to think that the Constitution intended for Congress to "substitute their will" for the will "of their constituents." By Hamilton's reasoning, the federal courts are designed to restrain the excesses of Congress and "keep the latter within the limits assigned to their authority." He added that his ruling did not mean that the courts were "superior" to or above the Congress but that "the power of the people is superior to both."

Thomas Jefferson, who was president at the time of *Marbury v. Madison,* disagreed. He thought the federal courts should be limited to reviewing the legal actions of other courts to decide if they conformed to provisions of the Constitution. But he did not think the federal courts had the right to rule over the other branches of government. In a letter to Abigail Adams, the wife of John Adams, the second president, President Jefferson wrote that the branches should be independent of each other and that Chief Justice Marshall's opinion transformed an equal branch of government into a "despotic branch." Jefferson, as author of the Declaration of Independence, resisted all forms of central government power, fearing the leadership would take on the arrogance of the British royalty. To accentuate the democratic protections for Americans under the Constitution, he favored independent lines of power among the three branches of the federal government. He believed each branch should make its own decision on the constitutionality of any action. The idea that the Supreme Court now claimed the right to monitor the actions of each branch of government was at odds with the balance of powers in the Constitution. Chief Justice Marshall's view of the power of the courts had turned the Constitution, wrote Jefferson in 1819, into "a mere thing of wax in the hands of the judiciary, which they may twist, and shape into any form they please."

The dispute between President Jefferson and Chief Justice Marshall reflected a genuine tension over the role of the courts, controlled as they are by unelected officials, that has remained a matter of debate in legal circles ever since. At times, the ability of the Supreme Court to have the final say on matters of national importance has made the Court a political target for charges of imperial arrogance. In the twentieth century, the debate over the courts' power became a point of contention during President Franklin Roosevelt's administration when he tried to reorganize the Court under his court-packing scheme, expanding the number of justices on the Court so that he could add more to the judicial branch for his controversial policies. Though he failed in this effort, the Supreme Court nonetheless played a central role in upholding central elements of President Roosevelt's New Deal programs. The Court soon broke new ground by finding existing laws of racial segregation to be unconstitutional. Later it stirred the culture war in the 1970s with its *Roe v. Wade* decision allowing for legal abortion.

Recently the Supreme Court under Chief Justice Roberts has been accused of playing politics with important rulings that favored conservative, Republican positions. In *Citizens United,* the Court allowed unlimited and anonymous financial contributions to political campaigns, in *Shelby County v. Holder,* the Court weakened the landmark Voting Rights Act, and in *D.C. v. Heller* and *McDonald v. Chicago,* the Court reversed almost a century of gun control measures to reaffirm America's commitment to gun rights. Ruth Bader Ginsburg, a liberal justice appointed by President Bill Clinton, a Democrat, has called the conservative majority on the Supreme Court one of "the most activist courts in history" in overturning major laws to further a right-wing political agenda. The *New York Times* reported in 2013 that "the Roberts court may not be especially activist in the classic sense of striking down a lot of laws. But there does appear to be an element of politics in its rulings."

Supporters and opponents see the Roberts-led Court and its controversial conservative majority as the realization of a long-term conservative Republican dream. The nation's top court now reflects conservative policy views and cultural values. While the rise of political conservatism in twenty-first-century politics has its roots in the 1964 Goldwater presidential campaign, the critical moment of triumph, including work to transform the courts, was the election of President Reagan and the power Reagan gave Edwin Meese.

Meese's reputation as President Reagan's enforcer of conservative policy positions and the patron saint of conservatives seeking top government jobs and judicial nominations made him a magnet for media attention and controversy. Conservative political groups featured him as their speaker, advertising him as the president's alter ego. One story about him was headlined "Is Ed Meese 'Assistant President'?"

Meese fed the political fires around him with speeches attacking liberals. In a 1981 speech to a group of California policemen, he described the American Civil Liberties Union as "a criminals' lobby." He publicly argued against the need for Congress to continue Voting Rights Act protections for minority voters in states with a history of racial bias in voting. He stirred liberal anger with his efforts to cut funding for programs that provided legal aid to poor people. And he was widely rebuked for questioning whether there are hungry children in the United States, saying that people were standing in line for food from charities "because the food is free, and that's easier than paying for it." President Reagan defended Meese by saying that his words had been taken "totally out of context." But then he claimed that Dr. Martin Luther King Jr., the black civil rights leader, would have been against affirmative action because it was contrary to King's call for the nation to be "colorblind."

Critics on the left portrayed the amiable Meese as in over his head in the world of national politics, a tragic, often stumbling figure. Even in conservative political circles, Meese was frequently treated as a political lightweight compared to the president's two other top aides, chief of staff James A. Baker III and Deputy Chief of Staff Michael K. Deaver. Meese's critics accused him of self-aggrandizement and spending more time giving speeches than advising the president. The *Chicago Tribune* later described Meese as "opposed to virtually every credo of late-20th-century American liberalism: legalized abortion; abolition of the death penalty; strong federal intervention in civil rights issues; increased rights for criminal suspects; and strong federal welfare programs." The story went on, "So was Ronald Reagan. As time went on, Reagan had to compromise; Meese did not. 'He is more Reagan than Reagan,' White

House aides would say in the first term. As long as Meese served in the administration, conservatives could comfort themselves that the Reagan Revolution had not been abandoned."

For all the first-term turmoil around Meese and all the criticism of him in the press, the former Oakland prosecutor retained the president's trust. When, at the start of the second term, Reagan made him the nation's seventy-fifth attorney general, Meese sharpened his determination to put a conservative imprint on the nation's legal structure.

"Having previously spent a lot of time on these issues in the White House, when I became Attorney General it was very easy to develop a jurisprudence of originalism as the basis for our policies within the Department of Justice," Meese later told the *University of St. Thomas Law Journal.* That focus included reshaping the nation's courts with judges who shared his conservative views, using the Constitution "for guidance in problem-solving, not only in terms of selecting judges but also in terms of handling issues in a way that perpetuates the principles of the Founders."

The height of his effort to get back to the Founders' original intent was to select judges on the basis of their fidelity to strictly interpreting the law on the basis of the Constitution. "I think our overall concern was with judicial activism as [liberal] judges were encroaching on legitimate concerns of the people's representatives—whether the representatives were legislators or executive officials," he told the law journal. "That militated against judicial activism as far as we were concerned."

As attorney general, Meese went public with his reformation of the nation's courts under the banner of getting back to basics in his 1985 speech to the bar association. He openly attacked liberal rulings that came from the Supreme Court under Chief Justice Earl Warren. "By seeking to judge policies in light of principles, rather than remold principles in light of policies, the Court could avoid both the charge of incoherence and the charge of being either too conservative or too liberal. A jurisprudence seriously aimed at the explication of original intention would produce defensible principles of government that would not be tainted by ideological predilection. This belief in a Jurisprudence of Original Intention also reflects a deeply rooted commitment to the idea of democracy. The Constitution represents the consent of the governed to the structures and powers of the government."

President Reagan affirmed Meese's approach when he spoke at the 1986 swearing-in ceremony for two of his Supreme Court nominees— William Rehnquist as the new chief justice and Antonin Scalia as associate justice. President Reagan said he nominated the two with the principle of judicial restraint "very much in mind." Looking back to the original Founding Fathers' work establishing the federal courts, the president said the Founders wanted a strong judiciary operating "within the boundaries of a written constitution and laws." Recalling the history of the writing of the Constitution and the debate among the Founding Fathers in 1787 about the proper role of judges, he said: "In the convention and during the debates on ratification, some said there was a danger of the courts making laws rather than interpreting them." He recounted the disagreement between Hamilton and Jefferson on the proper role of the federal government. But he said the two men and "all the Founding Fathers recognized that the Constitution is the supreme and ultimate expression of the will of the American people. . . . They understood that, in the words of James Madison, if 'the sense in which the Constitution was accepted and ratified by the nation is not the guide to expounding it, there can be no security for a faithful exercise of its powers.'" With Meese in the front row, President Reagan repeated what he called the "warning" from famed lawyer Daniel Webster that "miracles do not cluster," and without close adherence to the miracle of the Constitution as it was written, there was danger. For if "the American Constitution shall fall there will be anarchy throughout the world."

It was a high point of Meese's tenure at the Justice Department. He tried to hit another high note with the 1987 nomination of a committed originalist legal thinker, Robert Bork, for a seat on the Supreme Court. But Democrats in the Senate opened a debate on whether Bork's focus on the original intent of the Constitution was in conflict with the modern Court's agreement on the importance of upholding legal precedents. Some said that if appointed, Bork would reopen painfully difficult legal consideration of civil rights laws that had no point of reference in the Constitution. Even Bork's statement of support for the 1954 *Brown v. Board* decision ending legal segregation in the nation's public schools did not satisfy the critics. If Bork approved of *Brown*, a high court ruling not grounded in the Constitution, they asked, what did a strict judicial reading of the Constitution mean? The Senate rejected Bork by the biggest margin in history.

The strong antipathy to Bork led conservatives to claim that liberals had vilified an outstanding if conservative legal thinker. They created a new word to describe his harsh political rejection by liberals— "Borked." Liberals, on the other hand, celebrated Bork's defeat as a rebuke to Meese's ongoing effort to enshrine originalism at the top of the court system. The bell had sounded, signaling the start of an era of intense partisanship surrounding appointments to the federal courts and especially the Supreme Court.

The next year, 1988, Meese was forced to resign as a result of a special prosecutor's investigation into the Wedtech scandal. The *Chicago Tribune* described his tenure as attorney general as one of the most controversial in history, even without considering his strong advocacy of strict construction of the Constitution in service of conservative positions on abortion and other explosive political issues.

"In 7½ years in Washington, Meese has been investigated by two 'independent counsels' with the powers to prosecute him; subjected to the longest confirmation process in the history of the U.S. Senate—400 days between his nomination and confirmation as attorney general," the paper wrote. "He has been accused of cronyism, favoritism, selling federal jobs, influencing regulatory matters and manipulating federal investigations. . . . Why Meese survived so long, under so much duress, is a mystery even to Reagan insiders. In part it is Reagan's extraordinary loyalty to his friends. In part it is the conviction that the President could not abandon a symbol of conservatism."

Meese remains active in conservative politics as the living personification of Reagan-era calls for pressuring the courts to get back to the basic reading of the original intent of the Constitution. He claimed victory in the ten consecutive Republican nominees, from 1969 to 1991, who won confirmation as Supreme Court justices. As the keeper of the Reagan flame, he works with conservative think tanks and groups to advance strong conservative politicians, judges, and policies. But with the election of President Obama in 2008, the rise of conservatism on the federal bench has begun to fade.

In late 2014 the *New York Times* reported: "Democrats have reversed the partisan imbalance on the federal appeals courts that long favored conservatives. . . . For the first time in more than a decade, judges appointed by Democratic presidents considerably outnumber judges appointed by Republican presidents. . . . Democratic appointees who hear cases full time now hold a majority of seats on nine of the 13 United States Courts of Appeal."

But Meese's legacy lives on in the Supreme Court, where conservatives hold a 5–4 majority. Today, three out of nine Supreme Court Justices—Justices Thomas, Alito, and Scalia—describe themselves or have been described as originalists. Meese's efforts to shift the direction of the federal courts to strict constructionism remain at the heart of the partisan tug-of-war that defines politics at the start of the twenty-first century, and his success in the world of law and judges continues to reverberate across the new century, shaping the policies and law of the nation.

CHAPTER 16

THE SOCIAL SAFETY NET

Social Security, Medicare, and Robert Ball

America's Founding Fathers would be very surprised to discover that the federal government they established in 1776 now offers every one of the more than 300 million Americans health insurance.

Congressional Republicans opposed to the plan often cite the original Founders' vision of limited government to argue that national healthcare is unconstitutional, or at least extraconstitutional—that is to say, it is outside anything considered by the first Founders. When the Affordable Care Act passed Congress in 2010, Republicans unanimously voted against it.

Four years later, polling showed that most Americans were still opposed to the law, especially conservatives displeased with the idea of a government mandate for Americans to buy health insurance coverage. The Tea Party, born of opposition to the healthcare mandate, wore tricornered hats in the tradition of the American colonists who declared independence from King George, his high taxes, and mandates issued by his intrusive army of redcoats.

On the other hand, House Democratic leader Nancy Pelosi proudly cited the original Founding Fathers as supporters of healthcare for all Americans when she met with President Obama in 2014. There are "bumps in the road," she said, but "our founders wanted [the American people to have] a healthier life—liberty and the freedom to pursue their happiness."

The most compelling rebuttal to Pelosi's claim comes from conservative critics, who see the Affordable Care Act, often referred to as "Obamacare," as an "assault on individual liberty," in the words of Peter Berkowitz of the Hoover Institution. One opinion column in the *Wall Street Journal* lamented that the law will "change the structure of the American government as it has existed for 225 years."

There is no doubt the *Wall Street Journal* is right about the change to government. Until the new law took effect, the United States never had a national health insurance plan for all its citizens. The idea of healthcare for all is the triumph of the efforts, and failures, of a slew of new founding fathers—Presidents Franklin Roosevelt, Harry Truman, Dwight Eisenhower, John F. Kennedy, Lyndon Johnson, Richard Nixon, Bill Clinton, George W. Bush, and Barack Obama. Across the years they gradually pushed and revised and nurtured the very idea of healthcare as a fundamental right of citizenship for all Americans. They got national healthcare further and further up the mountain of American history until it reached the summit, visible and available to all as a twenty-first-century reality.

But one man's steady work guided the presidents' effort at reinventing the nation's healthcare system. This new founding father wasn't an elected official but a federal bureaucrat. Even now he remains unknown to most Americans. His name is Robert Ball. And he steadily expanded existing American social policy and public opinion to pave the way for the reality of a federal healthcare program.

Ball's work behind the scenes fits with the original Founding Fathers' embrace of revolutionary change. He overcame past resistance to federal involvement in healthcare by fighting opposition from doctors, insurance companies, hospitals, and unions. He faced down charges that national healthcare was a socialist infringement of America's free market capitalist principles.

At our nation's founding, several of the Founding Fathers agreed the federal government had some role to play in keeping citizens from sickness without regard to the size of their pocketbook. Healthcare was a concern in the colonies, and citizens were angry at the exclusive access the rich enjoyed to the few doctors available. In 1790, there was roughly one doctor for every one hundred and fifty Americans. By comparison, the United States has one doctor for every four hundred Americans today. Colonial anger at preferential healthcare for the rich came to a violent head over a private smallpox inoculation hospital in Marblehead, Massachusetts. A group of sailors burned down the hospital to protest the high cost of the inoculation, which made it available only to the rich. Later, when yellow fever swept the colonies in 1793, hitting Philadelphia, the biggest city, hard, the new federal government got involved. State governments needed federal officials to coordinate efforts to stop the disease from spreading across state borders. With its power to regulate interstate commerce, Congress passed several bills—one in 1796 and then a stronger one in 1799—to help states enforce quarantines to contain yellow fever.

Justification for the federal government getting involved with healthcare can be found in the Constitution's pledge that America's compact with its citizens begins with protecting their well-being as well as their individual rights—"promote the general welfare and secure the blessings of liberty," as it is worded in the Constitution.

James Madison wrote in *The Federalist Papers,* "If men were angels, no government would be necessary." And when asked why a nation based on personal freedoms needed the Constitution and a central government that defined and in some cases limited those freedoms, John Adams, the future second president of the United States, wrote in 1787 that the U.S. Constitution limits individual rights—and though he did not explicitly say free market—as it also provides a counter to the private financial interests of individuals, the parochial interests of local jurisdictions, and the preferences of any political party in order to "compel all to respect the common right, the public good, the universal law, in preference to all private and partial considerations."

Several of the nation's Founding Fathers became elected members of the congressional majority that expanded the federal role in healthcare in 1798 by passing the Act for the Relief of Sick and Disabled Seamen. In addition to funding the care of seamen at existing hospitals, the law also established the Marine Hospital Service, which funded construction of federal hospitals to care for sick sailors. The law was signed by President John Adams. Under the law, seamen were taxed twenty cents per month to finance the new marine hospitals. The tax had to be paid by ships' owners before entering any American port. The Public Health Service and the Office of the Surgeon General later grew out of the system of federal marine hospitals.

The early federal government did not attempt to extend the medical care they gave to sailors to all American citizens. Early American values put a premium on families taking care of their own, especially when a child or an elderly person got sick. Almanacs, medical pamphlets, and local newspapers featured stories on how to cure colds and other illnesses. Mothers passed home remedies to their daughters. Folk wisdom advised Americans to keep their homes clean, dig deep troughs for outhouses, and get their children outdoors for fresh air. Professional medical care was viewed as a luxury for elites. Organized medicine did not fit easily with the Colonial emphasis on individual rights and independence from any ruling upper class. Even for wealthy colonists it was hard to find a real doctor, someone with a medical education; slightly more common were people who had apprenticeships with doctors and opened their own office.

Most colonists in need of medical help beyond the family went to their church community. Ministers sometimes doubled as unlicensed doctors or "clerical practitioners." The men who ran taverns and coffeehouses often collected the best local treatments for illness, so people went to them for help, sometimes recuperating in a backroom.

In 1760 New York City established basic tests for anyone offering medical help. The federal government had no role in certifying the few doctors who claimed to have a degree from medical school. For nearly a hundred and fifty years after the first colonists arrived in North America the nation had no hospitals; the first hospital in the thirteen colonies, called the Pennsylvania Hospital, was founded in 1751.

In 1854 President Franklin Pierce, reflecting the attitude of American self-sufficiency, vetoed legislation to pay for land in the states for construction of insane asylums, as well as facilities for the "blind, deaf, and dumb." Political pressure from social welfare activists led Congress to approve the bill. President Pierce stood firm and rebuffed the appeals for compassion by reminding the Senate, in a famous veto message, that any powers not explicitly given to the federal government in the Constitution were the duties of the states. That led to the conclusion that sick people as well as those who are blind or mentally ill, without benefit of family or money, are the responsibility of state and local governments.

President Pierce's opposition to the national government caring for the sick was an accepted part of American politics and culture for the next half century. The only exception was the federal government's role in caring for injured soldiers during the Civil War. Historian Margaret Humphreys describes the war between the North and South as "the greatest health disaster that this country has ever experienced, killing more than a million Americans and leaving many others invalided or grieving." As a result, the federal army opened general hospitals to take care of injured warriors. Military leaders supported the hospitals out of fear that if the soldiers went back home to heal they would never come back to the battlefield. These military hospitals were the first hospitals in the United States that were not asylums or poorhouses. Initially, some soldiers were insulted by the government's Civil War medical hospitals. In that era, most hospitals had a stigma attached to them as a place of last resort for the insane. Also, many women did not want their husbands and sons in the care of strangers at a hospital when they felt it was proper for them to care for their family members at home.

But the need to treat serious gunshot and knife wounds led soldiers to the hospitals. The severe trauma suffered by the soldiers also compelled Congress to approve federal funding to train surgeons. This enabled anatomical research to improve the quality of surgery and the creation of laboratories to develop new painkilling drugs. There was a surge in American medical studies, which had always lagged behind European standards.

Almost all of those hospitals closed after the Civil War. It took nearly fifty years before the American Association for Labor Legislation (AALL), a group of progressive academics, began to call for the national government to care for sick workers by providing health insurance. In 1915 the association published a pamphlet that included a "Model Health Insurance Bill" for Congress. It recommended that employers, workers, and state governments jointly pay for half a year of sick pay for injured or sick workers, as well as a death benefit to cover funerals. These benefits were intended for people who made less than $1,200 per year and all manual laborers, though it excluded seasonal and domestic workers.

Typical of reformers in the Progressive Era, the AALL argued, in the words of one advocate, that workers "must learn to see that they have a right to force at least part of the cost and waste of sickness back upon the industry and society at large." Several leading doctors supported the bill as a way to bring more patients into their offices, though this initial excitement was soon replaced by fear that public health insurance would place doctors under government control. And political doubt about the plan came from top union leaders, including Samuel Gompers, head of the American Federation of Labor. Gompers worried that a federal medical insurance plan shifted workers' loyalty away from unions. Big business did not like the plan, either. The National Industrial Conference Board, a business think tank, argued that offering "sick pay" might lead workers to fake illness. The nation's growing private insurance industry also opposed the plan, fearing it would drive them out of business.

World War I got the federal government back into the medical care business as veterans came home. But when a 1917 California commission advised the state to create a compulsory health insurance plan for all residents, opponents quickly emerged. The critics called the plan a "dangerous device, invented in Germany, announced by the German Emperor from the throne the same year he started plotting and preparing to conquer the world." Halting, small steps toward federal support for people who could not afford medical care came in 1921 when Congress approved funding to bring doctors and medicine to Native American reservations. That year Congress funded grants to help states provide medical services to pregnant women and infants.

Anything more faced opposition from doctors worried about losing money and power to control the price of their services, and from the medical industry. Stricter laws for licensing doctors and higher tuition at the growing number of medical schools led doctors to increase their fees. Doctors became politically powerful, too, with the American Medical Association persuading Congress to end the program created to help pregnant women. The doctors argued that the women who ran the facilities were not "real" doctors, and condemned the whole effort as bringing European socialism to the United States.

The political climate for federal involvement with healthcare changed when FDR won congressional approval of the Social Security Act in 1935. There was no provision for medical care in the bill. But the intent of the law was to keep elderly people out of poverty, and that group had a lot of medical needs. In 1938, one Roosevelt commission on social welfare recommended to the president that the government offer money to the states to help pay for healthcare for children, their mothers, the poor, and the disabled. But according to historian Michael R. Gray, "The group's most controversial proposal was for the creation of a state-based insurance program, funded at least in part through public taxes, to provide medical care to the entire population." Excited about the proposal, President Roosevelt organized the National Health Conference in July 1938 that brought 150 doctors, farmers, and union officials to Washington. But the proposal died in the face of opposition from doctors, who feared that compulsory health insurance for all Americans would result in pressure on doctors to drop their prices if the government controlled the national market for healthcare. These concerns got sympathy from the many anti–New Deal conservatives who won seats in Congress during the 1938 elections. Attention to the idea also faded as the nation's focus turned to World War II. But even during the war President Roosevelt told aides he remained committed to a national plan to give medical insurance to all Americans.

Initially, Social Security was limited to workers in commerce and industry—roughly half of the working population and almost all white men. Social Security's old age insurance offered little for two groups of workers: women and blacks. Few women worked in the big industrial factories; they commonly worked as domestic help. And the majority of black people, due to racial segregation, worked as domestics, as farm laborers, and in part-time jobs. The Social Security Act of 1935 explicitly excluded these types of workers. Women and blacks overwhelmingly did not qualify for Social Security retirement annuities. Social Security did offer some money under the Old Age Assistance plan for the states to give out to poor people over the age of sixty-five no matter where they worked or how much they had paid in taxes. That program offered funds to supplement welfare payments to the elderly from state governments. A forerunner of Medicaid, Old Age Assistance was what we would now call an "entitlement program" or derided as "welfare." The

Social Security Act also created the first federal unemployment insurance program. But no provision in the Social Security law allowed for national health insurance to cover medical expenses.

Still, Social Security reshaped the national debate over federal involvement in helping Americans pay the rising cost of healthcare. Combined with the federal government's war effort, the presence of Social Security led far more people to agree that it was the proper role of government to solve the nation's major social problems.

In 1947, two years after the end of the war, the Republican majority in Congress voted to stop scheduled increases in the Social Security tax paid by workers and industry. They wanted the money to be used to spur the economy. It seemed like a killing blow to the growth of Social Security and any expansion to a national plan to provide federally funded medical care for Americans, especially the sickest group of Americans, the elderly.

To quiet charges from President Truman that the GOP was undermining Social Security, the Senate's Republican leader, Arthur Vandenberg of Michigan, agreed to fund a panel to study the economics of Social Security. Sen. Eugene Milliken, the Republican head of the Senate Finance Committee, named the panel's members, including representatives from Eastman Kodak, representing big business; Providential Mutual, on behalf of the insurance industry; the AFL and the CIO, from the labor movement; and economists from Harvard and Princeton.

The man selected to run the commission was Robert Ball, a former Social Security official. At the heart of Ball's behind-the-scenes work was the question of whether healthcare is a fundamental right for Americans. His attention to that matter reinvented the Social Security system and set the stage for Americans to accept a federal role in healthcare.

Ball was not a philosopher. He was not elected to office. His public profile was easily overshadowed by towering political figures. In fact, most people have never heard of Robert Ball. But his commitment to the idea of creating a federal government firewall between the elderly and poverty proved to be just as crucial as the work of any president. With Ball standing as an anchor among policy makers, politicians, and administrators, the federal safety net of guaranteed protection against poverty in old age was able to take hold in American life. Without Ball's principled stand through years of changing politics, economics, and demographics, there would be no Social Security, no Medicare to provide healthcare for the elderly, no Medicaid to provide healthcare for the poor, and certainly no Affordable Care Act in the twenty-first century.

Ball was unrivaled in his mastery of the inner workings of Social Security. And he used his superior understanding of those details to win support for expanding the program, including pushing it into federal medical insurance, Medicare. It was Ball's hand that made Social Security the most politically indestructible program in the federal government, the apocryphal "third rail" of American politics—any politician attempting to touch it would be defeated at the ballot box.

Ball won overwhelming public support for Social Security by painting it in different colors from other federal programs. It was Bob Ball who transformed it into a reward for a lifetime of hard work by American citizens. This was no poverty program and no giveaway. It bore no resemblance to welfare. In keeping with America's Puritan work ethic, Ball set up Social Security as a program that required workers to pay into the system throughout their working life in order to qualify for their benefits in retirement. In other words, Ball separated Social Security from politically unacceptable labels such as "government handout" or "welfare." Instead he created a system in which all citizens, rich or poor, felt they had *earned* the right to the government guarantee of benefits to keep them out of poverty in retirement.

When the system was threatened by failing support from Congress, it was Ball who revived it in the late 1940s and early 1950s. And in the 1960s Ball brought federally guaranteed medical coverage, Medicare and Medicaid, into the Social Security program. These stepping-stones paved the way for President Obama to sign the Affordable Care Act into law more than fifty years later.

Ball, the youngest of three children, was born in New York in 1914. His father, Archey Ball, was a minister; his mother was a public school teacher. Both graduated from a small Wisconsin school called Lawrence College with Phi Beta Kappa honors before his father attended divinity school. Rev. Ball moved among several Methodist churches in the Northeast.

Traveling ministers like Ball's father had a tricky role. They had to conform to the norms of different communities to gain acceptance and financial support, but they also had to serve as a spiritual guide, setting the bar for acceptable Christian behavior. Ball later told an interviewer that his dad was both a "lead man" and "a very social person who regardless of the seriousness of his goals, enjoyed almost every day as it went—he was full of laughter and full of humanness." Learning from his father's example, Ball took those skills as a bureaucrat into the federal government by demonstrating the capacity to stand on principle without alienating others.

Ball was just fifteen when the stock market crashed in October 1929, triggering the start of the Great Depression. He watched as his minister father worked late nights to help unemployed and often desperate people, especially the elderly, get enough food to eat.

Over six feet tall, Ball played football in high school. He enrolled in Wesleyan University in 1931, majored in English literature, and then stayed an extra year at college to get a master's degree in labor history and economics—hot topics at the time, as Congress had just passed the Wagner Act, giving employees the right to organize unions at private businesses.

The Social Security Act was passed during Ball's senior year of college. As the son of a minister and a student of economics, he understood that it signaled the start of a revolutionary government attack on poverty. Ball was thrilled by the legislation because, as he later recalled, "it [supplied] a continuing income to groups who without it would be most susceptible to poverty."

When he graduated from college, Ball intended to go to Washington to work on President Roosevelt's New Deal program, but he could not find a job. Instead, he went to work at Stern Brothers' department store in New York City as an accountant. He hated the work and left to take a job as a librarian in New Jersey. His interest in politics, economics, and unions finally was rewarded when he got a job as assistant editor of a pro-labor newspaper in East Orange that was circulated throughout heavily populated northern New Jersey. Ball also got directly involved in union politics, picketing at the Paterson silk factories and organizing a boycott to support workers striking at the Little Falls Laundry.

Though Ball enjoyed his work for the labor newspaper, in 1939 his dream of working for FDR's New Deal came true when he accepted a position as a field assistant with the Social Security Administration's local office in New Jersey. It was just four years after Congress had passed the Social Security Act. Social Security began collecting payroll taxes in 1937; the plan called for distributing benefits for the first time in 1940 to retired workers over age sixty-five.

Ball's job was to pursue and arrange meetings with employers who failed to list all their employees and pay their new Social Security taxes. Thus he had to make sure New Jersey employers were familiar with the old age and survivors insurance programs; the job required him to explain the programs to workers, as well. As a result, Ball became an expert on the benefits structure from both sides of the table. His goal was to ensure that employers and employees sent the right amount of money to the government. Northern New Jersey had lots of recent immigrants, including Poles, Slovaks, and Italians, many of whom were confused by the new government system with its abstract-seeming benefits. Ball had to win their trust.

Ball's commitment to the program coupled with his ease with the details of Social Security made him a star, and he was soon elevated to manager of the Bayonne, New Jersey, Social Security office. As the nation headed toward World War II, Ball's mastery of Social Security brought him to the attention of the national office, and he was hired to train other field workers. Ball's message to new recruits was almost religious in tone; he became famous for the passion with which he explained to labor unions, employers, and Congress that Social Security was far more than a simple welfare program for the poor. This was a program for those who worked. Ball spoke as an apostle for a new covenant between hardworking Americans and their government. The new system celebrated the productivity of the American economy, Ball liked to say, because it gave workers a reason to stay on the job until sixty-five, and it gave employers a way to reward long-serving employees.

The heart of the gospel of Social Security, according to Robert Ball, always returned to the idea that it was not aimed only at the poor. Benefits were based on the number of years and the amount of money that each worker paid in payroll taxes. Everyone paid the same percentage of income, but the total amount paid was different for a factory worker, with a working-class income, than for a wealthy banker. But both paid into the system in order to be entitled to a guaranteed pension, thus creating the image of a democratic program that rewarded work at every level of society.

There was little change to Social Security during the war, but in his 1943 State of the Union address, President Roosevelt spoke about the importance of building on the program with new plans to keep Americans out of poverty "from the cradle to the grave." He gave his support to a Senate bill to add a national health insurance plan to Social Security. The president raised the bar in his 1944 presidential campaign by calling for an "Economic Bill of Rights" for all Americans. The president said his plan included "the right to adequate medical care and the opportunity to achieve and enjoy good health . . . the right to adequate protection from the economic fears of old age, sickness, accident and unemployment." After the president won his fourth term, he fueled the expansion of Social Security to cover medical costs for all Americans by claiming that "good medical care" was a fundamental "right of American citizenship" during his January 1945 budget message. The idea was in the planning phase at the Social Security board when the president died in April 1945. In November 1945 President Truman, appealing to the public's adoring memory of President Roosevelt, gave his endorsement to congressional legislation calling for Roosevelt-style national health coverage.

With Roosevelt's death and the war's end, the idea began to get more attention. It also triggered a new round of opposition. Doctors and insurers complained it was "socialism" and "un-American." The American Medical Association hired a public relations firm to create a national "education campaign" to undercut long-standing public support for President Roosevelt's promise of a national health insurance plan. The doctors said the plan amounted to an attempt at "the enslavement of the medical profession." The U.S. Chamber of Commerce, the American Bar Association, the American Legion, and even the Catholic Church joined the opposition to a government-run medical plan, whether as an extension of Social Security or a separate program. Republicans ran advertising in the 1946 midterm elections with the political slogan "Had Enough." They made the case that the New Deal had already expanded government and taxes to the point of overwhelming private business. The Republicans won the political argument and took control of Capitol Hill for the first time since the Great Depression. Any talk of expanding Social Security by adding medical coverage was over. There was even fear that the entire Social Security system might be dismantled.

Big labor lost interest in bringing healthcare under the federal blanket of Social Security as well. Their focus was on using their right to bargain for healthcare with employers. The principle that healthcare insurance could be negotiated between unions and employers was affirmed in a 1948 Supreme Court case, *Inland Steel Co. v. National Labor Relations Board*. The court ruled healthcare benefits are understood to be included in the phrase "wages and conditions of employment," a phrase in the 1935 Wagner Act that established the right of unions to bargain for workers. By 1950, just two years after the Supreme Court ruling, the number of workers benefiting from union-negotiated health coverage had risen from 2.7 million to 7 million. By the mid-1950s two-thirds of the nation's blue-collar industrial workers paid union dues that provided them with healthcare coverage under a union contract. Consequently, the unions saw healthcare as key to keeping workers in unions. In 1954 a change in the tax laws would make payments by employers into medical plans for their workers tax free, dramatically increasing the number of workers getting health insurance coverage at their jobs. "By the end of 1954, 12 million workers and 17 million dependents were enrolled in collectively bargained health plans," wrote historian Paul Starr in his book *The Social Transformation of American Medicine*.

By the 1952 presidential campaign, the future of any government-backed medical coverage was strongly in doubt. The Democratic candidate, Adlai Stevenson, did not endorse it, and the Republican candidate, Dwight D. Eisenhower, openly condemned the idea. President Truman did not mention the issue but later wrote: "I have had some bitter disappointments as President, but the one that has troubled me most, in a personal way, has been the failure to defeat the organized opposition to a national compulsory health insurance program."

But all this was in the future. The immediate problem was that by 1946 the political climate for Social Security itself appeared so dire that Ball, despite his dedication to the government plan, left the Social Security Administration to join an effort by New Deal supporters to fight to keep Social Security alive. At the University-Government Center on Social Security, Ball wrote a 1947 article with the title "Social Insurance—the Right to Assistance."

That year the Republican Congress froze the Social Security tax rate. The move was one step away from killing off Social Security, leaving it to starve to death for lack of funding. Absent any political investment in the program from Democrats, the Republican majority in the Senate, feeling the pulse of opposition to Social Security, called attention to its weak vital signs, portraying its shaky finances as a threat to bankrupt the federal government.

Arthur Altmeyer, the U.S. commissioner for Social Security, pleaded for Senate Republican leaders to at least appoint a government advisory panel to study whether Social Security had a future. The Republican leaders agreed, but insisted on an independent group that included leading businessmen, a labor leader, doctors, and academics. The panel included no one from the Social Security Administration. The Senate-sponsored advisory panel was viewed by newspaper writers as the first step to ending the New Deal program, which some labeled as a well-intentioned but financially unsustainable response to the Great Depression. In Washington political circles, the big question was whether the panel was going to be run by someone intent on saving Social Security or ending it.

In the end, the Senate and the Social Security Administration agreed to appoint a man with knowledge of the system, a former employee who left the agency several years earlier, a little-known bureaucrat acceptable to both sides who had a reputation as a pragmatic technician without any glaring political ideology: Robert Ball.

Social Security's critics in the Senate did not know the quiet bureaucrat possessed his father's religious commitment to caring for the poor and viewed his bureaucratic work for Social Security as a kind of priesthood. To outside observers, it was hard to charge Ball with a personal preference for saving a dying program. He did not engage in advocacy. He did not have a preachy style. In the fashion of big business, Ball simply held seminars for experts. He arranged hearings. He focused on specifics. But the questions he put before every group assumed that Social Security's primary aim—federally guaranteed pensions for retired workers—was worthy of continued taxes on workers and employers.

As a result, the answers he got framed options for how to best expand the program. And the council then considered how to best devise a secure base of financing and boost public trust in the system. Ball won agreement from industry, labor, and even doubters in the medical business—the doctors and insurers—that the key for Social Security's future was that its minimum benefits had to exceed the amount of money given out to welfare recipients.

At a time when the Republican majority in Congress held powerful doubts about the financial future of Social Security, Ball got his group of businessmen, insurers, and unionists to propose extending coverage to a new set of workers: domestic workers, farm workers, the self-employed, and government workers. By expanding the base of eligible workers as wages went up across the economically booming nation, the advisory council argued that the Social Security program could claim a windfall and end the program's financial worries. In fact, the council said, there would be enough money to allow an increased payout for beneficiaries.

The Republican Congress found itself backed into a corner. Despite their concerns about the future cost of Social Security as more people retired, the program now had the blessings of a bipartisan panel of experts, industrial barons, and workers' unions. Polls also found widespread public support. And President Truman once again began speaking in favor of the plan. The fiscal hawks retreated. Congress had little political choice but to approve new life for Social Security. The answers provided by the advisory panel became the Social Security Act Amendment of 1950.

Those 1950 amendments transformed the American approach to helping the poor. Now that Social Security was a program for every American, it reaffirmed the idea that it was not just for the poor. Once again it stood out from other government programs. Social Security, as designed by Ball, remained a program of federal insurance for all working people, those "deserving" of help. It was never confused with freeloading or entitlements for the poor in public debate. Somehow Ball's tactics and language managed to prevent Social Security from being stigmatized by critics as a handout to the elderly and disabled, or confused with welfare for the poor.

When President Eisenhower was elected in 1952, he promptly fired several top officials in the Social Security Administration. The new president did not like the program, fearing both its future expense and the large surplus of cash building up in the Social Security trust fund and available to the government to further expand federal aid to the needy. His brother, Edgar Eisenhower, made the outright suggestion of abolishing Social Security. But Dwight Eisenhower sensed its popularity. His advisers reminded him that millions of workers had already contributed to Social Security for more than a decade with the understanding that their return on that money was a government promise or guarantee of retirement income.

The Eisenhower administration calculated that it was in the president's best interest to avoid being labeled by Democrats as the man who destroyed Social Security. "Should any political party attempt to abolish Social Security, unemployment insurance, and eliminate labor laws and farm programs, you would not hear of that party again in our political history," the president wrote in a letter to his brother.

The only reason Ball was spared from being fired by Eisenhower's new team was his reputation as an experienced guide to the inner workings of the system. Oveta Culp Hobby, Eisenhower's pick as secretary of health, education, and welfare, made Ball staff director of her brain trust of advisers on Social Security. Hobby's marching orders from the Eisenhower White House, in a memo the president sent to her, was to show America that the Democrats and their New Deal program did not have "a monopoly of the goals of a good society."

The Eisenhower administration decided the best political resolution was to make Social Security funds available to all—even people who had not paid into the system with their payroll tax deductions. In exchange, they proposed reducing the benefits. Democrats immediately protested that the program was being weakened to the point of offering little meaningful financial support to retired workers. The political backlash quashed the idea. Instead, Secretary Hobby, under the brilliant work of Ball, came up with a new idea. She advised the president to extend social security to more workers. That would benefit the government by lessening the need for welfare payments. But the critics of Social Security didn't quit. Congressional hearings were called by Rep. Carl T. Curtis (R-Neb.), "one of the most tenacious and vocal critics" of the program, according to one history of Social Security. The congressman's goal was to expose flaws in the program and depict it as an exercise in liberal New Deal thinking that could not work because its long-term costs outweighed its benefits.

Over six days of hearings, the chief witness sent by the government to attempt to defend the program was Robert Ball. Ball did not attempt an ideological defense of New Deal liberalism or Social Security. Instead, he offered statistics. And those numbers showed that Social Security was financially stable and that plans to expand the program to more Americans were feasible. The hearings faded from the news as conservative critics retreated in the face of the deluge of numbers and charts from Ball. With his defense further strengthened by the failure of the Republican attacks, Ball was able to win a 1954 congressional vote to expand Social Security once again.

And Robert Ball managed to use that congressional affirmation of Social Security to gain support for a breakthrough that changed the history of Social Security.

Working with Sen. Robert Kerr (D-Okla.), Ball persuaded Republicans to agree to a bipartisan plan to create a separate fund, within Social Security, to protect workers who became disabled. At the time, workers lost future increases in their benefit packages when illness or injury forced them out of work and they stopped paying their Social Security taxes. Though some, like Ball, believed that the United States needed a public mechanism to compensate disabled workers for extended periods of time that they missed work, many in Congress worried that the loss of payments from disabled workers might make the entire program too expensive, possibly leading to the collapse of the Social Security trust fund. To remedy the problem, Ball proposed a stand-alone fund, financed by a small increase in payroll taxes, to make contributions for disabled workers.

By 1957 the push for government-funded health insurance gained the support of the AFL-CIO. It was a major shift for the union, which preferred to put its stamp on healthcare for workers through union-negotiated wage and benefit packages. Union leaders believed they could have both company-sponsored medical plans and government guarantees. Newspapers reported that the Eisenhower administration, in its last days, considered a plan that would allow Social Security to provide Americans with money for "catastrophic" healthcare emergencies. The idea never came before Congress, but just the mention of it was revealing. The pressure was growing to help the elderly, the disabled, and the poor pay their medical bills.

Ball kept critics of Social Security on the defensive with his continued success in making the Social Security system run smoothly. There were no scandals. There were no failures to provide service. The program was a model of the federal government providing help to its hardworking citizens. Ball's "Statement of Bureau Goals and Objectives" became a celebrated mantra among corporate efficiency and design experts. In what he called "Bureau Objective Number One," Ball set out a clear mission: "The right check, to the right person, at the right time."

By 1957, with the success of Social Security's protection for disabled workers, Democrats in Congress enlisted Ball's expertise in support of a proposal advanced by Rep. Aime Forand (D-R.I.) to use Social Security payroll taxes to cover hospital, surgical, and nursing home expenses for senior citizens. With Ball guiding him, the congressman proposed increasing cash benefits for medical care and coverage for up to four months per year of hospital or nursing home care. The money to pay for the plan was to come from small increases in Social Security taxes of less than half a percent.

By the late 1950s, there were more old people, more expensive medical tests, and more hospitals than in 1935, when Social Security had been created. Dealing with medical payments had not been anticipated when benefit levels were first set. By the early 1960s, seniors who depended on Social Security checks every month found it tough to afford healthcare. And private insurance companies found people over sixty-five too risky to insure, because they were prone to illness and long, expensive hospital stays.

Despite continuing opposition from the American Medical Association, the Chamber of Commerce, and the Health Insurance Association of America, the idea of national healthcare worked its way into the 1960 presidential campaign. Support for the idea continued to grow. A later study of the history of Social Security by journalist Peter A. Corning found that there had been an "avalanche of mail" to congressmen about the devastating cost of medical care for the elderly. Major newspaper editorials concluded that helping to pay medical bills for seniors had become the "number one domestic issue" during the 1960 election campaign. When Democratic candidate John F. Kennedy won the election, a key part of his New Frontier program for the nation was a proposal to extend "Social Security benefits for 14 million Americans over 65 to cover hospital and nursing home costs," writes Kennedy biographer Michael O'Brien.

Momentum favoring the idea continued to build. The AMA accused the Kennedy administration of leading a "propaganda blitz" to put pressure on Congress to pass legislation for a Social Security–paid healthcare plan for the elderly. Part of the new Kennedy administration's plan was to use the popular young president to sell the plan. President Kennedy and his staff embraced it as the logical extension of the Democratic Party's tradition of New Deal legislation.

In a nationally televised speech from New York City's Madison Square Garden viewed by an estimated twenty million people, the president asked people to join him in petitioning Congress to pass the healthcare bill. The same year, 1962, President Kennedy selected Ball as the commissioner of Social Security, replacing William Mitchell, a Republican appointee whom President Kennedy had kept on at the start of his administration to show that Social Security had the support of both parties and was beyond politics. When Mitchell resigned, the president's top staff saw political advantage in keeping an apolitical gloss on Social Security. As the best-known bureaucrat in the Social Security Administration, Ball was seen as the man for the job. He had been a leader in the Social Security Administration under Democratic and Republican presidents; he had never run for office; and he was accepted by both sides as an expert on the mechanics of the program.

The Social Security trust fund was financially sound as Ball took over. The only cloud was fast-rising medical costs for the elderly. Ball felt it could be dealt with by passing the Kennedy healthcare bill. Doctors, however, through the American Medical Association, fought Ball's idea of federal subsidies for senior healthcare. They complained it was the first step toward a government takeover of the healthcare industry. Hospitals and insurance companies also saw it as a threat to their power and earnings. Even with his new position as the Social Security commissioner, Ball was not making much progress advancing his idea. In Congress, debate on various proposals for a healthcare subsidy plan for America's elderly was stalled by lobbying from the doctors.

But after President Kennedy's 1963 assassination, the healthcare plan gained a powerful advocate. Newly sworn in, President Lyndon Johnson made it part of his Great Society program of expanding civil rights and social programs. By 1964 the Congress had changed, too. President Johnson's landslide victory had brought more Democrats into the House of Representatives, where they held a supermajority of 295–140 over Republicans. The tone of the debate now shifted. The medical community's opposition to a national healthcare program was reduced to attempts to limit the program to just the elderly. With the new makeup of Congress there was an assumption that some form of the bill was inevitably going to pass. The only recourse for the critics was how to make sure Congress didn't take the program too far.

By early 1964 President Johnson had begun using the issue as a rallying point for his upcoming presidential race, telling one audience: "We are going to fight for medical care for the aged as long as we have breath in our bodies." In Congress, Democrats made progress advancing legislation by promising doctors and insurance companies that the changes would not amount to a federal takeover of the healthcare field. Medicare, as it was called, was only for people over 65 who qualified for Social Security, and the disabled.

The second part of the proposed 1965 Social Security amendment was for a plan to offer medical care to poor people who were not yet sixty-five and so did not qualify for Medicare based on age. This plan, called Medicaid, was conceived as a partnership between the federal government and the states to share the cost of medical care for poor families. Medicaid was to be administered as part of Social Security, but unlike Medicare, its federal funding came from general revenues, not from the withholding of taxes on workers that funded Social Security.

Even with its concessions to critics, the 1965 Social Security amendments were too much for the American Medical Association. They ran an advertisement asking Americans to write to Congress demanding an end to the bill and describing the congressional plan as the "beginning of socialized medicine."

Passing Medicare legislation "was really a long fight," Ball told NPR's Scott Simon in a 2003 interview. On April 8, 1965, the House passed the Medicare bill, inspired by Ball and Forand and designed by Chairman of the House Ways and Means Committee Wilbur Mills (D-Ark.), against surprisingly muted opposition. "This is a landmark day in the historic evolution of our Social Security system," said President Johnson, putting added pressure on the Senate to act quickly. On July 9 the Senate approved a similar bill. In just two weeks the House and Senate worked out differences over several Senate amendments to the House version, and a final bill was sent to President Johnson. In a historic ceremony, LBJ signed the bill on July 30, 1965, at the Truman Library in Independence, Missouri.

"It was a generation ago that Harry Truman said, and I quote him: 'Millions of our citizens do not now have a full measure of opportunity to achieve and to enjoy good health. Millions do not now have protection or security against the economic effects of sickness,'" President Johnson said as former president Truman and his wife, Bess, joined him for the ceremony. "Well, today, Mr. President, and my fellow Americans, we are taking such action. . . . Because the need for this action is plain; and it is so clear indeed that we marvel not simply at the passage of this bill but what we marvel at is that it took so many years to pass . . . There are more than 18 million Americans over the age of 65. Most of them have low incomes. Most of them are threatened by illnesses and medical expenses that they cannot afford. And through this new law, Mr. President, every citizen will be able, in his productive years when he is earning, to insure himself against the ravages of illness in his old age."

President Johnson said the benefits of the bill went beyond the elderly and the poor to all American families. "No longer will young families see their own incomes, and their own hopes, eaten away simply because they are carrying out their deep moral obligations to their parents, and to their uncles, and their aunts," he went on to a broadly smiling President Truman.

The program was an extension of Social Security's original old age and survivors insurance plan. Part A of the plan provided insurance to cover hospital stays, and Part B offered funding for seniors to pay for doctor's appointments, tests, and outpatient services. The man responsible for implementing the plan was the undisputed master of the Social Security system, Robert Ball. His first challenge was working with the very people who had tried to stop Congress from approving the new law—doctors, hospitals, and insurance companies. Ball made the case to this contingent with financial projections of higher profits from more patients for the entire healthcare industry. More seniors would be seeking treatment and filling doctors' offices and hospital beds, he explained, now that they had subsidies to pay the bill. Seniors still had to pay 25 percent of the cost, creating new business for private insurers. Ball also made clear there was no federal interest in expanding the program to younger people or in starting a federal healthcare plan that dictated pricing for medical procedures, care, and hospital stays for the entire medical industry.

Ball was faced with one major challenge. In order to get the more reluctant lawmakers to support the 1965 amendment, Congress had made Medicare Part B voluntary. Unlike Social Security's other program, it was not mandatory. Without large-scale voluntary participation from the nineteen million people eligible, the program might collapse from the multimillion-dollar cost of hiring and training nine thousand new Social Security employees to work on the plan, opening new offices nationwide and certifying hospitals and doctors to handle Medicare patients. Ball also faced potentially killing criticism for wasting money if only a few patients enrolled, especially if they waited until they got sick and called on the Social Security system to pay for the most costly, end-of-life medical care. Ball had less than a year to make it all work before Medicare payments were scheduled to be available to the public.

So Ball became a cheerleader. In a 1965 pamphlet for Social Security employees celebrating the thirtieth anniversary of the program, he wrote: "What a great time this really is to be alive. We are on the edge of greatness in America. We are taking steps to improve the position of the poor; the security of the old, the disabled, widows and orphans; the education of the young; and freedom and equality for all.

"And what a great time to work for Social Security and be a part of this program which is doing so much for so many!" he continued. "We all have a great opportunity, and a great trust to perform; let's get on with the job."

Ball devised a plan to have his Social Security staff advertise the Medicare program as if it were compulsory, just like the old age and survivors program. Ball put advertising on television and in newspapers and sent applications with government emblems in the mail. In addition, punch card applications were sent to the fifteen million seniors already getting Social Security benefits. There was an incredible response rate; according to the *Washington Post,* 93 percent of the nineteen million people eligible had signed up that summer of 1966.

Medicare's first patient was Mary Augustus, a sixty-eight-year-old from Hartford, Connecticut. The government paid $331.71 for her to have surgery in the hospital. It was the beginning of a successfully run program under Ball's stewardship; it was popular and proved that the federal government could play a role in easing poverty among the elderly without ruining life for doctors and the insurance industry.

Ball led the larger, more powerful Social Security Administration until his retirement in 1973. Before he left, he played a critical role in getting Congress to approve a cost-of-living adjustment to prevent inflation from draining the value of Social Security's benefit structure. He also helped to develop the Supplemental Security Income plan for elderly and disabled people with poverty-level income. And when Social Security seemed headed for financial trouble in 1981, Ball was selected to serve on President Reagan's National Commission on Social Security Reform. The panel, headed by economist Alan Greenspan, made a slight reduction in benefits to ensure the program's future solvency.

When Ball died in 2008, the *Washington Post* described him as "possibly the most influential person of any party in shaping the fate of the giant Social Security program." Journalist Carolyn Puckett wrote in the *Social Security Bulletin* that Ball played such an incredibly important role in the history of Social Security because of his "longevity" and because he managed to sell politicians and the public on the "philosophy that a successful social insurance program must provide an adequate level of benefits, have near universal coverage, and maintain benefit rates related to the level of an individual's earnings so that payments are an earned, not just a statutory, right."

According to Puckett, Ball "excelled in three roles: as a social policy expert, as an inspiring leader and administrator, and as a master negotiator and legislative tactician." Ball is credited with incredible success in sustaining and growing Social Security and the controversial idea that government played a key role in halting individual poverty for the elderly, for the disabled, for the orphaned, and more. Ball's greatest legacy, however, may be that he is the link between the New Deal's creation of Social Security in 1935, the expansion of Social Security to include Medicare and Medicaid in 1965, and congressional passage of the 2010 Affordable Care Act, which gave life to the nation's first federal health insurance plan for all Americans.

It is only because of the half-century of wide acceptance across political lines of Social Security, and the acceptance of the tax and funding system for the program—and for Medicare in particular—that the prospect of universal health coverage for all Americans could even be contemplated. Medicare "represented the nation's first (and very belated) stride toward some sort of national health insurance scheme, at least for more than twenty million of its older citizens," wrote legal scholar Susan G. Neisuler in her book *Justice at the City Gate: Social Policy, Social Services, and the Law.*

And Medicaid, the 1965 program to help the poor afford medical care, became the model for the twenty-first-century federal concept of how to offer insurance to every citizen. President Obama's plan did not adopt it across the board, as that would have meant adopting a single-payer plan for all Americans, something that Republicans in Congress refused to accept. Instead, the new plan set up state insurance markets of private insurance plans and subsidized the poor so they could afford to purchase insurance.

In the end, it is only because of the minister's son and his near-religious commitment to the idea of providing aid to the poor that the American public has come to accept that there is virtue and even a sense of obligation to their fellow citizens to offer healthcare coverage to all Americans. The strongest ropes supporting the twenty-first-century social safety net in America are there because of the vision and operational skills of Robert Ball and the determined political efforts of Presidents Roosevelt, Truman, Johnson, and Obama.

CHAPTER 17

SILENT SPRING

Rachel Carson and the
Environmental Movement

Hearing the grandiose pledge in Barack Obama's speech in St. Paul, Minnesota, some critics later said the promise from the presidential candidate had religious, messianic overtones.

"I am absolutely certain," an exuberant candidate Obama said after winning the 2008 Democratic nomination for president, "that generations from now, we will be able to look back and tell our children that this was the moment when . . . the rise of the oceans began to slow and our planet began to heal. . . . This was the moment—this was the time—when we came together to remake this great nation so that it may always reflect our very best selves, and our highest ideals. . . . [M]ay God bless the United States of America."

Yes, the candidate who went on to be twice elected president of the United States pledged to stop "the rise of the oceans" and "heal" the planet. Had they been listening, at that point Franklin, Jefferson, Hamilton, and Madison might begin to grumble. Halting the rise of the oceans? That's impossible, supernatural, beyond human capacity! For that matter, why would anyone even need to halt the rise of the oceans? The original Founding Fathers wouldn't know that the oceans had risen in the first place.

Even if they knew the sea level was higher, President Obama was speaking in terms of government responsibility unfamiliar to the original Founders. His speech was rooted in a mid-twentieth-century movement started by the writer Rachel Carson.

Of course, other presidents have used grandiose language. Franklin Roosevelt called the United States before World War II a global "arsenal of democracy." LBJ launched a "War on Poverty" as part of his plan for an idealistic "Great Society." All of these pledges go far beyond the scope of power and duties for the federal government as envisioned by the original Founding Fathers. But healing the earth exceeds even the scope of those ambitious plans.

Before Rachel Carson the idea of any government repairing damage to the natural world of the oceans, land, and the air did not make sense. It would have overwhelmed colonists who lived in the 1700s, the Americans who followed "manifest destiny" to push west to the Pacific Ocean in the 1800s, and even the Americans who crossed oceans to win two world wars in the twentieth century.

Carson's books tied together the conditions of the planet's water and air, life among humans and animals, and the quality of the food and water we consumed. Her 1962 book *Silent Spring*, on the dangers of the pesticide DDT, changed the nation by creating new federal and local government agencies to guard against pollutants and protect the land, air, and water. The Clean Air Act, the Clean Water Act, the Environmental Protection Agency, and the National Environmental Policy Act were all inspired by Carson's *Silent Spring*. Carson's work led her to be viewed as the mother of the nation's annual Earth Day celebration.

The original Founding Fathers did care about nature; they viewed the earth and the oceans as gifts from God. The ocean was a buffer of protection from political interference by the British and other European powers. The earth was the source of the nation's agricultural success and economic abundance.

At the time of the writing of the Declaration of Independence, southern plantation owners had a special regard for the earth as the basis of livelihood in growing cotton, sugarcane, and vegetables and in raising farm animals. Thomas Jefferson, himself a planter, wrote about farmers as the ideal Americans because "cultivators of the earth are the most vigorous, the most independent, the most virtuous." To Jefferson, farming allowed Americans to directly exercise the freedoms for which they had fought in the Revolutionary War. An economy based on small farming communities was a self-sufficient society able to meet its needs for food, clothing, and shelter. While he supported Free Trade, he also did not want America to have to answer to foreign demands and restrictions that reminded Jefferson of the taxes that England levied on the American colonies throughout the 1700s.

James Madison, another southern farmer, similarly called for the nation to celebrate its farmers, people trained in cultivating the land and raising animals, because more farmers would lead the nation to be "more free, the more independent" from economic worries.

Several of the original Founders considered themselves experts on farming. "The first four presidents of the United States—George Washington, John Adams, Thomas Jefferson, and James Madison—were all utterly obsessed with manure and recipes for compost," historian Andrea Wulf wrote in a 2011 *Los Angles Times* article titled "Gardening as Politics: Digging the Founding Gardeners." "Washington, Adams, Jefferson and Madison regarded themselves first as gardeners and farmers, not politicians," Wulf wrote. "They wove their passion for gardens and nature into the fabric of America; it was aligned with their political thought. Agriculture would be the foundation of the new republic, they believed." Jefferson wrote in a 1787 letter to Madison: "I think our governments will remain virtuous for many centuries; as long as they are chiefly agricultural."

Not all the Colonial-era Founding Fathers agreed. Alexander Hamilton, the nation's first secretary of the treasury and a northerner, predicted disaster if the young nation's economy became solely dependent on agriculture, with its reliance on forces beyond any man's control—from pestilence to disease to the weather with its storms, drought and heat waves. In two reports delivered to Congress in 1790 and 1791 on America's economic future—the "Report on Banking" and the "Report on Manufactures"—Hamilton expressed his preference for manufacturing as the foundation of the nation's economy, aided by a central bank to set policy for U.S. currency and global trade.

Hamilton's thinking extended to preparing the young nation for the possibility of conflict with Britain. After the Revolutionary War, President Washington, who led the victorious Continental Army against the British, advised Congress to promote domestic manufacturing to avoid

ever again having to depend on getting military support and goods
from other countries. Hamilton echoed Washington's concern about
the need for manufactured goods in any future war, such as guns and
gunpowder. Hamilton's attention to environmental policy called for
sacrificing farmlands and natural resources to build and supply factories.

The split between Hamilton and Jefferson over the economic pri-
macy of agriculture and the start of industry played out in small ways
during the Colonial era. In New England, farmers alert to potential
damage to their land won limits on how much timber could be cut down
to build expanding cities. In the city of Philadelphia, as local businesses
grew they ate up surrounding farmland. New mills and warehouses
as well as roads and ports for shipping spread the industrial bound-
ary line deeper into agricultural lands. There was also growing concern
about air quality. Franklin argued that the odors emitted by tanneries
that unceremoniously dropped their waste into Philadelphia's business
district caused illness and lowered property values.

Even as an advocate of an industrial economic base for the new nation, Alexander Hamilton never dared to advise Congress to "replace
farms with factories," according to Ron Chernow in his biography *Alexander Hamilton*. Hamilton did make the practical case to congressional leaders that "since manufacturing and agriculture obeyed different
economic cycles, a downturn in one could be offset by an upturn in
another." Hamilton also argued that for the country to grow economically it needed to have manufactured goods as well as farm produce to
trade with other nations. The complete shift to industrialization took
nearly a century, until the end of the 1800s, but even then farming remained critical to the U.S. economy. But the rise of manufacturing, as
Hamilton predicted, transformed the country from a middling international presence to a military and economic superpower.

The Industrial Revolution came with enormous benefits for the
United States. It produced jobs that paid wages far beyond those of the
farm economy, attracting workers from Europe and generating tremendous wealth that allowed for investments in the latest machinery. U.S.
industry also provided the backbone of the nation's military power.
And the military, in turn, protected trade routes for international commerce of American products.

The nation's incredible financial success did have a downside. Smoke from coal furnaces dirtied the air, and runoff from industrial processes turned streams gray. Americans lamented the changing landscape as forests were cut down, open spaces paved, and mountains left pockmarked from strip mines. In 1854, Henry David Thoreau published *Walden; or, Life in the Woods*, a meditation on the loss of simplicity and self-sufficiency among Americans as the country increasingly became an industrialized economy. In his view the nation was losing its appreciation of the power of nature.

Environmental historian Christine Meisner Rosen later described how in the 1840s and 1850s American industries "discharged foul, sometimes toxic, solid, liquid, and gaseous wastes and loud, repetitive, mechanical noises and vibrations into the surrounding air, water and land." Rosen's 2003 article described the changes to the American landscape with regret: "These emissions blackened air and water and disturbed ecosystems wherever rivers were dammed for power, wood or coal burned to power production processes, and slaughterhouses, mills, workshops, manufactories, mines, and smelters established."

Despite the popularity of *Walden,* industrial barons and politicians brushed aside complaints about damage to the environment in the name of producing jobs and economic wealth. Top politicians dismissed the complaints as bellyaching by a small, elite group who did not understand the need to make sacrifices in the name of industrial progress, create steady jobs for workers, and produce an abundance of products for consumers.

American reliance on manufacturing increased throughout most of the twentieth century. But by the twenty-first century, manufacturing makes up only 12 percent of the U.S. economy. Agriculture and mining have slipped to just 5 percent of the nation's gross domestic product. Today, far more American economic activity can be found in financial services, high technology, pharmaceuticals, energy, and education. Oil and natural gas production in the United States has grown to be the most productive in the world and a major boost to the economy.

In today's economy, the air, earth, and the ocean play a very different role in America's economic life. And they bear a burden never considered by the Founding Fathers.

The United States and China are now the source of one-third of the gas pollution emitted into the world's atmosphere. Those gases erode ozone in the atmosphere that shields the earth from the heat of the sun. As the ozone erodes, scientists report, icebergs melt in Antarctica, ocean levels rise, and new weather patterns arise—all referred to with the shorthand phrase "climate change."

American schoolchildren today talk about concepts totally alien to the original Founders—global warming, sustainability, and saving the planet. The United States deals with oil spills from offshore drilling as well as deep cuts into mountains to mine for coal and other minerals. Chemicals and water are forced into rock formations far under the surface of the earth to drive out natural gas in a controversial but lucrative process called fracking. At the same time more Americans are buying and driving hybrid cars and electric cars to limit their personal "carbon footprint" of damage to the environment. It is common for American families to recycle paper, glass bottles, and plastics, an activity unknown to the original Founders.

These twenty-first-century activities—recycling, driving energy-efficient cars—are not things that Americans give much thought to on a daily basis. Such practices are considered good behavior and virtuous citizenship. This illustrates the strength of American environmentalism. Ecologically friendly activities are so deeply entrenched in the modern American psyche that for many they have become habits, like brushing your teeth.

But even as these activities become commonplace, environmentalism remains a contentious national and international issue. One of President Obama's first trips as president was to a 2009 United Nations conference on climate change in Copenhagen, Denmark. The goal was to limit the rise in global temperatures during the twenty-first century by getting newly industrialized countries, including China, India, South Africa, and Brazil, to reduce the emission of greenhouse gases. President Obama called the Copenhagen Accords—the nonbinding treaty that the conference members produced—"a meaningful and unprecedented breakthrough . . . For the first time in history all major economies have come together to accept their responsibility to take action to confront the threat of climate change."

Yet there was no legally binding agreement, a major disappointment to environmentalists. The new president tried but failed to get Congress to agree to a "cap-and-trade" policy offering incentives to factories and energy plants to cut back on their use of polluting fuels in exchange for tax breaks. In 2014 President Obama announced a deal with China to reduce carbon dioxide emissions by having the United States cut back on its use of oil and coal to produce energy, while China eventually stops its use of those fuels. The *New York Times* hailed the deal as a "historic announcement." Yet others claimed the deal with China was no deal at all. Republican congressional leaders complained that while the United States had to immediately reduce its carbon emissions by 26–28 percent of their 2005 emission levels, China only agreed to stop increasing carbon emissions by 2030. Senator Jim Inhofe, a Republican from Oklahoma, wrote in a newspaper column: "The United States will be required to more steeply reduce our carbon emissions while China won't have to reduce anything . . . this deal is a non-binding charade."

These controversial efforts by President Obama to limit pollution have clear historical links to President Richard Nixon's creation of the Environmental Protection Agency in 1970. President Nixon created the Environmental Protection Agency to guide the nation to a future where Americans are not "choked by traffic, suffocated by smog, poisoned by water, deafened by noise," as he said in his 1970 State of the Union address. "The great question of the 1970s," Nixon continued, "is shall we surrender to our surroundings, or shall we make our peace with nature and begin to make reparations for the damage we have done to our air, to our land and to our water? Restoring nature to its natural state is a cause beyond party and beyond factions . . . Clean air, clean water, open spaces—these should once again be the birthright of every American."

Yet one woman's transforming work dwarfs even those historic steps. She changed American thinking about everyone's relationship with the oceans, pollution, animals, and even bug spray. Her books on the oceans depict animals as friendly creatures, humankind's neighbors, sharing a common environment and fate. Rachel Carson's work led to a ban on one notorious pesticide, DDT, and was the starting point for a change in local, state, and federal rules limiting industrial pollution. Her new view of the responsibilities of scientists prompted schools and universities to begin teaching environmental science and to focus on the ethics of scientific innovation. On a grand scale, Carson renewed Thoreau's reverence of unspoiled rivers, majestic mountains, and the wind-blown plains as America's sacred cultural heritage.

Silent Spring stands to this day as the continental divide in American environmental history. It gave birth to nationwide concern about endangered species and unsafe drinking water. It is the forerunner of concern over genetically modified foods and acid rain. President Nixon's monumental efforts in creating a national Council on Environmental Quality and the EPA have been described by one historian as "the extended shadow of *Silent Spring*."

Rachel Carson's book had such an enormous impact that she was immediately attacked by the chemical industry. The National Agricultural Chemical Association funded a $250,000 campaign—the equivalent of an effort costing roughly two million dollars today—to discredit the book, arguing that Carson did not have a doctorate and her facts were wrong. One chemical company sent a letter to her publisher, Houghton Mifflin, suggesting she was under communist influence: "Members of the chemical industry in this country and Western Europe must deal with sinister influences . . . [whose purpose is] to create the false impression that all business is grasping and immoral." Former agriculture secretary Ezra Taft Benson wrote a letter to President Eisenhower saying Carson is "probably a communist" and asking "why a spinster with no children was so concerned about genetics."

"Isn't it just like a woman to be scared to death of a few little bugs," read a letter published in the *New Yorker*. Monsanto, a company that produced chemical pesticides, mocked *Silent Spring* by distributing a parody in which pesticides are illegal and insects take over the world. A political cartoon in the *Saturday Review* showed a man saying: "I just got adjusted to radioactive fallout, and now along comes Rachel Carson." The head of biochemistry at Vanderbilt published a critique with the title "Silence! Miss Carson," and implied that women should not be taken seriously on matters of science. Those critical comments only hint at the opposition Carson faced.

Published in September 1962, *Silent Spring* sold more than 100,000 copies by Christmas, and stayed on the *New York Times* bestseller list for 31 weeks. William O. Douglas, associate justice of the Supreme

Court, declared that *Silent Spring* was "the most revolutionary book since *Uncle Tom's Cabin*," which challenged slavery as immoral.

In a book about Carson, former editor in chief of Houghton Mifflin Paul Brooks compared the controversy over the publication of *Silent Spring* to that of Charles Darwin's landmark *On the Origin of Species*. An excerpt of the book printed in the *New Yorker* in June 1962 generated the most mail in the magazine's history. By May 1963 President Kennedy's Science Advisory Committee sent the White House a recommendation calling for "the elimination of the use of persistent toxic pesticides."

In April 1963 CBS News presented an hour-long special titled *The Silent Spring of Rachel Carson,* watched by ten million viewers. The next day the U.S. Senate named a subcommittee to review the use of poisonous pesticides. Carson testified before the panel in June 1963, calling for limiting aerial spraying of pesticides and more research on the damage being done by pesticides to vegetables, fruit, livestock, wild animals, and humans. She sparked front-page headlines across the country by calling for the federal government to pass new laws protecting the environment and for a new federal agency to coordinate all farming and industrial actions that impact every part of nature, from the rivers to animals.

Widespread public debate about Carson's work led media to engage in the argument. News coverage came to assume that there are standards for responsible corporate, military, and agricultural stewardship of the world around us. And most of all, her work placed public pressure on the courts, Congress, and the federal bureaucracy to revise the laws governing American industry and to create new, more sustainable relationships to the natural resources on which industry—and all of us—depend for future use.

"If it wasn't for Rachel Carson, I never would have had these hearings," said Sen. Abraham Ribicoff. "I was not aware of the extent and the importance of the problem she raised." The hearings led to a new law requiring chemical companies to divulge what was in their bug sprays and the Agriculture Department to consult with the Interior Department and state governments before it agreed to any widespread use of pesticides.

Within five years of *Silent Spring*'s publication, a group of scientists founded the Environmental Defense Fund. In 1970 President Nixon created the Environmental Protection Agency to do the exact kind of monitoring of environmental policy that Carson recommended in her Senate testimony. And by 1972 the Environmental Defense Fund had won a federal ban on DDT, the pesticide identified in *Silent Spring*, as the single greatest threat to the environment.

Carson died of a heart attack in 1964, just two years after her book was published. But the book took on a life of its own, becoming the bible of the environmental movement in the United States. And other writers picked up the baton.

So who was Rachel Carson? At five feet four inches and 115 pounds, with reddish brown hair cut primly short and thin, tight lips, she was not a commanding presence. People remember her as a pale, impish figure with the subdued personality of a government bureaucrat. Her lack of natural charm and political skills led the *New York Times* to describe her as a "small, solemn-looking woman . . . not given to quick smiles or to encouraging conversation even with fans."

She was born in 1907 in Springdale, Pennsylvania, about eighteen miles from Pittsburgh. Pittsburgh was then a fast-growing center of factory production, located close to the coal mines and with easy access to major rivers. Eliza Griswold wrote in the *New York Times* that "from [Carson's] bedroom window, she could see smoke billow from the stacks of the American Glue Factory, which slaughtered horses." Two power plants, the West Penn Power Company and the Duquesne Light Company, soon moved nearby. The big plants brought in workers, buses, and cars, lunchrooms and bars, transforming Carson's quiet world of wooded landscapes, streams, and wildlife.

Her father was the son of Irish immigrants and worked various jobs—as an insurance salesman, a Realtor, and even an electrician—without much success. But he managed to buy sixty-five acres of woodland in Springdale and move his family to a cabin with no heating or plumbing. That home became the center of Rachel's childhood. The last of three children, Rachel walked the hilly land owned by her family. At age twenty-two she had never been more than sixteen miles from the cabin and never seen the ocean—the subject of so much of her future writing.

Her mother, Maria, was the daughter of a Presbyterian minister. After studying piano at a seminary, she became a piano teacher. But she stopped teaching music after her marriage, because local custom barred married women from teaching. Rachel was born well after her sister and brother, and as the family's baby, she became the central focus of her mother's attention. One of Carson's editors later described her mother as "undoubtedly the strongest single influence in her daughter's life." The mother's religious upbringing led her into a turn-of-the-century movement of people opposed to the nation's rapid industrialization. The "Nature-Study" movement led Maria to teach Rachel never to kill insects. The family rarely ate meat.

Maria Carson read books to Rachel as a child that featured animals with human qualities, such as Peter Rabbit and Benjamin Bunny. The tales and walks in the woods with her mother led Rachel, in the words of biographer Philip Sterling, to have "feelings about the fields and woods, about the small creatures, tame and wild, who were part of her personal world . . . that everything in the world may somehow be connected with everything else."

Her mother's seminary education provided Rachel with an introduction to stories of adventure on ships crossing the oceans to distant ports, such as the tales by Joseph Conrad, Herman Melville, and Robert Louis Stevenson. When she was ten, Rachel submitted a short story to a fiction magazine based on a story she had heard from her brother, who had fought in World War I, about a courageous pilot. It was published and became the first of several stories she did for the magazine.

Rachel's sister and brother didn't finish high school. But her mother saved money and made it possible for Rachel to be driven two miles every day to a high school in New Kensington, where she graduated first in her class. Rachel then won a scholarship to a nearby state college, Pennsylvania College for Women (now Chatham University). Rachel's mom was such a regular presence on campus that other students referred to her as "the commuter."

In her sophomore year Rachel took a basic biology class to fulfill her science requirement. Her professor was Mary Scott Skinker, who took an interest in Carson's fast mind. The combination of Carson's childhood love of nature and a teacher who delighted in classification of animals, plants, rocks, and water led the teenager to switch her major to biology the next year. She graduated magna cum laude and, at Skinker's prodding, applied to graduate school in biology at Johns Hopkins in Baltimore. Carson was one of two women accepted in a class of seventy students.

Professor Skinker also helped her get an internship at the Marine Biological Laboratory at Woods Hole, Massachusetts. Skinker had a strong interest in the lab because it had been founded by the Women's Education Association of Boston and was one of the few scientific research facilities where women did scientific work side by side with men. Skinker knew the director of research for the U.S. Bureau of Fisheries and arranged for Carson to talk with Elmer Higgins about possible future jobs.

That summer Carson had her first trip on a boat, and saw the ocean for the first time. She later wrote that her time at Woods Hole gave her a first taste of "the real sea world—that is, the world as it is known by shore birds and fishes and beach crabs and all the other creatures that live in the sea or along its edge . . . Probably that was when I first began to let my imagination go down through the water and piece together bits of scientific fact until I could see the whole life of those creatures as they lived them in that strange sea world."

The harsh reality of the Great Depression hit the Carson family while Rachel was in her first semester of graduate school at Hopkins. Her parents, as well as her brother and her divorced sister (who had two children), had no jobs. They moved to Baltimore in 1930 to live with Rachel. While in graduate school Carson was able to get work as a lab assistant and teaching assistant to help support her family. But by 1934 she could no longer afford tuition at Hopkins and withdrew to look for a full-time job. Money was such a challenge that when her father died in 1935 the family sent his body back to the Pennsylvania hill country for burial but none of the rest of the family could pay the fare to go back for the funeral.

Once again Professor Skinker helped Carson, arranging for her to visit Elmer Higgins, who had run scientific studies for the Bureau of Fisheries at Woods Hole. Now in Washington, D.C., directing a radio show on the oceans, Higgins needed a writer for his program, and hired Carson. The program, nicknamed "Seven-Minute Fish Tales," was about the world beneath the waves. Carson also began to write articles for the local newspaper, the *Baltimore Sun*, about the threat posed to fishing and hunting at the Chesapeake Bay by pollution; she published under the name R. L. Carson to hide the fact she was a woman, as she was afraid readers would not find a woman credible. While doing occasional stories for the *Sun*, Carson got a full-time job at the Bureau of Fisheries as a junior aquatic biologist. She wrote and edited brochures sent around the nation on the research being done by the Bureau of Fisheries.

Higgins wanted Carson to describe marine animals in terms that could excite people and get them to support funding for more research. Rachel produced a four-page story called "The World of Water" that described aquatic life through the eyes of sea creatures. At Higgins's suggestion she sent a copy to the *Atlantic Monthly*, and the editor, "impressed by your uncommonly eloquent little essay," published it in the September 1937 issue under the title "Undersea." The *Atlantic* article set her on a new path, opening opportunities and generating attention; according to Carson, "everything else followed."

She got an offer from the well-known chief editor of Simon & Schuster, Quincy Howe, to expand the article into a book about the secrets of life hidden from human eyes in the ocean. Representatives from Simon & Schuster proposed that Carson's book stay away from people and write from the point of view of the sea creatures. With a $250 advance and no book contract, Carson agreed to take on the project.

She wrote the book in longhand at night. Her mother typed up the pages while Rachel worked at the Bureau of Fisheries to support the family. With the death of her father and older sister, Rachel Carson now supported her mother and her sister's two children.

As she was writing her book, she continued to write articles about wildlife around the Chesapeake Bay for the *Baltimore Sun*, the *Richmond Times Dispatch*, and *Nature*. Her stories about hunting, fishing, and touring sold well. What sold best was Carson's detailed, scientifically accurate tales about bird life, especially the world of a very common mid-Atlantic bird, the starling.

Yet when she tried to write stories about the damage done by increasing pollution and rapacious commercial fishing, no one was interested. Newspaper editors told her it would bore readers and advertisers. Her lone success on that front came in 1938 when the *Times Dispatch*

ran a story of hers about how "draining marshland, cutting timber
[and] plowing under the grasses" has brought many animals to the
verge of extinction. She carefully presented the crisis as a threat to the
tourism and hunting industries, but hidden within the story was a telling line: "The home of wildlife is also our home . . . [Conserving natural
habitats] has a deeper significance than restoration of wildlife alone."
Carson ended the story with an argument for conservation, connecting the lack of prairie grass in the Great Plains—and the absence of the
animals who fed on the grass—to dust storms in states as far away as
Pennsylvania and New York. And those choking storms, she inferred,
killed off more wildlife, breaking the food chain that sustained life both
above and under the nation's waterways.

The idea of a natural world being thrown out of balance by human
damage was a central theme of Carson's book, *Under the Sea Wind*,
published in November 1941, a month before Pearl Harbor. The badly
timed book did not sell well, but it was praised by the *New York Times*
as "so skillfully written as to read like fiction, but in fact [it is] a scientifically accurate account of life in the ocean and along the ocean shores."
Under the Sea Wind presents the daily life and struggles of the animals
as drama. Carson had constructed her narrative without humans: the
stars in the book are a bird, an eel, and a mackerel. A sandpiper named
Blackfoot migrates from South America to the Arctic. Her mackerel
(named Scomber, because all mackerel belong to that genus) hatches,
grows, withstands predators, mates, and reproduces. In the third section an eel—named Anguilla for the biological classification that includes eels—makes a heroic journey home to the Sargasso Sea.

Carson gave her animals drive and ambition that human readers
could see in their own lives. What discomforted readers was that she
also took care to depict a world in which actual humans were not at the
center of the lives of her protagonists. They lived with the rhythms of
the tides, waves, and migration, realities beyond human control.

In the preface she wrote: "I have spoken of a fish 'fearing' his enemies, for example, not because I suppose a fish experiences fear in
the same way that we do, but because I think he behaves as though he
were frightened. With the fish, the response is primarily physical; with
us, primarily psychological. Yet if the behavior of the fish is to be un-
derstandable to us, we must describe it in the words that most properly

belong to human psychological states." In a letter to a friend about the book she said the animal characters "give us a little better perspective on human problems . . . Blackfoot, Scomber, Anguilla and the other characters . . . are as ageless as the sun and rain, or the sea itself."

The failure to make humans the center of the animal universe did not help sales. Book reviewers, however, praised the book for its scientific accuracy and strong writing. Scientists famous for denigrating "popular science" writing joined in applauding Carson for a detailed, accurate account of life under the water.

After the book came out, Carson continued working for the government. With the nation's attention on the war, she wrote a celebrated series of pamphlets on seafood for cooks, mostly housewives, coping with a wartime shortage of beef and poultry. The series was titled "Food from the Sea," and it took readers on a tour of the nation's various locales for seafood—from the coast of New England to the lakes of the Midwest to the southern Gulf Coast. She also continued to write for newspapers on topics such as the nation's best aquariums. Another article described the similarities between the sound waves used by bats to communicate with each other and the navy's radar system to scan for enemy ships. The story on the bats was reprinted by the navy for use by recruits being trained to work with radar.

Carson was now established as a top science writer for the government, and her salary increased. But she wanted to write books. In a letter to a friend she confided that she was bored: "I don't know where I am going! I know that if I could choose what seems to me the ideal existence, it would be just to live by writing—but I have done far too little to dare risk it."

The government work did require Carson to stay up to date on the latest studies being done by government scientists, including work done to support the war. That is how she noticed that scientists were using a new chemical mix to kill lice and insects that spread malaria and bubonic plague among American soldiers. The new chemical was dichlorodiphenyltrichloroethane, or DDT.

After the war, DDT was sold as a new, fuss-free spray for American families trying to eliminate bugs. Assigned to edit a report on the negative side effects of DDT by wildlife biologist Clarence Cottam and her boss at the Fish and Wildlife Service, Elmer Higgins, Carson was among the first to see research discussing the chemical's effect on fish. The 1945 study concluded that fish as well as birds were consuming DDT when they ate dead insects. Others suspected the harmful effects of DDT as well. An article in *Time* magazine described how the DDT that was sprayed in Toronto's Algonquin Park "killed not only the moths and other insects, but practically all invertebrates, especially crayfish; many minnows; some trout [those that ate poisoned insects]; more than half of the snakes and frogs. It also damaged a few broadleaved trees." The article cautioned that DDT's success in killing insects could be a "two-edged sword."

Three months later, in a July 1945 letter to a senior editor at *Reader's Digest,* Carson suggested a story for the magazine, then one of the nation's largest, on the hidden scandal of damage being done to animals by DDT. "We have all heard a lot about what DDT will soon do for us by wiping out insect pests," she wrote. She argued to the magazine's senior editor, Harold Lynch, that recent government experiments "show what other effects DDT may have when it is applied to wide areas: what it will do to insects that are beneficial or even essential . . . whether it may upset the whole delicate balance of nature if unwisely used." Lynch did not buy it; he said the readers had no interest in a negative story about potential damage that was not yet confirmed or evident to most people.

So Carson tabled the DDT piece for the time being. Her ongoing work for the government led her to write a series of guides for the nation's three hundred bird and wildlife refuges. Political pressure from developers who wanted to build houses and highways during the economic boom after World War II prompted Carson's bosses to approve of the guides as a way to spur public appreciation and respect for the sites. Carson celebrated the areas as perfect for camping as well as fishing and hunting, and made a strong case that they were worth protecting for future generations. The twelve-guide series, titled Conservation in Action, is notable for Carson's loving descriptions of birds living in the refuges and details about how the birds migrate, feed, and reproduce.

Carson's work on wildlife refuges and her access to federal science research led her back to the topic of her first book, the ocean, in a new book, published in July 1951. Carson wrote that the oceans pre-dated the continents that were home to mankind. The defining aspect of life

on earth, she wrote, is its existence as "a water world, a planet dominated by its covering mantle of ocean, in which the continents are but
transient intrusions of land above the surface of the all-encircling sea."

In *The Sea Around Us* Carson relied on work done by military scientists studying the tides, waves, and currents to help with sea battles
and coastal invasions (such as the famous landing at Normandy during Operation Overlord). The studies gave the desk-bound Carson fresh
knowledge about the history of ocean storms shifting land patterns and
creating islands, as well as revelations about the depth of the oceans
and the creatures hidden far from human sight.

Thanks to major magazines picking up excerpts, incredibly including the fashion magazine *Vogue* and the literary magazine the *New
Yorker*, *The Sea Around Us* became a bestseller. For the first time Carson saw her name on the *New York Times* bestseller list. In the postwar
period, readers, especially American women, took to Carson's book as
a joyful, spiritually uplifting story. It was also a clear escape from preoccupation with war and the ongoing Cold War threat of nuclear an-
nihilation.

Carson's detailed look at nature and her colorful, sophisticated
prose had the characteristics of the best fiction. "Many people have
commented with surprise on the fact that a work of science should have
a large popular sale," Carson said after the book won the National Book
Award for nonfiction. "But this notion that 'science' is something that
belongs in a separate compartment of its own apart from everyday life
is one that I should like to challenge."

The downside of the celebrity that came to Carson with the book's
commercial success were the constant expressions of doubt from male
scientists and book reviewers that a woman could know so much about
science. Early in her writing career Carson asked newspaper and magazine editors to avoid that kind of questioning by listing her name as
"R. L. Carson." She still kept her picture off the book cover. But the fact
that she was a woman attracted an unusual audience for books based
on scientific research—women.

The money she made with her second book allowed Carson to resign
from her writing job with the Fish and Wildlife Service in 1952 and
begin working on her third book full-time. Free from limits as a government employee, Carson began to voice political opinions. She had

long been troubled by the postwar increase in the use of petrochemi-
cal products—plastics, detergents, solvents, abrasives, and pesticides.
She wrote a letter to the *Washington Post* in 1953 criticizing President
Eisenhower, the former World War II Allied commander, for allowing the Interior Department to open federal land for coal mining and
timber harvesting. "It is one of the ironies of our time that, while con-
centrating on the defense of our country against enemies from without
we should be so heedless of those who would destroy it from within,"
she wrote.

Carson had her own dance with mortality during the early 1950s,
when she had surgery to remove a tumor in her breast. The health issues led her to buy a house near the seashore in Maine. She went there
with her mother, now an elderly woman, while helping her niece to care
for a new baby born out of wedlock. Carson was afraid family issues
could lead to a gossip scandal, and so she made a point of shielding her
family life from the press.

In 1955 she published the third book in what immediately was described as a "Sea Trilogy," titled *The Edge of the Sea.* The book shifted
the reader's attention from the oceans to the seashore. Carson went into
the life of the amazing variety of life and terrain found where waves
meet rocks, sand, and earth. The nature study was a perfect companion
to her two earlier books, and another bestseller.

Carson's status as a bestselling author helped her to expand her already strong connections with top research scientists. University scientists now joined the government scientists who reached out to her and
introduced her to new friends and colleagues doing scientific research.
One clear theme emerged from those letters and conversations: Carson's earlier concern with the use of DDT was justified, as it had become apparent that new damage was being done with more widespread
use of the chemical.

The opportunity for Carson to get some stories about DDT into
newspapers and magazines got a boost when Congress approved
$2 million for a July 1957 mass spraying of DDT to kill fire ants attack-
ing crops on southern farms. Newspapers wrote lots of stories about
the dreaded ants, the political response, and long-simmering concerns
about DDT. Attention to the dangers attached to the use of DDT were
heightened even further when New York State sprayed large areas of

Long Island to kill off gypsy moths, tent caterpillars, and mosquitoes. The bugs were indeed killed, but farmers found their fruit and vegetables contaminated, and the soil ruined for future crops.

Marjorie Spock, a well-known conservationist, sued the government for reckless use of DDT. Public awareness of the danger of DDT resulted in the creation of an activist group called the Committee Against Mass Poisoning. One official associated with Massachusetts's spraying program responded with assurances that DDT was safe, and characterized the protest movement as "hysterical." But Thanksgiving 1959 saw all cranberry sauces made from cranberries sprayed with herbicides taken off grocery store shelves, as scientific studies had suggested a link between the chemicals found in mass-produced food and thyroid cancer.

Carson attempted to take advantage of all the controversy to sell articles to the newspapers and magazines on the dangers of pesticides. But most magazines rejected her proposals by repeating the objections voiced ten years earlier: it was a depressing subject and not nearly as interesting as learning about the wonderful creatures hidden under the waves. It was also a threat to magazines' advertising revenues. It took the help of her literary agent and friends at the *New Yorker,* notably the celebrated author E. B. White, for Carson to finally get a deal to write a three-part story on the harm to humans being uncovered in the lawsuit that grew out of the use of DDT on Long Island gardens.

As Carson began reporting on the lawsuit, she pushed to do a bigger story. She told her editors about the rising concern from scientists concerning DDT's effect on underground water streams and wells, as well as its role in cancers in animals and humans. And she had documents that confirmed the problem. "Carson found [scientists] in key places who, at great risk to their jobs and reputations, were willing to give her confidential information if she protected them," according to one of her biographers, Linda Lear, author of the book *Rachel Carson: Witness for Nature.*

As previously noted, excerpts from *Silent Spring,* Carson's book on DDT, first appeared in the *New Yorker* in June 1962. The article became a sensation, stirring response from readers, politicians, scientists, farmers, doctors, and the chemical companies. When the book was released in September 1962 it was an immediate bestseller. In a 2012 *New*

York Times article titled "How 'Silent Spring' Ignited the Environmental Movement," author Eliza Griswold noted that the book begins with the story of a mythical, happy suburban town suddenly hit by a "mysterious blight." "Carson knew her target audience . . . included scores of housewives," wrote Griswold. She made suburban women the heroes of the book as they "discovered robins and squirrels poisoned by pesticides outside their back doors." In the book, Carson asked American women if by using dangerous pesticides like DDT they were not complicit in causing "suffering to a living creature." "Who among us is not diminished," she wrote, by such actions?

Silent Spring was packed with stark, apocalyptic language. She described DDT and other chemical cocktails as "elixirs of death." She challenged the nation's unrestrained trust in the virtues of scientific advances by writing: "Only within the . . . present century has one species—man—acquired significant power to alter the nature of his world. . . . The most alarming of all man's assaults upon the environment is the contamination of air, earth, rivers, and sea with dangerous and even lethal materials." She amped up the threat by later writing: "Along with the possibility of the extinction of mankind by nuclear war, the central problem of our age has therefore become the contamination of man's total environment with such substances of incredible potential for harm—substances that accumulate in the tissues of plants and animals and even penetrate the germ cells to shatter or alter the very material of heredity upon which the shape of the future depends." Near the end she adds a note of optimism to the sad tale by calling for "new, imaginative and creative approaches to the problem of sharing our earth with other creatures."

Carson's book was immediately attacked by the chemical industry. As noted earlier, one letter from a chemical company suggested she was an outright communist: "Members of the chemical industry in this country and in Western Europe must deal with sinister influences . . . [seeking] to create the false impression that all business is grasping and immoral . . . so that our supply of food will be reduced to east-curtain parity."

The attacks failed to stall book sales or quiet the uproar created by the detailed horror stories in the book. In the six months after excerpts of the book were published, more than forty bills were introduced in state legislatures to limit the use of pesticides. Congressional hearings followed, and President Kennedy referred to "Miss Carson's book" when he told reporters that the Agriculture Department and the federal public health officials had been ordered to review the use of pesticides.

Carson's appearance on television shows, her congressional testimony, and the new research on the use of chemicals shifted the way the American public viewed nature. After *Silent Spring* it became widely accepted that humans and the world of nature, animals, fruit, vegetables, trees—and everything reliant on the elements of air, water, and earth—are all connected and impact each other. That concern grew throughout the 1960s as the public became aware of the army's use of the powerful chemical napalm to firebomb the enemy in Vietnam, as well as chemical pollution leading to the Cuyahoga River catching fire in Cleveland, Ohio, and a huge oil spill off the scenic California town of Santa Barbara. As President Nixon said in his 1970 State of the Union address: "Clean air, clean water, open spaces—these should once again be the birthright of every American."

Later that year the president created the Environmental Protection Agency (EPA), giving it authority to enforce new laws on pollution and the use of chemicals. The establishment of the EPA took Carson's concerns to a new level, far beyond Earth Day celebrations and international conferences of concerned scientists. The power of the federal government was now on the side of clean air, pure drinking water, and animals threatened with extinction. Ranchers and farmers had to consider EPA regulations on endangered species. Mining companies had to respond to government monitoring of how they burrowed into the face of mountains to get at coal seams. Companies that sold chemicals for household use had to get approval for new products and worry about lawsuits. Car makers had to deal with government regulation of exhaust fumes.

Americans have always cherished the physical beauty and spiritual calm of their national forests. But Carson shifted our perspective on forests by bringing forests and lakes and the ocean into the suburbs and the city. She made nature into something that Americans touch and experience every day. She opened our eyes to the idea that Americans in the biggest cities depend on nature for air, water, and resources necessary for modern life. The Carson sea trilogy and *Silent Spring* revealed the threat beyond pollution from the billowing smoke coming out of a factory smokestack. Her readers came to understand the silent threat caused by some seemingly helpful, efficient new products—like DDT in bug spray.

In the wake of the environmental movement launched by Carson, Democrats made a political push to have government fund research into clean, renewable energy sources, notably wind turbines and solar panels. Republicans, who felt such regulations had gone too far, turned the other way. They lambasted the EPA for tying up American private sector efforts to compete against nations with no pollution controls.

The GOP labeled the increasing number of new government rules to protect the environment as "job-killing regulations." They complained about the federal penalties applied to companies for using fossil fuels, labeling it a "war on coal" and on the workers and communities who made money from mining. Republicans opposed new limits on emissions from coal-burning plants enacted through a policy, cap-and-trade, that gave tax breaks to companies that paid for new technologies to scrub pollutants from the smoke rising from coal operations.

Republicans sided with oil companies to call for more wells to be drilled on private and public land, including the Alaska National Wildlife Refuge. Conservative Republicans positioned themselves as pro-business and pro-jobs. Both Republicans and Democrats supported a controversial new procedure for forcing high-pressure blasts of air, chemicals, and sand into the ground—a practice called fracking—to release otherwise inaccessible pockets of natural gas and oil.

The early opposition to *Silent Spring* from chemical companies never went away; instead it got better funding and became more sophisticated. One Carson biographer told the *New York Times* in 2012 that "politicized and partisan reaction created by *Silent Spring* has hardened over the past 50 years."

Of course, Carson's work did not cause the political polarization that is a hallmark of today's political discourse. But it did trigger fierce polarization between liberals and conservatives over the modern environmental movement. At its core the debate still pits concern about nature against economic progress.

President Nixon's immediate political response in support of Carson's call for environmental protections allowed for policies intended to be mutually beneficial to protecting nature and providing for business growth. But the call for being good stewards of the environment has taken on a new color as businesses complain about overregulation and the high cost of reducing emissions and pollutants. At the same time, environmental science has revealed even more troubling consequences of the use of fossil fuels, and the resulting greenhouse gases that scientists claim are altering our planet's climate. New chemicals present new dangers, and scientists now regularly debate the benefits versus the cost of such new products. Political arguments against environmental regulation have taken on a decidedly anti-science tenor, including denials of scientific data that high levels of carbon emissions lead to global climate change.

In this, the hardened political conversation about the future of the nation's environment parallels the competing visions of the first Founders: between leaders in favor of protecting farmlands and leaders intent on unleashing industrial growth through the use of natural resources to produce economic expansion.

The current version of that divide is the work of Rachel Carson. This member of what I refer to as the new founding family began her environmental revolution growing up in the Pennsylvania woods talking to birds and watching the fish in nearby streams. Raised by a mother who told her not to step on bugs because they, too, are living creatures, she grew up to write politically potent, soul-stirring stories of the paradise under ocean waves and the cataclysm awaiting animals and humans from reckless treatment of nature. And her work continues to be at the center of the way Americans understand and debate nature today.

CHAPTER 18

A NEW BEGINNING

Martin Luther King Jr., Jesse Jackson,
and the Fight for Racial Equality

With more than a third of America's population made up of people of color, the political and cultural force posed by racial minorities in our country today lies far outside the Colonial experience. So, too, is a nation that retains a white majority population but twice elects a black man as president. Imagine Colonial Americans' shock at hearing that 43 percent of whites voted for Obama in his first election and 39 percent voted for him in his second winning campaign for the White House. The fact that a highly educated, wealthy black man was elected as the nation's top leader is outside any frame of reference for those who lived two hundred years ago.

The reality of race relations in late 1700s America was that close to half of the men at the Constitutional Convention in Philadelphia, twenty-five of the fifty-five, owned black slaves. Only 8 percent of blacks in all of Colonial America were free. In Philadelphia, the biggest city in the Colonies, even those black people who were not slaves could not vote or serve in the state militia. The idea of a black intellectual was also alien to the first Founding Fathers. To the Founders, a black newspaper columnist, book writer, and political commentator like me might as well be a visitor from another planet. Most blacks in the colonies, even free black people, were barred from attending public schools, and as a result were illiterate. To see me, a college graduate with a degree in philosophy, at lunch with President Obama, a Harvard law graduate, might strike the Founders as an absurd joke.

Michelle Obama, as the nation's First Lady, might be even more astounding to the nation's first Founding Fathers. Black women—as well as black men and white women—had no voting rights under the original Constitution. The sight of a Princeton- and Harvard-educated black woman dressed by top designers in elegant gowns would have been totally outside the experience of the men who founded the nation.

To fully grasp how a nation of slave owners could possibly elect a black president, the original Founders would have to meet two men: Martin Luther King Jr. and Jesse Jackson. Together, they transformed America from a nation that enforced segregation into a place that applauds racial diversity, and even requires it in the workplace. They created America's racial conscience, a fiery sense of duty on behalf of minorities whose flames have been recently stoked by the deaths of black men like Michael Brown and Eric Garner by white police officers. They set the terms for America's current conversation about race, and for this reason deserve spots in America's new Founding Family.

Dr. Martin Luther King, a preacher, an activist, and the President of the Southern Christian Leadership Committee, saw his mission as the logical extension of the work done by America's first Founding Fathers. By drawing on the idealistic words of the original Founding Fathers and calling on the nation's Christian morality, King transformed the nation's political conversation about race from a matter of law to a matter of right and wrong, creating a civil rights movement based on appeals to the conscience and ideals of America. His adherence to nonviolence fit with the nation's aspiration to be a model of freedom and rights to the world after World War II.

Here is King at the 1963 March on Washington, delivering his most famous speech—"I Have a Dream"—and calling up the moral spirit of the original Founding Fathers: "When the architects of our republic wrote the magnificent words of the Constitution and the Declaration of Independence, they were signing a promissory note to which every American was to fall heir," King told more than 250,000 people listening to him in front of the Lincoln Memorial as part of the call for

Congress to pass a new Civil Rights Act. "This note was a promise that all men, yes, black men as well as white men, would be guaranteed . . . 'life, liberty and the pursuit of happiness.' . . . Instead of honoring this sacred obligation, America has given the Negro people a bad check, a check which has come back marked 'insufficient funds.' But we refuse to believe that the bank of justice is bankrupt. . . . [We] demand the riches of freedom and security of justice."

When King was murdered nearly five years later, it was one of his lesser-known acolytes, a gifted organizer and orator named Jesse Jackson, who rose to succeed him as the nation's most influential black leader. Known as the "President of Black America," Jackson rose to fame by organizing boycotts against white-owned companies in order to get them to hire African Americans. He shifted the demands of the civil rights movement, transforming what was, under the leadership of Dr. King, a call for racial equality and integration into an all-out fight for a proportionate share of America's benefits: government jobs, political patronage, high school diplomas, admission to top schools, median income, home ownership, lower infant mortality rates, and higher life expectancy. It was Jackson who changed the way we measure racial equality for black people, as well as for Hispanic, Asian, and even white populations. Jackson personifies the leap in the American mind that took race relations beyond guaranteeing freedom from slavery, and fought for equal opportunity for blacks. The two men combined to move race relations forward and create vast advances for black Americans. The historic rise of King and Jackson laid the groundwork for the political possibility of a black president, a reality incomprehensible to the Founding Fathers.

Some of the original Founders were aware of the hypocrisy inherent in protesting the British king's control over their lives in the colonies while imposing despotic economic control over slaves. Thomas Jefferson wrote in his first draft of the Declaration of Independence that rebellion from the British was partly justified by the king's decision to wage a "cruel war against human nature itself, violating its most sacred rights of life and liberty in the persons of a distant people who never offended him, captivating and carrying them into slavery in another hemisphere." Jefferson also complained that the king was "exciting those very people [black slaves] to rise in arms" against American colonists rebelling against the king. Upon hearing complaints from delegates, mostly from the South, the Continental Congress cut the slavery portion out of the final version of the Declaration, realizing that it was a divisive issue capable of breaking apart the ranks of the revolutionaries.

At the Constitutional Convention the question of the morality of slavery came up again. James Madison recorded in his journal that Gouverneur Morris, a delegate from Pennsylvania, called slavery a "nefarious institution" and a "curse of heaven on the states where it prevailed." George Mason told the convention, "Every master of slaves is born a petty tyrant." John Rutledge, a South Carolina delegate, responded with anger: "Religion and humanity have nothing to do with this question." The critical issue, he warned, was whether delegates from the southern slaveholding states would support the new Constitution. And he made it clear they would oppose any document that hurt the South's economy by halting the stream of ships from Africa bringing in black slaves to harvest cash crops from plantations in the South.

The black people known to the men writing the Constitution as they gathered in Philadelphia were mostly domestic servants—cooks, coachmen, and gardeners. Carpenters, bricklayers, and other skilled white professionals of that time excluded blacks from their guilds in order to stop them from competing for jobs. Historian Nell Irving Painter describes free black people in the northern colonies as "poor, hard-working people with little access to formal education. Few enjoyed enough economic independence to permit their engagement with national political issues."

Blacks constituted about 20 percent of the population in Colonial America. In 1776, when the Declaration of Independence was signed, more than 90 percent of black people in the new nation were slaves, and more than 85 percent of those slaves lived in the South. With the invention of the cotton gin in 1793, the number of slaves in the South grew rapidly. From 1790 to 1810 the U.S. slave population climbed from less than 700,000 to more than 1.2 million. Almost all of the new slaves were sent to the southern states.

Between 1777 and 1804 every northern state set up a timeline to eliminate slavery within its boundaries. There was little opposition, since there were few northern plantations. In addition, the fact of so many southern slaves fighting alongside the British led to fears of future slave rebellions in the North, also depressing any appetite for black slaves there.

During the Constitutional Convention the delegates agreed that the new Congress would not act on the legality of the slave trade before 1808. In 1807 Congress did agree on a new law banning the import of new slaves, but it was the result of a debate over the North's economic interests versus the South's. Ultimately, the southern congressmen did not object to stopping the influx of new slaves because 1.2 million slaves already lived in the South. White plantation owners counted on their slaves having babies, who became slaves upon birth, so they did not need to rely on importing new slaves. And, in fact, the number of slaves increased after the states stopped bringing in slaves from overseas. By 1860, there were more than four million slaves living in the South.

The need to maintain political balance between free states and slave states, the North and the South, shaped the national conversation over race for the first half of the 1800s. As the nation expanded west, the South tried to maintain its voting power in Congress by increasing the number of slave states, while the northern states tried to halt any new states from endorsing slavery. Behind this debate was a contest of economic interests. Big business owners in the North backed tariffs on foreign goods to protect them from overseas competition. Major southern plantation owners opposed the tariffs for fear it would kill the European market for cotton. The contest of economic interests led South Carolina to threaten to secede in 1832. That threat and the southern insistence on allowing slavery in states being newly admitted to the Union led to the birth of an antislavery or abolitionist movement.

The only black political presence during this period was the result of slave revolts. Nat Turner, a Virginia slave, led a large revolt in 1831 in which roughly sixty whites and around one hundred blacks, including Turner himself, were killed. Historians' accounts of the number of black people killed during the revolt widely vary, but all agree on the savagery of the attack that ended the slave rebellion. The first political party calling for the abolition of slavery also emerged in the years before the Civil War; all of its members were white. Some newspapers allowed stories about the horrors of slavery to be told; some allowed former slaves, such as Frederick Douglass, a platform for speeches about the abuse of slaves. As the national debate increased on the morals of slavery, southerners in Congress managed to pass a gag rule in 1836 to prevent discussion of antislavery legislation. As the country continued to expand into new territories, it led to questions of the legal right of slave owners to claim runaway slaves as well as to establish new slave operations. These disputes gave new fuel to the debate on slavery. The congressional gag rule was repealed in 1844, and in 1850 Congress reached a political deal to admit California to the Union as a free state while citizens of New Mexico and Utah, newly formed territories, were given the right to vote on whether they wanted slavery.

Douglass and other free black people became popular speakers for white abolitionist events. In 1852 a white woman, Harriet Beecher Stowe, published *Uncle Tom's Cabin,* a novel about the abuse of black people under slavery. And a white man, John Brown, led a highly publicized fight to keep slavery out of settlements in Kansas. The politics of white America began to shift as the abolitionist movement gained momentum and lent its support to creation of the Republican Party. The new party's political purpose was to oppose the Democrats' advocacy for the political right of southern states to continue slavery. The Republican Party platform called on Congress to "prohibit [slavery] in the territories," and labeled slavery a "relic of barbarism."

The new party found a strong voice in Abraham Lincoln, a former congressman who ran for the Senate in 1858 against an incumbent Democrat, Stephen Douglas. Stories about their long, pointed debates over slavery became a regular feature of newspapers nationwide. Douglas called for territories and new states to set their own law on slavery. Lincoln stated that slavery was a "moral, social and political wrong." Lincoln lost the Senate race but gained national attention that vaulted him to the Republican nomination for president two years later. He won the 1860 election, and over the next few months, from December 1860 through May 1861, the southern states attempted to secede from the Union, igniting the Civil War.

Lincoln, despite his moral opposition to slavery, did not call for its end early in his presidency. In 1862 he wrote a letter to the *New York Tribune,* an abolitionist paper, to say that his entire purpose in going to war was to keep the southern states in the Union. "If I could save the Union without freeing any slave I would do it, and if I could save it by freeing all the slaves I would do it; and if I could save it by freeing some and leaving others alone, I would also do that." President Lincoln also told a group of black leaders that African Americans were the cause of the war: "Our white men are cutting one another's throats. . . . But for your race among us there could not be war."

The striking absence of a black perspective in the national debate extended to President Lincoln's desire to keep blacks off the battlefield. He initially refused to allow former slaves—in fact any African Americans—to enlist in the Union Army. But after the first year of the war, Congress gave permission for the Union to enlist African Americans. The prospect of bringing the war to an end with the added strength of black soldiers inspired Lincoln to act to free the slaves. In September 1862 the president acted to free slaves in all southern states that did not surrender and return to the Union by January 1, 1863. When none of the southern states met the deadline, he issued the Emancipation Proclamation, which freed over three million slaves. In total, roughly 4 million slaves would eventually be freed. By the time the South lost the Civil War in 1865, more than six hundred thousand Americans— the most in any war in the nation's history—had died. As the war was coming to an end, President Lincoln was assassinated.

After the war Congress passed a slew of laws and constitutional amendments to end slavery, guarantee black men the right to vote, extend equal rights to black citizens, and even give blacks a voice in southern politics for the first time, under what became known as Reconstruction. In 1866 Congress passed a Civil Rights Act to confirm that, with the exception of Native Americans, all people born in the United States, including former slaves, had citizenship rights equal to those "enjoyed by white citizens." During the next two years, Congress passed a series of Reconstruction Acts that admitted southern states back into the Union once they ratified the Fourteenth Amendment. Tennessee was excluded because they had already ratified it. The southern states also had to give black men the right to vote. According to historian Eric Foner, writing in the *New York Times*, "for the first time, African-Americans [in the South] voted in large numbers and held public office at every level of government. It was a remarkable, unprecedented effort to build an interracial democracy on the ashes of slavery." The effort continued in 1870 as the states ratified the Fifteenth

Amendment. Unlike the Reconstruction Acts, directed at the former Confederacy, the Amendment guaranteed all black men the right to vote, whether in the North or in the South. (In 1868, more than half of northern states still blocked blacks from voting.)

But the entire Reconstruction effort fell apart as whites still loyal to the Confederacy pressured the federal government to end support for the new political order. By 1877 the new president, Rutherford Hayes, pulled the remaining federal troops out of the South that had originally been sent there to enforce Reconstruction policies, including black voting rights. And in the 1896 *Plessy v. Ferguson* decision, the Supreme Court ruled that a "separate but equal" set of rules for blacks and whites was permitted under the Constitution. That new regime of government-enforced segregation led once more to blacks being treated as second-class citizens, with an inferior set of rights enforced by the government.

At the start of the twentieth century the discouraging reality for black citizens was that they were outcasts in their own nation, treated as an inferior caste. The idealistic goals of Reconstruction had been pushed aside both by the law and the white racists who used violence, from lynching to cross burning, to enforce a more familiar racial order, with blacks only a step away from their prior life as slaves. Black citizens remained physically and psychologically burdened by the acceptance of black slavery at the nation's birth and its many, continuing tragic consequences.

But black voices in the debate over race began to emerge with the creation of the National Association for the Advancement of Colored People (the multiracial NAACP) in 1909. By the 1930s the NAACP had enough money to support court challenges to the law of segregation. As we saw in Chapter 3, those cases led to the Supreme Court's 1954 *Brown v. Board of Education* decision ending legal segregation in public schools. The high court ruled unanimously for the argument made by a black man, the lead lawyer for the NAACP Legal Defense Fund, Thurgood Marshall, that separating students by race was a violation of the Fourteenth Amendment's guarantee of equal rights.

The ruling was dramatic. Just after midday on May 17, 1954, Chief Justice Earl Warren announced the decision from the bench at the Supreme Court. "What a wonderful world of possibilities have unfolded for the children," Ralph Ellison, the celebrated black author, immediately wrote to a friend after hearing about the *Brown* decision. At the NAACP's offices, "we just sat there looking at one another," one NAACP official later recalled, quoted in a book by historian James T. Patterson. "The only emotion we felt at that moment was awe. Every one of us felt it." Thurgood Marshall told news reporters: "It is the greatest victory we ever had."

But there was a countermovement. The *Brown* ruling provoked the rise of segregationist opposition to integration of schoolchildren, especially in the South. It also prompted the start of frequent protests, often led by black college students with loud, insistent voices (until then a rarity), calling for equal rights for all Americans. The best-known black protest leader was a twenty-six-year-old minister, a graduate of the historically black Morehouse College with a doctorate in theology from Boston University: Dr. Martin Luther King Jr.

Born in 1929 in Atlanta, King grew up in segregation, riding in the back of buses and going to all-black schools. He heard his father, a minister, dismissed by whites as "boy." In young King's racially separate America, the only place a black man could achieve stature was as a minister. In the pulpit black ministers were isolated from the power of segregationists thanks to a financial base secured by the black people who filled the pews. "I grew up in the church," King later said. "My father is a preacher, my grandfather was a preacher, my great-grandfather was a preacher, my only brother is a preacher, and my daddy's brother is a preacher. So I didn't have much choice."

Dr. King was in his first job after divinity school, leading the Dexter Avenue Baptist Church in Montgomery, Alabama, when he almost instantaneously gained national recognition for his work as the leader of a 1955 bus boycott held in support of Rosa Parks, a seamstress who was jailed for refusing to give her seat in the front of a bus to a white man. Speaking at the first meeting held to organize the bus boycott, King's captivating gospel cadence, his mastery of biblical imagery in service to the message of God's people fleeing captivity, elevated him as the lead voice of the growing nationwide civil rights movement: "There comes a time," King said that night, "when people get tired. We are here this evening to say to those who have mistreated us so long that we are tired—tired of being segregated and humiliated; tired of being kicked about by the brutal feet of oppression."

Segregationists bombed King's house. The local police arrested him. And yet, he managed to keep the movement active for an entire year until the Supreme Court affirmed a lower court ruling that the bus company's segregationist seating was a violation of the constitutional rights of black citizens. Jo Ann Robinson, one of the boycott's organizers, later said that the moment the ruling was announced, she felt as if the voice of black people was being heard for the first time in the halls of American power. "We felt that we were somebody—that somebody had to listen to us, that we forced the white man to give what we knew was a part of our own citizenship . . . It is a hilarious feeling that just goes all over you, that makes you feel that America is a great country and we're going to do more to make it greater."

King became the leading apostle of black America, delivering thoughtful speeches based on scripture and highlighted by inspired calls for compassion for all. He gave a new, more accessible national voice to all the legal, constitutional arguments for the federal government to protect the rights of black citizens. His 1963 speech at the Lincoln Memorial in Washington, D.C., is regarded as one of the great speeches of American history: Despite a painful record of slavery, violent oppression, and discrimination in the United States, King said, he still dreamed of America living up to "the meaning of its creed: 'We hold these truths to be self-evident: that all men are created equal.' I have a dream that one day on the red hills of Georgia the sons of former slaves and the sons of former slave owners will be able to sit down together at the table of brotherhood. . . . I have a dream that my four little children will one day live in a nation where they will not be judged by the color of their skin but the content of their character."

The "I Have a Dream" speech was a turning point in building public support for passage of the 1964 Civil Rights Act, the most important piece of civil rights legislation since the Civil Rights Act of 1866. This time, with a Democrat in the White House and a Democratic Congress, President Lyndon Johnson used public pressure, much of it the result of King's voice calling for Americans to force Congress to ensure that blacks had rights equal to those of whites, to get the bill through. The law Congress passed and that LBJ signed specified that discrimination based on race, color, religion, or sex at schools, workplaces, restaurants, hotels, and other public places was unconstitutional.

King's voice continued to resonate in Congress, in the courts, in the newspapers, and booming from radios. His marches created power-ful images of protesters, often dressed in their Sunday suits and hats, walking with quiet dignity. With television news coming to maturity during the 1960s, King's protests, his interviews with the media, and reports on his work made him a media star. For much of the nation the entire civil rights movement seemed to be about this one man. His voice and his message of peaceful protest and Christian brotherhood found welcome reception in black churches of every denomination—although it did stir some jealousy among other ministers—but it was also welcomed in many white churches outside the South.

The voices of segregationist politicians did not go silent. King was called "Liver-Lipped Luther," an "agitator," a "communist," and more. Southern governors engaged in so-called massive resistance to racial integration, beginning by stopping black and white children from going to school together. Ten years after the 1954 *Brown* decision, more than 97 percent of black children living in the old Confederacy and the rest of the South remained in schools that were segregated by race. There was only slightly more integration in the North, as white Ameri-cans looking to avoid the turmoil surrounding school integration left for suburban schools with fewer black people. In the 1964 presidential campaign, Republican Barry Goldwater had opposed Congress passing the Civil Rights Act to guarantee that black people had a right to be served in restaurants and stay in hotels. He lost badly, but increasing racial tensions persisted and became evident in the 1968 presidential race. Gov. George Wallace, an Alabaman, represented the short-lived American Independent Party, whose platform called for an end to federal government enforcement of racial integration. One historian later wrote that Wallace gave voice to southern white feelings of being "pushed around by an invasive federal government, threatened by crime and social disorder, discriminated against by affirmative action ... [fusing] a barely coded racism to populist anti-statism." Wallace's voice found an audience among alienated white southern Democrats. In the presidential election, Wallace carried the southern states of Arkansas, Louisiana, Mississippi, Alabama, and Georgia.

Meanwhile, riots erupted among the poor black people who left the South seeking jobs in the North. Most had been forced into cramped, low-income, racially separate ghettos in big cities across the country. Black rioting became a violent and fire-charred reality in Watts, the Hough neighborhood of Cleveland, Detroit, and other cities.

Then, on April 4, 1968, King's voice was silenced. His assassination by a white man set off yet another round of rioting nationwide. The angry, violent public reaction to his murder set loose powerful emotions among whites and blacks—anger, resentment, grief, and despair.

When the shot that killed King was fired, twenty-six-year-old Jesse Jackson was in the parking lot of the motel where King was staying. King was looking down from the balcony of his room, talking to people waiting for him to go to dinner, when the bullet struck him. Jackson rushed up to the balcony, where he found Ralph Abernathy cradling the dying King. Abernathy was King's best friend and a top aide at the Southern Christian Leadership Conference (SCLC), the group founded by King. In the awful death scene on the balcony, King's blood covered Abernathy, and some landed on Jackson's turtleneck. At least one historian said Jackson intentionally smeared the blood onto his shirt.

Coretta Scott King, King's widow, asked King's aides not to make public statements in the days following her husband's murder. But the next day, April 5, Jackson was on national television telling viewers that King "died in my arms." He still had on the bloodstained turtleneck as he told the nation he was "the last person on earth" to hear King's dying words. Jackson refused to take off the bloody shirt. His wife, Jackie Jackson, later said her husband wore it "about three days, four days, five days to a week."

Jackson spoke at a memorial service in Chicago wearing the same bloody turtleneck. He told mourners: "This blood is on the chest and hands of those who would not have welcomed him [King] here yesterday." Jackson spoke with raw emotion to a weeping crowd. The assassination, he warned, was not the time to "sit here looking sad and pious ... but to behave differently." King's death, he said, meant the slain leader had been "through, literally, a crucifixion—I was there.

And I will be there for the resurrection." Jackson's assertive voice and presence caused him to rocket past more senior people in the civil rights movement. He overshadowed the men who had been closest to King, as well as Mrs. King. Roger Bruns, one of Jackson's biographers, later wrote that King's family and aides saw Jackson as an "opportunist." But most of the nation saw him as the next Dr. King.

Born in 1941 to a seventeen-year-old single mother in South Carolina, Jesse Jackson had known King for only three years. The high-energy former college football quarterback was a seminary student when he met King in Selma in 1965. Jackson did not get to town in time to participate in the legendary Selma march for voting rights, and he left before King successfully led a second march from Selma to the state capitol in Montgomery. But Jackson was in town as King fought to get the courts to approve a permit for the march, and as King restrained the black community from violent outbursts following state troopers' vicious beating of people marching for voting rights.

Under all that pressure, King was not patient with Jackson. Biographies of King describe him as aggravated by Jackson's loud, pushy style of behavior. The young, attention-grabbing Jackson was not well received by those in King's inner circle. "So is this guy for real?" Andrew Young later recalled thinking when he saw Jackson plant himself at the head of a line of protesters. "Or does he just not know any better. And I decided that here was a natural-born leader . . . he just couldn't stand in line with everybody else." Meanwhile, Jackson pursued a relationship with King relentlessly. Young later wrote that he "always suspected that Jesse's childhood as the son of a single mother created in him a constant psychological need for a father figure."

Jackson, too, attributed his work in civil rights to the absence of his father, who lived in the same neighborhood but never supported his son. "I never slept under the same roof with my natural father one night in my life," he later said. Jackson is quoted by biographer Marshall Frady as having said that this was why "I have always been able to identify with those the rest of society labels as bastards, as outcasts and moral refuse." He went on: "I know [how it feels to have] people saying you're nothing and nobody and can never be anything. I understand when you have no real last name. I understand. Because our very genes cry out for confirmation."

As Jackson's father figure, King was a complex substitute. One story often told about Jackson's relationship with King involves a meeting of SCLC aides during protests in Memphis just five days before King's death. King had thrown his support behind striking garbage workers, mostly black men subsisting on low wages. He was chastising his staff for not taking the demonstrations seriously. King intended the sanitation strike to be a lead-up to his Poor People's Campaign, a rally for widespread economic equality that King's workers, including Jackson, worried would be unrealistic. Jackson's aggressive style, his self-important demands, set off King. "If you are so interested in doing your own thing that you can't do what the organization is structured to do, go ahead," King said, chiding Jackson in front of several SCLC staff members. "If you want to carve out your own niche in society, go ahead, but for God's sake, don't bother me."

After the assassination, Jackson did just that, creating his own niche based on King's standing as the top civil rights leader. Over the next twenty years it was the energetic Jackson who voiced black positions on key racial issues. No one succeeded in challenging his hold as America's preeminent voice on civil rights, a position once held by King.

Most important, Jackson changed the message. King's message felt like an uplifting gospel song, with its soaring, faithful, idealistic call for racial integration and promise that all people might be treated as equals without regard to race in a "beautiful symphony of brotherhood." Jackson moved past the poetry. He spoke in the prose of hard numbers. His voice defined racial brotherhood in terms of economic equality and shared political power.

Three years after King's assassination, Jackson left King's group behind. In 1971 he started a new civil rights organization. It was far different from King's faith-based organization of ministers. Jackson appropriately named the group PUSH—People United to Save Humanity. Jackson's new team pressured American corporations to set numerical goals, quotas, for hiring black workers, signing contracts with black-owned companies, selling franchises to black businessmen, and contributing to black churches and charities. When Coca-Cola refused to give in to PUSH's demands, Jackson got a famous black entertainer and Coke spokesperson, Bill Cosby, to back him, at which point Coca-Cola immediately accepted PUSH's agreement. Jackson used the threat of boycotts and unlimited access to newspapers and television shows to get beer company Schlitz, Coca-Cola and other soda companies, cosmetics company Avon, and Burger King to start doing business with black companies and make deposits in black-owned banks.

Jackson's message from the foremost pulpit in black America, the pulpit once occupied by King, was all about jobs and access to capital for black business: "If [black America] accounts for 20 percent of a firm's sales then that firm must give us 20 percent of its advertising dollar, 20 percent of its banking business, and 20 percent of its jobs," Jackson said in explicit terms to one reporter. In an earlier interview he explained that his advocacy for putting concrete markers on racial equality was "a defensive strategy evolved in order to stop whites from controlling our community and removing the profits and income that belong to black people."

Jackson's focus on the economic needs of black America led him to champion New Deal–style progressive government. That racially inclusive approach won wide support from white liberals as he moved past the tense black-power, blacks-only calls for white America to make amends for its racist past. Jackson maintained King's broader appeal for government help for people of all races—the poor in black ghettos, farmers struggling as corporations made agriculture into a commodity business, and the white working class being left behind as manufacturing left the United States in the 1970s and 1980s. Jackson was never a black-power militant demanding that government help only black people; King had viewed the term "black power" as an "unfortunate choice of words" because it alienated so many white supporters, and Jackson shared that opinion, inasmuch as "black power" might scare white corporate leaders away from the bargaining table, where Jackson wanted to cut deals over jobs, contracts, and charitable contributions.

To critics who saw his focus on money as being at odds with King's legacy, Jackson emphasized that the economic focus was an extension of King's work. At the time of his death, King was scheduled to travel to Washington to lead a Poor People's Campaign. That protest called for people to live on the National Mall in front of the Capitol to impress on Congress the dire need for federal programs offering the poor economic protections, beginning with guarantees of jobs, housing, and healthcare. Jackson did end up leading the Poor People's Campaign.

The effort did not succeed in prompting the major congressional action it had intended, but it clearly stirred the nation.

Jackson's steely commitment to bring more money and political power into black America set a different tone in the press and among civil rights activists. Even if King had been heading toward calls for economic justice for the poor, his entire effort was rooted in the church. King went to black churches and white charities for money. And King never ran for office. Jackson aimed his appeals for financial support at corporations as well as churches. Jackson backed the election of black politicians in order to share their power over budgets and patronage. As a result, Jackson never achieved King's level of popular acclaim. The Nobel Peace Prize was not offered to him. King had never positioned himself as a corporate or political insider; his public image was as a prophet.

Nevertheless, Jackson held tight to his claim to be King's heir. While he became the lead cheerleader for black capitalism, he remained the leading black voice on every racial controversy. His dominance in black America led to jealousy, especially since he personally profited by pressuring corporations to contribute to his group, his black festivals, his conventions of black business, and his job-training program. But Jackson's premise that black America needed to become financially self-sufficient went unchallenged. White corporate boardrooms looking to avoid racial tensions found him a convenient, one-stop way to insulate themselves from trouble with black folks.

Jackson's political ambition provided another point of difference from his predecessor. King lived at a time when there were few black politicians; the powerful voices in black America during King's era came from the pulpit. By the early 1970s, as Jackson took the lead, the most powerful black voices could be heard speaking from the political platform. The tremendous growth in the number of black politicians resulted from the rising power of the emerging black middle class as a voting bloc.

Between 1969 and 1972 the total annual income in black America rose by a stunning 34 percent. In 1974, the wealthiest 5 percent of non-white (mostly black) families were making over $7,000 more per year than they were in 1969. In 1977 black male professionals and technical workers saw their unemployment rate drop to just 6 percent. The number of black-owned businesses nearly doubled from 1969 to 1977, reaching a record 231,000. From 1960 to 1975, thirty-five black-owned banks were established, twenty-four of them between 1970 and 1975.

With white residents and businesses leaving urban areas after the riots of the late 1960s and rising tension over school integration, the power of the black voters and black business in big cities created a surge of black mayors and city council members. Between 1950 and 1970 the proportion of African Americans living in cities doubled. By the late 1970s the nation reached a record of more than three thousand black elected officials, including more than two hundred black mayors, almost all Democrats. Jackson was their leader, their touchstone on national issues, and their link to the top levels of big corporations.

Jackson relied on access, favors, and deal making with black mayors as well as corporate executives. He encouraged his black political allies to do business with his network of financial supporters and corporate allies. Jackson's clout in the Democratic Party, particularly in cities with rising black populations, made him a powerful voice and a power broker within the party.

"The tendency is to always want to compare personalities, or make it an either-or situation," said Rev. Joseph Lowery, one of the men who succeeded King as the leader of the SCLC. "Jesse Jackson is not extending Martin King. Jesse Jackson is extending Jesse Jackson, and the movement, into the political arena."

Jackson's chief political mission was to maximize the value of black political power. Having more attention given to the black vote and black politicians was a sure path to more power for Jackson. He did not want white Democrats taking black votes for granted while chasing after white southern voters with GOP-flavored opposition to busing and affirmative action. From his national civil rights movement perspective, Jackson made the case that Democrats were dependent on black voters to win local, state, and national elections. As President Nixon's base of white "silent majority" voters moved away from the Democrats, the party became more dependent on black political power. An essential part of Jackson's strategy for maintaining the Democrats' fidelity to blacks was his push to have more black people and women in the party leadership and as delegates to the national convention. That would allow them to define the party as the party of racial minorities, of women, and of younger people as they wrote the party platform and picked the presidential nominee.

When Democrat Jimmy Carter was elected president in 1976, he made Andrew Young, a former top aide to King, his ambassador to the United Nations. President Carter also named the first black woman, Patricia Roberts Harris, to the cabinet as secretary of housing and urban development. Jackson used his influence at the White House to win multimillion-dollar funding to implement his PUSH EXCEL program to better educate children in big-city school districts.

Jackson stood taller in the public mind than any of the black officials who won elections. He was not tied into any one city's politics. He did not deliver for any one set of voters. As a nationally famed civil rights leader and a cultural hero on the left, he had politicians come to him to ask for his political endorsement, to help with white corporate leaders, and to deliver their message with his powerful voice in the media. Jackson was everywhere. He appeared on the popular children's television show *Sesame Street* to recite a poem he often performed at his rallies: "I am—Somebody / I may be poor, but I am—Somebody." He had access to reporters and newspaper editorial boards in every big city. His Saturday morning meetings held at PUSH headquarters in Chicago provided a forum for black-made products and businesses to gain attention, as well as for top gospel choirs to perform, with Jackson giving inspiring speeches. The weekly meeting was broadcast nationally. Such an influential voice meant that congressional leaders opened their doors for him, as did the White House. Jackson's media presence made his comments on every racial issue the measure of black opinion. He combined the moral authority of an heir to King and a civil rights leader with his political power to become the unofficial "president of Black America."

In November 1983, Jackson announced that he was running for the Democratic nomination for the presidency. Ronald Reagan, who had defeated Jimmy Carter in 1980, was not popular in black America. He was the champion of white conservatives opposed to increasing federal spending and taxes for government programs to help blacks. In 1964 Reagan campaigned for Goldwater, the Republican presidential nominee opposed to the Civil Rights Act of 1964. In 1980 Reagan was

widely quoted as saying the Voting Rights Act of 1965, which called for
federal oversight of voting laws to protect black voting rights in most
of the former Confederate states, was "humiliating to the South." During a 1980 campaign speech in the same Mississippi town where three
civil rights workers had been killed by segregationists in 1964, Reagan called for a return to "states' rights," a phrase that meant an end
to federal oversight and the return of local, segregated political power.
During Reagan's two terms in office, the decline in Justice Department
lawsuits to protect the civil rights of blacks led to major headlines. All
of Reagan's political signals to his base in the southern GOP led black
historian Manning Marable to write that the "ideological glue of Rea-
ganism was racism."

In December 1983 Jackson bolstered his already high national profile by going to Syria and winning the release of an American lieutenant
being held hostage after his military plane had been shot down. After
the successful mission, President Reagan welcomed Jackson and Lieutenant Robert Goodman to the White House, saying, "All Americans
must be pleased" with the release of the hostage "as a result of the efforts of the Rev. Jesse Jackson." No black American politician and no
other civil rights leader, including King, had ever taken on such high-
level international diplomacy.

In the 1984 Democratic primaries Jackson received 3.5 million votes
and won five primaries. It was a groundbreaking performance for a
black American politician. And he succeeded despite major mistakes,
including disparaging New York Jews as "Hymies" who he doubted
would vote for him. Even so, he came in third in the delegate count,
behind former vice president Walter Mondale and the widely known
Colorado senator Gary Hart. Jackson's performance attracted two million new voters to the political process. Before the July 1984 Democratic convention, the *New York Times* quoted Jackson as saying, "In
1964 we [black Democrats] were trying to get into the convention . . .
now we have a place on the stage." Jackson took the black movement
for equal rights from a rebellious effort outside the halls of political
power and transformed it into a movement of political insiders. After
the 1984 campaign the black novelist James Baldwin saw new horizons
for black America, even the most desperate souls. "Nothing will ever

again be what it was before," he said. "It changes the way the boy on the street and the boy on Death Row and his mother and his father and his sweetheart and his sister think about themselves."

Much of Jackson's success in the 1984 campaign hinged on changing the way Americans talked about race. He established markers for racial progress apart from King's poetic appeal for fairness and brotherhood. Jackson's mileposts for racial justice hinged on increasing the black percentage of delegates, the number of black party officials, and the number of contracts the party signed with black business.

In 1988 he ran again for the Democratic presidential nomination and did better, winning thirteen primaries and caucuses; this time he got the votes of nearly seven million Democrats. Jackson lost the nomination to former Massachusetts governor Michael Dukakis, but his strong performance elevated him beyond the novelty of a black man running for president. His campaigns attracted record numbers of black voters. Jackson's historic candidacy also drew in surprising support from whites, Asians, and Hispanics. Support from Jackson's "Rainbow Coalition" was key to Douglas Wilder's 1989 victory in the race for governor of Virginia, which made him the first black governor in the nation since Reconstruction. Jackson's success in transforming the 1960s civil rights movement into a 1980s political movement contributed to the rising number of blacks elected to Congress. In 1967 there were five blacks in the House of Representatives; by 1969 the group had grown to ten. A little more than a decade later, the number had nearly doubled to nineteen members. And by 1993, with a boost from the political excitement generated by Jackson's two national campaigns, black politicians held thirty-nine seats in the House.

As the voice of newcomers to the party, Jackson complained bitterly about the lack of minorities and social activists among the delegates to the national political convention. After the 1984 primaries he loudly lamented that the winner, former vice president Walter Mondale, was awarded 55 percent of the delegates despite having gotten only 38 percent of the votes. The disparity was the result of a winner-take-all primary system in which the winning candidate in any state took all the delegates from that state. That meant even a narrow victory in a state with a large population translated into a windfall of delegates. Jackson argued for a proportional system, awarding delegates to candidates on the basis of their share of the total vote in any state. Under pressure to show respect for the high-energy campaigns run by the civil rights leader turned politician, the party's leaders agreed to the change.

Jackson did not seek the Democratic nomination in 1992. Instead, he stirred black support for Bill Clinton, a former Arkansas governor. Clinton won the nomination and the presidency. The changes to the nominating process made little difference in the nominating process from 1992 through 2004. In those four campaigns the Democratic Party's candidate for president claimed the nomination overwhelmingly and would have won under the old system as well as the new proportional system. But that changed in 2008, when the first major black candidate since Jackson ran for the nomination.

Illinois senator Barack Obama had no ties to the civil rights movement. He had never known Dr. King, much less been covered in his blood. The son of a white American mother and a black Kenyan father, he was educated at Harvard Law School. Except for the color of their skin, Obama and Jackson had little in common.

In the 2008 primaries, Obama won 47 percent of the popular vote, and Hillary Clinton, the former first lady and senator from New York, won 48 percent of the vote. Her victories in big states with a lot of delegates—California, Texas, New York, and Ohio—would have defeated Obama under the winner-take-all system. But because the new system was in place, Obama was given a proportion of the delegates from the big states based on the votes he won in those states. With his victories in many of the smaller states Obama was able to claim more total delegates than Mrs. Clinton. He won the nomination and the general election to become the first black president.

Jackson and Obama never became close friends or political allies. Jackson viewed Obama as an Ivy League–educated outsider among black politicians. For Jackson, Obama's background was outside the crucible of the 1960s movement and even the experience of racial segregation. Obama never lived in the South. His highly educated white mother had taken him to Indonesia before he was sent back to the States to attend a private school in Hawaii. So when Obama came onto Jackson's turf as a community organizer in Chicago after graduating from Harvard Law School, Jackson gave him the cold shoulder. When Obama ran for political office in Chicago against older black politicians who were veterans of civil rights battles, Jackson opposed him at every turn.

Even after Obama won election to the U.S. Senate from Illinois and was starting his run for president in 2007, Jackson complained that he was "acting like he's white" for not aggressively backing blacks during a controversy at a Louisiana school in which black students were threatened with being lynched. In 2008 Jackson publicly scorned Obama for calling on black men to be better fathers and halt the epic rise in single black mothers by taking more responsibility for raising their children. Jackson was overheard by a television microphone whispering that "Barack's been talking down to black people . . . I want to cut his nuts off."

Obama's principal sin, in Jackson's mind, was changing the black message on race. Obama was speaking to black America about the need to look in the mirror and deal with its own problems as a first step toward solving the race problem with whites. Jackson's outbursts against Obama led Sheryll Cashin, a Georgetown Law School professor, to tell the *Washington Post* that "personal jealousy" separated the two men. "It must be hard," she explained, "for a generation of black men who came up in an era when nothing was easy to see this young man rise, almost effortlessly."

As Obama raced to victory, Jackson publicly praised him. But Jackson put the forthcoming victory in the context of the long history of civil rights, including his own contributions. "He is running the last lap of a 54-year tag-team race," Jackson told reporters, pointing to the Supreme Court's 1954 *Brown* ruling ending school segregation. "Man, there's excitement to see this in my lifetime . . . If you're part of the team, whoever scores a touchdown, the victory goes to the team."

Even as Obama was taking the black movement in a new direction, Jackson held tight to his insistence on black voices delivering the message of black grievance against white society. The difference between Jackson and Obama extended to their style. Where Jackson was a dramatic, charismatic figure, Obama was widely depicted as "cool" and "intellectual." Even as a black U.S. senator and presidential candidate, "Obama's manner, his accent, his pedigree, his broad approach to the issues, told white voters, among other things: I am not Jesse Jackson," wrote David Remnick in a biography of Obama.

Obama was one of several black politicians in the early 2000s adopting a more moderate voice on race. The era of racial identity politics was being pushed from center stage, because the new president was black. The rapid change in the demographics of the nation also played a role. For the first time Hispanics outnumbered blacks. An influx of immigrants further mixed the nation's racial picture, as more than a third of the nation was now made up of people of color. The rising generations of minority politicians made a show of being willing to talk across racial lines in situations where Jackson had made financial and affirmative-action-style demands for more black faces in jobs and on boards. These new black politicians without a chip on their shoulder included Obama; Cory Booker, the former mayor of Newark who went on to win a New Jersey Senate seat; Harold Ford, who served as a congressman from Tennessee; Deval Patrick, the assistant attorney general in the Clinton administration who became governor of Massachusetts; and Adrian Fenty, the mayor of Washington, D.C.

Obama and the new generation of black politicians viewed Jackson with respect while dismissing him as a man whose time was passing. Some went as far as to say that Obama's presidency had ushered in a "postracial America," where the nation was finally able to see beyond "black" or "white."

Yet even as Obama distanced himself from Jackson, the contemporary conversation about race in America remains deeply indebted to Jackson's work. Obama would not have been elected president if not for the reforms forced on the Democrats by Jackson that led to quantifiable increases in political power for minorities, women, and young people. The incredible reality of a black president is testament to Jackson's success in transforming the racial debate in America from a mid-twentieth-century movement for equal rights for black Americans to a twenty-first-century fight for equal outcomes for blacks seeking jobs, income, and political office.

Over the past few years, several racially loaded events have given America's racial debate a new sense of urgency: the murder of an unarmed black man in Ferguson, Missouri; the dangerous riots following the death of a black man in Baltimore; the slaughter of nine black South Carolinians at a historically black church in Charleston by a white supremacist. What, Americans ask, is responsible for these tragedies? Should we blame the strained relations between Ferguson's police department and its black community on the lack of minorities in its police force? Should we blame the Baltimore riots on the fact that 41 percent of Baltimore black men between the ages of twenty-five and fifty-four are unemployed? What should we blame for these shocking statistics: a racist society unwilling to recognize historical injustices, or some lack of personal responsibility on African Americans' part? The answers depend on the person you ask. But these conversations share a focus on better jobs, more money, and equal representation that is far from the King era's concentration on abstract notions of racial justice. This is the legacy of the Reverend Jesse Jackson, a man who taught us how to quantify racial change.

Dr. King's morally based approach to civil rights has and will remain an important guidepost for future battles for social justice. The post-Ferguson rallying cry "Black Lives Matter" resonates with Dr. King's vision of a country where we judge others not by the color of their skin but by the content of their character. Black Lives Matter has sparked a national conversation about race that has forced us to recognize the forms of racism that persist even in a society that some believe is fully colorblind. If nothing else, these symbolic gestures keep Americans motivated in their quest to build a more equal future.

Yet if recent events have taught us anything, we've learned that concepts such as "equality," freedom," and "opportunity" are only as meaningful as the tangible results they yield. For making that the baseline for conversations about race in the twenty-first century, we can thank Jesse Jackson, who built on Dr. King's dreams and poetic prayers for change with an insistence on real, concrete measurements.

CHAPTER 19

THE RIGHT TO
BEAR ARMS

Charlton Heston and the NRA

The fight over guns in twenty-first-century America takes place in the bright, unrelenting light of a constitutional right. The Second Amendment is a beacon guaranteeing that private citizens have the right to own a gun.

But according to many there is another side to the Second Amendment, one illuminated by the chalk outlines of the corpses on America's streets of those killed by gunfire. The ever-rising daily death toll from gun violence—more than thirty thousand Americans die by gunfire each year—burns brightly in the American eye. While millions of Americans celebrate the shining principles of the Second Amendment as a necessary right to secure individual liberty and prevent government tyranny, others are stunned by grief at the thought of so many lives lost to gun violence.

No matter what side of the debate one is on, the reality of gun violence is frightening to us all. That is one reason so many feel the best answer is to be armed ourselves. So many issues and concerns come into play in terms of our reactions to guns in American life. There is our fear of armed criminals with guns. On the other hand, there is our fear of accidents involving guns. There is the sad reality of people using guns to kill themselves—more than 60 percent of gun deaths are suicides. And there is the terrifying specter of people who are mentally ill committing mass murder using guns. But there is also a lively gun culture, where people get enormous pleasure from engaging in recreational shooting and in hunting; for many of these people, gun ownership is part of their family tradition. They see gun ownership as a precious right, on par with the right to life, liberty, and the pursuit of happiness.

In all this, we shouldn't forget the high profits that accrue to gun makers, or the unstoppable flow of illegal guns. And we should be aware of the huge campaign contributions to politicians from gun lobbyists and their opponents. As for the law, the Supreme Court ruled in separate cases in 2008 and 2010—one focused on guns in federally controlled jurisdictions and the other on the states—that every American has the right to own a gun for self-defense, for fun, or for any other legal purpose, without regard to military service. It all makes for big, bitter political fights over gun rights and gun control in city halls and in the state house, in Congress and across the dinner table.

If the Founding Fathers came back to life today, what could they add to the frustrating debate over gun violence in twenty-first-century America? How would George Washington and Thomas Jefferson—or any other American patriot who prized gun ownership in the 1700s—grapple with what happened on December 14, 2012? On that day, twenty-five minutes after the first graders at Sandy Hook Elementary School said the Pledge of Allegiance, a twenty-year-old man carrying three guns shot through a glass window in the small, quiet Connecticut town of Newtown. Once inside, he shot the principal and the school psychologist. Then he went into the first-grade classroom, where he shot and killed the teacher and a behavioral therapist. Then he fired his guns at the children repeatedly, killing fifteen. Still he was not done. In the next classroom he shot and killed the teacher and her aide along with five students. The children who were killed were only six or seven years of age. Before the police arrived, the young gunman, Adam Lanza, killed himself. In all, he shot to death twenty children, six adults, and himself. The police allowed only the most experienced paramedics to enter the school to remove the bodies; they feared most would collapse at the sight of the carnage. Candlelight vigils and prayer circles for the dead took place around the nation. So many children and adults had died that their photos had to be reduced to thumbnail size in the newspapers and on television newscasts in order to fit. The stories of the lives of the people slaughtered were heartbreaking. The boyfriend of one teacher killed in the massacre had planned to propose marriage to her later that month.

But this was not a singular, tragic event.

In 1999, after Eric Harris and Dylan Klebold gunned down thirteen people at Columbine High School in Colorado, President Clinton said he was "profoundly shocked and saddened by this tragedy" and stunned that it could happen in a calm, middle-class suburb like Littleton.

In 2007, after thirty-two people were killed by a gunman at Virginia Tech, President Bush said the impact hit "every American classroom and community."

In 2012, after the bloody scene described earlier at Sandy Hook Elementary School, President Obama made a similar speech, wiping tears from his eyes: "We've endured too many of these tragedies in the past few years. . . . I know there's not a parent in America who doesn't feel the same overwhelming grief that I do. The majority of those who died today were children—beautiful little kids between the ages of 5 and 10 years old. They had their entire lives ahead of them—birthdays, graduations, weddings, kids of their own . . . As a country, we have been through this too many times. Whether it is an elementary school in [Newtown, Connecticut], or a shopping mall in Oregon, or a temple in Wisconsin, or a movie theater in [Aurora, Colorado], or a street corner in Chicago . . . we are going to have to come together and take meaningful action to prevent more tragedies like this, regardless of politics."

And in 2015, after nine people were shot to death at a prayer meeting in South Carolina an aching, grief-weary President Obama spoke to reporters once again about gun violence: "I've had to make statements like this too many times. Communities like this have had to endure tragedies like this too many times. . . . At some point, we as a country will have to reckon with the fact that this type of mass violence does not happen in other advanced countries. . . . [I]t is in our power to do something about it."

But gun violence remains a stubborn, disturbing fact of American life. Along with abortion, it is perhaps the nation's most politically divisive issue.

In addition to the horror of mass shootings, there is a consistently high death toll from gunfire in big cities, usually in poor black and Hispanic neighborhoods where youth gangs and drug dealers exchange gunfire. Sixty percent of American gun homicides take place in the sixty-two largest cities. Black men between the ages of twenty and twenty-four are five times more likely to be killed by a gun than white men of the same age. Black people kill most of the black people killed by guns. White people kill most of the white people killed by guns. But overall, African Americans are twice as likely to be killed by gunfire as white Americans.

It is mass shootings, however, that get the most attention. The victims are more likely to be white, and the people pulling the trigger are more likely to be white men. Of the seventy-two mass shootings since 1982, forty-four have been by white men, according to a statistical study by *Mother Jones* magazine. "Thirty-five of the mass shootings [an event with more than four fatalities] have occurred since 2006," the magazine reported in 2015 after the Umpqua Community College shooting in Oregon. "Seven [mass shootings] took place in 2012 alone, including Sandy Hook," according to *Mother Jones*. In addition, the study found that "of the 143 guns possessed by the killers, more than three-quarters were obtained legally. The arsenal included dozens of assault weapons and semi-automatic handguns with high-capacity magazines." The report concluded that a majority of the shooters "were mentally troubled" and "more than half of the cases involved school or workplace shootings."

From 1980 until the 2012 Sandy Hook attack, there were 137 fatal school shootings that resulted in 297 people being killed in the United States. And since the Sandy Hook shootings there have been well over 100 school shootings in the United States. Overall, guns in the hands of civilians caused 31,672 deaths in 2010, the year the statistics were last tallied nationally. Sixty-one percent of those deaths were suicides—in other words, 19,392 people killed themselves with a gun. Guns caused 606 accidental deaths that year, and roughly 81,300 people were injured by gunfire.

In terms of fatalities, that means that between homicides and suicides, an average of 87 people are killed by gunfire every day. That does not include shootings by police, military, and other government agents. Nor does that include the people who were shot but lived.

According to Everytown for Gun Safety, a gun control nonprofit organization, in nearly 60 percent of mass shootings that occurred from 2009 to 2014, the offender murdered either a family member or an "intimate partner."

Nearly 70 percent of 2011 homicide victims were killed with a firearm. Among the homicides in which the FBI was able to uncover the relationship between the victim and murderer, 54 percent of victims personally knew their killer and 25 percent were killed by a member of his or her family.

Between 270 and 310 million guns are owned by American civilians, according to a 2013 report by the Pew Research Center. With a population of about 300 million, that means there is a gun for nearly everyone in the country. In reality, about 24 percent of Americans own at least one gun. Another 13 percent of Americans live with someone who owns at least one gun. That means that 37 percent of Americans live in a residence where there is a gun.

The plentiful supply of guns is one reason the United States is the most violent industrialized nation in the world, by a wide margin. The gun homicide rate in the United States is more than seven times as high as it is in Australia, Canada, Germany, France, India, Japan, or Britain. Another way to understand the impact of guns in the United States is a statistical comparison. While there are currently 88 civilian-owned guns per 100 people in the United States, there are only 30 guns per 100 people in Germany, 10 per 100 in Spain, and 6 per 100 in the United Kingdom. U.S. citizens make up 5 percent of the world's population but own about 50 percent of all civilian firearms.

The bull's-eye of the nation's dispute over gun regulation and gun violence is the Founding Fathers' pledge in the Second Amendment to the Constitution that individual Americans have a right to "keep and bear arms."

The most passionate, uncompromising defense of every American's right to a gun comes from the nation's most powerful lobbying group, the National Rifle Association (NRA). Even after the devastation of so many elementary school children killed at Sandy Hook, the NRA—representing 4.5 million members and gun manufacturers—managed to stop Congress from passing new laws to strengthen background checks on people buying guns. The NRA also stopped efforts to restrict ownership of semi-automatic guns. The *Washington Post* described the NRA in the days after Sandy Hook as "arguably the most powerful lobbying organization" in the capital and "certainly one of the most feared." The *Post*'s story after Sandy Hook on the consistent political power of the group over the years sought to identify the key to the NRA's methods: "There is no single secret to its success, but what liberals loathe about the NRA is a key part of its power. These are the people who say no."

By saying "no" time and again in absolute terms to gun control laws, even in the wake of Sandy Hook, the NRA forced politicians to pick one side or the other, with no middle ground, no equivocation. That approach led to the defeat of the congressional bill. By sounding the alarm over the threat of future gun control efforts, the NRA attracted a hundred thousand new dues-paying members to its existing base of more than four million. The power of "no" risked charges of extremism, but it was unrivaled in bringing in members and money.

At a press conference after the Sandy Hook elementary school shooting, the NRA's leader, Wayne LaPierre, said easy access to automatic guns was not the cause of the massacre; criminal behavior was. "The only thing that stops a bad guy with a gun is a good guy with a gun," he said. In other words, the only way to stop gun violence is to have more guns.

When Senator Dianne Feinstein, a California Democrat, introduced legislation banning the sale of assault weapons, the NRA accused her of denying law-abiding Americans their Second Amendment right. The group accused her of trying to reduce a constitutional right to a "privilege" to be granted to chosen citizens by elite politicians. NRA officials suggested that the senator instead crack down on crime and get busy fixing the nation's mental health system.

When the Obama White House and Democrats in Congress continued to call for new laws to control the sale of semi-automatic weapons, LaPierre countered by suggesting the government put armed guards in all schools. Even the conservative *New York Post* condemned LaPierre's performance with a front-page headline that read "Gun Nut!" But an NRA television advertisement asked: "Are the president's kids more important than yours? Then why is he skeptical about putting armed security in our schools when his kids are protected by armed guards at their schools?" The White House told reporters the NRA advertisement was "repugnant and cowardly."

In the days after the Connecticut slayings, when public opinion clearly favored the legislation, the NRA won again: the assault weapon ban lost by a vote of 60–40 in the U.S. Senate. All but one Republican voted for it, and fifteen Democrats voted against it. To date, the Sandy Hook massacre and subsequent shootings have not led to any new federal gun control laws.

After the 1999 Columbine High School shooting, President Clinton tried to ban the sale of guns at gun shows, where the weapons used in that shooting had been bought. Gun show sellers are not required to perform background checks on a buyer. With the NRA against him, Clinton failed to gain the votes to win. In addition, seven gun control bills were introduced in the Colorado legislature after the Columbine shootings. None passed. The NRA spent $600,000 to lobby against the new laws.

COLONIAL-ERA GUNS were heavy and difficult to shoot. It took thirty seconds simply to load a musket. By comparison, it took Adam Lanza five minutes to kill twenty-six people.

When the Dutch, British, Spanish, and French settlers arrived in the New World, they brought guns with them. And by the mid-1600s, the colonists had acquired more guns through trade with Europe. Ever since John Smith anchored at Jamestown, Virginia, the settlers used guns to fight the Native Americans. They relied on guns in their battles with French soldiers to the north. One history of the Colonial era and the American Revolution, written in the nineteenth century, described how "the near neighborhood of the Indians and French quickly taught them the necessity of having a well regulated militia" armed with guns. Citizen soldiers in the militias often had to bring their own guns with them. The men also served as a police force in times of peace, responsible for breaking up brawls and enforcing curfews. Historian Saul

Cornell describes gun owners as a high-status group. They got together to train at events called "musters." Those events served an important social function as the scene for local political discussions. "It would be impossible to overstate the militia's centrality to the lives of American colonists," writes Cornell.

By the late 1760s the local militias became the colonists' prime opposition to the dictates and taxes being imposed by the British crown. When John Hancock was caught smuggling wine into Boston Harbor, the British seized the boat. The colonists responded by rioting against the British officials. The British governor in Boston ordered all the colonists to hand over their guns; the colonists refused.

Samuel Adams wrote in a 1769 newspaper broadside headlined "An Appeal to the World" that living without guns but under the control of British forces with guns was an injustice. He advised that all Bostonians should "have arms for their defense," and proposed a law to require that every able man must have a "well-fixed firelock." Adams's sentiment was widely held in the colonies. Several local declarations of rights written during the same period promoted the use of guns to check British tyranny.

To increase the supply of guns available to locals, early German settlers in Pennsylvania began making their own guns, and by 1774 half of the landowners in the colonies owned a gun. The first battle of the American Revolution, the Battle of Lexington and Concord in 1775, was won by Colonial militiamen bearing guns. They are often referred to as "Minutemen" because with their own gun they were ready to enter battle quickly. The need to create a more unified force to fight the British led the Continental Congress, in the summer of 1775, to form the Continental Army as a collection of state militias, consisting primarily of colonists who privately owned a gun. General George Washington frequently complained about the shortage of guns for his troops; one year into the war, a quarter of his Continental Army lacked a gun. And the rifles given to his men in the Revolutionary War often fell apart. In a July 1776 letter, General Washington instructed a colonel to dismiss soldiers who did not have guns, saying that it was "absurd and unjust" to keep them: "it is in fact amusing ourselves with the appearance of Strength, when at the same time we want the reality."

Even when they worked, long rifles took so long to reload that British redcoats could attack with knives before the American soldiers could get off a second shot. A rainstorm during the aptly named Battle of the Clouds near Philadelphia caused the muskets of several Continental Army regiments to completely break down. Despite the problem with poorly maintained guns from private stockpiles, the revolutionaries wrote the 1781 Articles of Confederation—the first constitution for their independent nation—forbidding the federal government from creating a standing army and, as a result, its own arsenal of guns. The new central government would have to rely on state militias, and the state militias relied on the goodwill and support of local communities within the states. Yet even with their faulty guns, the Colonial forces managed to defeat the British in 1783.

The concept of state-run, locally controlled militias remained an important part of the young nation's psyche. But keeping the national army under local control created fears of slow national response to new military threats. Even some Anti-Federalists, people who favored a small, less involved federal government, agreed that the new government needed a reliable army, capable of speedy action, to face off against Native American tribes as well as the French, British, and Spanish armies, all of which still occupied land in North America. Pressure to create a central standing army grew stronger when Revolutionary War veteran Daniel Shays led an anti-tax protest in western Massachusetts that shut down several courthouses and harassed supporters of the new national government, including prominent lawyers and merchants. The Shays group was upset with merchants who went to court to demand money from farmers who failed to pay for goods sold on credit. The farmers resisted court orders to seize their produce and farms to pay the merchants. The Massachusetts militia eventually defeated Shays's men in February 1787. But the threat of future rebellion inspired the Constitutional Convention to look at enhancing the power of the federal government.

George Washington, president of the Constitutional Convention, let it be known that he viewed the local militias as too weak to defend the country or halt local rebellions. In a 1776 letter he denigrated the local militias as unmanageable in the face of a major threat: "Come in, you cannot tell how; Go, you cannot tell when; and Act, you cannot tell where." During the convention, James Madison wrote in his journal that "the discipline of the militia is evidently a national concern and ought to be provided for in the National Constitution."

Enough votes emerged to support a central government army as protection against insurrection and to defend the country against ongoing threats from Native Americans and foreign forces. The resolution to the dispute was to have both state militias and a national army. Constitutional power was given to the federal government to "raise and support armies." Article 1, Section 8, Clause 12 of the Constitution also allowed for a militia under control of both state and federal governments, with Congress given the power to call on those soldiers to enforce federal laws. But the leaders of each state were given the power to pick militia leaders and train militia soldiers.

The argument over creating a permanent federal army with a stockpile of guns was key to debates in the states over ratification of the Constitution. Anti-Federalists worried that a national army with its own arsenal would protect a tyrannical president—a new version of King George. They wanted the ability to fight that army just as they fought the British. As a result, one key issue was whether the federal army had the right to confiscate guns from the state militias. It was the British attempt to confiscate the colonists' guns that, in part, had prompted the Revolution. Virginia's governor Patrick Henry, speaking at his commonwealth's ratifying convention, voiced his concern openly: "Have we the means of resisting disciplined armies, when our only defense, the [state] militia, is put into the hands of Congress?" But despite those concerns, the bigger fear at the ratification conventions was the threat of another war with the British, battles with Native tribes, and future local insurrections like Shays's Rebellion. The Anti-Federalists had to admit that local militias needed federal coordination to handle these threats. For the young nation, its fear of external enemies ultimately outweighed fear of an internal threat from a militarized centralized government.

The Constitution was ratified in June 1788 with the proviso that it be open to amendment. In keeping with that promise, James Madison, then a congressman from Virginia (and one of the authors of the *Federalist Papers,* which made the case to the public for states to ratify the Constitution), wrote out a list of the strongest reservations voiced at state conventions. Madison, who feared that opponents of a strong federal government would call for an entirely new constitutional convention if their concerns were not taken seriously, made passage of the amendments a central concern. Of the list he submitted to Congress, one of them became the Second Amendment, which in its final form said: "A well-regulated militia being necessary to the security of a free state, the right of the people to keep and bear arms shall not be infringed." Madison saw the future Second Amendment as the answer to concerns about a too-powerful national army. The new law's focus on privately owned guns kept local militias in place as a check on any federal government that became too strong and defiant of the will of the states.

Nothing in debates about the Second Amendment addressed the "right to bear arms" for self-defense or hunting. In fact, common law, inherited from the British, already allowed private citizens to have a gun. In a draft of one Virginia state constitution, Thomas Jefferson wrote that "no free man shall ever be debarred the use of guns." Jefferson later wrote a friend that he felt guns "give boldness, enterprise and independence to the mind."

Virginia's General Assembly did propose a law to restrict the use of guns. James Madison drafted the law. It would have punished people who disobeyed hunting laws by forbidding them to carry any gun off of their private property "unless whilst performing military duty." In Boston, citizens were not allowed to have loaded guns in their homes. In Pennsylvania the Test Act required everyone buying a gun to first pass a test of loyalty to the nation. Those local laws had nothing to do with the right to own a gun—for the sake of participating in a militia— which the Second Amendment protects.

And that is why the original Founding Fathers, if present for the twenty-first-century gun control debate, would be confused by the emphasis on personal protection from crime. They *assumed* anyone could own a gun. The Second Amendment was entirely debated in terms of maintaining a "well-regulated militia."

Today the gun lobby's efforts to dismiss calls for gun control goes far beyond the Constitution's protection of gun rights as needed for a militia. The NRA, frequently citing the Second Amendment, contends that law-abiding, gun-owning Americans are the best way to stop criminals. As the NRA's LaPierre argued after the school shooting in

Newtown, the real problem is criminals, not guns. This argument has wide support among gun owners. Polls show that 50 percent of civilian gun owners say they purchased a gun for protection; only 32 percent say they have a gun for hunting. No one mentioned obtaining a gun in preparation for joining a militia.

In truth, only one of every forty-four gun homicides is committed in self-defense, according to a 2013 study. The remaining deaths cover a range of circumstances, from accidents to outbursts of anger that lead to gunfire. A 2008 study published in the *New England Journal of Medicine* revealed that living in a home where there is a gun increased the chance of getting killed by a gun by at least 40 percent. A 2009 study in the *American Journal of Public Health* concluded that civilian gun owners are about four and a half times more likely to be shot than people who do not carry guns.

When police searched the home of Adam Lanza, the man who committed the Sandy Hook shooting, they found a well-stocked gun collection and fourteen hundred rounds of ammunition, all purchased legally. His mother, whom he shot in the head before driving to the Sandy Hook school to shoot the children, had bought the guns. She had frequently taken him to local gun ranges to practice his marksmanship. She had planned to buy her son, who was mentally ill, even more guns for Christmas that year. She had felt the guns and shooting had a positive, empowering effect on him. It is an argument used by supporters of the right to private ownership of guns. Seventy-five percent of gun owners say they enjoy owning guns. Guns, writes religious historian Donovan Schaefer, have an "affective pull" on the emotions of Americans, reminding us of the rebellious spirit of the Founding Fathers, who used guns to escape the yoke of British tyranny. Schaefer connects gun ownership with liberty, freedom, and the right to pursue happiness; gun ownership offers power as well as the exercise of personal responsibility.

That connection was clear in the Colonial era, but it was specific to keeping wild animals at bay and hunting for fresh meat. In Colonial times there was no refrigeration and far fewer slaughterhouses. George Washington went hunting several times every week. One of Thomas Jefferson's slaves told a writer that Jefferson regularly shot squirrels and partridge. The young John Adams famously skipped school to go hunting. One visitor from England wrote in the 1700s, "There is not a man born in America that does not understand the use of firearms . . . in the cities you can scarcely find a lad of 12 years that does not go a gunning."

The American male enthusiasm for guns grew over the centuries into a powerful image of the capable, independent man who provided food for his family. It was the spirit of the Minuteman, the colonist ready to fight the British at a moment's notice, and the independence of the Old West, where settlers and cowboys protected their lands and herds and where lawmen kept the peace with their six-shooters. In the twentieth century it morphed into the brave federal agents who battled syndicate crime in big cities. At the start of the twenty-first century, the moment that captured the country's passion for guns came in a speech from an actor, Charlton Heston.

Speaking during the presidential election of 2000 as president of the NRA and a supporter of the Republican candidate, George W. Bush, Heston criticized the Democratic presidential nominee, Al Gore, for his opposition to the NRA. Heston predicted Gore's campaign would be willing to slander NRA members as "gun-toting, knuckle-dragging, bloodthirsty maniacs who stand in the way of a safer America." Heston, in a flourish he had been using in speeches to NRA crowds since the late 1980s, picked up a flintlock rifle—the same gun used by George Washington's Continental Army in the Revolutionary War—held the long gun over his head, waved it back and forth, and declared: "So, as we set out this year to defeat the divisive forces that would take freedom away, I want to say . . . 'From my cold, dead hands.'"

Heston's defiant stand linked gun ownership to manliness and America's history of rugged individualism in his defense of the Second Amendment to the Constitution. His statement had religious overtones as well, given Heston's famous role as Moses in the 1956 blockbuster movie *The Ten Commandments*. Emilie Raymond, his biographer, wrote that Heston came to represent "rugged masculinity" in American culture. Later he went on to play other mythic figures in Hollywood cinema, including Ben Hur, a daring chariot racer in the Roman Empire; El Cid, a heroic Spanish knight; and an American astronaut in *Planet of the Apes*. One film critic joked that "if God came to earth, most moviegoers would not believe it unless he looked like Charlton Heston."

It was Heston's heroic image that attracted the NRA's public relations team to hire the actor to appear in advertisements beginning in the late 1980s and to orchestrate his election to the honorific but highly visible post of NRA president. His celebrity status as a movie star and his enthusiasm for guns led some people to assume Heston had been with the gun-lobbying group from its inception. In fact, the NRA was founded in 1871 by veterans of the Civil War.

The first president of the NRA, the Charlton Heston of his time, was a former Civil War hero, General Ambrose Burnside. And the principal founders were two former journalists and army men, Colonel William C. Church and General George W. Wingate. A former *New York Times* employee, Church had left his writing job to join the Union Army. His family had served in the American Revolution and the War of 1812. During the fighting, Church and Wingate complained about the poor marksmanship of American soldiers. They worried that having so many poor marksmen in a future war would lead the United States to defeat. They complained, too, about the poor shooting ability of the New York City police in the late 1800s, a time of social turmoil as cities filled with dislocated people from farms as well as immigrants from other lands looking for work in urban factories.

Only fifteen people, mostly Union Army officers from the Civil War, attended the NRA's first meeting in the New York City offices of the *Army and Navy Journal,* a newspaper that often carried their writings. It was a modest beginning. In an early stroke of public relations genius they realized General Burnside's celebrity could help their cause. Although the general was a mere figurehead, he brought his rank and military connections into play to help the group get attention from newspapers and funding from the military. Over the next century and a half the organization grew rapidly, coming to dominate and define gun politics in the twentieth and early twenty-first centuries.

In the beginning, however, the NRA was not political. Its charter simply promised members a commitment "to promote rifle practice, and for [that purpose to construct] a suitable range or ranges." They got off to a good start on that limited task when the New York State legislature granted them $25,000 to build a shooting range away from the city on Long Island. Boy Scouts, policemen, and reserve officers in the National Guard were among their first clients. But almost immediately the rifle range at Creedmoor, Long Island, became an attraction for the rich.

In 1874 the NRA hosted the nation's first international shooting competition, attracting New York's top businessmen, who rode to the range in a line of fancy horse carriages. The crowd, estimated at eight thousand, was warned to avoid cheering during the contest to allow the marksmen to concentrate on their targets. Gen. Wingate wrote that "pandemonium broke loose, and the sky was darkened with hats that were thrown into the air," when the U.S. contingent beat the favored Irish team.

The NRA's success with shooting contests inspired construction of more shooting ranges around the country, and private clubs joined the NRA. In addition, the colonel and the general used their access to U.S. military leaders to begin conversations about how the NRA could train marksmen for future wars. At the urging of the NRA and its supporters in the military, Congress created the National Board for the Promotion of Rifle Practice (NBPRP) to build more civilian shooting ranges. One-third of the group's members served as trustees of the NRA. Most newcomers to the federally funded shooting clubs joined the NRA.

With its rising influence inside the military and on Capitol Hill, the NRA began pushing to make surplus military guns available for people practicing at its shooting ranges. Passed by Congress in 1905, Public Law 149 authorized the sale of surplus army guns to the NRA rifle clubs. The promise of cheap guns attracted more American gun enthusiasts; at points the government even gave NRA members surplus weapons for free. Two years later, in 1907, the NRA had become entrenched in Washington politics, and decided to move its headquarters to the nation's capital. By 1912 the federal government began funding NRA-certified shooting competitions.

As the NRA was growing, there was also a rise in concern about criminals using guns. Big-city newspaper headlines went into detail on the bloody killing in 1911 of a popular novelist shot to death by a mentally ill man. New York's mayor was wounded by gunfire the year before. And the New York papers began giving sensationalistic coverage to stories of gunplay among newly arriving immigrants, particularly Asian newcomers in what the papers called the "tong wars." New York State senator Timothy Sullivan, responding to alarm in New York

City, successfully pushed through a law requiring New Yorkers to get a license to own a handgun. The Sullivan Law also required keeping records of gun sales and made it a felony to sell or give guns to anyone under the age of sixteen.

The NRA immediately opposed the new law as interference with its mission of training expert shooters. As other states began to debate putting in place similar laws, the NRA's president, James Drain, wrote a newspaper column stating that the law might keep criminals from getting guns, but it must come with a "warning" if it makes "it very difficult for an honest man and a good citizen to obtain" a gun. "Such laws," Drain cautioned, "have the effect of arming the bad man and disarming the good one to the injury of the community." The argument failed, and the Sullivan Law became the first effort at gun control in the United States since the antebellum period.

In 1813 Kentucky had passed a law banning concealed guns in public places. Similar laws against concealed guns passed during the 1820s and 1830s in several states. Louisiana's ban was motivated, according to the preamble to the law, by "assassinations and attempts to commit the same that have of late been of such frequent occurrences as to become a subject of serious alarm to the peaceable and well-disposed inhabitants of the state." The next major gun control laws came toward the end of the century. As slaves were freed during the post–Civil War period, white segregationists in several southern states passed laws to keep guns out of the hands of black people. But for the country's white majority there was little or no restriction on gun ownership. Yet the NRA did not fight federal gun legislation passed during this period. For instance, there was no political dispute over the passage of the 1927 Mailing of Firearms Act, a law that banned the sale of guns through the mail to prevent gangsters from shopping widely to build up their arsenals. The NRA's indifference to this early gun control law was old-fashioned Washington deal making, a politically astute move to protect the NRA's ties to Congress and federal funding.

After Franklin D. Roosevelt, the former governor of New York and a supporter of the Sullivan Act, was elected president in 1932, he pursued national gun control legislation. With the public in fear of the famed mobsters of the "Tommy gun era," including Al Capone and John Dillinger, the president won passage of the first nationwide gun control law, the 1934 National Firearms Act, which discouraged the sale of shotguns, machine guns, and other firearms used by mobsters by levying a huge tax on them. And in 1938 President Roosevelt passed still more gun control legislation. The Federal Firearms Act made it a crime for a convicted felon to carry a gun across state lines. Once again the NRA was willing to support the new laws to protect its relationship with the federal government. It was smart politics.

Between World War I and World War II the federal government sold twenty thousand surplus guns to NRA members. At the end of World War II President Truman gave his blessing to the NRA's work by celebrating its "splendid program" of training Americans as marksmen. The group's membership tripled in just three years after the war ended, as American soldiers, having grown attached to their guns, signed up to continue shooting. That led the NRA into a new field— training former soldiers to be recreational hunters. Throughout the 1950s, the NRA remained "thoroughly mainstream and bipartisan," according to the *Washington Post*. But that politically neutral approach changed in the 1960s.

On November 22, 1963, President Kennedy was assassinated. On April 4, 1968, Martin Luther King Jr. was assassinated. On June 5, 1968, Senator Robert Kennedy was shot to death. Meanwhile, the nation's crime rate tripled and its gun homicide rate doubled. The day after RFK's assassination, President Johnson pressed for strong gun control. "Weapons of destruction," he said in a speech to Congress, "can be purchased by mail as easily as baskets of fruit or cartons of cigarettes." The president asked the lawmakers "in the name of sanity . . . in the name of safety and in the name of an aroused nation to give America the gun control law it needs." That same month, June 1968, Congress passed the Omnibus Crime Control and Safe Streets Act.

Four months later another, more expansive effort at gun control, the Gun Control Act of 1968, was signed by President Johnson. The president's attempt to require all gun owners to register their firearms with the government didn't make it through Congress, but Johnson did win most of what he wanted. The new law halted the sale of handguns and rifles across state lines. It also made it illegal for Americans to buy handguns outside of their home state. The sale of all guns to anyone under eighteen was banned, and people under twenty-one lost their right to buy handguns. And the law banned the sale of all firearms to the mentally disabled and convicted felons. Given the rash of assassinations, the NRA found itself in a weak political position to stop anything but the call for registration of guns, which it made into a red line as an outright violation of the Second Amendment.

The NRA's willingness to negotiate with politicians was evident when its top officer, Franklin Orth, testified before Congress in support of the Johnson bill: "We do not think that any sane American . . . can object to placing into this bill the [gun] which killed the president of the United States." He later told *American Rifleman* magazine that the law is "one that sportsmen of America can live with." His willingness to compromise on the biggest gun control bill in the nation's history provoked criticism from hard-line activists within the NRA. The leader of that opposition was Harlon Carter.

Carter, a rural Texan, joined the NRA in 1930 at age sixteen. At age seventeen, he shot and killed a Mexican teenager. His mother suspected the boy might have been involved in a car theft, and Carter grabbed a shotgun and tracked down the Mexican near a swimming hole. When Ramon Casiano refused to go back to Carter's home for questioning by his mother, Carter shot him in the chest, killing him. Carter was convicted but had his three-year sentence overturned on appeal. Then he changed the spelling of his first name from Harlan to Harlon to confuse state officials and newspaper reporters researching his past. For years he succeeded in hiding the record of his murder conviction. Carter was a bright, driven man who had earned a law degree before going to work as a Border Patrol agent and then rising to the NRA's board of directors in the early 1950s. From his earliest days, Carter took a purist position on people having a right to guns. The 1968 bill angered him. He was famous among NRA members for a simple position: "You don't stop crime by attacking guns—you stop crime by stopping criminals." He pushed the board and NRA staff to cut back its focus on sports shooting and marksmanship, wanting money and energy put into arguing the case for gun ownership as a constitutional right. His unapologetic approach to gun rights went so far as to tell people worried about gun violence committed by criminals and the mentally ill that he viewed such tragedies as the "price we pay for freedom."

The husky, bald Carter's anger at the new gun control law gained traction with more gun owners in 1972 when the federal government consolidated what had formerly been the Alcohol, Tobacco, and Firearms Division of the IRS into its own agency—the Bureau of Alcohol, Tobacco and Firearms (ATF)—in part, to enforce the 1968 law, in light of the spread of cheap handguns, widely called "Saturday Night Specials." At a 1977 NRA meeting, Carter led a revolt against the moderates in the NRA's leadership. "Beginning in this place and at this hour this period in NRA history is finished," he told the group. He was right. In the 1980 presidential election the NRA endorsed its first candidate, Ronald Reagan, a conservative Republican. Harlon Carter condemned the Democrat in the race, incumbent president Jimmy Carter, for putting gun control advocates on the federal courts and having aides who are "literally the Who's Who of the antigun movement." With President Reagan, a gun rights advocate, in the White House, the NRA still could not eliminate the ATF, but they managed to force sharp cuts in the agency's staff and budget, limiting enforcement of the Gun Control Act of 1968.

Inspired by their high-profile ties to the president, the NRA hired an aggressive public relations firm to counter critics who demeaned them as rowdy, stupid, beer-bellied louts who loved to play with guns. Nearly two-thirds of the NRA's members lived in rural areas (35 percent) or a small town (26 percent), and 57 percent of its members called the South or Far West home. Carter felt the geographic distance from big media led to a cultural bias in East Coast media portrayals of the NRA and also in Hollywood television comedy sketches and in the movies. The negative portrayals of gun enthusiasts increased after John Lennon, the former Beatles musician, was murdered with a gun in 1980 and President Reagan was shot during a 1981 assassination attempt.

Carter hired Ackerman McQueen, a big public relations firm from Oklahoma, for a multimillion-dollar campaign beginning in 1982. Their first ad campaign was called "I'm the NRA!" The first newspaper advertisement featured a blond boy, no older than five, holding a BB gun to his chest. The text below the picture read: "Each year, NRA members teach thousands of young people safe gun handling and basic marksmanship skills." Other advertisements featured an astronaut, a Dallas Cowboys cheerleader, and Chuck Yeager, an Air Force general and test pilot who was the first man to travel faster than the speed of sound. A later advertisement featuring a threatening man approaching a woman bears the headline "Should you shoot a rapist before he cuts your throat?" The ad then explains that "American women are realizing that they must take responsibility for their own self-defense." In the same period the public relations firm helped to place a story in a 1983 edition of *Reader's Digest* that gave a family-friendly, traditional-values image to people who owned a gun. One gun owner was quoted as saying that when he looked at his collection of eighty guns he wondered who owned them: "They kind of hook me up with history and make the days of George Washington, Lincoln and the pioneers more real than the pages of a history book ever could."

In 1983 President Reagan became the first president to speak at an NRA convention, walking onstage with Harlon Carter. By this point Carter was lionized among gun rights activists. Historians later described him as stirring such passion among gun owners that "even macho hunters grow misty-eyed at the mere mention of his name." After being introduced by Carter, President Reagan in his speech quoted President Lincoln as saying, "Important principles ... must be inflexible." Later Reagan added: "The NRA believes America's laws were made to be obeyed and that our constitutional liberties are just as important today as two hundred years ago. And by the way, the Constitution does not say government shall decree the right to keep and bear arms. The Constitution says 'the right of the people to keep and bear arms shall not be infringed.'"

With President Reagan's backing, the NRA took a newly aggressive stand against the 1968 Gun Control Act. Their fight to dilute the law gained even more clout when Republicans took control of the Senate in the early 1980s. The chairmanship of the Judiciary Committee shifted from Ted Kennedy, who had seen two brothers assassinated with guns, to Strom Thurmond, a South Carolina conservative ready to work with the newly political NRA. Thurmond and the GOP benefited from the highly energized NRA membership. The NRA promised three million members who voted, and who often voted on the basis of one issue— whether a politician supported gun rights. There were also campaign contributions and funding for independent advertising (one popular bumper sticker read "Gun Control Is Not Crime Control"). As the bill to rescind parts of the 1968 law made its way through Congress, the

NRA urged its members to write letters to their representatives. One letter from NRA headquarters to members said that any politician opposed to removing limits imposed by the Gun Control Act was "not working for gun and hunting rights in America—it is that plain and simple—either he is with us or he is against us."

The NRA's aggressive attitude was even directed at police departments, with whom the gun lobby had previously had a positive relationship. Several top police officials tried to stop the NRA's push for Congress to allow the sale of armor-piercing bullets and the Glock 17, a plastic gun reputed to be able to pass undetected through airport security (actually, it couldn't). The NRA opposed those amendments and attacked their leading proponent, San Jose police chief Joseph McNamara. An NRA spokesman claimed the chief was soft on criminals and wanted to legalize marijuana. Rep. William Hughes, a New Jersey Democrat, said, "The NRA can put fifteen thousand letters in your district overnight" and "have people in your town hall meetings interrupting you the next day." Another Democrat told the Washington Post it was costly to defy the NRA: "We made the hard political calculus, 'Do I want to spend the next five months debating one crummy vote on gun control?' The NRA's got the network, the head counts, they know who is wavering."

The NRA bid to weaken the 1968 law won out. New legislation allowed more gun sales to take place across state lines and for the first time made it illegal for the federal government to create a list of Americans who own guns.

Having spent $1.6 million lobbying to loosen gun control laws, the NRA followed up with close to $2 million in campaign funding to help their favorite House and Senate candidates in the 1986 midterm elections. "Few lobbies have so mastered the marble halls and concrete canyons of Washington," said a Washington Post editorial. The NRA is "the most persistent and resourceful of all single-issue groups," said a New York Times editorial. Again and again they exercised their power to say no to any gun control law. At every turn they argued that gun control—even small efforts to delay or limit the ability to buy and fire a gun—was the proverbial slippery slope that would lead to the federal government making a grab for everyone's guns.

Several years later a retired ATF official, William J. Vizzard, captured the essence of the NRA's approach to gun control legislation in a newspaper interview after the Sandy Hook shooting. "The NRA is a populist lobby," he told the *Washington Post*. "They get support when people are mad and stirred up. . . . [So] they are not interested in fixing things. . . . [T]he more they stir things up, the more members they get and the more money they make. What do they gain by compromise? Nothing."

After a mass shooting in Stockton, California, in 1989 in which five children were killed and thirty-two others injured with a semi-automatic AK-47, two senators sponsored a bill to ban the sale of the gun. The NRA responded fiercely. They sent 50,000 letters to their members that compared one of the senators, Dennis DeConcini, an Arizona Democrat, to Soviet communists.

The harsh, hostile political voice emerging from the NRA was politically effective. But it also opened the group to being portrayed as extremist. The NRA's campaign against the ban on armor-piercing bullets and the Glock 17s alienated police departments across the country. By 1991 former President Reagan, who had survived being shot in an assassination attempt and seen his press secretary, Jim Brady, suffer a debilitating head wound that confined him to a wheelchair for the rest of his life, moved away from the NRA. The former president eventually supported a bill named for Brady that required mandatory background checks for all gun purchases. In the same period NRA membership declined from 3 million in 1989 to 2.3 million in 1991. And in 1992 the Democrats, now clearly positioned as the NRA's political opposition, won the White House for the first time since 1976.

Meanwhile, resentment against the ATF smoldered in NRA newsletters and speeches. It began to burst into public after ATF agents played a major role in defeating an anti-government militia-style group at Ruby Ridge in 1992 and a cult at Waco in 1993.

In 1995, as violent crime in big cities spiked, President Clinton proposed new gun control laws. The NRA responded aggressively. One March 1995 advertisement showed federal agents dressed in black with a submachine gun as they forced their way into a private home. "Tell the Clinton White House to stay out of your house," said the NRA advertisement, signed by LaPierre. An April 1995 fundraising letter warned that any ban on weapons was just the start of a reign by "jackbooted government thugs" who would "take away our constitutional rights, break in our doors, seize our guns, destroy our property and even injure or kill us . . . [N]ot too long ago it was unthinkable for federal agents wearing Nazi bucket helmets and black storm trooper uniforms to attack law-abiding citizens. Not today."

Days after the fundraising letter was sent, a federal government office building housing the ATF offices in Oklahoma City was bombed. The death of 168 people, including 19 children in the day care center in the office building, led to a backlash against the NRA. Former president George H. W. Bush canceled his NRA membership and wrote a public letter to the NRA that said the group's advertising describing federal agents as thugs and Nazis was an insult to the brave Americans who worked for the ATF, especially a former Secret Service agent who protected him at the White House. "He was no Nazi," the president wrote. He added that the NRA attacks offended "my own sense of decency and honor; and it offends my concept of service to country." The NRA was knocked back. Richard Riley, a former NRA president, told the *New York Times* that the NRA had worked for a century to create an image "akin to the Boy Scouts of America . . . and now we're cast with the Nazis, the skinheads and the Ku Klux Klan."

It was during this dark political period that Carter and his advertising executives at Ackerman McQueen found a new star to replace President Reagan: Charlton Heston. The man who played Moses and other iconic leading men in the movies became a gun rights advocate in 1982. He first joined the movement when California Democrats pushed a law to require California gun owners to register their guns with the state government. Californians Against the Gun Initiative, a group opposed to the law, worked with the NRA to recruit Heston as their spokesman. Heston appeared in speeches and videos. In a thirty-minute documentary narrated by Heston, the movie star interviewed lawyers, criminologists, and sociologists about gun violence. The selected experts agreed that the new law would not stop violent crime. Heston's work raised $5 million and helped to stop the new law.

In 1989 the NRA discovered Heston's power as an advocate of gun rights at a Missouri fundraiser. As the keynote speaker, Heston described several days of pleasure spent hunting in northern Michigan. Heston told the NRA faithful that gun control advocates did not understand the joy of hunting. He took the audience back to his days as a boy in northern Michigan, "a skinny hick from the woods." As the child of divorced parents and with few friends, he had gained confidence and skill by going into the woods to learn how to use a rifle to hunt deer, rabbits, and ducks. His stories connected his childhood lessons from handling a gun to masculinity. Heston's belief in gun rights was tied to his respect for American individualism. That appreciation for individual rights, Heston would often explain, had made him an anti-communist and also had led him to become a man who marched with Dr. Martin Luther King Jr. for equal rights for black people and got his fellow Hollywood stars, including Paul Newman, Frank Sinatra, and Steve McQueen, to endorse the civil rights movement. To those outside the NRA who saw an unyielding organization refusing to agree to gun control and who labeled the group as barbarians and relics of a time long past, he said he believed in the Constitution and specifically the Second Amendment.

"I went to war when they asked me to go," he said. "I raised my family, none of them are in jail. I pay my taxes, I contribute to charity, I vote in every election. Now because I support the Bill of Rights, I am a zealot? Like hell!" He urged the NRA members to take pride in gun ownership, and in the first example of a trademark gesture he raised up a rifle that had been given to honorary guests and growled his famous slogan that the only way his gun could be taken away from him was if someone took it from his "cold, dead hands."

The standing ovation was thunderous. The picture of the lanky, handsome Heston waving the gun appeared in newspapers and magazines nationwide. He was not the first to use the powerful line. It was initially a catchphrase for the Second Amendment Foundation, another gun rights group. But Heston's personal authority, his fame, and his stature made it his signature saying, the highlight of future speeches he gave in support of gun rights.

The speech also convinced Ackerman McQueen to use Heston in a series of television advertisements. One well-known advertisement featured Heston in front of a graffiti-covered wall in a bad neighborhood in Washington, D.C. "This is the most dangerous place in America," he said. "These streets once ruled by Jefferson, Lincoln, Truman are now ruled by criminals. I'm one of seventy million gun owners who want to stop crime. Tough judges and jail time will do that . . . [a] gun ban approach won't."

Heston became the instantly recognizable face of the NRA's response to attacks on gun rights from the political left wing. Heston made appearances to combat negative portrayals of gun owners in Hollywood movies. He spoke out against rappers who attacked cops in their lyrics. Heston made headlines when, at a 1992 Time Warner shareholder meeting, he condemned the company for signing deals with rap musicians who glorified pornographic sex, drugs, and lawlessness. Heston read the profane lyrics of a song called "Cop Killer" by a Time Warner artist, rapper Ice-T, out loud to the older, mostly white shareholders. The music, Heston claimed, was sabotaging American culture; Time Warner subsequently dropped the rapper.

Heston enjoyed jousting with the NRA's critics. He told a 1997 National Press Club audience: "Today I want to talk to you about guns: why we have them, why the Bill of Rights guarantees that we have them, and why my right to have a gun is more important than your right to rail against it in print." Heston continued fighting the culture war for the NRA in 1998 when Barbra Streisand, the legendary singer, produced a pro-gun-control movie for television about a bloody Long Island Railroad shooting. Heston told reporters that Streisand was the "Hanoi Jane of the Second Amendment" and dismissed her as "not widely informed on the Constitution," all the while predicting that debating her would be "like shooting fish in a barrel."

Wayne LaPierre and the Ackerman McQueen public relations team made a strategic decision to pull Heston into an official role at the NRA by arranging for him to be elected to the board of directors. They then elevated him to vice president, and in 1998 made a grand show of pushing out older NRA hard-liners to usher the movie star into the presidency of the NRA. No one could deny the brilliant symbolism of having Heston as the public face of the group. The man who had delivered Jews from slavery in the movie role of Moses would deliver the NRA out of its political wilderness. In his speeches he often spoke of "parting the waters" and driving chariots to victory against the NRA's opponents. His speeches attracted wide coverage, and in them he repeated that gun owners were the heart of America—not extremists, but traditional people who wanted to exercise their constitutional rights. In his mind gun owners were being maligned and shunned in much of America simply for being gun owners. "I can tell you why they think that," he said by way of expressing his sense of alienation as a gun owner. "Year after year of lie after lie by the press and politicians who are hook, line and sinker stupid about lock, stock and barrel freedom."

The NRA flourished under Heston. He was so successful that LaPierre, the actual operational leader of the organization, and Ackerman McQueen discarded the two-term limit and kept Heston on as the NRA's president. He ended up serving a record five terms from 1998 to 2003. By the end of his tenure, NRA supporters shouted "We love you" whenever the seventy-year-old stood up to speak. His star power was so great that he drew in record numbers of new members, increasing the size of the group from 2.6 million in 1998 to more than 4 million in 2002.

He even took on President Clinton. Heston had just been inaugurated as NRA president when President Clinton backed new gun control measures in response to the mass shooting at Columbine High School. In his first speech in the job, Heston challenged Clinton for not enforcing existing gun laws and not prosecuting criminals who illegally obtained guns. "Mr. Clinton, America didn't trust you with our healthcare system," he proclaimed in his distinctively deep, theatric voice. "America didn't trust you with gays in the military, America doesn't trust you with our twenty-one-year-old daughters, and we sure, Lord, don't trust you with our guns." In the end, none of the Clinton-backed legislation on gun control made it past the NRA's opposition and political clout in Congress.

Heston's answer to the Columbine tragedy was to insist two days after the massacre that every school should have an armed guard. He did not know that there had been an armed policeman at the school who failed to stop the murders. The NRA's opponents ridiculed him, but his supporters wrote it off as part of a long history of antagonism aimed at the NRA by the mainstream press.

The NRA and Heston had scheduled their annual meeting for a week after the Columbine killings in nearby Denver, Colorado. Despite calls to cancel the event or find another locale, the group defiantly kept their meeting in Denver. As they met, hundreds of gun control advocates surrounded the convention site in protest. Heston used the confrontation to attack the critics as "elitists" who were too busy "screeching hyperboles" to remember Second Amendment guarantees for American gun owners.

In *Bowling for Columbine,* a scathing film documentary look at the culture of gun lovers, liberal director Michael Moore featured an interview with Heston. The elderly Heston appeared confused, bumbling, and uncertain in an embarrassing interview. Moore, a gun control supporter, got Heston to sit for the interview by pretending to be a lifelong NRA member who wanted to meet his hero. At one point he asked why Heston kept loaded guns in his house. The NRA president replied, "For self-defense." But when pressed as to whether he had ever had to defend himself, Heston admitted that he never had to do so. Looking unsteady, Heston finally resorted to saying he kept the gun loaded "because the Second Amendment gives me the right to have it loaded." Later, when Moore asked why the United States had such a big gun violence problem, a once more uncertain Heston suggested that it had to do with the amount of "ethnic" people coming into the country. The film gained wide circulation and became a hit in movie theaters, with Heston looking foolish. At around the time the movie was released Heston announced that he had been diagnosed with Alzheimer's disease. He formally stepped down as president of the NRA in 2003.

Even after Heston died in 2008, the ridicule from critics of the NRA did not stop. In 2013 the comic actor Jim Carrey made a music video called "Cold Dead Hands." In a whiny, over-the-top country-western voice, Carrey sang: "Charlton Heston movies are no longer in demand / His immortal soul may rest forever in the sand / The angels wouldn't take him up to heaven like he planned / Because they couldn't pry that gun from his cold, dead hands."

The snide treatment of Heston, however, can be seen as a backhanded testament to his success in winning support for the right to own a gun. It was Heston as the face and voice of the NRA who brought hundreds of thousands of new members to the NRA. In 2010 the NRA's annual budget was $220 million. It paid no taxes thanks to its tax-exempt status as a group dedicated to "protect and defend the U.S. Constitution . . . and the national defense." It used that money to fund more than $20 million in campaign contributions to politicians who took the organization's side in opposing gun control. It spent more money on advertising to criticize politicians who favored gun control.

And Heston's legacy endures in recent Supreme Court rulings in favor of the right to own a gun, as well as in the power of the NRA to stop efforts at limiting gun rights. Until 2008 the federal courts had maintained a consistent view of the Second Amendment based on the understanding that the Founding Fathers had a need for private citizens of the colonies to keep guns in case of war. In 1939 the Supreme Court had ruled against two men who argued that government-imposed taxes on guns conflicted with their constitutional rights to own a gun free of interference by the government. And in 1980 the Supreme Court had ruled that there was no Second Amendment right that allowed a convicted felon to object to local laws preventing felons from buying a gun. The court's ruling rested on the idea that gun ownership had nothing to do with individual rights but was solely tied to the government's interest in having civilians ready to join a fight against a common enemy of the state.

All this changed with the 2008 *District of Columbia v. Heller* Supreme Court case. Despite past court opinions directly tying gun ownership to the Constitution's desire to preserve an armed militia, the Supreme Court ruled for the first time that apart from any military need, every individual American—with the exception of criminals convicted of a felony and the mentally ill—has a legal right to own a gun "for traditionally lawful purposes, such as self-defense within the home." The words echoed Heston's.

The ruling in that case involved a D.C. police officer, Dick Heller, who wanted to keep a handgun at home in a crime-riddled big-city neighborhood. But the local law required a license before anyone could buy a gun, and it also required that all guns in private residences be kept "unloaded and disassembled or bound by a trigger lock." Heller's application was denied on the basis of previous court rulings tying gun ownership to military purposes. Heller responded with a lawsuit based on his Second Amendment right to bear arms. The case went all the way to the Supreme Court, and the Court's conservative majority ruled in Heller's favor. The only reservation expressed by the Supreme Court was to allow the government of the District of Columbia to control "conditions and qualifications on the commercial sale of arms." Other than that clause, the Supreme Court ruling was a complete victory for the NRA.

Heston's name is nowhere to be found in the Supreme Court's 2008 majority opinion that reversed all the prior decisions. But the ruling was everything he had fought for. It decoupled the link between gun rights and possible military service.

"Somewhere Charlton Heston is smiling," *Investor's Business Daily* wrote in an editorial the day the ruling was announced. A conservative website, Wake Up America, put a picture of Heston next to its story on the Court ruling and wrote: "Charlton Heston fought hard for this type of ruling before he passed away."

Echoing through the opinion was the conceptual connection Heston famously made in his speeches to the Founding Fathers' fears of a government-sponsored military being the only people in the country armed with guns. The *Las Vegas Review-Journal,* on the day after the ruling, wrote: "Would the Founding Fathers—who had just defeated the greatest military power on earth thanks to the fact that the American yeoman farmer carried a serviceable rifle—have enacted a Second Amendment to guarantee the right of the central government to disarm the common populace . . . ?"

Two years later, in 2010, the Supreme Court affirmed its decision in the *Heller* case in a 5–4 decision that extended the right of individuals in any state to own a gun for self-defense. The case *McDonald v. Chicago* established that the earlier ruling in *Heller* applied beyond a federal jurisdiction (the District of Columbia) to every individual state.

The two rulings had lots of critics. The *Wall Street Journal's* editorial page wrote that the high court's decision in *Heller* would "shred the collective interpretation [of the Second Amendment]." Washington, D.C.'s mayor said the ruling opened the door to more guns in the city and "more handgun violence." Chicago's mayor lambasted the Court for a decision that takes the nation "back to the Old West." In fact, since the rulings guns have been used to kill an average of thirty thousand people annually. But the Court's ruling and the power of Heston's work to tie gun rights to the traditions and culture of the nation have combined to make owning and carrying guns a reality of twenty-first-century life. During the 2014 midterm elections, Michael Bloomberg, the three-term mayor of New York City and a longtime supporter of expanded background checks for gun buyers, spent most of a $40 million campaign chest backing candidates in support of gun control. The NRA responded by spending $2 million on ads attacking Bloomberg, even though he was not running for office. And Bloomberg-backed candidates had mixed success at best.

A majority of Americans express concern about gun violence, yet they also tell pollsters that with so many guns in private hands they don't see any way to deal with the problem. And supporters of gun control, unlike gun rights advocates, tend not to be single-issue voters. Polls show most Americans want some limits on gun ownership and strong background checks. But the lobbying power and political power of the NRA have stood in the way.

The vexing reality of easy access to guns and the ideological fight over the right to own a gun are now ingrained features of the American experience. They are tied to politics, region, race, family tradition, and culture. The issue touches big emotional buttons for people on both sides of the gun rights/gun regulation divide.

Heston and the NRA have pushed the prominence of guns in American culture far beyond the Founding Fathers' concerns about arming a militia. Guns today are a simple fact of American life. And a great deal of the reason gun rights advocates dominate the debate, and so many state legislatures, is because of the efforts of Heston and the NRA.

BIBLIOGRAPHY

Chapter 1: The Founding Fathers and Modern America

"2012 Presidential Race—Election Results by State." NBCNews.com. Last modified November 6, 2015. http://elections.nbcnews.com/ns/politics/2012/all/president/.

"Age and Sex Composition: 2010." U.S. Census Bureau, May 2011. http://www.census.gov/prod/cen2010/briefs/c2010br-03.pdf

Amira, Dan. "Michele Bachmann Stands By Ridiculous Thing She Said About Slavery." *New York,* June 28, 2011.

Bailyn, Bernard. *To Begin the World Anew: The Genius and Ambiguities of the American Founders.* New York: Alfred A. Knopf, 2003.

"Belief in Economic Opportunity Unites Americans Across Ethnic/Racial Lines." *PR Newswire,* June 3, 2011.

Bernstein, R. B. *The Founding Fathers: A Very Short Introduction.* New York: Oxford University Press, 2015.

Buchanan, Pat. *The Death of the West: How Dying Populations and Immigrant Invasions Imperil Our Culture and Civilization.* New York: St. Martin's Griffin, 2001.

Buckland, Robert. "Speaker's Resignation Is a Testament to Founding Fathers' Wisdom." *Boston Globe,* September 30, 2015.

Carlyle, Thomas. *On Heroes, Hero-Worship, and the Heroic in History.* London: Chapman and Hall, 1840.

"Census: Women Equal to Men in College Degrees." MSNBC, April 20, 2010. http://www.nbcnews.com/id/36663479/ns/us_news-census_2010/t/census-women-equal-men-college-degrees/.

Chernow, Ron. "What Would the Founding Fathers Think of Election Day 2012?" *Wall Street Journal,* November 6, 2012.

Crowley, Michael. "The New Generation Gap." *Time,* November 14, 2011.

Cohen, Elizabeth. "Who Would the Founding Fathers Deport?" *Washington Post,* February 3, 2013.

Ellis, Joseph. *Founding Brothers: The Revolutionary Generation.* New York: Alfred A. Knopf, 2000.

"Inside Obama's Sweeping Victory." Pew Research Center, November 5, 2008. http://www.pewresearch.org/2008/11/05/inside-obamas-sweeping -victory/.

Jefferson, Thomas. *Jefferson: Political Writings,* edited by Joyce Appleby and Terence Ball. Cambridge: Cambridge University Press, 1999.

Kurzweil, Ray. "The Law of Accelerating Returns." *Kurzweil Accelerating Intelligence,* March 7, 2001.

Lepore, Jill. *The Whites of Their Eyes: The Tea Party's Revolution and the Battle over American History.* Princeton: Princeton University Press, 2011.

Perlo-Freeman, Sam, Aude Fleurant, Pieter D. Wezeman, Siemon T. Wezeman. "Trends in World Military Spending." *SIPRI Fact Sheet,* April 2015.

"The Rise of Neo-Nativism: Putting Trump into Proper Context." *Ipsos Ideas Spotlight.* http://spotlight.ipsos-na.com/index.php/news/the-rise-of-neo -nativism-putting-trump-into-proper-context/.

Sanchez, Claudio. "Women Outnumber Men Earning Doctoral Degrees." NPR, September 15, 2010. http://www.npr.org/templates/story/story.php ?storyId=129874290.

Stathis, Stephen W. *Landmark Debates in Congress: From the Declaration of Independence to the War in Iraq.* Washington, D.C.: CQ Press, 2008.

"Women Outnumber Men Earning Doctoral Degrees." NPR, September 15, 2010. http://www.npr.org/templates/story/story.php?storyId=129874290.

Yetman, Norman R. *Majority and Minority: The Dynamics of Race and Ethnicity in American Life.* 6th ed. Needham Heights, Mass: Pearson, 1998.

Chapter 2: The Great American Melting Pot

"America's Foreign Born in the Last 50 Years." U.S. Census Bureau, February 13, 2013. http://www.census.gov/how/pdf/Foreign-Born--50-Years -Growth.pdf.

Barkan, Elliott Robert, ed. *Immigrants in American History: Arrival, Adaptation, and Integration,* Volume 1. Santa Barbara: ABC-CLIO, 2013.

Boller, Paul F., Jr. *Essays on the Presidents: Principles and Politics.* Fort Worth: TCU Press, 2012.

Borjas, George J. *Heaven's Door: Immigration Policy and the American Economy.* Princeton: Princeton University Press, 1999.

Canellos, Peter. "Obama Victory Took Root in Kennedy-Inspired Immigration Act." *Boston Globe,* November 11, 2008.

Chaddock, Gail Russell. "Kennedy and Immigration: He Changed the Face of America." *Christian Science Monitor,* August 28, 2009.

Cortes, Carlos E., ed. *Multiracial America: A Multimedia Encyclopedia,* Volume 1. Los Angeles, London, New Delhi, Singapore, and Washington, D.C.: Sage, 2013.

Editorial Board. "Immigration Impasse." *New York Times,* June 18, 1965.

Ekins, Emily. "Meet the Millennials: Reason-Rupe Surveys." Reason.com, July 10, 2014. https://reason.com/poll/2014/07/10/meet-the-millennials.

Grieco, Elizabeth, Edward Trevelyan, Luke Larsen, Yesenia D. Acosta, Christine Gambino, Patricia de la Cruz, Tom Gryn, and Nathan Walters. "The Size, Place of Birth, and Geographic Distribution of the Foreign-Born Population in the United States: 1960 to 2010." *U.S. Census Bureau Population Division Working Paper No. 96* (October 2012).

Hulse, Carl. "Kennedy Tactics on Immigration Vex Democrats." *New York Times,* April 12, 2006.

Jacobson, Matthew Frye. "The Quest for Equality: European Immigration Part I." Lecture, The Gilder Lehrman Institute of American History. https://www.youtube.com/watch?v=9HvaR3bnt2o.

———. "Whiteness and the Normative American Citizen." Lecture, University of Wisconsin-Whitewater, October 2014. https://www.youtube.com/watch?v=r_WbWd4fw4g.

Johnson, Lyndon B. "Remarks at the Signing of the Immigration Bill." LBJ Presidential Library, October 3, 1965.

Jordan, Miriam. "Heartland Draws Hispanics to Help Revive Small Towns." *Wall Street Journal,* November 8, 2012.

Kennedy, Edward. "Q&A: Sen. Kennedy on Immigration, Then & Now." Interview by Jennifer Ludden. NPR, May 9, 2006.

Kennedy, John F. "Letter to the President of the Senate and to the Speaker of the House on Revision of the Immigration Laws," July 23, 1963. Online by Gerhard Peters and John T. Woolley, The American Presidency Project. http://www.presidency.ucsb.edu/ws/?pid=9355.

———. *Nation of Immigrants.* 1964. Reprint, New York: HarperPerennial, 2008.

———. *Public Papers of the Presidents of the United States: John F. Kennedy, January 1 to November 22, 1963.* Washington, D.C.: U.S. Government Printing Office, 1964.

Kibria, Nazli, Cara Bowman, and Megan O'Leary. *Race and Immigration.* Cambridge, UK: Polity, 2013.

Kirkendall, Richard S., ed. *The Civil Liberties Legacy of Harry S. Truman.* Kirksville, Mo.: Truman State University Press, 2013.

Lowe, Lisa. *Immigrant Acts: On Asian American Cultural Politics.* Durham: Duke University Press, 1996.

Ludden, Jennifer. "1965 Immigration Law Changed Face of America." NPR, May 9, 2006. http://www.npr.org/templates/story/story.php?storyId=5391395.

Meacham, Jon. "Voices of Obama's America: Who We Are Now." *Newsweek,* January 16, 2009.

"Michele Bachmann's Misplaced Immigration Nostalgia." *Washington Post,* September 14, 2011.

Passel, Jeffrey S. and D'Vera Cohn. "US Population Projections: 2005–2050." Pew Research Center, February 11, 2008. http://www.pewhispanic.org /2008/02/11/us-population-projections-2005-2050/.

"The Rise of Asian Americans." Pew Research Center, June 19, 2012. http:// www.pewsocialtrends.org/2012/06/19/the-rise-of-asian-americans/.

Roberts, Sam. "Listening to (and Saving) the World's Languages." *New York Times,* April 29, 2010.

Salamone, Frank A. "Kennedy Family." *Class in America: An Encyclopedia,* Volume 1: A–G. Edited by Robert E. Weir. Westport, Conn.: Greenwood Press, 2007.

"Selected U.S. Immigration Legislation and Executive Actions, 1790–2014." Pew Research Center, September 28, 2015. http://www.pewhispanic.org /2015/09/28/selected-u-s-immigration-legislation-and-executive-actions -1790-2014/.

Shannon, William. "The Emergence of Senator Kennedy." *The New York Times Magazine,* August 22, 1965.

Smith, James P. and Barry Edmonston, ed. *The New Americans: Economic, Demographic, and Fiscal Effects of Immigration.* Washington, D.C.: National Academy Press, 1997.

"Three Decades of Mass Immigration: The Legacy of the 1965 Immigration Act." Center for Immigration Studies, September 1995. http://cis .org/1965ImmigrationAct-MassImmigration.

Toness, Bianca Vázquez. "Kennedy Shaped Modern-Day Immigration System." WBUR, August 27, 2009. http://www.wbur.org/2009/08/27/ kennedy-immigration.

Truman, Harry S. *Public Papers of the Presidents of the United States: Harry S. Truman, January 1, 1952, to January 20, 1953.* Washington, D.C.: Government Printing Office, 1966.

Chapter 3: The Living Constitution

Altschuler, Bruce E. *LBJ and the Polls.* Gainesville, Fla.: University of Florida Press, 1990.

Ball, Howard. *A Defiant Life: Thurgood Marshall and the Persistence of Racism in America.* New York: Crown Publishing, 1998.

Blackman, John. *A Memoir of the Life and Writings of Thomas Day.* London: J.B. Leno, 1862.

Cray, Ed. *Chief Justice: A Biography of Earl Warren.* New York: Simon and Schuster, 1997.

Daley, James, ed. *Great Speeches by African Americans: Frederick Douglass, Sojourner Truth, Dr. Martin Luther King, Jr., Barack Obama, and Others.* Mineola, N.Y.: Dover Publications, 2006.

Eichelberger, Erika, Jaeah Lee, and A. J. Vicens. "How We Won—and Lost—the War on Poverty, in 6 Charts." *Mother Jones,* January 8, 2014.

Finkelman, Paul, ed. *Encyclopedia of African American History, 1896 to the Present: From the Age of Segregation to the Twenty-First Century Five-Volume Set.* New York: Oxford University Press, USA, 2009.

Hampton, Henry, Steve Fayer, and Sarah Flynn. *Voices of Freedom: An Oral History of the Civil Rights Movement from the 1950s Through the 1980s.* New York: Bantam Books, 1990.

"Inventory of the Earl Warren Papers: 1924–1953." Online Archive of California. http://www.oac.cdlib.org/findaid/ark:/13030/tf4b69n6gc/.

Johnson, Lyndon B. "Remarks in the Capitol Rotunda at the Signing of the Voting Rights Act." LBJ Presidential Library. August 6, 1965. http://www.lbjlib.utexas.edu/johnson/archives.hom/speeches.hom/650806.asp.

———. "Transcript of the Johnson Address on Voting Rights to Joint Session of Congress." *New York Times,* March 16, 1965.

———. "Remarks at the Welhausen Elementary School, Cotulla, Texas, November 7, 1966." Online by Gerhard Peters and John T. Woolley, The American Presidency Project. http://www.presidency.ucsb.edu/ws/?pid=28003.

Kluger, Richard. *Simple Justice: The History of Brown v. Board of Education and Black America's Struggle for Equality.* 1975. Reprint, New York: Vintage Books, 2011.

"NAACP: 100 Years of History." NAACP. http://www.naacp.org/pages/naacp-history.

Plessy v. Ferguson, 163 U.S. 537 (1896).

Taylor, Stuart Jr. "Marshall Sounds Critical Note on Bicentennial." *New York Times,* May 7, 1987.

Transcript, Earl Warren Oral History Interview I, 9/21/71, by Joe B. Frantz, Internet Copy, LBJ Library.

Warren, Earl. *The Memoirs of Chief Justice Earl Warren.* Garden City, New York: Doubleday & Co., 1977.

White, G. Edward. *Earl Warren: A Public Life.* New York: Oxford University Press, 1982.

Williams, Juan. *Thurgood Marshall: American Revolutionary.* New York: Times Books, 1998.

Zelden, Charles L. *Thurgood Marshall: Race, Rights, and the Struggle for a More Perfect Union.* New York: Routledge, 2013.

Chapter 4: Broken Windows, Urban Crime, and Hard Data

Alexander, Michelle. *The New Jim Crow: Mass Incarceration in the Age of Colorblindness.* New York: New Press, 2010.

Andrews, William and William J. Bratton. "What We've Learned About Po-
    licing." *City Journal,* Spring 1999.

Archbold, Carol A. *Policing: A Text/Reader.* Los Angeles, California: SAGE,
    2013.

Bratton, William J. "Cutting Crime and Restoring Order: What America
    Can Learn from New York's Finest." The Heritage Foundation, Oc-
    tober 15, 1996. http://www.heritage.org/research/lecture/hl573nbsp
    -cutting-crime-and-restoring-order.

"Brief History of the FBI." FBI. https://www.fbi.gov/about-us/history/brief
    -history.

Bush, George W. "President Bush's Speech on Department of Homeland Se-
    curity." *USA Today,* November 25, 2002.

The Editorial Board. "A Real Debate on Surveillance." *New York Times,*
    June 10, 2013.

Friedman, Thomas L. "Blowing a Whistle." *New York Times,* June 11, 2013.

Gibbons, Jordan. "Commissioner William Bratton: NYPD's Top Cop to Ad-
    dress Community Policing." *Press of Southeast Queens,* February 20, 2015.

Grogan, Paul S. and Tony Proscio. *Comeback Cities: A Blueprint for Urban
    Neighborhood Revival.* Boulder, Colo.: Westview Press, 2000.

Kelling, George L. and William J. Bratton. "Policing Terrorism." Manhattan
    Institute for Policy Research, September 1, 2006. http://www.manhattan
    -institute.org/html/policing-terrorism-5636.html.

Kelling, George L. and James Q. Wilson. "Broken Windows: The Police and
    Neighborhood Safety." *The Atlantic,* March 1982.

Keough, Robert. "Bill Bratton on the New Crime Paradigm." *CommonWealth
    Magazine,* January 1, 2002.

Kramer, Mattea and Chris Hellman. "What's Homeland Security?" *Mother
    Jones,* February 28, 2013.

Krauss, Clifford. "The Bratton Resignation: The Legacy; Bratton Hailed as
    Pioneer of New Style of Policing." *New York Times,* March 27, 1996.

Lardner, James. "THE C.E.O. COP." *The New Yorker,* February 6, 1995.

"The Life and Times of Incoming NYPD Commissioner William Bratton."
    New York Daily News, December 5, 2013.

Lobo, Arun Peter and Joseph J. Salvo. "The Newest New Yorkers: Character-
    istics of the City's Foreign-Born Population." New York City Department
    of City Planning, 2013. http://www.nyc.gov/html/dcp/html/census/nny
    .shtml.

Obama, Barack. "Statement by the President." White House Office of the
    Press Secretary, June 07, 2013. https://www.whitehouse.gov/the-press
    -office/2013/06/07/statement-president.

Press, Gil. "Bill Bratton on Data and Analytics, Homeland Security and
    Hometown Security." *Forbes,* April 27, 2013.

Priest, Dana and William M. Arkin. "A Hidden World, Growing Beyond Control." *Washington Post,* July 19, 2010.

Rosenthal, Elden M. "Patriot Act Is a 'National Security' Threat to Constitutional Rights: Guest Opinion." *Oregonian,* June 13, 2013.

Sengupta, Somini. "In Hot Pursuit of Numbers to Ward Off Crime." *New York Times,* June 19, 2013.

Siegel, Fred. *The Prince of the City: Giuliani, New York, and the Genius of American Life.* San Francisco: Encounter Books, 2005.

"Timeline of New NYPD Commissioner Bratton." *New York Daily News,* December 5, 2013.

Chapter 5: "No Apologies, No Regrets"

"The Abrams Tapes: Insight to the MACV Headquarters During the Vietnam War." *HistoryNet,* June 12, 2006. http://www.historynet.com/the-abrams-tapes-insight-to-the-macv-headquarters-during-the-vietnam-war.htm.

Bidwell, Allie. "Majority of Americans Don't Trust Newspapers and Television News." *U.S. News & World Report,* June 18, 2013.

Bliss, Edward, Jr. *Now the News: The Story of Broadcast Journalism.* New York: Columbia University Press, 1991.

Brokaw, Tom. *The Greatest Generation.* New York: Random House, 1998.

Brownlee, Romie L. and William J. Mullen III. *Changing the Army: An Oral History of General William E. DePuy, USA Retired.* Washington, D.C.: Government Printing Office, 1988.

CNN Staff. "By the Numbers: Women in the US Military." CNN, January 24, 2013. http://www.cnn.com/2013/01/24/us/military-women-glance/.

"Confidence in Institutions." Gallup, June 2015. http://www.gallup.com/poll/1597/Confidence-Institutions.aspx.

The Editors of Boston Publishing Company. *The American Experience in Vietnam: Reflections on an Era.* 1988. Reprint, Minneapolis: 2014.

"Eisenhower." *American Experience,* PBS: WHYY. http://www.pbs.org/wgbh/americanexperience/films/eisenhower/.

Flanagan, Ed. "China Brings Its First Aircraft Carrier into Service, Joining 9-Nation Club." NBC News, Sept. 25, 2012.

Gambone, Michael. *Small Wars: Low-Intensity Threats and the American Response Since Vietnam.* Knoxville, Tenn.: Univ. of Tennessee Press, 2012.

"General Frederick Carlton Weyand." Campaign for the National Museum of the United States Army. 2015. https://armyhistory.org/general-frederick-carlton-weyand/.

Gole, Henry G. *General William E. DePuy: Preparing the Army for Modern War.* Lexington, Ky.: University Press of Kentucky, 2008.

Grace, Francie. "Vietnam War Gen. Westmoreland Dies." CBS News, July 18,

2005. http://www.cbsnews.com/news/vietnam-war-gen-westmoreland -dies/.

Jones, Brian. "One Chart Shows the Magnitude of US Naval Dominance." *Business Insider,* November 13, 2013.

"Man of the Year: Gen. Westmoreland, the Guardians at the Gate." *Time,* January 7, 1966.

McCaffrey, James M. *The Army in Transformation, 1790–1860.* Westport, Conn.: Greenwood Press, 2006.

Mills, C. Wright. *The Power Elite.* 1956. Reprint, Oxford University Press, 2000.

Onuf, Peter S., ed. *Congress and the Confederation.* New York: Garland, 1991.

Patton, Benjamin and Jennifer Scruby. *Growing Up Patton: Reflections on Heroes, History, and Family Wisdom.* New York: Penguin, 2012.

Ricks, Thomas E. "Forgotten Warrior." *Washington Monthly,* August 2009.

Romjue, John L. *American Army Doctrine for the Post–Cold War.* Fort Monroe, Va.: Military History Office, United States Army Training and Doctrine Command, 1996.

Smith, Bruce. "Gen. William Westmoreland, Who Led Troops in Vietnam, Dead at 91." Associated Press, July 19, 2005.

Stewart, Richard W., ed. *American Military History: The United States Army in a Global Era, 1917–2003.* Washington D.C.: Center of Military History, 2009.

Tucker, Spencer C., ed. *The Encyclopedia of the Wars of the Early American Republic, 1783–1812: A Political, Social, and Military History* [3 Volumes]. Santa Barbara: ABC-CLIO, 2014.

"The Way of the Soldier: Remembering General Creighton Abrams." Foreign Policy Research Institute, May 2013. http://www.fpri.org/articles/2013/05/ way-soldier-remembering-general-creighton-abrams.

Chapter 6: It's the Economy, Stupid

Belluck, Pam. "Recession Anxiety Seeps into Everyday Lives." *New York Times,* April 8, 2009.

Bischoff, Kendra and Sean F. Reardon. "Residential Segregation by Income." *US2010: Discover America in a New Century.* October 16, 2013. http:// www.s4.brown.edu/us2010/Data/Report/report10162013.pdf.

Cassidy, John. "After the Blowup." *The New Yorker,* January 11, 2010.

Denning, Steve. "The Origin of 'The World's Dumbest Idea': Milton Friedman." *Forbes,* June 26, 2013.

Dollars and Deficits: Inflation, Monetary Policy and the Balance of Payments. Englewood Cliffs, N.J.: Prentice Hall, 1968.

Ebenstein, Alan O. *Milton Friedman: A Biography.* New York: Palgrave Macmillan, 2007.

Erickson, Amanda. "Renowned Economist Friedman Dies." *Columbia Daily Spectator,* November 17, 2006.

Feeney, Mark. "Milton Friedman, 94; Economist Propelled Shift Toward Markets." *Boston Globe,* November 17, 2006.

Fleming, Thomas. *What America Was Really Like in 1776.* New Word City, Inc., 2011.

"Five Years after Market Crash, U.S. Economy Seen as 'No More Secure.'" Pew Research Center, September 12, 2013. http://www.people-press .org/2013/09/12/five-years-after-market-crash-u-s-economy-seen-as-no -more-secure/.

Friedman, Milton. *Capitalism and Freedom: Fortieth Anniversary Edition.* Chicago: University of Chicago Press, 2002.

"Milton Friedman." *Commanding Heights,* PBS, October 1, 2000. http://www .pbs.org/wgbh/commandingheights/shared/minitext/int_miltonfried man.html.

Friedman, Milton and Rose D. Friedman. *Two Lucky People: Memoirs.* Chicago: University of Chicago Press, 1998.

"The Goldwater View of Economics." *New York Times,* October 11, 1964.

Goodman, Peter S. "A Fresh Look at the Apostle of Free Markets." *New York Times,* April 13, 2008.

Hardy, Quentin. "Milton Friedman: Legalize It!" *Forbes,* June 2, 2005.

Hutchison, T. W. *Economics and Economic Policy in Britain, 1946–1966.* London: Allen and Unwin Ltd., 1968.

"Interview: Milton Friedman." *Playboy* 28, no. 2 (1973): 51–68.

Kennedy, David M. *Freedom from Fear: The American People in Depression and War, 1929–1945.* New York: Oxford University Press, 1999.

Klein, Daniel B. "Economists Against the FDA." The Independent Institute, September 1, 2000. http://www.independent.org/newsroom/article.asp ?id=279.

"The Lost Decade of the Middle Class." Pew Research Center, August 22, 2012. http://www.pewsocialtrends.org/2012/08/22/the-lost-decade-of-the -middle-class/.

Martin, Roger L. *Fixing the Game: Bubbles, Crashes, and What Capitalism Can Learn from the NFL.* Boston, Mass: Harvard Business Review Press, 2011.

"Milton Friedman—Biographical." Nobelprize.org. Last Modified 2014. http:// www.nobelprize.org/nobel_prizes/economic-sciences/laureates/1976/ friedman-bio.html.

"Milton Friedman Interviewed." *Times Herald,* December 1, 1978.

Noble, Holcomb B. "Milton Friedman, 94, Free-Market Theorist, Dies." *New York Times,* November 17, 2006.

Perlstein, Rick. *Before the Storm: Barry Goldwater and the Unmaking of the American Consensus.* New York: Hill & Wang, 2001.

Piketty, Thomas. "Inequality in America: The 1% in Historical and Comparative Perspective." *Penn Social Science & Policy Forum,* November 9, 2012. https://www.sas.upenn.edu/sspf/event/2012/inequality-america-1 -historical-and-comparative-perspective-thomas-piketty.

Rank, Mark Robert, Thomas A. Hirschl, and Kirk A. Foster. *Chasing the American Dream: Understanding What Shapes Our Fortunes.* New York: Oxford University Press, 2014.

Raum, Tom. "Poll: One-Third of Americans Fear They May Lose Jobs." *Huffington Post,* November 20, 2008.

Rodgers, Daniel T. *Age of Fracture.* Cambridge, Mass.: Belknap Press of Harvard University Press, 2011.

Shierholz, Heidi and Elise Gould. "Already More Than a Lost Decade: Poverty and Income Trends Continue to Paint a Bleak Picture." Economic Policy Institute, September 12, 2012. http://www.epi.org/publication/ lost-decade-poverty-income-trends-continue-2/.

Skidelsky, Robert Jacob Alexander. *John Maynard Keynes: The Economist as Saviour 1920–1937.* London: Macmillan, 1992.

"The Social Responsibility of Business Is to Increase Its Profits." *New York Times Magazine,* September 13, 1970.

Summers, Lawrence H. "The Great Liberator." *New York Times,* November 19, 2006.

Will, George F. *One Man's America: The Pleasures and Provocations of Our Singular Nation.* New York: Crown Forum, 2008.

Chapter 7: Liberty and Justice for All

Anderson, Carol Elaine. *Eyes Off the Prize: The United Nations and the African American Struggle for Human Rights, 1944–1955.* Cambridge, UK, and New York: Cambridge University Press, 2003.

Antieau, Chester James. "Natural Rights and the Founding Fathers—The Virginians." *Washington and Lee Law Review* 43 (1960): 43–79.

"Biography: Eleanor Roosevelt's Life." PBS: WHYY. http://www.pbs.org/ wgbh/americanexperience/features/biography/eleanor-biography/.

Clinton, Hillary. "Remarks at the Eleanor Roosevelt Human Rights Award Ceremony" (December 10, 2010.) U.S. Department of State. http://www .state.gov/secretary/20092013clinton/rm/2010/12/152661.htm.

Conklin, Wendy. *Eleanor Roosevelt.* Huntington Beach, Calif.: Teacher Created Material, 2007.

Cook, Blanche Wiesen. *Eleanor Roosevelt: Volume 2, The Defining Years: 1933–1938.* New York and London: Viking, 1999.

———. "Eleanor Roosevelt's Human Rights Legacy." *Peace & Freedom* 66, no. 1 (Spring 2006): 4–5.

Glendon, Mary Ann. *A World Made New: Eleanor Roosevelt and the Universal Declaration of Human Rights.* New York: Random House, 2001.

Goodman, J. David and Jennifer Preston. "How the Kony Video Went Viral." *New York Times,* March 9, 2012.

Goodwin, Doris Kearns. *No Ordinary Time: Franklin & Eleanor Roosevelt: The Home Front in World War II.* New York: Simon and Schuster, 1994.

Newport, Frank, David W. Moore, and Lydia Saad. "Most Admired Men and Women: 1948–1998." Gallup. December 13, 1999. http://www.gallup.com/poll/3415/most-admired-men-women-19481998.aspx.

Peyser, Marc and Timothy Dwyer. "Eleanor Roosevelt's Anything-but-Private Funeral." *The Atlantic,* November 4, 2012.

Revkin, Andrew C. "'A Girl with a Book'—Malala's Day at the United Nations." *New York Times,* July 12, 2013.

Roosevelt, Eleanor. "Speech to the Democratic National Convention Urging Support for the United Nations." July 22, 1952. *Eleanor Roosevelt Papers Project.* http://www.gwu.edu/~erpapers/documents/displaydoc.cfm?_t=speeches&_docid=spc041708.

Roosevelt, Eleanor. "On the Adoption of the Universal Declaration of Human Rights, December 9, 1948." *Great Speeches by American Women.* ed. James Daley. Mineola, N.Y.: Dover Publications, 2008.

Sears, John. "Eleanor Roosevelt and the Universal Declaration of Human Rights." *Celebrating Eleanor Roosevelt,* 2008. http://www.fdrlibrary.marist.edu/library/pdfs/sears.pdf.

Stevenson, Adlai. "Eleanor Roosevelt, October 12, 1882–November 7, 1962, Eulogy Delivered by Adlai E. Stevenson at a Memorial Service, Cathedral of St. John the Divine, New York City, November 17, 1962." *In Tribute: Eulogies of Famous People,* ed. Ted Tobias. Lanham, Md., and London: Scarecrow Press, 1999.

Tapp, Robert B. "The Universal Declaration of Human Rights: Still Ahead of Its Time?" *The Humanist,* October 17, 2008.

"The Universal Declaration of Human Rights," December 1948. United Nations. http://www.un.org/en/universal-declaration-human-rights/.

Winter, Jay. "Review of *A World Made New: Eleanor Roosevelt and the Universal Declaration of Human Rights,* by Mary Ann Glendon." *Ethics & International Affairs* 15, no. 2 (January 2001): 167.

Chapter 8: The Bridge and Tunnel Crowd

Auch, Rober, Janis Taylor, and William Acevedo. "Urban Growth in American Cities: Glimpses of U.S. Urbanization." U.S. Geological Survey, January 2004. http://pubs.usgs.gov/circ/2004/circ1252/#Purpose.

"Biography: Robert Moses." The New York Preservation Archive Project. 2014. http://www.nypap.org/content/robert-moses.

Brooks, Wesley C. *Finding New Neighbors: Clearing the Way to . . . 'Clear to Close.'* Bloomington, Ind.: AuthorHouse, 2013.

Butkiewicz, James L. "Fixing the Housing Crisis." *Forbes,* April 30, 2009.

Caro, Robert. *The Power Broker: Robert Moses and the Fall of New York.* 1974. Reprint, New York: Alfred E. Knopf, 2012.

Cohen, Rich. "La Belle Simone." *New York,* November 10, 2013.

Dim, Joan Marans. "Did Robert Moses Ruin New York City?" *Barron's,* March 17, 2012.

Glaeser, Edward. "Great Cities Need Great Builders." *New York Sun,* January 19, 2007.

Goldberger, Paul. "Robert Moses, Master Builder, Is Dead at 92." *New York Times,* July 30, 1981.

Hayden, Dolores and Jim Wark. *A Field Guide to Sprawl.* New York: W. W. Norton & Company, 2004.

King, John. "Jane Jacobs vs. Robert Moses." *SFGate,* July 28, 2009.

Knott, Sarah. *Sensibility and the American Revolution.* Chapel Hill, N.C.: University of North Carolina Press, 2009.

Kaufman, Michael T. "Tough Times for Mr. Levittown." *New York Times,* October 22, 1989.

Lacayo, Richard. "Suburban Legend William Levitt." *Time,* December 7, 1998.

Morrone, Francis. "Longing for Robert Moses." *New York Sun,* August 22, 2005.

"Northeast." *America 2050.* http://www.america2050.org/northeast.html.

Pace, Eric. "William J. Levitt, 86, Pioneer of the Suburbs, Dies." *New York Times,* January 29, 1994.

Peltz, James F. "It Started With Levittown in 1947 : Nation's 1st Planned Community Transformed Suburbia." *Los Angeles Times,* June 21, 1988.

"Robert Moses and the Modern Park System (1929–1965)." New York City Department of Parks and Recreation. http://www.nycgovparks.org/about/history/timeline/robert-moses-modern-parks.

Rodgers, Cleveland. *Robert Moses: Builder for Democracy.* New York: Holt, 1952.

Sarachan, Sydney. "The Legacy of Robert Moses." PBS: WHYY, January 17, 2013. http://www.pbs.org/wnet/need-to-know/environment/the-legacy-of-robert-moses/16018/.

Schiff, Judith. "Robert Moses and the World's Fair." *Yale Alumni Magazine,* March and April 2014.

Teaford, Jon C. *The Twentieth-Century American City: Problem, Promise, and Reality.* Baltimore: Johns Hopkins University Press, 1986.

Young, William H. and Nancy K. Young. *World War II and the Postwar Years in America: A Historical and Cultural Encyclopedia.* Santa Barbara: ABC-CLIO, 2010.

Chapter 9: "Keep the Boys Happy"

Blake, Aaron. "The End of Unions?" *Washington Post,* June 11, 2012.

Carter, Jimmy. "Labor Day Remarks at a White House Picnic. Washington, D.C., September 3, 1979." Online by Gerhard Peters and John T. Woolley, The American Presidency Project. http://www.presidency.ucsb.edu/ws/?pid=32824.

Cohany, Harry, Theodore Reedy, John Brumm, Nelson M. Bortz, Witt Bowden, Joseph W. Bloch, and Joseph P. Goldberg. *Brief History of the American Labor Movement.* Bureau of Labor Statistics. Washington, D.C., U.S. Government Printing Office, 1976.

Compa, Lance A. "An Overview of Collective Bargaining in the United States." *El derecho a la negociación colectiva: Monografías de temas laborales.* ed. J. G. Hernández. Seville: Consejo Andaluz de Relaciones Laborales, 2014.

"Controls Needed to Halt Inflation, Meany Says." *Reading Eagle,* August 31, 1969.

Coolidge, Calvin. "Address to the American Society of Newspaper Editors, Washington, D.C., January 17, 1925." Online by Gerhard Peters and John T. Woolley, The American Presidency Project. http://www.presidency.ucsb.edu/ws/?pid=24180.

Debs, Eugene V. "The Canton, Ohio Speech (June 16, 1918)." *Writings of Eugene V. Debs: A Collection of Essays by America's Most Famous Socialist.* ed. Lenny Flank. St. Petersburg, Fla.: Red and Black Publishers, 2008.

Dolan, Jay P. *The Irish Americans: A History.* New York: Bloomsbury Press, 2008.

Dubofsky, Melvyn and Warren R. Van Tine. *Labor Leaders in America.* Urbana and Chicago: University of Illinois Press, 1987.

Gass, Nick. "Poll: Americans' View of Labor Unions Improving." *Politico,* August 17, 2015.

"George Meany (1894–1980)." AFL-CIO. http://www.aflcio.org/About/Our-History/Key-People-in-Labor-History/George-Meany-1894-1980.

Gurr, Ted Robert, ed. *Violence in America: Protest, Rebellion, Reform, Vol. 2.* Newbury Park, Calif.: SAGE, 1989.

Greenhouse, Steven. "Defeat of Auto Union in Tennessee Casts Its Strategy into Doubt." *New York Times,* February 15, 2014.

———. "Union Membership in U.S. Fell to 70-Year Low Last Year." *New York Times,* January 21, 2011.

———. "Volkswagen Vote Is Defeat for Labor in South." *New York Times,* February 14, 2014.

Hirsch, Barry T. "Unions, Dynamism, and Economic Performance." *Institute for the Study of Labor Discussion Paper No. 5342* (November 2010).

Johnson, Dennis W. *The Laws That Shaped America: Fifteen Acts of Congress and Their Lasting Impact.* New York and London: Routledge, 2009.

Jones, Jeffrey M. "Approval of Labor Unions Holds Near Its Low, at 52%." Gallup, August 31, 2011. http://www.gallup.com/poll/149279/approval -labor-unions-holds-near-low.aspx.

"Legacy of George Meany." *Christian Science Monitor,* January 14, 1980.

Leonhardt, David and Kevin Quealy. "The American Middle Class Is No Longer the World's Richest." *New York Times,* April 22, 2014.

Lewis, John L. "Speech by John L. Lewis in Opposition to Taft-Hartley Statute, Delivered Before the AFL Convention, October 14, 1947." *Labor Standard.* http://laborstandard.igc.org/Vol4No2/John_L_Lewis_Speech .htm.

"Life and Impact of George Meany." C-SPAN.org, August 25, 2001. http:// www.c-span.org/video/?165762-4/life-impact-george-meany.

Moore, David W. "Public Support for Unions Remains Strong." Gallup, August 30, 2012. http://www.gallup.com/poll/6706/public-support -unions-remains-strong.aspx.

Morris, Richard B. "The Emergence of American Labor." United States Department of Labor. http://www.dol.gov/dol/aboutdol/history/chapter1.htm.

O'Connor, David E. *Deciphering Economics: Timely Topics Explained.* Santa Barbara, Calif.: Greenwood, 2014.

Pomerleau, Kyle. "Summary of Latest Federal Income Tax Data." Tax Foundation, December 18, 2013. http://taxfoundation.org/article/summary -latest-federal-income-tax-data.

"Polling." Raise the Minimum Wage, January 2015. http://www.raisethe minimumwage.com/pages/polling.

Priddle, Alisa. "Detroit Blight Part of Anti-Union Fight in Tenn." *USA Today,* February 6, 2010.

Rayback, Joseph G. *History of American Labor.* 1959. Reprint, New York: The Free Press, 1966.

Robinson, Archie and George Meany. *George Meany and His Times: A Biography.* New York: Simon and Schuster, 1981.

Saad, Lydia. "Americans' Support for Labor Unions Continues to Recover." Gallup, August 17, 2015. http://www.gallup.com/poll/184622/americans -support-labor-unions-continues-recover.aspx.

Sabadish, Natalie and Lawrence Mishel. "CEO Pay and the Top 1%: How Executive Compensation and Financial-Sector Pay Have Fueled Income Inequality." Economic Policy Institute, May 2, 2012. http://www.epi.org/ publication/ib331-ceo-pay-top-1-percent/.

Stinson, Linda. "DOL's Historian on the History of Labor Day." United States Department of Labor. http://www.dol.gov/laborday/history-elevator.htm.

"The Truth About Unions." *Alabama Construction News,* April 10, 2015. http://alabamaconstructionnews.org/2015/04/10/the-truth-about-unions/.

"Union Members Summary." Bureau of Labor Statistics, January 23, 2015. http://www.bls.gov/news.release/union2.nr0.htm.

Western, Bruce and Jake Rosenfeld. "Unions, Norms, and the Rise in U.S. Wage Inequality." *American Sociological Review* 76, no. 4 (August 2011): 513–37.

Young, Angelo. "Here Are the December 2013 'Big Eight' US Auto Sales Numbers: GM, Ford, Chrysler, Toyota, Honda, Nissan." *International Business Times,* January 3, 2014.

Chapter 10: One Nation Under God

"About the 700 Club." CBN. http://www1.cbn.com/700club/about-700-club.

Aikman, David. *Billy Graham: His Life and Influence.* Nashville, Tenn.: Thomas Nelson, 2007.

Applebome, Peter. "Jerry Falwell, Moral Majority Founder, Dies at 73." *New York Times,* May 16, 2007.

Associated Press. "Falwell Remembered for Impact on Conservative Movement." Fox News. May 15, 2007.

"Billy Graham: Pastor to Presidents." Billy Graham Evangelistic Association. February 19, 2012. http://billygraham.org/story/billy-graham-pastor-to-presidents-2/.

"Billy in India." *Time,* February 13, 1956.

Brinkley, Alan. *Voices of Protest: Huey Long, Father Coughlin, & the Great Depression.* New York: Alfred A. Knopf, 1982.

Carter, Jimmy. *White House Diary.* New York: Farrar, Straus, and Giroux, 2010.

"Dr. James Dobson Offers Romney Some Advice." WND, August 15, 2012. http://www.wnd.com/2012/08/dr-james-dobson-offers-romney-some-advice/.

"Election 2012 Post Mortem: White Evangelicals and Support for Romney." Pew Research Center, December 7, 2012. http://www.pewforum.org/2012/12/07/election-2012-post-mortem-white-evangelicals-and-support-for-romney/.

Fessenden, Tracy. *Culture and Redemption: Religion and the Secular in American Literature.* Princeton, N.J.: Princeton University Press, 2007.

———. "Nineteenth Century Bible Wars and the Separation of Church and State." *Church History* 74, Issue 4 (2005): 784–811.

Franklin, Benjamin. "Letter to Ezra Stiles, March 9, 1790," in *Benjamin*

Franklin: Autobiography and Other Writings. ed. by Ormond Seavey. Oxford: Oxford University Press, 1993.

Gibbs, Nancy and Michael Duffy. "Billy Graham: 'A Spiritual Gift to All.'" *Time,* May 31, 2007.

Goldfield, David. *Black, White, and Southern: Race Relations and Southern Culture, 1940 to the Present.* Baton Rouge, La.: LSU Press, 1990.

Goodstein, Laurie. "Falwell: Blame Abortionists, Feminists, and Gays." *Guardian,* September 19, 2001.

Graham, Billy. *Just As I Am: The Autobiography of Billy Graham.* 1997. Reprint, New York: HarperCollins, 2007.

Gunn, T. Jeremy. *Spiritual Weapons: The Cold War and the Forging of an American National Religion.* Westport, Conn.: Praeger Publishers, 2009.

Harrell, David Edwin, Jr. *Pat Robertson: A Personal, Religious, and Political Portrait.* San Francisco: Harper and Row, 1987.

Harris, Matthew L. and Thomas S. Kidd, eds. *The Founding Fathers and the Debate over Religion in Revolutionary America: A History in Documents.* Oxford and New York: Oxford University Press, 2012.

Heclo, Hugh and Wilfred M. McClay, eds. *Religion Returns to the Public Square: Faith and Policy in America.* Washington, D.C.: Woodrow Wilson Center Press, 2003.

"How the Faithful Voted: 2012 Preliminary Analysis." Pew Research Center, November 7, 2012. http://www.pewforum.org/2012/11/07/how-the-faithful-voted-2012-preliminary-exit-poll-analysis/.

Hunter, James Davidson. *To Change the World: The Irony, Tragedy, and Possibility of Christianity in the Late Modern World.* New York: Oxford University Press, 2010.

Inskeep, Steve. "Author Examines Founding Fathers' Views on Religion." NPR.org. November 23, 2006.

"Liberty University Quick Facts." Liberty University. http://www.liberty.edu/aboutliberty/?PID=6925.

Lincoln, Abraham. "Second Inaugural Address, March 4, 1865." Online by Gerhard Peters and John T. Woolley, The American Presidency Project. http://www.presidency.ucsb.edu/ws/index.php?pid=25819.

Madison, James. "Letter to Thomas Jefferson (January 22, 1786)." *The Writings of James Madison,* vol. II, *1783–1787.* ed. Gaillard Hunt. New York: G.P. Putnam's Sons, 1901.

Madison, James. "Letter to William Bradford, Jr., (January 24, 1774)." *Letters and Other Writings of James Madison,* vol. I, *1769–1798.* Philadelphia: J.B. Lippincott & Co. 1865.

McCollum v. Board of Education of Champaign 333 U.S. 203 (1948).

Meacham, Jon. *American Gospel: God, the Founding Fathers, and the Making of a Nation.* New York: Random House, 2006.

Merritt, Jonathan. "The Religious Right Turns 33: What Have We Learned?" *The Atlantic,* June 8, 2012.

Miller, Steven P. *Billy Graham and the Rise of the Republican South.* Philadelphia: University of Pennsylvania Press, 2009.

Newport, Frank, Jeffrey M. Jones, and Lydia Saad. "Democrats More Liberal, Less White Than in 2008." Gallup, November 7, 2011.

"'Nones' on the Rise." Pew Research Center, October 9, 2012. http://www.pewforum.org/2012/10/09/nones-on-the-rise/.

Page, Susan. "Churchgoing Closely Tied to Voting Patterns." *USA Today,* June 3, 2004.

Paine, Thomas. *Age of Reason.* 1794. Reprint, London: Aziloth, 2011.

Pellegrini, Ann. "Religious Liberty v. Sexual Freedom?" Lecture, Harvard Kennedy School Carr Center for Human Rights Policy, Cambridge, Massachusetts, December 5, 2012. https://www.youtube.com/watch?v=kXY-ESHpC4M.

Putnam, Robert D., David E. Campbell, and Shaylyn Romney Garrett. *American Grace: How Religion Divides and Unites Us.* New York: Simon and Schuster, 2010.

Radner, Ephraim. "New World Order, Old World Anti-Semitism—Pat Robertson of the Christian Coalition." *Christian Century,* September 13, 1995.

Reagan, Ronald. "Address Before a Joint Session of Congress on the State of the Union, January 25, 1984." Online by Gerhard Peters and John T. Woolley, The American Presidency Project. http://www.presidency.ucsb.edu/ws/?pid=40205.

Reitman, Janet. "The Stealth War on Abortion." *Rolling Stone,* January 15, 2014.

"Religion: More Important to Americans Than Western Europeans." Pew Research Center, April 16, 2012. http://www.pewresearch.org/daily-number/religion-more-important-to-americans-than-western-europeans/.

Stanley, Tiffany. "The Culture Warrior in Winter." *National Journal,* July 10, 2014.

Tooley, Mark. "Eisenhower's Religion." *American Spectator,* February 14, 2011.

Truman, Harry S. "Radio Address as Part of the Program 'Religion in American Life,' October 30, 1949." Online by Gerhard Peters and John T. Woolley, The American Presidency Project. http://www.presidency.ucsb.edu/ws/?pid=13345.

Vedantam, Shankar. "Walking Santa, Talking Christ." *Slate,* December 22, 2010. http://www.slate.com/articles/health_and_science/the_hidden_brain/2010/12/walking_santa_talking_christ.html.

"Welcome to Deism." World Union of Deists. http://www.deism.com/deism_defined.htm.

Williams, Daniel K. *God's Own Party: The Making of the Christian Right.* New York: Oxford University Press, 2010.

Worthen, Molly. "How Billy Graham Became an American Icon." CNN.com, November 9, 2013. http://religion.blogs.cnn.com/2013/11/09/how-billy -graham-became-an-american-icon/.

Chapter 11: Girls to Women to Your Boss

"Betty Friedan Interview." PBS: WHYY. http://www.pbs.org/fmc/interviews/ friedan.htm.

Blackman, Ann. "The Friedan Mystique." *Time,* April 23, 2000.

DeCrow, Karen. "Leading Lady; Betty Friedan's Memoir Chronicles the Progress of Feminism." *Syracuse New Times,* September 20, 2000.

Dreier, Peter. "The Feminine Mystique and Women's Equality—50 Years Later." *Huffington Post,* February 18, 2013.

Fox, Margalit. "Betty Friedan, Who Ignited Cause in 'Feminine Mystique,' Dies at 85." *New York Times,* February 5, 2006.

Friedan, Betty. *The Feminine Mystique.* 1963. Reprint, New York and London: W.W. Norton & Company, 2013, with an introduction by Gail Collins.

———. *It Changed My Life: Writings on the Women's Movement.* 1976. Reprint, Cambridge, Mass.: Harvard University Press, 1998.

———. *Life So Far: A Memoir.* New York: Touchstone, 2000.

———. *The Second Stage.* 1981. Reprint, Cambridge, Mass.: Harvard University Press, 1998.

Ginsberg, L. "Ex-Hubby Fires Back at Feminist Icon Betty." *New York Post,* July 5, 2000.

Greer, Germaine. "The Betty I Knew." *Guardian,* February 7, 2006.

Horowitz, Daniel. *Betty Friedan and the Making of the Feminine Mystique: The American Left, the Cold War, and Modern Feminism.* Amherst, Mass.: University of Massachusetts Press, 1998.

Horowitz, David. "Feminism's Dirty Secret." *Jewish World Review,* June 12, 2000.

Kaplan, Marion. "Betty Friedan: 1921–2006." Jewish Women's Archive. http:// jwa.org/encyclopedia/article/friedan-betty.

Kurtz, Howard "Abuse Reports That Smack of Unfairness." *Washington Post,* June 5, 2000.

Lindsay, Rae. *The Presidents' First Ladies.* 1989. Reprint, Englewood Cliffs, N.J.: Gilmour House, 2001.

Maslin, Janet. "Looking Back at a Domestic Cri de Coeur." *New York Times,* February 18, 2013.

Menand, Louis. "Books As Bombs." *The New Yorker,* January 24, 2011.

Sullivan, Patricia. "Voice of Feminism's 'Second Wave.'" *Washington Post,* February 5, 2006.

"Ten Most Harmful Books of the 19th and 20th Centuries." *Human Events,* May 31, 2005.

Vagianos, Alanna. "23 Ways Gloria Steinem Taught Us to Be Better Women." *Huffington Post,* March 25, 2014.

Wolfe, Alan. "The Mystique of Betty Friedan." *Atlantic Monthly,* September 1999.

"Women in S&P 500 Companies." Catalyst, November 15, 2012. http://www .catalyst.org/knowledge/women-sp-500-companies.

Chapter 12: The Power of Diplomacy

Dallek, Robert. *Nixon and Kissinger: Partners in Power.* New York: Harper-Collins, 2007.

Gertz, Bill. *Failure Factory: How Unelected Bureaucrats, Liberal Democrats, and Big Government Republicans Are Undermining America's Security and Leading Us to War.* New York: Crown Forum, 2008.

Hanhimaki, Jussi M. *The Flawed Architect: Henry Kissinger and American Foreign Policy.* New York and Oxford: Oxford University Press, 2004.

Hersh, Seymour. *The Price of Power: Kissinger in the Nixon White House.* New York: Summit Books, 1983.

Isaacson, Walter. *Kissinger: A Biography.* 1992. Reprint, New York: Simon & Schuster, 2005.

Judis, John B. *The Paradox of American Democracy: Elites, Special Interests, and the Betrayal of Public Trust.* New York: Pantheon Books, 2000.

Kaplan, Robert D. "In Defense of Henry Kissinger." *The Atlantic,* May 2013.

Kissinger, Henry. *The White House Years.* Boston: Little Brown & Company, 1979.

Kissinger, Henry and Charlie Rose. "An Hour With Henry Kissinger." *Charlie Rose.* Directed by Chris da Cunha and Joe Nocerito. PBS. May 31, 2011, Season 5, Episode 21.

Komine, Yukinori. *Secrecy in US Foreign Policy: Nixon, Kissinger and the Rapprochement with China.* Burlington, Vt.: Ashgate Publishing Company, 2008.

Mazlish, Bruce. *Kissinger: The European Mind in American Policy.* New York: Basic Books, 1976.

Monroe, James. "Seventh Annual Message, December 2, 1823." Online by Gerhard Peters and John T. Woolley, The American Presidency Project. http://www.presidency.ucsb.edu/ws/?pid=29465.

Newport, Frank, David W. Moore, and Lydia Saad. "Most Admired Men and Women: 1948–1998." Gallup, December 13, 1999. http://www.gallup .com/poll/3415/most-admired-men-women-19481998.aspx.

"Nixon's China Game." *American Experience.* PBS: WHYY. http://www.pbs .org/wgbh/amex/china/filmmore/index.html.

Nixon, Richard. "Remarks to the Nation Announcing Acceptance of an Invitation to Visit the People's Republic of China, July 15, 1971." Online by Gerhard Peters and John T. Woolley, The American Presidency Project. http://www.presidency.ucsb.edu/ws/?pid=3079.

Reimer, Mirco. "The Quest for Peace: Henry Kissinger on Germany." *American Diplomacy,* February 2014. http://www.unc.edu/depts/diplomat/item/2014/0105/ca/reimer_quest.html#_ftnref29.

Reagan, Ronald. "Letter to Mr. and Mrs. Elwood H. Wagner, August 3, 1971," *Reagan: Life in Letters.* ed. by Kiron K. Skinner, Annelise Anderson, and Martin Anderson. New York: Free Press, 2003.

Small, Melvin, ed. *A Companion to Richard Nixon.* Malden, Mass.: Wiley-Blackwell, 2011.

Snow, Edgar. "A Conversation with Mao Tse-Tung." *LIFE,* April 30, 1971, 46–48.

Studwell, Joe. *The China Dream: The Elusive Quest for the Last Great Untapped Market on Earth.* London: Profile Books, 2002.

Suri, Jeremi. *Henry Kissinger and the American Century.* Cambridge, Mass.: Belknap Press of Harvard University Press, 2007.

Washington, George. "Farewell Adress, September 19, 1796." Online by Gerhard Peters and John T. Woolley, The American Presidency Project. http://www.presidency.ucsb.edu/ws/?pid=65539.

Chapter 13: One-Third of a Nation

"After Years of Debate, Welfare Reform Clears." *CQ Almanac,* 1988. https://library.cqpress.com/cqalmanac/document.php?id=cqal88-1141998.

"Child Poverty." National Center for Children in Poverty. http://www.nccp.org/topics/childpoverty.html.

Desilver, Drew. "Who's Poor in America? 50 Years into the 'War on Poverty,' a Data Portrait." Pew Research Center, January 13, 2014. http://www.pewresearch.org/fact-tank/2014/01/13/whos-poor-in-america-50-years-into-the-war-on-poverty-a-data-portrait/.

Dowd, Maureen. "Washington Talk: Q&A: Daniel Patrick Moynihan; Welfare and the Politics of Poverty." *New York Times,* February 19, 1987.

Dunn, Alan. "Average America vs the One Percent." *Forbes,* March 21, 2012.

Franklin, Benjamin. "Arator: 'On the Price of Corn, and Management of the Poor,'" November 29, 1766. Founders Online. http://founders.archives.gov/documents/Franklin/01-13-02-0194.

Heilbrunn, Jacob. "The Moynihan Enigma." *The American Prospect,* July–August, 1997.

Hodgson, Godfrey. *The Gentleman from New York: Daniel Patrick Moynihan, a Biography.* New York: Houghton Mifflin Company, 2000.

Johnson, Lyndon B. "President Lyndon B. Johnson's Commencement Address at Howard University: 'To Fulfill These Rights.'" LBJ Presidential Library. June 4. 1965. http://www.lbjlib.utexas.edu/johnson/archives.hom/speeches.hom/650604.asp.

Kristof, Nicholas. "Our Banana Republic." *New York Times,* November 6, 2010.

Luhby, Tami. "Welfare Spending Cut in Half Since Reform." CNN Money, August 9, 2012.

Macartney, Suzanne. "Child Poverty in the United States 2009 and 2010: Selected Race Groups and Hispanic Origin." U.S. Census, November 2011. http://www.census.gov/library/publications/2011/acs/acsbr10-05.html.

Moynihan, Daniel Patrick. *Daniel Patrick Moynihan: A Portrait in Letters of an American Visionary.* ed. Steven R. Weisman. New York: PublicAffairs, 2010.

———. *Miles to Go: A Personal History of Social Policy.* Cambridge, Mass.: Harvard University Press, 1996.

———. "Text of the Moynihan Memorandum on the Status of Negroes." *New York Times,* March 1, 1970.

"'The Moynihan Report.' The Negro Family: The Case for National Action," March 1965. Black Past: Remembered & Reclaimed. http://www.black past.org/primary/moynihan-report-1965.

Nichols, Austin. "Explaining Changes in Child Poverty Over the Past Four Decades." Urban Institute, September 2013. http://www.urban.org/research/publication/explaining-changes-child-poverty-over-past-four-decades.

Paine, Thomas. "Agrarian Justice." Social Security Online. https://www.ssa.gov/history/paine4.html.

Patterson, James T. *Freedom Is Not Enough: The Moynihan Report and America's Struggle over Black Family Life from LBJ to Obama.* New York: Basic Books, 2010.

"Policy Basics: Where Do Our Federal Tax Dollars Go?" Center on Budget and Policy Priorities, March 11, 2015. http://www.cbpp.org/research/policy-basics-where-do-our-federal-tax-dollars-go.

Reaves, Jessica. "Appreciation: Daniel Patrick Moynihan." *Time,* March 27, 2003.

Schoen, Douglas. *Pat: A Biography of Daniel Patrick Moynihan.* New York: Harper & Row, 1979.

Tankersley, Jim. "Economic Mobility Hasn't Changed in a Half-Century in America, Economists Declare." *Washington Post,* January 23, 2014.

Trattner, Walter I. *From Poor Law to Welfare State: A History of Social Welfare in America.* 1977. 6th ed. New York: Free Press, 1999.

Vobejda, Barbara. "Clinton Signs Welfare Bill Amid Division." *Washington Post,* August 23, 1996.

Chapter 14: Equal Protection Under the Law

Arana, Gabriel. "The Conservative Parent Trap: Why I Love Seeing Republicans Have Gay Kids." *Salon,* August 20, 2014.

Barlow, David. *Sexually Transmitted Infections: The Facts.* New York: Oxford University Press, 2006.

Bronski, Michael. *A Queer History of the United States.* Boston: Beacon Press, 2011.

Buchanan, Pat. Syndicated column. *Seattle Times,* July 31, 1993.

Carter, David. *Stonewall: The Riots That Sparked the Gay Revolution.* New York: St. Martin's Press, 2004.

Cook, B. W. "Barry Goldwater: How Right Is Right?" *Orange Coast,* October 1995.

Delaney, Samuel. *Motion of Light in Water: Sex and Science Fiction Writing in the East Village.* Minneapolis: University of Minnesota Press, 2004.

D'Emilio, John. *Making Trouble: Essays on Gay History, Politics, and the University.* New York and London: Routledge, 1992.

Duberman, Martin. *Cures: A Gay Man's Odyssey, Tenth Anniversary Edition.* 1992. Reprint, Boulder, Colo.: Westview Press, 2002.

———. *Stonewall.* New York: Dutton, 1993.

Eskridge, William. *Dishonorable Passions: Sodomy Laws in America: 1861–2003.* New York: Viking, 2008.

"Excerpts from Goldwater's Remarks." *New York Times,* September 16, 1981.

Franklin, Marcus, Associated Press. "Stonewall Rebel Reflects 40 Years After NYC Riots." *USA Today,* June 27, 2009.

Goldwater, Barry M. "America Must Realize There Is No Gay Exemption to Constitutional Principles." *Sun Sentinel,* July 17, 1994.

———. *Conscience of a Conservative.* 1960. Reprint, Princeton and Oxford: Princeton University Press, 2007.

———. "The Gay Ban: Just Plain Un-American." *Washington Post,* June 10, 1993.

Grove, Lloyd. "Barry Goldwater's Left Turn." *Washington Post,* July 28, 1994.

Hay, Harry. *Radically Gay: Gay Liberation in the Words of Its Founder.* ed. Will Roscoe. Boston: Beacon Press, 1996.

Katz, Jonathan Ned. *Gay American History: Lesbians and Gay Men in the USA.* New York: Crowell, 1976.

Kelley, Ken. "Cruising with Anita." *Playboy* (May 1978).

Kopkind, Andrew. "After Stonewall." *The Nation,* July 4, 1994.

McCabe, Scott. "Crime History: Stonewall Riots Spark Gay Rights Movement." *Washington Examiner,* June 27, 2012.

Obama, Barack. "Inaugural Address by President Barack Obama." The White House Office of the Press Secretary. January 21, 2013. https://www.white

house.gov/the-press-office/2013/01/21/inaugural-address-president -barack-obama.

O'Keefe, Ed and Jon Cohen. "Most Back Repealing 'Don't Ask, Don't Tell,' Poll Says." *Washington Post,* December 15, 2010.

Press, Bill. "The Sad Legacy of Jerry Falwell." *Milford Daily News,* May 18, 2007.

Timmons, Stuart. *The Trouble with Harry Hay: Founder of the Modern Gay Movement.* Boston: Alyson, 1990.

Unnamed Secretary for George Washington. "General Orders on March 14, 1778." *The Writings of George Washington from the Original Manuscript Sources, 1745–1799.* ed. John C. Fitzpatrick. U.S. Government Printing Office, 1939.

Watercutter, Angela. "Gay Activist Harry Hay Dies." Associated Press News Archive, October 24, 2002.

Wallenberg. Christopher. "In 'The Temperamentals,' a Tale of Two Early Gay Rights Pioneers." *Boston Globe,* April 1, 2012.

Whetzell, Keeley. "The 1969 Stonewall Riots." Hanscom Air Force Base, June 17, 2014. http://www.hanscom.af.mil/news/story.asp?id=123414727.

Chapter 15: Back to the Future

Biskupic, Joan. "Reagan's Influence Lives On in US Courts." *USA Today,* May 12, 2008.

Brennan, William J., Jr., "Address Before the Text and Teaching Symposium, Georgetown University (1985)." *Classics of American Political and Constitutional Thought.* vol. 2, *Reconstruction to the Present.* eds. Scott J. Hammond, Kevin R. Hardwick, and Howard L. Lubert. Indianapolis, Ind.: Hackett Publishing Company, 2007.

Brest, Paul. "The Misconceived Quest for Original Understanding." *Boston University Law Review* 60 (1980): 204–238.

Broder, David S. "Mr. Meese Versus Civil Liberties." *Washington Post,* May 27, 1981.

Cannon, Lou. *Governor Reagan: His Rise to Power.* New York: Public Affairs, 2003.

Clines, Francis X. "If One American Is Going Hungry, Reagan Says, It's One Too Many." *New York Times,* December 15, 1983.

Cross, Frank. *The Failed Promise of Originalism.* Stanford, Calif.: Stanford University Press, 2013.

Edwards, Lee. *To Preserve and Protect: The Life of Edwin Meese, III.* Washington, D.C.: The Heritage Foundation, 2005.

"Edwin Meese III." Heritage Foundation. http://www.heritage.org/about/ staff/m/edwin-meese#.

Ehrlich, Daniel D. "The Elder Statesman Series Inaugural Interview: A Conversation with Former United States Attorney General Edwin Meese, III." *St. Thomas Journal of Law and Public Policy* 3, no. 1 (Spring 2009): 1–14.

Greenhouse, Linda. "Law in the Raw." *New York Times,* November 12, 2014.

Hamilton, Alexander. "The Federalist No. 78: The Judiciary Department," June 14, 1788. Constitution Society. http://www.constitution.org/fed/federa78.htm.

Horrock, Nicholas M. "More Reagan Than Reagan." *Chicago Tribune,* July 6, 1988.

Jefferson, Thomas. "Thomas Jefferson to Spencer Roane (September 6, 1819)." Library of Congress. http://www.loc.gov/exhibits/jefferson/137.html.

———. "To Mrs. Adams," September 11, 1804. *Memoirs, Correspondence, and Private Papers of Thomas Jefferson.* vol. III, ed. Thomas Jefferson Randolph. London: Henry Colburn and Richard Bentley, 1829.

Keck, Thomas. *The Most Activist Supreme Court in History: The Road to Modern Judicial Conservatism.* Chicago: The University of Chicago Press, 2004.

Liptak, Adam. "How Activist Is the Supreme Court." *New York Times,* October 12, 2013.

Marbury v. Madison 5 U.S. 137.

Meese, Edwin. "Address before the American Bar Association (1985)." *Classics of American Political and Constitutional Thought.* vol. 2, *Reconstruction to the Present.* eds. Scott J. Hammond, Kevin R. Hardwick, and Howard L. Lubert. Indianapolis, Ind.: Hackett Publishing Company, 2007.

Nixon, Richard. "Address to the Nation Announcing Intention to Nominate Lewis F. Powell, Jr., and William H. Rehnquist to Be Associate Justices of the Supreme Court, October 21, 1971." Online by Gerhard Peters and John T. Woolley, The American Presidency Project. http://www.presidency.ucsb.edu/ws/?pid=3196.

O'Neill, Jonathan. *Originalism in American Law and Politics: A Constitutional History.* Baltimore and London: The Johns Hopkins University Press, 2005.

Peters, Jeremy W. "Building Legacy, Obama Reshapes Appelate Bench." *New York Times,* September 13, 2014.

Reagan, Ronald. "Remarks at the Swearing Ceremony for William H. Rehnquist as Chief Justice and Antonin Scalia as Associate Justice of the Supreme Court, September 26, 1986." Online by Gerhard Peters and John T. Woolley, The American Presidency Project. http://www.presidency.ucsb.edu/ws/?pid=36494.

Reagan, Ronald. "A Time for Choosing." October 27, 1964. Ronald Reagan Presidential Library and Museum. http://www.reagan.utexas.edu/archives/reference/timechoosing.html.

Rorabaugh, W. J. *Berkeley at War: The 1960s.* New York: Oxford University Press, 1989.

Sperling, Godfrey, Jr. "Is Ed Meese 'Assistant President'?" *Christian Science Monitor,* May 4, 1981.

Sweeney, Louise. "Presidential Counselor Ed Meese." *Christian Science Monitor,* August 26, 1982.

Chapter 16: The Social Safety Net

Adams, John. *The Works of John Adams, Second President of the United States: With a Life of the Author, Notes and Illustrations.* vol. IV, ed. Charles Francis Adams. Boston: Little, Brown, 1851.

Berkowitz, Edward D. *Robert Ball and the Politics of Social Security.* Madison, Wis.: University of Wisconsin Press, 2003.

Conan, Neal and Andrew Wehrman. "Founding Fathers Faced Health Care Revolt, Too." NPR.org. http://www.npr.org/templates/story/story.php?storyId=113543985.

Corning, Peter A. *The Evolution of Medicare: From Idea to Law.* Social Security Online. https://www.ssa.gov/history/corning.html.

Humphreys, Margaret. *Marrow of Tragedy: The Health Crisis of the American Civil War.* Baltimore: Johns Hopkins University Press, 2013.

Johnson, Lyndon B. "President Lyndon B. Johnson's Remarks with President Truman at the Signing in the Independence of the Medicare Bill, July 30, 1965." Online by Gerhard Peters and John T. Woolley, The American Presidency Project. http://www.presidency.ucsb.edu/ws/index.php?pid=27123&st=&st1.

Kliff, Sarah. "When Medicare Launched, Nobody Had Any Clue Whether It Would Work." *Washington Post,* May 17, 2013.

Madison, James. "The Federalist No. 51: The Structure of the Government Must Furnish the Proper Checks and Balances Between the Different Departments." Constitution Society. http://www.constitution.org/fed/federa51.htm.

Neisuler, Susan G. *Justice at the City Gate: Social Policy, Social Services, and the Law.* Lincoln, Nebr.: Writers Advantage, 2003.

O'Brien, Michael. *John F. Kennedy: A Biography.* New York: Thomas Dunne Books/St. Martin's Press, 2005.

Pelosi, Nancy. "Transcript of Pelosi Press Stakeout Following Meeting at the White House," April 1, 2014. Congresswoman Nancy Pelosi Serving California's 12th District. https://pelosi.house.gov/news/press-releases/transcript-of-pelosi-press-stakeout-following-meeting-at-the-white-house.

Pierce, Franklin. "Veto Message, May 3, 1854." Online by Gerhard Peters and John T. Woolley, The American Presidency Project. http://www.presidency.ucsb.edu/ws/?pid=67850

Puckett, Carolyn. "Robert M. Ball: A Life Dedicated to Social Security." *Social Security Bulletin* 68, no. 3 (2008). https://www.ssa.gov/policy/docs/ssb/v68n3/v68n3p67.html.

"Public Approval of Health Care Law." *Real Clear Politics.* http://www.realclearpolitics.com/epolls/other/obama_and_democrats_health_care_plan-1130.html.

Roosevelt, Franklin D. "State of the Union Address, January 7, 1943." Online by Gerhard Peters and John T. Woolley, The American Presidency Project. http://www.presidency.ucsb.edu/ws/?pid=16386.

———. "State of the Union Address, January 11, 1944." Online by Gerhard Peters and John T. Woolley, The American Presidency Project. http://www.presidency.ucsb.edu/ws/?pid=16518.

———. "State of the Union Address, January 6, 1945." Online by Gerhard Peters and John T. Woolley, The American Presidency Project. http://www.presidency.ucsb.edu/ws/?pid=16595.

"Social Security Act of 1935: Old-Age Benefit Payments." Social Security Online. https://www.ssa.gov/history/35actii.html#Old%20-Benefit.

Starr, Paul. *The Social Transformation of American Medicine: The Rise of a Sovereign Profession and the Making of a Vast Industry.* New York: Basic Books, 1982.

Sutphen, Debra Lynn. "Conservative Warrior: Oveta Culp Hobby and the Administration of America's Health, Education, and Welfare, 1953–1955." Ph.D. diss., Washington State University, 1997.

Trattner, Walter I. *From Poor Law to Welfare State: A History of Social Welfare in America.* 1977. 6th ed. New York: Free Press, 1998.

Chapter 17: *Silent Spring*

Banning, Lance. *Jefferson and Madison: Three Conversations from the Founding.* Madison, Wis.: The Madison House, 1995.

Brooks, Paul. *Rachel Carson: The Writer at Work.* San Francisco: Sierra Club Books, 1998.

Carson, Rachel. *The Sea Around Us.* 1951. Reprint, New York: Oxford University Press, 1989.

———. *Silent Spring.* 1962. Reprint, New York: Houghton Mifflin, 2002.

———. *Under the Sea Wind.* 1941. Reprint, New York: Penguin Group, 2007.

Carson, Rachel and Linda Lear, ed. *Lost Woods: The Discovered Writing of Rachel Carson.* Boston: Beacon Press, 1998.

Davenport, Coral. "Strange Climate Event: Warmth Toward U.S." *New York Times,* December 11, 2014.

"Fact Sheet: U.S.-China Joint Announcement on Climate Change and Clean Energy Cooperation." The White House Office of the Press Secretary. https://www.whitehouse.gov/the-press-office/2014/11/11/fact-sheet-us-china-joint-announcement-climate-change-and-clean-energy-c.

Gottlieb, Robert. *Forcing the Spring: The Transformation of the American Environmental Movement.* Washington, D.C.: Island Press, 2005.

Griswold, Eliza. "How 'Silent Spring' Ignited the Environmental Movement." *New York Times,* September 21, 2012.

Hunt, Gaillard, ed. *The Writings of James Madison: 1790–1802.* New York: G.P. Putnam's Sons, 1906.

Hynes, H. Patricia. *Recurring Silent Spring.* New York: Pergamon Press, 1989.

Kaplan, Lawrence S. *Alexander Hamilton: Ambivalent Anglophile.* Wilmington, Del.: Scholarly Resources, 2002.

Kress, Stephen. "The Legacy of Rachel Carson." *Huffington Post,* May 24, 2013.

Lear, Linda. *Rachel Carson: Witness for Nature.* New York: Henry Holt, 1997.

Leonard, Jonathan Norton. "Rachel Carson Dies of Cancer; *Silent Spring* Author Was 56." *New York Times,* April 15, 1964.

Martinez, J. Michael. *American Environmentalism: Philosophy, History, and Public Policy.* Boca Raton, Fla.: CRC Press, 2013.

Meisner Rosen, Christine. "Knowing Industrial Pollution: Nuisance Law and the Power of Tradition in a Time of Rapid Economic Change, 1840–1864." *Environmental History* 8, no. 4 (October 2003).

Mutikani, Lucia. "U.S. Manufacturing Weakness Persists; Worst May Be Over." Reuters, November 2, 2015.

Nakamura, David and Steven Mufson. "China, U.S. Agree to Limit Greenhouse Gases." *Washington Post,* November 12, 2014.

Nixon, Richard. "Annual Message to the Congress on the State of the Union, January 22, 1970." Online by Gerhard Peters and John T. Woolley, The American Presidency Project. http://www.presidency.ucsb.edu/ws/?pid=2921.

Obama, Barack. "Remarks by the President During Press Availability in Copenhagen." The White House Office of the Press Secretary, December 18, 2009. https://www.whitehouse.gov/the-press-office/remarks-president-during-press-availability-copenhagen.

"Obama's Nomination Victory Speech in St. Paul." *Huffington Post,* June 3, 2008. http://www.huffingtonpost.com/2008/06/03/obamas-nomination-victory_n_105028.html.

Quaratiello, Arlene Rodda. *Rachel Carson: A Biography.* Westport, Conn.: Greenwood Press, 2004.

"Science: DDT Dangers." *Time,* April 16, 1945.

Shabecoff, Philip. *A Fierce Green Fire: The American Environmental Movement.* New York: Hill and Wang, 1993.

Smith, Michael. "'Silence, Miss Carson!' Science, Gender, and the Reception of *Silent Spring.*" *Feminist Studies* 27, no. 3 (Fall 2001).

Souder, William. *On a Farther Shore: The Life and Legacy of Rachel Carson.* New York: Crown Publishers, 2012.

Sterling, Philip. *Sea and Earth: The Life of Rachel Carson.* New York: Crowell, 1970.

Wills, John. *US Environmental History: Inviting Doomsday.* Edinburgh, UK: Edinburgh University Press, 2012.

Woods, Brett F. ed. *Thomas Jefferson: Thoughts on War and Revolution: Annotated Correspondence.* New York: Algora Publishing, 2009.

Wulf, Andrea. "Gardening as Politics: Digging the Founding Gardeners." *Los Angeles Times,* May 29, 2011.

Chapter 18: A New Beginning

Blight, David. "HIST 119: The Civil War and Reconstruction Era, 1845–1877." Open Yale Courses. http://oyc.yale.edu/history/hist-119.

Bober, Natalie S. *Thomas Jefferson: Draftsman of a Nation.* Charlottesville: University of Virginia Press, 2007.

Boyd, Gerald M. "The Democrats in San Francisco; Entire Party Watches Jackson's Show." *New York Times,* July 16, 1984.

Breen, Patrick H. "Nat Turner's Revolt: Rebellion and Response in Southampton County, Virginia." Ph.D. diss., University of Georgia, 2005.

Bruns, Roger A. *Jesse Jackson: A Biography.* Westport, Conn.: Greenwood Press, 2005.

Cannon, Lou. *President Reagan: The Role of a Lifetime.* New York: Simon & Schuster, 1991.

Carson, Clayborne, ed. *The Autobiography of Martin Luther King, Jr.* New York: IPM in association with Warner Books, 1998.

Ellis, Catherine and Stephen Drury Smith, eds. *Say It Plain: A Century of Great African American Speeches.* New York: The New Press, 2005.

Ezra, Michael, ed. *The Economic Civil Rights Movement: African Americans and the Struggle for Economic Power.* New York: Routledge, 2013.

Finkelman, Paul, ed. *Slavery and the Founders: Race and Liberty in the Age of Jefferson.* Armonk, N.Y.: M.E. Sharpe, 1996.

Foner, Eric. *Reconstruction: America's Unfinished Revolution, 1863–1877.* New York: Harper & Row, 1988.

———. "Why Reconstruction Matters." *New York Times,* March 28, 2015.

Frady, Marshall. *Jesse: The Life and Pilgrimage of Jesse Jackson.* 1996. Reprint, New York: Simon & Schuster, 2006.

Frymer, Paul. *Uneasy Alliances: Race and Party Competition in America.* Princeton, N.J.: Princeton University Press, 1999.

Horwitz, Robert B. *America's Right: Anti-Establishment Conservatism from Goldwater to the Tea Party*. Cambridge and Malden: Polity, 2013.

Jackson, Jessie Jr. and Steve Cobble. "Proportional Primaries Working for Democrats." *Politico,* February 26, 2008.

Jakoubek, Robert E. and Gloria Blakely. *Jesse Jackson: Civil Rights Leader and Politician*. New York: Chelsea House Publishers, 2005.

"Jo Ann Robinson." *Voices of Freedom: An Oral History of the Civil Rights Movement from the 1950s Through the 1980s*. eds. Henry Hampton, Steve Fayer, and Sarah Flynn. New York: Bantam Books, 1990.

Levine, Bruce. *Half Slave and Half Free: The Roots of Civil War*. 1992. Reprint, New York: Hill and Wang, 2005.

Lincoln, Abraham. *Speeches and Writings, 1859–1865: Speeches, Letters, and Miscellaneous Writings, Presidential Messages and Proclamations*. New York: Library of America, 1989.

Marable, Manning. *Race, Reform, and Rebellion: The Second Reconstruction and Beyond in Black America, 1945–2006*, 3rd ed. Jackson, Miss.: Univ. Press of Mississippi, 2007.

Maraniss, David. "Jackson and King, Examining the Legacy After 20 Years." *Washington Post*, April 3, 1988.

Merida, Kevin. "A Leader Left Behind?" *Washington Post,* July 14, 2008.

Painter, Nell Irvin. *Creating Black Americans: African-American History and Its Meanings, 1619 to the Present*. New York: Oxford University Press, 2006.

"The Pilgrimage of Jesse Jackson: Interviews with Andrew Young, Calvin Morris, Jackie Jackson, Richard Hatcher, and Roger Wilkins." *Frontline*. http://www.pbs.org/wgbh/pages/frontline/jesse/interviews/index.html.

Remnick, David. *The Bridge: The Life and Rise of Barack Obama*. New York: Alfred A. Knopf, 2010.

Sitkoff, Harvard. *The Struggle for Black Equality, 1954–1980*. New York: Hill & Wang, 1981.

Sok, Emy. "Record Unemployment Among Older Workers Does Not Keep Them Out of the Job Market." Bureau of Labor Statistics, March 2010. http://www.bls.gov/opub/ils/sumrmary_10_04/older_workers.htm.

Patterson, James T. *Brown v. Board of Education: A Civil Rights Milestone and Its Troubled Legacy*. New York: Oxford University Press, 2001.

Williams, Juan. *Eyes on the Prize: America's Civil Rights Years, 1954–1965*. 1987. Reprint, New York: Penguin, 2013.

Chapter 19: The Right to Bear Arms

Achenbach, Joel. "NRA History: The Making of the Gun Lobby." *Washington Post*, January 13, 2013.

Achenbach, Joel, Scott Higham, and Sari Horwitz. "How NRA's True Believers Converted a Marksmanship Group into a Mighty Gun Lobby." *Washington Post,* January 12, 2013.

Allen, Mike. "Bloomberg Takes His Money Local." *Politico,* November 11, 2014.

Altimari, Dave. "Shooting Records Provide Details from Inside School." *Hartford Courant,* December 28, 2013.

Associated Press. "Final Newtown Police Report Yields Chilling Account of Massacre." *Guardian,* December 28, 2013.

Bell, Larry. "Shooting Holes in Mayor Bloomberg's Anti-Gun Propaganda: Ten Bullet Points." *Forbes,* April 2, 2013.

Bowling for Columbine. Directed by Michael Moore. United States: United Artists and MGM, 2002.

Branas, Charles C., Therese S. Richmond, Dennis P. Culhane, Thomas R. Ten Have, and Douglas J. Wiebe. "Investigating the Link Between Gun Possession and Gun Assault." *American Journal of Public Health* 99, no. 11 (November 2009): 2034–40.

"Bull's Eye." *Investor's Business Daily,* July 27, 2008.

Bush, George W. "Honoring the Victims of the Tragedy at Virginia Tech: A Proclamation by the President of the United States." White House Office of the Press Secretary, April 17, 2007. http://georgewbush-whitehouse.archives.gov/news/releases/2007/04/20070417-1.html.

Carrey, Jim. "Cold Dead Hands with Jim Carrey," *Funny or Die,* 5:56. March 24, 2013. http://www.funnyordie.com/videos/0433b30576/cold-dead-hand-with-jim-carrey?_cc=__d___&_ccid=7kmiml.nhv9hw.

Carter, Gregg Lee. *Gun Control in the United States: A Reference Handbook.* Santa Barbara, Calif.: ABC-CLIO, 2006.

Chadwick, Bruce. *George Washington's War: The Forging of a Revolutionary Leader and the American Presidency.* Naperville, Ill.: Sourcebooks, Inc., 2004.

Chapman, Steve. "Chicago Defies Forgotten 2nd Amendment." *Chicago Tribune,* November 27, 2008.

"Charlton Heston Has Alzheimer's Symptoms." FoxNews.com, August 09, 2002. http://www.foxnews.com/story/2002/08/09/charlton-heston-has-alzheimer-symptoms.html.

Christoffersen, John, Associated Press. "New Report Provides the Most Disturbing Picture Yet of Nancy Lanza's Relationship with Her Son." *Business Insider,* December 28, 2013.

Cohn, D'Vera, Paul Taylor, Mark Hugo Lopez, Catherine A. Gallagher, Kim Parker, and Kevin T. Maass. "Gun Homicide Rate Down 49% Since 1993 Peak; Public Unaware." Pew Research Center, May 7, 2013. http://www.pewsocialtrends.org/files/2013/05/firearms_final_05-2013.pdf.

"Colorado School Shooters Identified." CNN.com, April 21, 1999. http://www
.cnn.com/US/9904/21/school.shooting.01/.

"Continued Bipartisan Support for Expanded Background Checks on Gun
Sales." Pew Research Center, August 13, 2015. http://www.people-press
.org/2015/08/13/continued-bipartisan-support-for-expanded-back
ground-checks-on-gun-sales/.

Cooper, Alexia and Erica L. Smith. "Homicide Trends in the United States,
1980–2008." Bureau of Justice Statistics, November 16, 2011. http://www
.bjs.gov/index.cfm?ty=pbdetail&iid=2221.

Cornell, Dewey G. "Gun Violence and Mass Shootings—Myths, Facts and Solutions." *Washington Post,* June 11, 2014.

Cornell, Saul. *A Well-Regulated Militia: The Founding Fathers and the Origins
of Gun Control in America.* New York: Oxford University Press, 2006.

Davidson, Osha Gray. *Under Fire: The NRA and the Battle for Gun Control.*
New York: Henry Holt and Company, 1993.

"To Deadly Effect." *Washington Post,* December 27, 1980.

DeConde, Alexander. *Gun Violence in America: The Struggle for Control.* Boston: Northeastern University Press, 2001.

Desilver, Drew. "A Minority of Americans Own Guns, but Just How Many
Is Unclear." Pew Research Center, June 4, 2013. http://www.pewresearch
.org/fact-tank/2013/06/04/a-minority-of-americans-own-guns-but-just
-how-many-is-unclear/.

———. "Suicides Account for Most Gun Deaths." Pew Research Center,
May 24, 2013. http://www.pewresearch.org/fact-tank/2013/05/24/suicides
-account-for-most-gun-deaths/.

District of Columbia v. Heller, 554 U.S. 570 (2008).

Dolak, Kevin. "Newtown, Conn., Shooting: Teacher's Aide Rachel D'Avino's
Boyfriend Was Set to Propose." ABC News, December 17, 2012. http://
abcnews.go.com/US/newtown-shooting-teachers-aide-rachel-davinos
-boyfriend-propose/story?id=17999719.

Duclos, Susan. "Supreme Court Rules on Second Amendment 'Protects an Individual Right.'" *Wake Up America,* June 26, 2008. http://
www.wakeupamericans-spree.blogspot.com/2008/06/supreme-court
-rules-on-second-amendment.html#.VnmtpuuJnzI.

Eggen, Dan. "Another Victory for the Bulletproof NRA." *Washington Post,*
June 17, 2010.

"Firearm Justifiable Homicides and Non-Fatal Self-Defense Gun Use." Violence Policy Center, June 2015. http://www.vpc.org/press/self-defense
-gun-use-is-rare-study-finds/.

Follman, Mark, Gavin Aronsen, and Deanna Pan. "A Guide to Mass Shootings in America." *Mother Jones.* Modified October 2, 2015.

Goad, Benjamin. "NRA Strikes Back at Bloomberg." *The Hill,* October 1, 2014.

"The G.O.P. and the N.R.A." *New York Times,* May 12, 1995.

Groer, Annie and Ann Gerhart. "Heston Sticks to His Guns." *Washington Post,* September 12, 1997.

Harwood, William. "Gun Control: State Versus Federal Regulation of Firearms." *Maine Policy Review* 11, no. 1 (Spring 2002): 58–73.

Heston, Charlton. "Presidential Address." Speech, 1999 NRA Annual Members' Meeting, Denver, Colo., May 7, 1999. https://www.nranews.com/series/speeches.

———. "Presidential Address." Speech, 2000 NRA Members' Annual Meeting, Charlotte, N.C., May 20, 2000. https://www.nranews.com/series/speeches.

"History of Gun Control Legislation." *Washington Post,* December 22, 2012.

"It Means What It Says." *Las Vegas Review-Journal,* June 27, 2008.

Johnson, Lyndon B. *Lyndon B. Johnson: Containing the Public Messages, Speeches, and Statements of the President.* Washington D.C.: U.S. Government Printing Office, 1968.

———. "Letter to the President of the Senate and to the Speaker of the House Urging Passage of an Effective Gun Control Law, June 6, 1968." Online by Gerhard Peters and John T. Woolley, The American Presidency Project. http://www.presidency.ucsb.edu/ws/?pid=28911.

Kirk, Chris. "Since 1980, 297 People Have Been Killed in School Shootings." *Slate,* December 19, 2012.

Kopel, David. "A Survey of Legislation on Second Amendment Issues in 2015." *Washington Post,* July 20, 2015.

———. "Handgun Bans for Persons under 21: A Hidden Problem in Everytown's 'Universal Background Checks.'" *Washington Post,* November 5, 2015.

Kurtz, Howard. "House Votes to Weaken Gun Controls." *Washington Post,* April 11, 1986.

"Letter of Resignation Sent by Bush to Rifle Association." *New York Times,* May 11, 1995.

Logan, Rayford W. *Memoirs of a Monticello Slave: As Dictated to Charles Campbell in the 1840s by Isaac, One of Thomas Jefferson's Slaves.* Charlottesville, Va.: University of Virginia Press, 1951.

Malcolm, Joyce Lee. *To Keep and Bear Arms: The Origins of an Anglo-American Right.* Cambridge, Mass.: Harvard University Press, 1994.

Maxey, Edwin. "Federal Quarantine Laws." *Political Science Quarterly* 23, no. 4. (December 1908): 617–636.

Mays, Terry M. *Historical Dictionary of the American Revolution.* Lanham, Md.: Scarecrow Press, 1999.

"Newtown Probe: Shooting Took under 5 Minutes." CNN.com, March 28,

2013. http://news.blogs.cnn.com/2013/03/28/newtown-probe-1-4k-ammo
-rounds-in-lanza-home/.

Obama, Barack. "Statement by the President on the Shooting in Charleston,
South Carolina." White House Office of the Press Secretary, Washington,
D.C., June 18, 2015. http://www.people-press.org/2013/03/12/why-own-a
-gun-protection-is-now-top-reason/.

———. "Statement by the President on the School Shooting in Newtown, CT."
White House Office of the Press Secretary, December 14, 2012. https://
www.whitehouse.gov/the-press-office/2012/12/14/statement-president
-school-shooting-newtown-ct.

"159 School Shootings in America Since 2013." Everytown for Gun Safety, October 3, 2015. http://everytownresearch.org/school-shootings/.

Overby, Peter. "NRA: 'Only Thing That Stops a Bad Guy with a Gun Is a
Good Guy with a Gun.'" NPR.org. December 21, 2012. http://www.npr
.org/2012/12/21/167824766/nra-only-thing-that-stops-a-bad-guy-with-a
-gun-is-a-good-guy-with-a-gun.

Pelley, Scott, Nicole Young, Bob Anderson, and Michael Radutzky. "Tragedy
in Newtown." *60 Minutes.* December 17, 2012. http://www.cbsnews.com/
news/60-minutes-reports-tragedy-in-newtown/.

Raymond, Emilie. *From My Cold, Dead Hands: Charlton Heston and American Politics.* Lexington, Ky.: University Press of Kentucky, 2006.

Saletan, William. "Unfit to Bear Arms." *Slate,* April 1, 2013.

Sanger-Katz, Margot. "Gun Deaths Are Mostly Suicides." *New York Times,*
October 8, 2015.

Savas, Theodore P. and J. David Dameron. *A Guide to the Battles of the American Revolution.* New York: Savas Beatie, 2006.

Schaefer, Donovan. "Theses on Guns, Apocalypticism, and American Religion." *Bulletin for the Study of Religion,* May 26, 2014.

Schrager, Allison. "The Very Stark Numbers on Young Black Men and Gun
Violence." *Bloomberg Business,* August 20, 2014.

"Silver Bullet." *Wall Street Journal,* June 30, 2008.

Spitzer, Robert J. *Gun Control: A Documentary and Reference Guide.* Westport, Conn.: Greenwood Press, 2009.

———. *Politics of Gun Control.* Chatham, N.J.: Chatham House Publishers,
1995.

"Statistics on the Dangers of Gun Use for Self Defense." Law Center to Prevent
Gun Violence, May 11, 2015. http://smartgunlaws.org/dangers-of-gun
-use-for-self-defense-statistics/.

"Statistics on Gun Deaths & Injuries." Law Center to Prevent Gun Violence,
November 16, 2012. http://smartgunlaws.org/gun-deaths-and-injuries
-statistics/.

Sugarman, Josh. "The New Equality." *Frontline*. 1997. http://www.pbs.org/
wgbh/pages/frontline/shows/guns/procon/equality.html.

"Timeline of Shooting at Sandy Hook Elementary School." ABC News. http://
abcnews.go.com/US/fullpage/newtown-ct-shooting-timeline-sandy
-hook-elementary-school-18014080.

Washington, George. "To the President of Congress (December 20, 1776)."
The Writings of George Washington. vol. IV. ed. Jared Sparks. Boston: Fer-
dinand Andrews, Publisher, 1840.

Wead, Doug. *The Raising of a President: The Mothers and Fathers of Our Nation's Leaders*. New York: Atria Books, 2005.

"Why Own a Gun? Protection Is Now Top Reason." Pew Research Center,
March 12, 2013. http://www.people-press.org/2013/03/12/why-own-a
-gun-protection-is-now-top-reason/.

Winkler, Adam. *Gunfight: The Battle Over the Right to Bear Arms in America*.
New York and London: W. W. Norton & Company, 2011.

Wintemute, Garen J. "Guns, Fear, the Constitution, and the Public's Health."
New England Journal of Medicine 358, no. 14 (2008): 1421–24.

ACKNOWLEDGMENTS

We the People tells the story of how every American—known and unknown—puts their fingerprints on the face of the nation.

Well, true to that theme, this book is also the product of generations of family, friends, and colleagues—my very own Founders. A special thank you goes to Joshua Bucheister—my researcher.

Thank you to Delise, Antonio, Rae, Raffi, and Patrick—my home team. With newcomers Elias, Pepper, and Wesley, we have more championships on the way.

Congratulations to Tonio and Erika on their wedding. Marriage bells ring this year in the family for Christopher and Aubrey Samost and Jonathan and Alyse Mauro.

Roger and Elena—my loving brother and sister are boosters; so, too, are their families—Ginger, Beat, Jonathan, Alexandria, Ashley, Christopher, Aubrey, Kevin, Veronique, Patrick, Chiara, Raphael, and Paul. My brother-in-law, Dr. Arthur (Scooter) West, and his wife, Leathia, are friends as well as family. That goes for their children, Chip and Marissa. Thanks to my cousins: Calito, Gracie, Haroldo (his wife, Lulu; children, Omar and Nadia; daughter-in-law, Andrea; and son-in-law, Jorge), Javier, Ligia and her terrific son, Jonathan Mason, Ricardo, Rilda, Rogelio, Armonia, Donna, and Ruby-Linda.

Thank you—to Eric Lupfer, my agent at William Morris Endeavor Entertainment, for his faith in the idea. His intellectual help, along with Michael Santorelli, was critical in conceiving its structure. A hug for two more WME agents: Henry Reisch and Suzanne Gluck.

A few more words of thanks to Joshua Bucheister: My fellow Haverford graduate cares deeply about the craft of writing and the research behind a good story. Josh, you came on board in the middle of the journey and became a terrific first mate. Thank you to Joe Sangiorgio and Meredith Nnoka for their research help. Bill Frey, at Brookings, thanks for your demographic studies.

Thank you to my editor, Roger Scholl, and his assistant, Dannalie Diaz.

Roger's hard work to make this book a success counts as a blessing. Dannalie wrangled schedules, changes, and people to keep the book running on time. Molly Stern, the publisher, and Annsley Rosner, the associate publisher, have been believers in the power of this story from the very first mention of it. I am grateful for the Crown team that launched this book: Liz Esman, Sarah Pekdemir, Claire Posner, and Rachel Rokicki.

Roger Ailes, the president and CEO of Fox News, loves a good story, politics, and people. His support for my writing, my freedom to speak my mind—even when he disagrees—is the definition of a great boss and even a better friend. He is an American legend as a political strategist. As a news executive he has changed media. That incredible track record makes his generous spirit with me all the more amazing. I can testify to his personal kindness and caring in dark moments.

Shari Berg, Porter Berry, Bryan Boughton, Dianne Brandi, Michael Clemente, John Finley, Brian Jones, Jessica Loker, John Moody, Bill Sammon, Suzanne Scott, Bill Shine, David Tabacoff, and Jay Wallace are Fox executives who have spurred and guided me. I am grateful.

A big, sincere word of thanks to my cohosts and friends—incredibly smart and good people—on *The Five*: Eric Bolling, Kimberly Guilfoyle, Greg Gutfeld, and Dana Perino. That team is the best. The production team is way too cool: Megan Albano, Brooke Halsey, Amanda Hooshangi, Allie Novak, Sean O'Rourke, Mina Pertesis, Susan Wertheim, and Stefanie Wheeler.

My inner circle of Fox hosts is always there with a good word, pushing to new heights: David Asman, Bret Baier, Shannon Bream, Lou Dobbs, Harris Faulkner, Sean Hannity, Bill Hemmer, Brit Hume, Megyn Kelly, Howard Kurtz, Bill O'Reilly, Charles Payne, Geraldo Rivera, Shepard Smith, Stuart Varney, and Chris Wallace.

Jimmy Finkelstein, publisher of *The Hill,* is passionate about the news business and loves figuring out the future of how people get their news. So is his wife, Pamela Gross Finkelstein. Niall Stanage, the editor of my *Hill* column, and Bob Cusack, the *Hill*'s top editor, are excellent journalists at the ready with guidance and always good friends.

Thank you to my personal friends!

My church family, the wonderful people at Trinity Episcopal Church: You keep me growing in the Spirit. Thank you Father John Harmon and Rev. Reggie Simmons.

"Youth for Tomorrow"—led by Gary Jones and founded by Joe Gibbs—inspires with its love of children. Thanks to Oakwood Friends School.

My family of friends: Arthur Aidala; Susan Alexander; Jodi Allen; Jim Arrington; David Axelrod; Don Baer; Fred Barnes; Bishop Nathan Baxter; Fritz and Diane Bech; Lucille Blair and Liam Blair-Ford; David Brand; Donna Brazile; Sheldon Bream; Bob Brown; Lonnie Bunch; Donna Butts; Morgan Chalfant; John Chandler; Ron Christie; Raul Cisneros; Charles Cobb; David Cohen; Catherine Cook-Holmes; Doe Coover; Bill Coleman; Chris and Lynne Cowan; Spencer Crew; Tanya Davis; Sandya and Vijay Das; Jesse Jane Duff; Eric and Tina Easter; Ron Elving; John Eshun; Karen Finney; Michael and Ulrika Francis; David Garrow; Cheryl Gibert; Paul Gigot; Ken Gormley; Don Graham; Milton Grant; Warren Graves; Josh Greenman; Gina Wishnick Grossman; Cherie Grzech; Scot, Karen (Vossler), and Gavin Hagerthey; Ed Henry; Bill and Gail Herald (my fellow grandparents); Michael Hicks; Jim and Ann Hudson; Kim Hume; Alphonso Jackson; Dante James; Rhonda Jenkins; Scott Keeter; Ron and Pam Kessler; Colby King; Joel Klein; Bill Kristol; Tova Ladier; Brian Lamb; Lars Larson; Mark Lasswell; Marsha Levick; Bob Ley; Bill and Cynthiana Lightfoot; Charisse Lillie; James Loadholt; Joe Madison; Lynne Jordal-Martin; Lori Martin; Cam MacQueen; Nancie McPhail; Jennifer Pond; Thurgood Marshall Jr.; Gabe Mehretaab; Michael Meyers; Courtland Milloy; Sarah Mullins; Vincent and Lisa Napolean; Nick Nasrallah; Ruben Navarette; Jerralynn Ness; Arthel Neville; Dr. Michael Newman; Kojo Nnamdi; Barrett and Judy Nnoka; Ali Noorani; Franco Nuschese; Cathleen O'Brien; Kevin O'Keefe; Jeremy Peters; Bret Perkins; Amb. Edward Perkins; Jim Pinkerton; Joe Piscopo; Joe Quinlan; Diane Rehm; Jason Riley; Ed Rogers; Bob Schwartz; Sen. Tim Scott; Steve Scully; Steve Selden; Scott Simon; Brent Smith; Dr. Sian Spurney; Richard Strauss; Susan Swain;

Jessica Tarlov; Johnny Taylor; Chris and Brook Teal; Paul and Mendy Thaler; Julie Talarico; Justice Clarence Thomas and Ginny Thomas; Diane Thomson; Robert Traynham; Sterling Tucker; Jose Antonio Vargas; Fay Vincent; David Webb; Bob Wilson; Armstrong Williams; Philip Winder; Jason Wrenn; Ryan Yeisley; David Zinn; Barry Zubrow.

Thank you to my Fox family—Peter Barnes, Addisu Bekele, Dana Blanton, Tom Bowman, Betsy Burkhard, Carl Cameron, Steve Carlson, Dana Cash, Andrew Conti, Kevin Corke, Francisco Cortes, Mitch Davis, Janice Dean, Mary Pat Dennert, Andrea DeVito, Steve and Peter Doocey, Brian Doherty, Nina Easton, Mike Emanuel, Michelle Fields, Tom Fox, Nate Fredman, Bernie Goldberg, Don Grannum, Jennifer Griffin, Lacey Halpern, Mary Katherine Ham, Stephen Hayes, Jonathan Hoenig, Cory Howard, John Huber, Tony Jarrett, Queenette Karikari, Brian Kilmeade, Dana Klinghoffer, Ashley Koerber, Charles Krauthammer, Mary Kreinbihl, Judy Laterza, Mara Liasson, Stacia Lynds, Lori Martin, Gwen Marder, Dagen McDowell, Angela McGlowan, Bernard McGuirk, Connell McShane, Chris Mills, Ron Mitchell, Jennifer Montalvo, Andrew Napolitano, Heather Nauert, Iraida O'Callaghan, Patricia Pert, Lauren Cowan Pick, Kirsten Powers, Clay Rawson, Katy Ricalde, Craig Rivera, Isabella Rivera, Cristina Robbins, Tamara Robertson, Doug Rohrbeck, Ed Rollins, James Rosen, Karl Rove, Lauren Schneider, Doug Schoen, Anita Siegfriedt, Amy Sohnen, Seneca Stevens, Chris Stirewalt, A. B. Stoddard, John Stossel, Joe Trippi, Lamont Tyler, Leland Vittert, Jesse Watters, Caroline Whiteman, Lis Wiehl, George Will, Eboni Williams, Gerri Willis, Makeda Wubneh, and Eldad Yaron.

I really mean it—thank you.

INDEX